Treasures from the Attic

Goshen Library:

It wonderful to be able to talk with your book club. I met a lot of very nice people.

Thank you for having me.

Chuck Webb (Bucky)

7/17/12

Charles A. Welsh, Jr.
Seaman First Class United States Navy – April, 1944 to
November, 1945
Born June 10, 1912 – Deceased June 23, 2008

Treasures from the Attic

My Father's Letters 1943-1945, from the States
and aboard ship in the Pacific

Charles Welsh

Outskirts Press, Inc.
Denver, Colorado

Treasures from the Attic
My Father's Letters 1943-1945, from the States and aboard ship in the Pacific
All Rights Reserved.
Copyright © 2010 Charles Welsh
V4.0

Cover Photo © 2010 Charles Welsh. All rights reserved - used with permission.

Outskirts Press, Inc.
http://www.outskirtspress.com

ISBN: 978-1-4327-5925-4

Outskirts Press and the "OP" logo are trademarks belonging to Outskirts Press, Inc.

PRINTED IN THE UNITED STATES OF AMERICA

Table of Contents

Acknowledgements

This project started in the fall of 2004 and continued for nearly six years. It required many hours of being hunched over a computer and printer. It carved a big chunk out of my family life. My heartfelt appreciation and thanks go out to my wife Joan for her patience, understanding and encouragement. Without her support this project would never have been completed.

My sister Betty Bradley and my brother Francis Welsh pressed me to continue this effort and helped fill in the blanks when I got stuck or needed additional information or clarification. Dad's only surviving sister, Margaret Lutz, and his cousin Dick Welsh also provided background information. Janet Lembke, a local author, edited my copy and provided some writing and marketing tips. The pictures of the USS *San Francisco* were courtesy of *Classic Warships Publishing*. Vince Pici, my son-in-law, helped prepare all of the pictures for publication.

This has been a very rewarding albeit time-consuming effort. I learned much about my parents from the letters and gained a true appreciation of their feelings for each other. I only wish some correspondence from my mother had been available for inclusion.

The letters will not be returned to another dusty attic. They will be housed in the Associated Press Corporate Archives in New York City along with his other papers – a fitting place for their final resting place.

Introduction

It was a cool day in early April of 1944. The war in Europe was in full swing and the battle in the Pacific was heating up. Three friends – one from eastern Pennsylvania and two from western Pennsylvania – fulfilled a pact made a year or so earlier. They enlisted together in the United States Navy.

All were in their thirties and had families. The three did not have to disrupt their lives and go to war. They wanted to! On April 6, 1944, Jess James, Morgan Vone Jones and Chuck Welsh were sworn in at the courthouse in Altoona, Pennsylvania, and boarded a train taking them to boot camp at Great Lakes, Illinois.

This book tells the wartime story of my father, Chuck Welsh, as revealed by the more than 400 letters that he wrote to his family during his nineteen-month stint in the Navy. The letters were found in an obscure place in the attic of his home in Metuchen, New Jersey. They run the gamut from love letters to travelogues to battle descriptions.

He was a compelling writer. His prose is formidable whether describing boot camp, weekend liberty, a cross-country train trip, a typhoon, a battle, a coral atoll, a war ravaged city, V-J Day or just a day in the life of an ordinary seaman. He had a wonderful way of expressing his love for our mother and his family. A veteran journalist, he was a correspondent with the Associated Press (AP) in Philadelphia, Pennsylvania, prior to enlistment.

Prologue

It was the summer of 2003. My father, Charles A. Welsh Jr., age ninety-one, was moving out of his Metuchen, New Jersey, home of nearly 40 years into an assisted living facility. My mother passed away on Christmas Day, 1994, and Dad had been the sole occupant during the ensuing nine years. Although still very active, he had started to slip somewhat. He no longer drove and taking care of the home became increasingly difficult for him. He reluctantly agreed to sell the house, interestingly enough to one of his grandsons, and relocate to the Clara Barton facility just about two miles from his residence.

My sister and I were rummaging through the clutter in the attic of the house shortly after his departure. Sequestered away were many treasures depicting both happy and sad times of his life. Among them was an old seaman's chest filled with pictures, some framed and some loose, and other memorabilia from his long career with the Associated Press. However, we were particularly intrigued by two very dusty cardboard boxes which were hidden in the dark recesses of the attic – Heinz Sweet Preserved Gherkins and Kraft Salad Products.

Both boxes were filled with letters that Dad had written to our mother during the 19 months he served in the Navy during World War II. They were in the original envelopes with the censor's stamp prominently displayed. We were both very surprised since we had not been aware of the letters' existence. My sister and I perused them and they appeared to be chronologically in order by year and month but not by day. We told Dad about our find and he registered surprise that the letters were in the attic. He gave me permission to take them to my home.

Off the letters went to Virginia. I very quickly put them in complete chronological order and placed them in a filing cabinet where they continued to gather dust. Somewhere along the way I decided that it would be a good idea to transcribe the letters so Dad could read them. He was very excited about the project, which was termed "War Letters," and looked forward to reading them. I determined that I would not jump ahead, choosing to read and transcribe each day in order. In retrospect this was a big mistake.

I sat down at the computer and began to type – in two-finger fashion – starting in May, 2004. I worked on them intermittently as using two fingers is quite arduous and very slow and 400-plus letters means a lot of typing. Furthermore, there was no real sense of urgency.

In going through the letters a disturbing factor was revealed – there was no correspondence from our mother despite the fact she wrote as frequently as Dad, probably more often. Unfortunately space limitations in boot camp and aboard ship precluded their retention.

Volume I, which covered the period from April, 1944, to August, 1944, was completed in December of that year. Dad seemed to enjoy them as did the rest of the family. I kept on plugging and Volume II, September, 1944, to December, 1944, rolled out for Dad's review in March, 2006.

I intended to complete the final Volume III in time for his ninety-sixth birthday on June 10, 2008, but didn't get it done. Dad passed away on June 23 before the task was finished. I continued on after his death, typing the last letter on October 7, 2008. Volume III, January, 1945, to September, 1945, went to my sister's home, giving her the complete set of "War Letters."

In one of the later letters, Dad indicated that Mother had

suggested doing something with them, possibly in conjunction with the Associated Press. Dad felt they should wait until the war was over and he returned home. However, they didn't pursue this idea. After reading this particular letter it became clear what should be done now. A book was in order!

Although my family and I termed them "War Letters," they are not war letters in the strict sense of the word although the ship to which Dad was assigned participated in the battles of Leyte, Iwo Jima and Okinawa while he was aboard.

The letters tell the story of a sailor – an ordinary seaman, a husband and a father – as related by the almost daily letters that he wrote to his wife. They show his love for her, his family and his country. They depict his struggles during boot camp and the physical rigors of training with men ten to fifteen years his junior. They describe relationships with fellow sailors. They illustrate his exhileration when he achieved his goal – assignment to a fighting ship, the USS *San Francisco*, a heavy cruiser soon to be deployed in the Pacific. They tell about life aboard ship – the routine, the monotony, the relationships, the frightening storms, the rigors of battle and fear. Finally, they express the overwhelming sadness and helplessness of being thousands of miles away from home when a family tragedy occurred.

Of course, not all of the letters were included in this book – there were just too many. Some had to discarded and others edited in order to preserve space and eliminate repetition. This was an extremely difficult task.

The letters are treasures to be savored and enjoyed. However, to get a full and complete understanding of them it is necessary to go back to Dad's pre-war roots.

Prelude To The Letters

In 1910, Charles A., Sr. and Mary Welsh moved to Somerset, Pennsylvania, where they operated a newspaper stand and a newspaper delivery business. Somerset was a small town in the mountains of western Pennsylvania with a coal mining and agricultural base.

Charles A. Welsh, Jr. (Chuck) was born in 1912 and four sisters followed him – Eleanor, Mary, Margaret and Jean who was born in 1922. A young cousin, Dick Welsh, also lived with the family in Somerset. He was an Army Air Force officer during the War.

Chuck was an active boy. Naturally, he carried newspapers for his father, and also served as an altar boy at the local Catholic Church. He was big for his age and an excellent football player. He graduated from high school in 1929, intending to attend college and play football but was bitten by the journalism bug. He joined the fledging *Somerset Daily Herald* as a seventeen-year old cub reporter at the salary of $8 a week and advanced through the ranks, finally becoming managing editor. During his tenure the newspaper's name was changed to the *Somerset Daily American*.

By all accounts he was an energetic young man who had many friends. He and his buddies hunted, fished and went swimming together. They chased girls and moonshine along the winding mountain roads of western Pennsylvania.

On a summer day in 1930 he walked out his front door and

spied a pretty girl sitting on the stoop of a house across the street. According to his sister Eleanor, he was smitten immediately and vowed that day to wed the young lady, Elizabeth (Betty) Dresser, who was visiting her grandmother.

She hailed from Allentown in the eastern part of Pennsylvania. Betty's parents were Carl and Julia Dresser and she had three younger siblings, sisters Minette and Cathy and a brother Bob, the youngest. Bob and Cathy's husband, Wilbur Sechler, served in the Army during World War II. A long-distance courtship ensued which culminated in their wedding on October, 12, 1935.

They established their home in Somerset and Chuck took a second job in the State Liquor Store to supplement his income. Their first child, Charles A. III, (Bucky) was born in March, 1937, followed by a daughter Elizabeth (Chubbin) in November, 1938, and a son Francis in June, 1942.

In 1940, Chuck accepted a position with the Johnstown, Pennsylvania, *Democrat*. While in Johnstown, Chuck became friendly with John (Jess) James, the newspaper's editor, and James' brother-in-law, Morgan Vone Jones, a prominent attorney. The three often talked about joining the Navy even though they all had families and were in their early 30's. They were pretty much draft-proof.

The Associated Press (AP) became aware of Chuck's journalistic talent and offered him a position as correspondent in the Philadelphia, Pennsylvania, office. In the late summer of 1942, the young family moved east and settled in Kirklyn, a Philadelphia suburb.

Chuck continued to keep in contact with James and Jones. Early in 1944 the three decided that their previous discussions would become a reality – they would enlist in Navy together. Chuck talked to Betty, saying that he felt an obligation to go into the service even though the possibility of his being drafted was very slim. Betty supported him saying "If you feel the need to go, go." This quote came from a story written by Jerry

Schwartz of the Associated Press in 2000.

The question of where to locate during Chuck's Navy deployment was answered by an invitation to live with his parents. The Welsh Jr. family moved to Somerset in March of 1944. Chuck finished his work in Philadelphia and was given a rousing going-away party by his AP compatriots. After that it was goodbye to Betty, the kids, his parents and his siblings and on to Altoona, Pennsylvania, to join up with Jess and Vone.

On April 6, 1944, James, Jones and Welsh arrived at the Altoona courthouse in mid-morning for the swearing-in ceremony. They weren't sworn in until after 5 o'clock, experiencing the first of what would be many Navy "long waits." At 9:30 P.M. the threesome boarded a Pullman car for the train trip to Great Lakes, Illinois, and boot camp. Their civilian life was over. They now belonged to the United States Navy. Newly-christened "Sailor" Welsh began writing letters immediately.

THE LETTERS

Chapter 1
BOOT CAMP
GREAT LAKES, ILLINOIS
4/8/44 to 5/31/44

The First Letter

Dearest Betty (and everybody):   4-?-44 Friday afternoon
    Well, here I am, nearing the end of the first day and dashing off a note before chow, so this may end very abruptly. If it does, I'll not be caught short by failing to tell you that I love you very much - - you and your little ones.
    So far it's been interesting and not too difficult - - in fact not difficult at all. I'm still in civvies but will remedy that tomorrow morning and about Tuesday you ought to get my old clothes.
    We had a long wait at Altoona before we were sworn in about 5 o'clock. Then we wandered the town, visited the cathedral and finally pulled out on the 9:30 train - - in Pullmans, no less. Sat and talked until 11:30, then I crawled into the hay and slept like a baby until 7 a.m. Breakfast in the diner, pinochle in the club car brought us to Chicago about 9:30. Then we had 90 minutes to kill so Jess, Vone and I walked around town, took a long ride on the El to see the city, and then hopped another train for here. So far we've gone through some minor routine and had our teeth inspected

which brings us up to the present few minutes of liberty.

The crowd is a <u>good</u> one, with some fellows about my age who have several kids. I find it very interesting. Right now most of the boys seem to be writing, which should be a good indication of something or other. By tomorrow night I should know a good deal more about what's going to happen, and how long we'll be here. By then, too, we should be in our permanent barracks. I'll try to write then, and I suppose you know I'll be looking forward to hearing from you. All my love to everybody and I miss you all very much. Give my Bucky, Elizabeth and Fran a big kiss from me. And mark in the calendar one I owe you.

Love- Tonie.

4-8-44 Saturday Evening

I want to start this for a few minutes before I officially become a "Boat" which is accomplished by the not-so-simple process of putting on one's boats - - a short, laced-canvas legging. From now on we live and work in them. This should be the tip-off that I apparently am over the last hurdles, and am a sailor for the duration. My clothes are on the way to you and you can start when you please on the job of putting them away.

The end of the second day finds us more than somewhat tired. We were up at 5:30 - - that's standard procedure - - and cleaned the barracks, then went to chow. The rest of the morning was spent going through the final (?) physical and then issuance of clothes - - everything was included and the only difficulty was dress pants. They were out of my size, so I'll wear dungarees for Easter - - 'twill be a strange holiday.

Then we went back to the barracks, packed our stuff and went to chow again, followed by my (our) first march, over to our permanent barracks. This is barracks 3004, one of at least a million in this tremendous place, and as the newest recruits in the area we're naturally subject to considerable razzing. It will be that way until sometime next week when we get our haircuts and "shots" (We're "barber bait" and "needle bait" up to now.) then we'll be veterans and razzing the rest, I assume.

Scuttlebutt - - the source of all rumors - - has it that we're a five-week company which would mean going home on furlough about mid-May. Don't tell me you're surprised I'm looking forward to that already.

Well, I've taken time out for a few minutes, and now am officially a boat. Which somewhat startling transformation causes me to wonder if you love me as much as you used too?

Tonight, I'm considerably more tired than last and looking forward to hitting the sack. Also, I'm quite a bit more lonesome for all of you, but there's nothing to be done about that for some weeks.

We had a minor tragedy today, a big guy named Ted Rose, who was in charge of our Johnstown group all the way from Altoona to here, was jerked mysteriously out of the line during the physicals and apparently has flunked. As I said, I came out OK, but they noticed my slightly crossed eyes, labeled them as stralisunus (or something similar) and marked my physical sheet as <u>NOT</u> qualified for submarine duty. I had no intention of asking for such service, but would have preferred a clear record.

That's about all for now, Dearest. Give my love to everybody and write to me soon all you can about your kids, yourself and our family.

4-9-44 Sunday (To Bucky)

By the time you get this your first day in the new school will be over and I'm expecting you to write to me and tell me about it. Remember always to call the teacher "Teacher" and not Sister. And you must continue studying so your marks will stay good.

Since your Daddy is a sailor it's up to you to help Mother care for Elizabeth and Francis. I know you'll be a big help.

Do you still like your bunk bed? My bed here is just like yours, and like you I sleep on top. The only difference is that I do not have a ladder and have to climb up.

Write to me soon, and be a good boy. I'll see you in a few weeks. You can tell your mother for me that sailors don't spend much money. I had $20 when I left Somerset and have spent only $5. Can you tell her how much I have left?

I know you are going to be happy in Somerset. Be a good boy and tell me all about what you are doing. Lots of Love from Your Daddy

4-9-44 Sunday (To Elizabeth)

Dear Chubbin:

Did you get into kindergarten all right, little one? I suspect that they kept you out because of the vaccination which means that you will be going to see Dr. Barchfield. If you do, please tell him hello for me. And tell him that I'll try to get in to say hello myself when I come home on furlough.

I suppose you are helping Mother with the house work, because you live in a very big house now and she must have lots of help. Is Francis being a good boy? I'll bet he's talking more every day. Pretty soon he'll be a chatterbox just like you.

Perhaps I forgot to tell you that your bicycle, and the others, is in the cellar. It's beginning to look like spring here, and I'll bet the weather is nice back there.

Tell Mother that if she can find one I'd like to have a cloth money belt, the kind you tie around your waist. It should be blue. I don't think now of another thing I need.

Give my love to Grandma and Grandpa and Jean, and give Fran a big kiss from me. Lots of love from Your Daddy

4-12-44 Tuesday evening

Well the biggest of all events happened today - - two letters from you and they were welcome. It was a beautiful day before that, and perfect ever since.

I don't suppose you'd know me now, for we're no longer barber-bait, having had our first 20 cent boat haircut. You wouldn't believe it but one of those four barbers AVERAGED LESS THAN one and one-half minutes per haircut. The resulting product was better than what you would expect, but they couldn't find enough hair to give me 20 cents worth.

Another big event was the famed "Flying Five." The enclosed $2 is what I had left + 25 cents. What happened was this: we signed a slip saying we had received $5 from the paymaster, then lined up past said paymaster handed him the slip, and 8 steps ahead was a cashier who took the $5, handed us the $2.25, and we went a couple of steps further to get our package. It contained, among other things, the money belt I wanted (You'll not need to send one now.), a soap holder, razor outfit, miscellaneous toilet articles, stationery and a sailor's manual. The $5 had flown.

Oh yes, we had tests too and I sailed right through the general stuff in the morning - - got far more done than Jess and Vone. The afternoon was a lot harder and the electrical stuff was tough but I think I did ok.

Tomorrow (probably) we start the shots. For the last two days we've been going to classes in ship recognition, completing our tests, and beginning to learn to drill. It has been a busy life, will get busier as we go along. I couldn't write last night because I had to do my laundry and there was an awful lot of work to do around the barracks.

You can believe this or not: I'm having NO difficulty (up to now) in rolling out of the hay at 5:30. Probably going to bed every night has something to do with it. Aren't I wonderful? The Navy hasn't changed me yet, except the haircut. My guess is I've gained weight, for I'm eating far more than I did before. But I feel fine, and still like it very much.

Nevertheless, I'm lonely, here in the midst of the mob. Most of all I miss you, darling for there just isn't anything in the Navy or, anywhere else in the world, that can take your place. And then too, there aren't any little ones climbing all over me when I come in the barracks, and that is something that can't be replaced.

Betty, will you ask Mother to have my medal and rosary blessed and send them to me? I'd like to have them. Goodbye darling, take care of yourself and our family and I'll see you soon. I love you all very much.

4-15-44 Saturday evening

The ink will be the only thing blue about this letter, for I feel swell and the world is a reasonably pleasant one although it's raining, blowing like hell and really miserable outside. I'm sorry about that letter last night but I felt pretty miserable, what with all the shots - - double typhoid, diphtheria and vaccination - - and we had a helluva job in front of our detail.

But we did the best we could; I worked out a lot of the soreness from my arm and slept very well. We were up at 5, worked like dogs till 7, ate and then came back and cleaned up the ragged edges. About 11, the commander and his staff inspected, seemed pleased, and we heard this afternoon that our company and another older one came out tied for first place in the 20 companies of the regiment. We're, needless to say, quite happy and proud of it.

Then after chow we marched two miles in the rain for our classification interviews. I asked for sea duty, specifying that I wanted to try gunnery, and the examiner said (after looking at my marks on the test) "No, I think you'd better go to school." So I'm down for a test as a possible sound locator (They're the devices that detect submarines.) operator next Saturday, with gunnery school also a possibility. However, what they told us today was NOT official and we likely won't know where we go from here until a week or so before graduation day. And just in case you're mildly interested, that day is now tentatively set for May 13. It's reasonably sure it won't be any longer than that and - - if we are an honor company - - it may be a week or so less. How's that for news?

About the tests, I was proud of my marks. The interviewer told me that on the grading system 83 was the highest possible on some and 84 on others, with the general over-all average 50-54. Here are my marks: General classification 68, Clerical work 69, Reading 78, Radio 66, Arithmetic 74, Mechanical 68, Aptitude Matching 71, Electrical 66 (an involved job — aptitude counting and visualizing clocks), Spelling 83 and Overall Average 71.5. I should have been 10 points better if I had not made a mistake on how to handle the thing.

By the way, I suppose you're saving these letters. They might be a useful day-to-day record of my Navy service. Furthermore, I expect to send you a will to be filed away. The Navy says every man in the service should make one out and I'd have to do it some day anyhow. While I'm on this slightly morbid (but none the less sensible side) nobody has come around yet to fix us up for life insurance. Of course, I'll take the full $10,000, and it will cost me $7.10 a month. After the war I can convert it to ordinary life for about twice as much premium, which will be my first concrete dividend from the Navy.

To get back to today, after we walked back from the interviews I went to the hospital (sick bay) to see Jess. He wound up with catarrh fever, plus the shot reaction, hopes to be released tomorrow but likely will have to stay a day or two longer. He seemed OK.

Then I went to the canteen, had a great big sundae (two 10 cent dips of ice cream and 2 kinds of syrup for 15 cents), wandered around for a while, took a swim for pleasure and then beat it back to the hospital with some stuff for Jess, then to the barracks for chow. Came right back after eating and here I am.

My first week in the Navy has done me a lot of good. I feel fine physically, the food and routine (I'm even becoming "regular" if you can imagine that, maybe it's the bran every morning.) agree with me and I even imagine my "muscles" are hardening. I've still a much-too-big roll of fat on my belly, but I'm hoping to get rid of it, especially if we get some warm weather.

The whole station blossomed out in white hats today, traditional changeover date from the blue wool watch caps, and we donned our summer underwear. I guess I didn't tell you that we've worn longies - - woolens with both legs and sleeves, and I guess I ought to confess they really felt good and we missed them today.

When you write to Mary Smith [a Philadelphia neighbor] tell her for me I miss them a helluva lot. Next to just being with you and the kids and our family tonight, I'd like nothing better than to settle down with you and the two of them to a cheerful Saturday evening of bridge chatter and a few beers. Boy, them were the days, and I'm sure looking forward to picking up where we left off - - if the fates are willing.

Tell my Chubbin I'm very proud of her not crying when she was vaccinated. She's just like her daddy 'cause I didn't cry either when I was vaccinated yesterday. I hope she'll be very happy in kindergarten and know she'll be a <u>very</u> good girl.

I can well believe the apples sensation for even at this long range, and second hand, I feel sort of like that myself.

So our big boy has a girl friend! You tell him that his daddy says <u>NO</u> notes to girls in school. They can cause you to feel very foolish, if my memory is correct. Be sure that he keeps up his studies, and don't forget to keep him going on the catechism. Do they still have Saturday catechism classes?

Fran's washing sounds very interesting. If he gets good enough by the time I come home he can do my laundry. <u>I DON'T LIKE TO!</u>

That's enough for now darling. I love you and miss you like all hell, but the number of days we must stay apart is shrinking and while the end isn't in sight it's not too terribly far away.

4-18-44 Tuesday morning

I'm so sorry that I let you down two days in a ROW but it just wasn't possible to write. Let me tell you why and I think you'll see that at least while I'm in boot it won't be possible to do as I used to.

Sunday morning I commanded the detail going to Mass, first time I've tried anything like that, and got by all right. Enjoyed it too, and maybe before this is over I may be an acting petty officer. We need 'em.

Then after chow I read the Sunday paper and in the afternoon went to the canteen with Jess and Vone. Again we went to chow and before leaving I put a bucket of clothes to soak, intending to come back, write and then wash. But when I arrived Dick Pitzer and Don Mowry from Somerset were waiting to see me and of course we had to go for a walk and gab while they took me over to see Fred Hare [another Somerset friend], and it was after 8 when I got back, not nearly enough time to do my washing and get my detail through the cleanup job and as a result, I didn't get into bed until lights out at 9:30.

Then yesterday, I got back from chow intending to write and we had a last-minute order to get ready for a bag layout today. So Lou Ward, my bunkmate from Lansing, and I slaved like dogs until 9, rolling all our clothes in the Navy way. So you see the Navy just squeezed out your letters, and I'm afraid it will happen more and more often as the schedule gets tougher. And believe me it's getting tougher, much tougher and fast!

Yesterday started out with a very rigorous physical fitness test, a series of six stiff calisthenics. You get so many minutes to do each one, and try for a maximum number. I didn't press myself too far, being smart enough to know that I'm in lousy condition and sensible enough not to try to prove I'm not. As a result I made a miserable showing, and may have to take a special calisthenics course that will take four hours a week of my already limited free time. I hope so. I need it. But I forgot to tell you that we started the day with 15 minutes of calisthenics at 5:45 a.m. - - and a run around the small drill field, about ¼ mile.

Then after the test, with everyone really exhausted, we very sensibly marched and drilled for an hour, to cool out gradually. Then there were a couple of classes in the afternoon, I don't even remember what they were. After that rolling spree last night I was literally exhausted. Nevertheless, I hit the deck promptly at 5:30, and 20 minutes later we were out for a few exercises and ran around the big drill field, nearly a mile. I ran it slowly, but barely had enough strength left for a short sprint at the finish - - and it wasn't much of a sprint.

Then a couple of classes (We didn't do well.) and we've had a free hour here in the barracks so I started this letter, intending to finish it tonight but I think I'll mail it now and maybe try another one later if I can.

Dad will be interested to know that our new batallion commander is Ensign Paul Brown, the former Ohio State football coach.

This afternoon we ran the obstacle course for the first time, Oh Boy. My muscles aren't too stiff now, but I'm afraid they'll be worse tomorrow. Sorry to chop it off now, darling, but I must go. I love you all very much and I will write when I can.

4-24-44 Monday night

I've only time for a note tonight since I am - - for the first and last time - - on the sh-t list. I've just come back from a "happy hour." It all went wrong today when the regimental commander, inspecting the barracks, decided my display towel was dirty. Why

I don't know, and couldn't see, for I hung it up clean on Sunday, and haven't touched it since. But he said it was, put me down for 5 demerits and scheduled me with 15 others for the "happy hours." I'm on the sh-t list because the personal bad work also reflects on the company.

S0 - - after 2 hours of drill this morning, and more drill and a long hike this afternoon, we headed for the drill hall after chow and for an hour and 15 minutes were required to stand rigid for 10 minute stretches at present arms, port arms and attention. Try it one time for 10 minutes, not even moving a muscle. It's <u>tough</u>! But it didn't hurt me a bit and the actions of the C.P.O. trying to catch men moving, and his lecture on "This is the mildest form of punishment the Navy has - - it will be tougher from now on, etc." made it the most fascinating experiment in practical psychology I've ever seen. There's enough Irish in me to make it backfire, but some of the boys were scared plenty. I won't be back there again, but not because I'm afraid of anything they might do to me.

As a result of my hike today I am now for the first time, a real sailor, all tagged out in blues. I didn't think I had lost much weight or any waistline, but the 38-inch trousers I got today are too big (not too much so) and I think I look pretty trim. Don't know that you'll see anything of it before I come home, but that will be time enough. I'd like then to have a family picture taken if we can.

But now that I look like a sailor, I feel I'm getting somewhere and my checked-off calendar (Yes I use rings around <u>certain</u> dates too.) shows only 19 more days until I reach paradise again. That's what it will be like to have my arms around you, again.

Yesterday we filed out our requests for train tickets home and back. The Navy buys the tickets and gives you whatever is left from your pay. In my case that will be the grand sum of 25 cents - - my first official Navy pay.

Your letter was grand today, Bettsy, and I'm just a little bit glad you didn't share it with the others. Somehow we seem just a little closer because of it. Must quit now darling, for it's bedtime. I love you very very much.

4-30-44 Sunday night

Well, here I am another day and another week nearer the re-union that has become more important to me than anything in the world. It seems to be coming closer, too, praise be. I'm a little sleepy tonight, but otherwise feel good after a long but not overly strenuous day. I've been up since 3:30 a.m., when I went on guard, and haven't had as much as a wink. I was on guard until 7 a.m., went to chow and then came back and wrote a flock of letters - - notes, really - - to some of the guys in Philly

The latest bit of scuttlebutt says we'll leave here May 9 (Oh Happy Day). Rumor has it that the two companies in the next barracks, scheduled to leave May 6, have been set back 3 days, and will be graduated with us and the company downstairs which came in at the same time we did. I do not believe it, though it's a pleasant bit of speculation.

After going to Mass, writing and then chow, I pitched in on my laundry this afternoon, got it all done including the under-wear and socks I had on, then took a shower and put on clean stuff and felt wonderful.

Tonight after chow, Vone and George Knox, a 6 foot 3 Nashville banker, and I went for a long walk, stopping at the hostess house for a couple of smokes. I enjoyed it a whole lot, too. Knox is a fine fellow.

The inspections lately have really been rough as though the Navy is determined to show us how tough it can be. Most of the 15 of us caught the other day were convinced that our stuff was passable, at least as good as some that were not caught, and many of the 29 today were the same. On the list are both Jess and Vone, and they'll have a lot of fun.

You mentioned the other day that you hadn't seen the cleaning bill for my clothes, which makes it a logical deduction that you got the box containing my suit, etc. that I shipped home when I landed here (Gosh that seems a long time ago!). However you haven't said anything specific about it, so I'm sending you the Railway Express receipt, and if you haven't gotten the box check up as soon as you can with the agency there.

I'm counting on a couple of letters from you tomorrow, since I drew a blank at mail call today. (Jess just walked over and said: "Tell Betty I said hello and that my ass is dragging and I'm going to bed"). Mail service is highly irregular, with two letters in the same mail call. But you have been very faithful, as always, and it's the brightest spot of the day. That's because I love you more than anything in the world, my Bettsy, and I'm counting the minutes until I can put my arms around you and kiss you again and again and again.

Now about Jess. He never before in all his life has done such terrific physical work, nor been at it so long. The first two nights he was in bed and asleep, 10 minutes after he got here, but to-night he sat around for a whole hour, and seems to be standing up pretty well. On the whole, I think it will be good for him - - if it doesn't kill him.

You can't help but feel sorry for the guys who work in the chow house, for while the rest of us are having long hard days theirs are almost always the longest, and by far the toughest. Truthfully, I don't know whether I'm glad or sorry I didn't have to go. For while the work would be brutal I feel like a heel sitting back and letting them do it. But by and large I guess I've done my full share here.

Tomorrow I'll probably be on guard duty all or most of the day, since we have to take over two whole barracks, as well as our own. But I guess it won't be too bad.

Think I'll stop now, sweetheart, for there's some work to be done and then I'll hit the sack for a few hours until 5 a.m. Tell our little ones and Mother and Dad that I'll be home before too much longer, and that I can hardly wait to see them - - and you.

5-1-44 Monday morning

That month of May looks so good to me I just couldn't hold myself down when I wrote it. From now on the days will be the big ones, but that end-of-April hurdle was one I've been waiting to jump over for a long time.

It's now 9:20, and your husband has been up and stirring for four whole hours. The morning cleanup which took about two hours is over and there are 25 or 30 of us sitting around waiting for orders or for inspection, whichever happens first. I, and probably most of the gang, could sleep very soundly if I could get into bed, but of course that's not allowed.

Today is a dismal, rainy one, and I'll be satisfied to take it easy. Couldn't get my work finished until 10:30 last night, so considering I was awakened at 4 a.m. you can see I didn't get too much shut-eye. Then too I have a guard assignment that means getting up at 3:30 tomorrow morning. Don't know why I'm boring you with all this lack-of-sleep guff; guess it's the dull day which makes me even foggier than usual.

Then too, there's nothing to tell you, for of course nothing has happened since I wrote you last night. Oh yes there has, too. You may be interested in knowing that your husband starched a pair of shorts some time between 4 and 5 a.m. All I know about it is that I was somewhat damp when I got up, but guess it's no shame. Insofar as I know I'm the first in line, and either they haven't been feeding us saltpeter, or it's in the soup which I rarely eat. Who cares? You? (I don't if it doesn't mean extra laundry.)

Your husband is a very happy man right now, for he's just received a letter from his sweetheart for the first time in three days. That alone would be enough but better still it came just a few minutes after Lieut. Brown, just as he was leaving, turned to our commander and said: "A good inspection Mr. Reilly." Don't actually know why that should make me feel good, for it won't get me out of here one minute sooner, but after working so hard to get the place in shape it's a very considerable consolation.

Then too there was a very swell letter from my oldest son, and please tell him his Daddy has read it three times already, and will read it more. You probably would be surprised just how much of a thrill it is to hear from him, so please ask him to keep writing, and I'll answer just as soon as I can.

Got the check all right, too, but somehow it doesn't seem to mean a whole lot. I'm still holding a $10 bill of my original $20, plus the $30 check. Have been spending a few cents lately, since we've been admitted to the hostess house. Vone and I went down again last evening; this time managed to get into the coffee line and enjoyed it very much.

After I wrote that note yesterday, we went to chow and I did some laundry, then went up to the chaplain's office and went to confession. We have a brand-new chaplain, Lieut. Bogumil, from Buffalo. He arrived Tuesday and has been in the Navy for 6 months. Here in the Navy weekday Mass is at 5 p.m., and to go to communion we need only abstain from food for four hours and from liquids one hour. Our company was the one designated to attend Mass yesterday, (It's done to make sure there are some men at daily Mass.) but with so many of the boys in the kitchen there were only five of us to go.

I was one of the altar boys, and it surely seemed strange to serve for the first time in 12 years or so. Remembered the Latin pretty well, but had forgotten most of the ritual. But I did get a thrill out of it. It's very strange to go to confession in a sun-lit office, and stranger still to go to Mass in the evening, in the big, empty gymnasium, with only a few men sitting in the folding chairs which replace pews. But the Mass is always the same.

Had me a very easy day yesterday, spending most of my time on my own gear, and it looks like pretty much the same thing today. I have a little laundry to do (Yeah, there's ALWAYS laundry.) this afternoon, and since Jess seems to be stuck think I'll do some for him too. Had to get up and go on watch at 3:30 a.m. again today.

Think I'll stop now darling, since it's close to chow time. Will try to write again soon, probably tonight. Lots of love darling, and I'll be seeing you soon.

5-4-44 Thursday morning

This is just your own personal note, for what I want to say to you - - and do to you - - we shan't share with anybody. Your recent reference to a "burned cinder" and some other passages in the letters, tells me pretty plainly that you are feeling just about as I am - - you hussy!

I shall be a very aggrieved husband if the circle on your calendar coincides with the circle on mine, for above anything in the world I want to kiss you and hold you and put my hands on you and - - - - - - - !

Even thinking about it makes me tingle all over, darling, and there's a strange stirring in my belly when I remember how your smooth, soft skin feels under my hands, and the taste of your breast in my mouth. I'm afraid that for a few minutes, at least, I must be very rough with you for I'm hungry, my Betty, for you in my arms. Seems like a million years since I laid down beside you and held you close.

Nothing, and nobody else in all the world can make me feel like that and think like that except you, little darling but soon I'll be in heaven again, and I tell you I can hardly wait. I want to feel your arms around me, and slip my hand down against you, feel you there so close to me and loving me with all your heart.

Until I see you Betty, I know you'll understand how I feel, and why my breathing just now is so fast and shaky. I can remember what we have been to each other so often, and can only count the minutes until I take you in my arms again, and love you with all my heart.

5-8-44 Monday noon

Yours has been a lazy husband over the weekend, but somehow after talking to you Friday night I just couldn't bring myself to write, knowing that I'll be with you soon. Actually I may get to Somerset before this letter, for it seems certain now we'll graduate Wednesday. That leaves an outside chance we'll leave Wednesday evening, but Thursday morning or afternoon more probable. At any rate we should be together again by Friday, and I know that will be a real red-letter day in my life.

I'm sitting here on my bunk scribbling this, because it's a rainy day and the whole company is congregated indoors, around the tables. So far I've done nothing except go over to the main camp to exchange my 38 waist blue trousers for 36. You can call me "Skinny" when I get home, altho I've not lost any weight - - just waistline.

Gee but I'm getting sleepy. This business of regular hours and early rising finally is getting me down, so that when I get home you can expect me to spend a lot of time in bed (not necessarily asleep, said the hussy).

We had a pretty full program Saturday, starting with our final swimming test which included a jump off a 15-foot catwalk. Then some classes and an athletic period during which your husband played softball. We walked around a little in the evening then came back and went to bed early.

Sunday I went to communion again, took a walk with Vone, ate and then spent 3 hours with Jess in the regimental office typing our leave papers. Not an altogether unpleasant task, you understand.

Sorry must go now, for something or other.

Later: Now we're back in the barracks again since it's pouring, and I can take up my story and get this in the mail shortly.

The most important development is the schedule for tomorrow, which has just come out and looks like a total blank. As a result I'm somewhat discouraged about when we're leaving for there are a number of classes etc. we must complete before we can go. Best guess now seems to be Thursday afternoon before we get out of here, which would mean getting into Johnstown about 5 or 6 a.m. Friday. In any event I'm still hopeful of being with all of you Friday evening. What I plan to do is telephone again just as soon as I can be <u>certain</u> of when I'm getting to Johnstown. If you get this in time, please have a bus schedule handy so we can tell if there's a reasonable bus that will save Dad a drive in the middle of the night.

To go back to Sunday, after I got through typing, Jess, Vone and Marv Smith and I went to the canteen and played bridge for a couple hours then went to the hostess house for supper, came back to the barracks and talked for an hour, then went to bed. As I said, I just couldn't bring myself to write after talking to you, and to tell the truth don't want to write now but I feel like a heel for having neglected you so long. I will make it up to you when I hold you in my arms again - - Soon!

Boot Camp is officially over and Chuck went on leave to Somerset on May 10.

5-23-44 Monday

Well here I am back in the Navy and back to writing, when it would be so wonderful to be with you- - and all of ours. Things are very muddled, so you'll forgive me if this is screwy too. However, I'm still headed for school.

The trip wasn't too bad. Got to Johnstown OK, stopped at Vone's and drank beer until Jess came at 9, and we hit the train all right. But every aisle of every coach was jammed and we stood to Pittsburgh where half a dozen of us gambled and waited for a later train. We won, got seats, and I dozed fitfully to Chicago. Got there just in time to catch a train out here and we arrived in good time.

Then the muddle began and I must confess that as the train pulled into the Lakes I would gladly have tossed the whole thing overboard and headed for home, had I been able. But I guess the worst is over now and I'll be all right, though I miss you very, very awfully much.

Note the changed rating and address, which will get my mail to me until I leave for school. When that will be I don't know. The company is all split up, and probably 100 out of the original 140 ship out tomorrow morning, I suspect for the amphibians, and many of them are very unhappy. Jess, Vone and some others are going into the pharmacy corps which means they'll get 3rd class petty officer ratings. This place is called O.G.U., a transitory stage between boot camp and the next assignment.

Four or five guys on the schools list when we left boot camp came back today to find they are on general assignment and will be shipped tomorrow, perhaps to San Diego, and may not get home again. I'm over the first and probably biggest hurdle, and feel fairly safe, but it can still happen to me. I might not get home either.

This is a very mixed up place I'm in now, apparently without any officers or direction. It looks like I'll get on K.P., but I'm keeping my fingers crossed and hoping I'll be shipped out to my school soon. Unless I get on K.P., my biggest job will be dodging work.

There seems to be a distinct chance I'll get a weekend of liberty if I'm still here and don't quite know what to do with it. Suspect I'll probably go to Chicago first, then try to get to Milwaukee later, if things work out all right. Jess and Vone say they'll have a 35-hour liberty, but don't know whether we will be able to get together. They're about ¼ mile away, and I suspect we won't see much of each other until we've settled, and then only if we land on the same station.

I'm going to stop now Bettsy. It's rough writing with a pencil, but I'll try to do better tomorrow. Give the kids a big kiss from me and tell 'em I love them lots - - as I do you.

5-24-44 Tuesday evening

Really I should have done a lot better by you in the way of a letter today, but I just didn't get it done so I'll do what I can tonight and tomorrow if I'm still around I'll try to really write something.

After writing to you last night we cleaned up the barracks a little and climbed into bed. From 9:30 to 5:30 this morning your husband slept like a log, then got up and had a wonderful leisurely shower and shave, went to chow and then came back and helped clean the joint again, then we sat, and sat, and sat - - waiting for someone to come out and tell us we're going - - somewhere, anywhere will do. We played a little friendly pinochle, went to chow again and then came back and sat again until 3 when I did me a little laundry. By the time I finished it was chow time again, and since then I've been to the canteen.

I think I told you we've all been split up, with 8 or 10 here, and the rest of the 30-odd who stayed split up in a half dozen barracks. As a result, it's almost like a letter from home to see some of the old guys, and I enjoyed the talk. The vast majority of the old company, nearly 100 of them, climbed into their special train this afternoon and shoved off, for somewhere in California, we understand. I saw most of them last night, and a couple when I dropped into their barracks at noon for a minute.

Jess, Vone and a couple of the others from the old company are on liberty in Milwaukee tonight. Jess came up to see if I could go along, but I couldn't get a pass since I haven't been assigned to a work detail to earn one, and apparently am <u>NOT</u> (dammit!) in imminent danger of being shipped to a school. Incidentally, Jess said they come up for draft Friday, which may mean they'll be on their way somewhere by evening. They don't know where, either.

But while I was inquiring about the possibilities of a pass this afternoon I also asked the yeoman in the office about what I could expect here, and got the disheartening reply that gunners mates (that's me) usually stick around 3 to 5 weeks. That will be unpleasant for believe it or not I don't like loafing as a steady diet. As a result, I'm going to sit tight here over the weekend, will volunteer for a work detail Monday if nothing happens. Even K.P. would be better than sitting on your fanny. I'll probably have liberty from noon to midnight Saturday, and guess I'll go to Chicago to see a baseball game. Then next week, when I may get a longer liberty, I'll go to Millwaukee to see Ginny and Leo. [Ginny Shaulis was Betty's aunt on her mother's side and she and her husband Leo formerly lived in Somerset.] Of course that's all on the if-and-when basis, for you never know where you'll be one minute of any given day

You know I told you I had only seen a corner of this place while in boot camp, but I'm only now beginning to realize what a small corner it was. I'm inclined now to guess there must be upwards of 200,000 men here, and I haven't any idea how far upwards that might go.

Chow is really something here - - the food is much better than on the other side, and if I keep on loafing and don't hold myself in check I'll get fat as a pig. Last night we had pork chops, at noon today it was steak and browned potatoes, tonight a very fine stew. The food is served better here, in much bigger mess halls, and is much better prepared, especially in the seasoning.

On the whole life isn't so bad, but I'm hoping to get started somewhere soon, I don't like wasting all this time away from my darlings now, so goodbye, and all my love, to all of you - - and You.

5-26-44 Friday afternoon

If you got the card I mailed last night you already know that

I've been to Milwaukee and had a very swell visit with Ginny and Leo. They're just the same as always and we had a swell time.

It all came about very suddenly. We had worked around the barracks all morning yesterday, and were sitting there playing pinochle when a guy came upstairs and asked for someone to be on guard. So I stuck my neck out, thinking it meant a couple of hours of standing, and would keep me busy thru the evening. Instead, I learned, I had volunteered for a permanent (?) detail, and was told to move my gear to another barracks, where I roost on the top of a triple decker bunk.

By the time I was moved it was 4 p.m., and I was told then that since I was on a detail I was entitled to a liberty from 5 to midnight last night, and 1 to midnight tomorrow. So I promptly decided to go to Milwaukee and Don Clark, a Johnstown boy who caught a detail about the same time said he'd go along. So at 5 we shoved off with the liberty party, and took the trolley train to Milwaukee. The train is much like your well-remembered Liberty Bell, only there are four cars hooked together - - and it goes faster.

It's pretty country up that way, rolling, rich-looking farm-lands, with lots of trees, and nice homes. Milwaukee is a pretty city, clean, and with lots of lawn around the homes. Ginny and Leo have a big one-room and kitchenette apartment just about 25 blocks from the center of town. We hadn't eaten, so Ginny dug out some bacon, sausages, eggs, etc. and fed us royally.

Then Leo brought out the beer and we sat and drank and talked until 9:30, then they walked to the bus stop with us and we took the train back in plenty of time. As I said before, it was fun, and Don enjoyed it too, so much that he asked Ginny to get him a date for Saturday night and I guess we'll be going back then.

There isn't much change here from my former berth, except I'm on guard 4 hours a night 5 nights a week, in return for which I'll have 2 nightly liberties each week, and a 35-hour one (from 1 p.m. Saturday to Sunday midnight) every other weekend.

However we worked hard all day today cleaning up the joint and I'm slightly tired. I'm waiting now to go to chow, and then must come back and do some laundry, and I go on guard at midnight.

Had a wonderful haul at mail call today. (There's chow and I must go.) - - - One hour later - - - Two letters from you, and letters from Rusty and BB [two associates from the Philadelphia AP office] plus a letter from Joe Brennan [a friend from Somerset who is in the Navy].

So my big son lost another tooth. I'm glad he was so brave about it; in fact I'm downright proud of him. Did Dr. Straub say what the trouble was? And did you have him check the rest of his teeth? And above all how about your own?

Still no sign of where I'll be going, and it seems to look as though the four of us going to gunnery will be just about the last of the Mohicans from the old gang. Jess et al pulled out early this afternoon, they thought for the base hospital here. A half-dozen others go tomorrow or Monday, and I guess there are about a dozen of us left here and scattered around a few other barracks.

I'm finding ways to keep busy now, so that's not so bad, and liberty - - I learned - - is fun, and that helps a lot, but dammit I want to get on with this war and get it over with and come back to you. Every hour here is an hour wasted!

Then too, this isn't like the old crew, being mostly younger boys and a noisy and often annoying bunch. Further, the group changes daily, and you never get to know anyone. Clark is all right, but tho he seems and acts older he's still an 18-year old, and there's a gap between us.

While waiting for the train last night we met a gunners mate 3/c and spent a half hour quizzing him about what's in front of us. He had 12 weeks of school, in Florida, firing everything up to 5-inch guns. Then when he finished in the top 30 % of his class he got his ratings and was assigned here for 10 more weeks as an instructor. Lordy, that, if it happens to me, means six months on shore before I even see the sea, and in addition whatever time I waste here. Phooey.

I think, darling, I'm going to sign off now and do me a little laundry - -might as well get it over with so I'll be clean and ready to move along just in case I'm lucky. Guess that's all for now. Goodnight darling, with all my love.

5-30-44 Tuesday afternoon

This probably will be a sectional letter, or I may have to settle for just a note because I honestly don't know what I'm going to tell you. I'm starting it anyhow, just after lunch, while I'm sitting here waiting for one of the interminable roll calls they must have to keep track of so many strangers.

There's nothing further to report on when or where I'm going. It's still Thursday, but there's no clue to whether I'll stay here or ship out somewhere although I will be going to Gunnery School. I'll phone you as soon as I find out where I'm going.

I don't really care a whole lot, but rather think I'd like to move, for I should have at least an even chance of being closer to home, and I understand the only liberty we get in Gunnery School at Great Lakes is 32 hours every other weekend, and that's not enough time to come home, which would be the only way a liberty would be worthwhile. At some other station I might be able to get back more quickly, or might have a few hours longer, which would be something to cheer about.

Had me a card from Jess this morning, and his hunch was right, they landed at the station hospital. However, unless I stay here, I'll probably not see him for some time, because his card said he was out on liberty Saturday night, apparently in Waukegan, and would not be able to get out again for two weeks. So I suspect our journey together is ended. It's entirely probable we'll not meet again until all of this is over.

It's muster time now, and a helluva mob is flocking in here now, and I'll try to pick it up again in a little while.

Later: Actually that little while turned out to be some several hours for it's now 6:45 and I'm just getting back to finishing. After muster Don wanted to play pinochle and we sat over there all afternoon. Since the cards were running to me I won nearly a dollar playing for 10 cents a game and 5 cents a set, which makes for a profitable, as well as a pleasant, session. Now I'm back from chow, having stopped to watch a mushball game for a little while, and I guess I'll spent the rest of the night cooped up in here.

As you probably have guessed from the general tone of my letters, I'm finding it hard to readjust myself here again. It would have been a helluva lot better for me and a lot of others if we had plunged into the heavy work right away instead of spending days just loafing around. It gives you too much time to wish you were back home with your darlings. And to listen to discouraging gossip how tough the service schools are here, the rigorous class schedules, strict regulation of your behavior and in a lot of other ways.

I guess the horrible truth is that I'm wishing, sort of subconsciously as yet, that I weren't in the damm thing at all. However that's very foolish, and I'll just have to settle down and make the best of it when I get going - - soon.

Further, I wish I weren't going to school at all, but instead could be shoving off directly to sea. Think I would have tried to do just that, if it hadn't meant going away for Lord only knows how long without seeing you again. Then too, to be honest, I'm more than a little bit scared about the whole thing. So I guess I'll just have to be a drifter and let the dear old Navy do with me whatever it pleases.

There is not a whole lot longer to wait, praise be. Two more nights in here, then Thursday morning we should know where we're going. I still would like to get away from here, but don't think I will.

Tell Bucky I was sorry to hear he was so banged up but I know he was a good soldier about it, and will be all over it before he gets this. Don't fret about it Sonny (and you too Betts) for a boy just has to get a certain amount of that kind of stuff. There will be more, and you must always be brave Bucky, for that's the only way to take it.

And my girl is getting all dolled up and beginning to collect boy friends! Well I guess it must be she takes after her mother, but she'd better keep me as her # 1 boy friend or I'll be very angry. A good man must have two girls you know.

Guess that will have to be about it for tonight darling. I'll try to- - and almost certainly will - - write again tomorrow and you may hear from me before that, if I'm going away somewhere. All my love, darling, and believe me the only thing I really want in this world is to get back to you - - to stay - - as soon as possible.

5-31-44 Wednesday evening

Tomorrow is the big day, but we still don't know where or when we're going - - I still think it will be a stay here proposition, though there's no majority of opinion among the men here. Guess I'm just expecting the worst. Anyhow, I've spent most of the day getting the odds and ends of my clothes washed and ready to go.

Had a few tense moments this morning when the acting commander announced at muster he had a message for me. It turned out that the payroll office had just discovered my pay account, and was startled to learn that I'll be drawing the magnificent sum of $6 a month, and the lieutenant was perturbed about it because the Navy doesn't like to pay anyone less than $10 a month.

So I had to go over to the office and listen politely while a lady explained in words of one syllable what was going to happen to my dough. When I assured her I understand that, and could count to 10 without removing my shoes she shook her head dubiously and after receiving assurance that neither you or I will have to go to Navy relief for money, she said she guessed it was all right, and I could go.

The money situation is pretty tight here, with a few of the boys dead broke, and many more nearly so. I donated a couple of packs of cigarettes to a couple of the boys from the old outfit who were shoving off for parts unknown, without any moola, but still have $16.10 of my own after spending some money today for cigs, soap and razor blades. Dad will be interested to hear that I bought five-blade packs of Gillette blue blades for 6 cents a pack. Don't ask me how, but that's the price set on them at the canteen. If he wants some I'll be happy to get them.

Haven't heard anything more from Jess, so I still don't know exactly where he is or how he's getting along. I'm afraid he's not doing to well because he and Vone are most likely going to be pill rollers and needle pushers.

I plan to call you tomorrow morning if we're going away, and sure am looking forward to it (I mean talking to you). Seems a million years instead of 10 days, since I was home, and even if we don't move I'll probably blow myself to a call within the next few days. Will try to let you know sufficiently in advance so Mother and Dad and the kids can be there too.

I was very glad to hear today that Bucky is better, knew he would be all the time although something like that would have maimed you and I. Ain't kids wonderful? And that was a grand letter from my daughter, sounded for all the world like she was sitting there talking to me and I enjoyed it immensely.

Saturday and Sunday, unless we're on the road, I plan to spend a lot of time catching up with my correspondence, and I surely will write to both Bucky and Sis, just to show them how much their Dad appreciated their letters. That will have to be all for now, Darling except that I want more than anything else in the world to be with you. Far away from you, life is deadly monotonous, and very very lonely. Some day, soon I hope, I can hold you in my arms again and tell you how much - - I love you!

Chapter 2
GUNNERY SCHOOL
GREAT LAKES, ILLINOIS
6/1/44 to 7/15/44

6-1-44 Thursday evening

Well it's happened as I expected and here I am for 13 more weeks in Gunnery School, with every reason to believe I'm facing a vastly more difficult program than boots, both physically and in studies.

But I'm glad it's over and fully ready to settle down and do the damnedest best job I can. We won't get started to school until Monday, and because of the barracks we drew we will go to night school all through the course. Night school means classes from 4 to midnight at least 5, possibly 6 or 7 days a week.

We'll have an hour daily of "physical hardening," which probably includes very rigorous calisthenics, obstacle courses and a lot more things not overly pleasant to contemplate. To tell the truth it's the one part I dread most, for I fear it will be pretty hard on an old man. But if I survive I ought to be quite a man when it's all over.

Most of the rest of our time will be spent in mechanics, tearing guns apart and putting them together again. As I understand it, we're to be mechanics, rather than guys who do the shooting, which isn't altogether what I bargained for but something I can't change - - at present. Maybe I'll have a chance to try later.

Today started out just like all the rest of the time I spent in O.G.U., waiting and in doubt as to what and where. We were up at 5:30, ate an hour later and had the place cleaned before 8. Then we were told to wear whites, the first real evidence we were staying here, and to roll our gear. That was done by 9, and we had to do the cleanup again. After that we stood in formation outside for 30 minutes until a couple of the boys who had gone somewhere on their own decided to come back. Then we marched a mile to the main O.G.U. barracks, and were dismissed at 11:30 with orders to eat and be back in an hour.

Back again, we waited and waited, in 2 hours had to march twice past the clerks and give our names, then finally we were assigned bunk numbers, then a barracks off in the most distant corner of the service school section, and away we went to get our gear and move in.

This is a much smaller group than we had before, only 54 men altogether, and there are only two of us, Don Reed and me, left from the old company. I'm in the bottom bunk again as I was in boots, and located with a couple of nice-seeming fellows altho I know little about them as yet.

Guess that's about all for now, darling, for I've got to get to tailoring, shortening a pair of dungarees. I should have time to write you a reasonable letter tomorrow, and will catch up on a lot of letters, I think, over the weekend.

Anyhow, I still love you very very much, and always will, my Bettsy. It will be very wonderful to come back to you. Give the kids a big hug and kiss for me, and tell Mother and Dad not to worry. I've still got my pecker up, as Shakespeare would have phrased it.

6-6-44 Invasion Day

I've seen everything now and it's <u>NO</u> picnic - - but I'll probably survive. The worst, as I feared, is physical hardening, and
I'm not sure how much it hardened me today, but it damm near
mowed me down. Maybe I'd better put it altogether chronologically. I don't know how else I can make it coherent.

We went to class yesterday afternoon and ran into a bad break
at the start when our instructor was missing. Another teacher left
his own class to come over and show us a little about the .45 automatic pistol - - what the parts are, how to take it apart and put
it together again. Then they sent in a boy from an advanced class
to help us, and we spent the night working on the gun, except for
an hour for chow, a one-hour recognition class, and a 10-minute
smoke period.

Guess I learned a little bit about the gun, but it was a bad
start. The recognition class, taught by a stiff-necked lieutenant,
was a distinct disappointment because he talked in a monotone,
as though he didn't care anything about his job or whether or not
we learned. I sure hope he doesn't teach us all the time or it won't
be much fun. That was the extent of our classes, not a difficult
start at all, but we were a sleepy bunch when we got back here at
midnight, and hit the sack pretty promptly.

It had turned from hot to cool last evening, and by midnight
it was downright chilly. Some time during the night I woke up
wishing I had brought my potent back-warmer with me. But all
I could do was grab my extra blanket and snuggle down trying
to keep warm. I seem to be becoming a light sleeper, for I woke
several times in the night, then dozed off before reveille at 7:30.
That made seven hours of sleep.

We had to hustle then to be out of here at 8 for our first
calisthenics and when we got there the fun began. First there
was a sold half hour - - and I do mean solid - - of exercises var-
ied so as to practically exhaust every muscle. I managed to stick

through most of them, but a couple of times I just got bogged down, couldn't go any farther. From there we went to a half hour of tumbling, starting with somersaults across a big mat. It takes three of them to get across, and you do it fast all the way across. I made it four times, but the last two were right together and when I finished I was dizzy and sick, felt on the verge of passing out. I was standing up leaning against the wall and trying to hang on when a chief petty officer came over and tapped me on the shoulder and said come over here I've something for you to do.

Scared me at first, for I was afraid he'd think I was loafing, but I guess he diagnosed my trouble correctly, for he put me to sweeping up the dirt for 10 minutes, long enough to catch hold of myself. Then I was able to get in on the final phase, 3 laps around the drill hall, which would be something over a half mile.

Anyhow, as you can well guess, I was exhausted when it was all over. So was Reed, perhaps a little worse than I for nobody took pity on him. He worked himself sick, tried to vomit but couldn't because we had eaten nothing. A number of the other older men were pretty hard hit too.

So far as I can see, no allowance is made for older men in poor physical condition. Several hundred men, of all ages, take it at the same time with all sizes and all ages mixed in. The instructor, or director, is on a platform up front using a microphone, and anybody whom he thinks is loafing catches hell. And to top that off, I've just finished 15 minutes of swinging a sickle in tall grass, and my wrist is stiffened so that it doesn't want to write. I've got several other stiff spots, notably my fanny, but nothing really sore up to now. I'll know more tomorrow.

By the way, I forgot to tell you that I served the 6:30 and 9:30 Masses last Sunday - - there's a shortage of altar boys here. It's a strange sensation to sit in a big auditorium with 1,000 other sailors, listening to a grand organ and great choir and watching the unchanging Mass while the guns roar outside.

Don't know much else to write now, darling. I hope this hasn't sounded like too much moaning for I don't feel too badly about the whole thing, and know I'll be all right when I get hardened. In the long run it will do me a world of good, but it ain't going to be fun. Meanwhile I'll try to keep the letters coming, and you do it too for they sure are a ray of sunshine in this place.

Also, don't forget to let me know about your finances, for I think we may get paid about Friday and I'll have some to spare. My funds are running down a little because I've had to buy some school supplies (sounds funny for an old man, doesn't it ?), cigarettes and stuff but I still have 12 or 13 bucks, and won't need over a couple of bucks before the next regular payday, which will be about the 20th. I'm looking forward to going back to Milwaukee next weekend, when I expect to have liberty.

That will have to do for now, Bettsy, for I've a couple of things to do before we go to chow. Lots of love my dearest, and I wish I could be there to tell you about it.

6-7-44 Wednesday afternoon

Once again I find my time limited, so I can't promise to do much in the way of a letter. But I've got things pretty much under control (I think) and should be able to do better today and from now on.

Probably you're interested in my physical condition. I'm glad to report I'm not as stiff as I expected to be, and only a little bit sore. When I woke at 8:30 this morning I tried (very tentatively) to do a sit-up, and found my belly muscles locked. They just wouldn't answer. So I gingerly crawled out of bed, managed to get dressed and made my bunk in a half hour, and turned out for exercise.

This morning it was a hike - - about 4 miles in an hour, which is fast going, so we were at double time part of the way, and had only one momentary stop, at the half-way point. It wasn't nearly as tough as some of the hikes other outfits have told us about, and to tell the truth I really enjoyed it, especially because it meant no calisthenics. It was a beautiful crisp, cool morning, with the sun shining brightly, and we hiked up through North Chicago Junction and out into the country. Back in the barracks I took a grand hot shower, changed clothes and went to breakfast, then came back to read the paper for an hour.

I'm disappointed to see that the censors aren't letting the correspondents tell us any more about the invasion than they have of other major operations in the early stages. It's a stupid policy, and no reasonable man can say that censoring a story to delete the location of the fighting can be keeping information from the enemy, for his forces are fighting there too.

I suspect the present operation between Le Havre and Cherbourg is just the first of several. Look for one or more additional beachheads, further North toward Belgium, and a strike into the Balkans, perhaps a double-pronged affair with one army crossing the Adriatic from Italy into Yugoslavia or Albania, and the other heading North into Greece, hitting towards the Vandar River valley. It's a big show, and will take many months. There may be an additional drive into Southern France, probably under command of DeGaulle, toward Marseilles or Toulon.

After reading I went to work to clean up my laundry, and just finished it a little bit ago. Now all my work is caught up for tomorrow except rolling the clothes that will be dry by then - - but by then I'll have more laundry. It never ends - - or did you know?

Class last night was a repetition of the night before, minus recognition, and I suspect tonight we'll have a new teacher for that. We had no teacher, again, for our gun class, but I guess we made out all right with the Springfield rifle. Lordy we were a sore, tired bunch when we got home at midnight and it didn't take long to get to sleep. Needed both blankets, too, for it was quite cold. We wore our overcoats yesterday afternoon and last night.

I'm still ashamed of myself for not being able to write to

Bucky or Sis, especially since I had another letter from him today. But tell the kids their Daddy hasn't forgotten about them, and will write in a day or so, just as soon as I get a moment. Bucky's new stationery is very swell but he sure needs lines to guide by.

It's time to quit now, darling, for it's nearly chow and there are few odds and ends to be cleaned up before I go. Lots of love, dearest, and I'll be calling you on Sunday afternoon, so get yourself a little speech ready. You know what I want most to hear. Should be easy to guess, for I love you an awful lot, and miss you twice as much. By the way, I will be home on our 66 [this is a 66-hour liberty scheduled to take place in the 12th week of school], count on it, but that's a long time away.

6-10-44 Saturday evening

Herewith a birthday resolution: Not to have any more birthdays. It's not that I fear I'm getting old, but it seems that on birthdays I'm destined to be away from you, and I don't like it a little bit, consider it good and sufficient reason to abandon the practice. This makes it three times in the last four years that we're separated on June 10, and if my memory is correct it's about six times since we've been married. Phooey on that from me.

After chow yesterday we went to class, and started out with a test on airplane recognition. I got an 85, somewhat disappointing but not too bad. A couple (2) of the 54 guys made 100, and I should have been in the half dozen or so who made 90 or better.

Then we went to gun class, and got our marks from the previous night's test, an 88, also fair but should have been better. Later we had another test on the 3 important guns we studied during the night, and I had a 90. Not bragging about any one of the marks, and I mean to do better.

My brief sleep was further curtailed by a fire drill at 12:45, so that I had about 2 and 1/2 hours of sleep when I was called for guard duty at 3:30. There I was stuck until 8:30, with 15 minutes out for breakfast, then had to rush like hell to get shaved and change clothes in order to get to class at 9. That was our first weekly review test, and I made out all right, I think. Should get a 90 or better. The test, like all the rest we'll get each Saturday, was a multiple choice affair, to be graded by machine. We'll get the mark Monday, along with our first week's grade, and it should be a good indication of how I'm getting along. Our instructor told us that we're graded daily on personal appearance, neatness, effort and our daily test. The average daily grade counts 2/3, the weekly test 1/3, toward your weekly grade.

After today's test we were stuck with a share of the cleanup detail at the school building. Reed and I were the last 2 released, for some reason, and it was just in time for noon chow. Then it was rush, rush, rush again to get back to the barracks, change clothes and prepare for the weekly inspection, which was cleaned up passably at 3 p.m. and everybody in the other section went out on liberty, leaving 20-odd of us to hold down the joint until midnight tomorrow.

Reed and I played cards for a couple hours, then walked a while and at 6 went to the hostess house to splurge on a dinner, partly for a change but mostly because the chow has been very lousy lately. It seems that as night school students we get the short end of the food stick, eating an hour or two after the day pupils. We get what's left, sometimes even cold, as was the case with the fish and noodles (replacing potatoes) on Friday dinner. Suffice it to say that the hamburger steak, potatoes, green beans, pineapple and cottage cheese salad, rye bread, ice cream and 2 cups of coffee, which cost me 65 cents, tasted better than swell.

As I said it wasn't a bad birthday, considering I'm so far from my loved ones. Had a card from Peg, and a letter from Jess, in addition to the flock you sent. I got a terrific kick out of the card from Sis, the first sample of her writing I've seen, and appreciated Bucky's an awful lot too. Tell them I think they're grand kids to remember their Dad, and he'll do his absolute best to write to both of them tomorrow.

Incidentally, I'll have a full schedule then, for I'll have to go to Mass at least once, perhaps twice, and I have considerable laundry to do, as well as that awful backlog of correspondence that I'm still facing. Seems somehow that my days are always full, but perhaps that's best for it doesn't leave me too much time to dwell on the fact that the things which count most are much too distant from me.

But there's no use moaning about that, since I can't change it, and, the Lord only knows I'm not alone. Jess' letter should prove that to you. I'm enclosing it FYI, and please pass over the Navy verbiage, since it wasn't intended for your tender eyes.

Anyhow, I love you an awful, awful lot, Bettsy dearest, and couldn't think of a thing in the world I want more than to have you in my arms. Some of these days I'll be able to do just that again, and be able to tell you how much I love you

This is a letter written to Chuck by Jess James which was enclosed in the June 10, 1944 letter to Betty. It was written when they were separated from each other shortly after completion of Boot Camp.

Dear Chuck   Friday 7:15 P.M.

In the first place, I haven't given in yet to Navy time. I refuse to go into the mathematical progressions simply to convey the information that it is now 7:15 p.m. – even if all is not as well as it might be.

Your Thursday a.m. letter arrived at 4:30 p.m. today – nearly 30 hours to travel less than two miles. I gather the definite information that you can't get out of hock to get over here to visit us. Neither can Vone and I break out of this jail to see you. I'm in the abdominal surgery ward and he's in SOQ (Sick Officer's Quarters).

In many respects Boot Camp was a sailor's dream. The following is a typical day's schedule here:

5:45 a.m. – Rise and shine; 6 a.m. – Exercise; 6:10 to 6:30 – Shave, shower and dress; 6:30 to 6:45 Shit; 6:45 to 7:15 – Breakfast; 7:15 to 11.45 – Ward work (bed pan commando); 11:45 to 12:15 – Stand in chow line; 12:15 to 12:45 – Eat; 12:45 to 12:50 – Smoke; 12:50 to 1:00 – Walk to class; 1:00 to 4:15 – School; 4:15 to 5:00 – Fuck the dog (if he isn't all fucked out); 5:00 to 5:30 – Eat; 5:30 to 9:00 – Work in ward; 9:00 to 10:00 – Wash (!!!!!!!!!!!) the parenthesis is mine; 10:00 – Lights out.

Every other week we get three nights off. The other week we got off only two. Depends on which watch you're on. I'm on Starboard; Vone's on Port. When I say off, I mean free to sit around here. We've been given only two liberties in the first month. Two weekends – from noon Saturday till Monday at 9 a.m.

As for phoning you – that's impossible. I'm occupied during those hours that you're free.

We moved this week. We're now in a kind of double-jointed barracks you occupied when I left O.G.U. only there are no tables. Bunks are solid all the way. To smoke you stand in the hall. No lockers and incessant noise – radios and drunks. Also night turn men you don't feel like waking (although why not, I don't know; everybody else wakes them).

Something must be eating my ass tonight. All this griping. Maybe it's the invasion. Maybe it's the weather. (Have you ever seen anything like Great Lakes weather?) And aren't the Chicago papers doing a hell of a coverage job? I'm not as charitable toward the AP as you are. They're guilty in my book – by their own admission – until you prove they were left holding the bag by Hdq.

What did I start to say? Oh yes, your Milwaukee plan suits me – if I'm not barging in on your friends. Let me know what time you expect to catch the train (you get it at Downey's) and I'll meet you there providing it's not earlier than noon Saturday (in time for the noon train I mean). If you're shoving off earlier, I'll meet you anywhere you say in Milwaukee. Let me know definitely, please.

I think maybe what's irking me tonight is the thought that Vone's meeting Midge in Toledo, Ohio on Saturday night. She and the kids are spending a couple of nights at her parent's home near there. I'm thinking how nice it would be to see Janie and the kids.

I'm still getting out of this Navy what I started out to get, but the process could be more pleasant – in addition to giving one the notion he was contributing something to the war effort. As it is, I'm doing what any nurse's aid would turn up her nose at.

I'm ship-thinking again. Let me know as soon as possible about Milwaukee. I have a hotel clerk all fixed up to reserve a room for me 6/17. It'll cost the three of us $1.25 each. The room's not big, but the double bed's good – and we can toss for the cot – it's good too; I slept on it last week. All I have to do is give the hotel (the Belmont, across the street from the U.S.O.) 3 or 4 day's notice.

This's enough for this time. The competition's too much. There are at least 12 conversations going on here at the same time.

<u>Jess</u>

Dear Son [Bucky] : 6/11/44

I have been a long time getting around to writing your letter, but it's your turn tonight. It sounded swell to hear you on the telephone tonight, although I thought you sounded as though you had a cold.

Are you having a good time playing baseball? We play a little mushball here, when we get a chance, and the other afternoon I played basketball for a while. Then we can go swimming if we get the chance, in a great big indoor pool. If you were here I could teach you to swim pretty quickly, I think.

Fishing would be fun, too, if we could get to it. Lake Michigan, which is much, much bigger than the rivers we used to see in Philadelphia, is as close to our barracks as the gas station is to Grandpa's house. I'm hoping to be able to take both you and Sis fishing the next time I come home.

Lake Michigan is very big, so big that you can't see across it, and big ships, bigger than the ferries we rode on in Philadelphia go up and down it all the time. Most of the time it is foggy, and at night you can hear the fog whistle blowing on the breaker a mile away. Whoo, whoo, it sounds, soft and very deep-throated from this far away.

You really would have a good time seeing all the guns we have to study - - pistols, rifles, tommy guns, machine guns, and real cannons. We didn't get a chance to shoot any of them yet, but we will one of these days.

Have you kept on studying your catechism? You must keep up with it so you can make your first communion this summer and I'd like you to ask Father Gartland about when you can start learning to be an altar boy. I think I started when I was your age.

Write and tell me all about what you are doing, Son, and don't get into any fights unless somebody else starts trouble. Remember nobody likes a boy who is fighting all the time.

Be a good boy, be sure to do what Mother tells you, and help her all you can. I'll be home just as soon as I can make it.

Your Dad

6-16-44 Friday afternoon

This husband of yours is a very tired one right now, weighted down with a new job, too, for I've just been made master-at-arms of the section, second in command. Most of the time it's a glorified version of my boot camp job, for the MAA (We use initials and wear an arm band.) is in charge of the cleanup and the barracks. I didn't ask for the job, but now that I've got it I'll do the best damm job I can.

I'm tired mostly because the calisthenics this morning were even a little more brutal than usual, and lasted 10 minutes longer, which was anything but fun. However, the physical end is getting easier for me and I'm pretty much able to keep up with these young kids. It's still hard, brutal work.

Then I came back and took a shower, which helped some, but while I was standing in line after chow to buy my ticket to Milwaukee my right leg started to stiffen a little, and now one muscle is so sore it's downright annoying. Then I had to come back and do a little laundry before cleanup time, and it was then I got my new job.

The change has been brewing for several days, almost since we came in, in fact, for the little Italian — we call him Shorty — who was picked for the job at the beginning just didn't have the stuff. He was funny as hell, only 5 feet tall, but too loud and no idea about how to organize. Then too he can read and write only a little, which put him under a real handicap in school.

That wouldn't have been too much if he had tried, but he spent most of his time clowning, disrupting the class, and just didn't care. He was an awful braggart, too, but despite all that could be a likable chap when he tried. His trouble started last week when he turned in a blank examination paper one night, and most of the time he tried to copy and make others do his work for him. Anyhow he failed last week, but was doing a little better this week, copying for his Tuesday test, but seemingly getting by, possible because of the rookie instructor.

But last night, he went too far, not writing anything during the test, holding his own paper when the rest of us were ordered to exchange to correct them. While the instructor read the answers, Shorty scribbled frantically, and at the end announced he hadn't exchanged papers and asked the instructor to correct his.

Carson, the instructor, had seen what was going on, told Shorty to go to the supervisor if he wanted a grade, and the brazen little guy did just that. Sauls, the supervisor, came back to ask Carson how come, and Carson told him everything except how the paper was filled in. Sauls threw it away, offered Shorty another test, and when Shorty got smart even offered to let him take the same test again. Finally when Shorty kept on talking back, Sauls took him down to the C.P.O., and it wound up with Shorty being ordered to Captains Mast, where punishments are ordered.

As I said, this has been brewing for some time, and a couple days ago the section leader had called me aside and asked if I would take the job, saying he would recommend me. After the blowup last night he took me into the C.P.O. and told them I was the guy he wanted for the job. I said I'd take the job, or do anything else I was told.

I was offered the job just before cleanup this morning and took charge of it, which was finished just as I started this. It's the beginnings of a new job and it's going to be tough. The authority I have to order the guys to work is mighty slim, so I'm counting on getting it done without ordering, simply by asking. It will be a lot better if I can, but even so I'm bound to be an S-O-B to some of the lazy ones all of the time and probably the same to all the guys some of the time.

Rumor has it that the section leader and MAA get ratings as third class petty officers at the end of the course if they do a good job and get reasonably good marks. Don't know how much truth there is to that but it sounds logical as a means of repaying a guy for handling a nasty job. Anyhow, I don't care much about the rate, if I can get where I want to go.

Did fairly well last night, making 97 on the guns test, would have had 100 except I misunderstood what the instructor wanted on one question and failed to complete it. Then I got 88 on the recognition test, best mark in the section and tonight we get our weekly gun test, which I'm hoping to handle OK.

Tomorrow we go on the small arms range for the first time, and it will be tough getting ready for inspection. Must go now, darling, for it's school time. All my love.

P.S. This stolen note is being tacked on in school, where I've completed my test and now must sit around and wait for a couple of the slower ones to wind up. What happens then I don't know, for it's 40 minutes to chow time and I'll be surprised if they start teaching us anything new. What's more I can't figure what we'll do tonight, for we've four more hours of classes, and nothing in sight to do - - except clean up the durn school for Saturday inspection.

About the range tomorrow - - we'll fire 4 automatic guns, the Browning automatic rifle, the Thompson submachine gun (it's the "Tommy Gun" to Bucky), M-1 carbine and .30 caliber machine gun. Don't know how much we'll fire them but I guess only a few rounds, enough to get acquainted with them.

Our test today seemed easy, and if I don't make over 90 on it I'll be both surprised and very much disappointed. Furthermore, I have a 91 average so far this week, so I'd have to fall below 83 on the test to fail to better my overall 87 average of last week. Told you I could do better (business of eating eggs before hatching chicken to lay 'em). I plan to keep it up, too. That's enough bragging for one day Bettsy, so I'm going to cut it out, as of now.

Golly, I wish I were going somewhere else than Milwaukee tomorrow. Not that I won't enjoy myself there, but there's <u>one</u> other place I would prefer but can't reach. So I'll do the best I can, go see Ginny and Leo, have a reunion with Jess and drink a few beers, which ought to be a pretty fair weekend. But I'll be thinking of you, and wishing, no matter what I do, that I were with you instead. Bye darling, and take care of yourself and ours. I love you.

This was enclosed in a letter dated 6-17-44.

Dear Daddy

Do you get Weaties at Great Lakes? I will ask Father Gartland when I can be an altar boy soon. I don't know what is the matter with my appetite? Here is what I ate, four helpings of bran. Ha! Ha! I have folled you. Heh! Heh!

Mrs. Neilan has a new grandson. I am studying the Confiteor out of my catechism.

Lots of love Bucky

6-19-44 Monday noon

Can't say just now how much this will amount to for I'm short of time. As you probably can guess I'm way behind with my laundry, and doubt very much whether I'll be able to catch up tomorrow.

Anyhow, it was a very pleasant weekend, a grand change to be away for a while, and now I'm back and into the grind for another two weeks. Hope they'll pass faster than the last two. We had a pretty stiff hike this morning but I honestly enjoyed it and the exercise felt good after the loafing.

We got our identification cards a few minutes after I finished that note to you on Saturday, and there must have been 10,000 men going out. They split us into three groups, the biggest going to Chicago and points west, east and south, next largest to Milwaukee and the north, and the third and smallest the "local" party, for Waukegan and other nearby towns.

Then they marched us down to the railroad and out along the tracks to the waiting trains, and at a signal everyone scrambled to get in. Reed and I first landed in an old parlor car, with 25 big round single seats, and 75 guys there ahead of us. We sat on the arms of the chairs until we reached Kenosha, then moved back into another car where there were steel benches. I was able to doze for a few minutes, having had only 2 and ½ hours sleep before getting up to go on guard at 3:30 a.m.

When we got to Milwaukee Reed and I walked 8 or 10 blocks to the hotel where Jess had reserved rooms. We got a couple of beers, changed from blue uniforms to white, then went hunting the tailors for my pants, and Jess had a couple of jumpers at another place, so by the time we wandered around and picked them up it was 7:30 and we were due at Ginny's.

Well, we got there and had a couple more beers, then some food, the first thing I'd eaten except a bowl of cereal, since Friday evening. Another married couple, the same folks who had been there when Don and I were there before, dropped in and we were sitting there talking when I started to feel sick and sleepy like I'd never been before in my life. We went back to the hotel and I went to bed while Don and Jess went touring.

I was told later that Don brought Jess back about 3, then kept going until 5. I remember waking up and seeing Don asleep on the other bed. A little while later I woke with a start to find Reed gone, the door open, and hearing some man in the hall shouting "Get the hell out of here before I get a pistol"!

Don, it seems, had been awakened by screams from the next room, and when the screams kept getting weaker, and finally stopped, he was afraid someone had been or was being killed and went to investigate. That was when I woke up to hear the pistol business, and Don got back to the room pretty quickly for the guy sure sounded like he meant business. Finally we decided to call the desk and report the situation, but the clerk said a family quarrel had been reported before and suggested we pay no attention, saying they were checking. Later in the day we saw the man and a woman in the hotel lobby, and they seemed friendly enough.

So I went out to Mass, while Don tried to get Jess up, but it was no go. Jess had been sick most of the night, and had one of the world's worst hangovers, couldn't possibly crawl out even when I came back at noon. After giving Jess up as a bad job, Don and I went to Ginny's for a very swell dinner, and sat and talked until it was time for us to come back and check out of the hotel before 5 p.m.

There we finally got Jess up and dressed and after he got some tea and toast he recovered rapidly. A little while later, we went into a cocktail bar, ran into Jess's roommates and sat talking and drinking beer. That lasted until 7 when Jess, Reed and I went to the USO and checked our bags, then wandered down to the AP office in the Milwaukee Sentinel building. It's a dinky little office and only one man was working, but it was a lot of fun to hear the teletypes clattering and talk shop for a little while.

We were ready to come "home" then, so took the 8 o'clock train, and Reed and I got off at one station while Jess stayed on to the next. Don and I bought some ham and eggs at a restaurant just across the street from the gate then wandered in, and when we arrived at 10 p.m., were the first men from our entire barracks to return.

I slept like a log until 7:30, and then hiked and that brings us up to date on what happened. It was, as I said, a pleasant weekend, and a relief to get away.

I'm going to stop now darling, for it's time we went to work, and besides the pay list has just come out, letting us know how much money we can draw tomorrow. I'm on the list for $20, which is $5 less than I had expected to take down, but should be plenty (I'll let you know if I need more, never fear). Bye now dearest, I love you lots and will try to write some more later, if I get a chance. Tell Bucky and Sis I do look forward to their letters, and to keep them coming.

6-22-44 Thursday noon

Right at this moment I'm just a little more lonely than usual, if that's possible, and wishing above everything that I could be with you, even for just a little while. Can't say exactly what causes such a feeling but it's there and there's no use trying to hide it.

Our third week is nearing an end, only eight more to go before I see you, and already I'm beginning to tick off the days, something like I do at calisthenics when I'm beginning to play out. Sometimes it happens on pushups. I think I just can't go any longer until I say to myself - - only 3 (or however many) more to go, sure I can do that. And you'd be surprised how well it works. Hope it works as well counting off the weeks and days - - if you still have any idea I'm not coming home on my 66 you know what you can do with it.

Coming home from school last night we ran into some trouble. We were marching out of class when someone in the line started to get noisy. When the noise didn't stop a petty officer came out and stopped the whole section. The PO wanted to know who was making the noise and when no one stepped forward he marched the whole section to the duty office to put us all on report.

Fortunately, the duty chief wasn't around, but the chief who came out was from gunnery school and he proceeded to bawl us out, and wanted to know who was doing it. Then our friend Shorty stepped out, got a mild scolding, and it was then the chief told the section they would have to obey the section leader and MAA because "They are training to be petty officers, and will be made PO's when they finally finish school."

Too many people around here seem to think the end of the war is in sight, and I believe a majority of students and instructors I've talked to are firm in the belief that practically no men now in our stage of training will ever get on a warship. I still can't subscribe to that, and still think we've years of war ahead.

The European invasion is going faster than I expected, but still has a helluva long way to travel. And as for Japan, even the very big naval engagement which is hinted for the past few days would only be a start on the road to Tokyo. Somehow I can't be overly optimistic about the thing I want most.

I'm woefully behind with my laundry, damm it, so I now have underwear, sox, towel, hat to do, will have the same amount more, plus dungarees, tomorrow. Phooey. This is a helluva life. You must change underwear and hat and sox at least once every day, and with only four suits of underwear you've gotta keep right on the ball, as the Navy phrase goes.

Sorry darling, if I seemed snide yesterday when you confessed you had been ill. Honestly you did a good job covering up, but somehow you are too close to me (I don't mean physically close right now dammit.) to really deceive me on something like that, altho I'll admit you fooled me on the sciatica. On which note, I think I'll shut up for today. Always remember, Bettsy, that I love you with all my heart, and always will. This is a lonely life for both of us, but some day it will all be over and we can go back to living. Bye, dearest, and sleep tight.

6-26-44 Monday morning

Yours is a somewhat happier husband at the moment, probably because of a combination of pleasant factors. First and of course the most important was my phone call last night, and it surely was wonderful to talk to all of you. I could just see Dad grinning and my how Franny has improved in his language. Wish I could be there to talk with him. My Chubbin sounded like a sleepy gal and Bucky wide awake as usual. And this time I believe you are all right, praise be, so altogether it was pretty wonderful.

Then I got two letters from you and one from Eleanor this morning, plus my package. At the moment I'm sitting here in my new slippers, which brought anguished (jealous really) howls from some of the gang who fear I'll go clomping about the barracks in the middle of the night. But they're exactly what I wanted, and I thank you very much. All the rest of my presents were grand, too, seemed like an almost real birthday. I shared the nuts with the rest of the gang, and they lasted about two minutes, but the candy is safely hidden in my sea bag until a little later. You weren't, by any chance, hinting with the Mum were you? I'll have you know I use the stuff faithfully, after every bath, and I sometimes get two of those a day.

Right now I'm using the pen you sent. I wish you had kept it for as I told you I bought another last week and this time it's a good one, in addition to which I have I have the 75 cent job so at the moment I'm a man with three pens. But no matter how many pens I have I can only write only one letter at a time, so first chance I get I'll send the one back to you, and you can save my new set.

By the way how are you getting along with your baths now? What I mean, I wonder who's scrubbing your back. Wish - - Well, I will one of these days, see if I don't.

The only thing wrong with me at the moment is I'm sleepy as the deuce. Slept fitfully last night, and we were all wakened by a ruckus at 6 a.m. so I could sure use some shut eye. The other section had liberty this weekend, and about half of them came in all boiled up. What's worse, a couple brought bottles, strictly against the rules, and from what I can learn there was some drinking going on in the barracks in the wee small hours. Glad I didn't see any of it, for I would have had to make some trouble over it.

We had boxing for our physical hardening this morning, and this time it was 7 rounds instead of 5. Reed and I, who box together, work pretty hard at it but at the same time try not to hurt each other. Nevertheless my nose is a little crooked and I caught one good left on the jaw, but the 16 ounce gloves we wear don't let you get hurt very much, and it's lots of fun. Tomorrow we go back to calisthenics, and I'm getting so tough I don't even mind that - - much. Maybe there'll even come a day when I enjoy it.

I'm sorry to see Jess and Vone go – they're off to California – but guess I'll be catching up to them one of these days. They'll have no chance to get home before they go and Vone says they'll have at least 6 months in San Diego, and then don't know where they'll go.

Looks like I won't get to see Red Sabin [a friend from Somerset] until he comes back from boot leave. I was refused a pass to go to Green Bay area yesterday and don't suppose there will be another chance before he goes. I'm going to phone him, and tell him how to get here when he's on O.G.U.

Strange, but I seem to be running out of words again, durn it, so I'm going to call a halt and go in and shave. We'll be ready to clean up shortly, and then chow and school, so here we go again.

Tell my kids to write to me and let me know what they're doing. Know Dad will have a wonderful time at the retreat, and only hope Mother won't work too hard while he's away. 'Bye, darling, and I do love you very much.

Dear Son: 7/4/44 Tuesday

Since I'm going to vary my usual practice of writing all the letters to your mother, I thought I would sit down here this morning and see if I can't answer your letter of last week.

I've just come from breakfast, not a very good one, and when I finish writing I'll have to get to work with some washing. It seems we never do get caught up on that. Our breakfast this morning was a cooked cereal, which I don't like, bacon, hard boiled eggs, bread and butter and milk. Doesn't sound good and doesn't taste good either, but when you have been up for three hours, and had an hour of calisthenics and tumbling you are ready to eat almost anything.

Mother tells me you will be making your First Communion soon, and I very much wish I could be there with you. Communion is a great and wonderful gift from God, and while you are much too young yet to understand fully what it is, you'll learn as you get older. Pray hard, son, and we'll receive together when I come home again.

I do hope you are studying hard in vacation school, and not acting like a smart aleck because you already know many of the answers. Remember, none of the others had a chance to go to a real Catholic School and of course that gives you a big start. Next weekend, if I can find a moment, I'm going to try to write at least a note to Mother Incarnata [the principal at St. Lawrence School in Philadelphia] and tell her all about us.

My own school is going along pretty well. My report card (We really don't get a card, the teacher just tells us our marks.) shows I made a 95 on the test last week and had a 92 average for the week. The fellow who sleeps above me in the bunk bed had the same marks, and ours were the best in the section. I think my average of 91 for the first four weeks is as good as any in the class.

Just now we are studying the 20 millimeter cannon, an automatic gun that shoots a bullet 8/10 of an inch thick and nearly two inches long. It is used against enemy airplanes, and we are also studying Japanese fighting planes, which have funny names like Jake, Hamp, Rufe, Betty, Nell, Lillie and some more.

We had a pretty tough session of calisthenics this morning, starting out doing 90 jumping jacks without a stop. I'll show you what that is when I get home, and maybe I'll be able to teach you some tumbling, too, turning cart wheels, flip flops and such things like the acrobats in the circus - - only I'm not that good. But I find it fun and have a notion to try to get into the advanced class to learn a little more about it.

Haven't as yet played any baseball, although I would like to. There just is never as enough time here to do all the things you want to do.

Today is much the strangest Fourth of July I've ever spent. We work and go to school just as usual, for the war doesn't stop for holidays. Outside we can hear airplanes most of the time, and in a little while the cannon will be cracking on the aircraft range. That's as close as it will come to firecrackers today. How well I remember the Fourth of July celebrations we had when I was your size.

For weeks all of us kids saved their money to buy firecrackers, and always we got up at the crack of dawn and started to shoot them - - little crackers that we set up in slings; pop pop poppety pop pop, they sounded and the big ones we shot one at a time made a wonderful and very terrifying boom. The afternoons were for family picnics, sometimes at Edgewood Grove, and there were always two baseball games. At night there were more fireworks in the Grove, wonderful pinwheels and sparklers and roman candles that burned with a million colors and boomed like thunder. And late at night I used to sit up in my window and watch the skyrockets leaving trails of fire across the sky before they exploded in showers of red and green and orange balls of fire.

It was pretty, but an awful waste of money and always some youngsters were hurt, sometimes horribly burned. So while I'm sorry in a way you can't do it, I'm much happier because I know you're safe. And some time in the future, I'll take all of you to see a night fireworks display so you'll know what it's like.

That's just one of the many things I've planned for all of us when we get this war over. It will be lots of fun to go to baseball games and all sorts of things with your mother, you, Sister and Fran, and I'm not going to miss it any more than I have to.

Until we can, be a good boy for Mother and help her as much as you can. Sis properly should be Mother's best helper around the house but there are lots of things for a big boy to do when his Dad's away. Be careful too and write when you can.

Your Dad

7-4-44 Tuesday afternoon

Darling, a little while ago I finished a long letter to Bucky that will do for the family, so this is just between you and me.

It's hard to talk intelligently at this distance, but if we can both imagine we're lying in bed talking with the lights out, as we used to do in those happy days that seem so long ago, it may work out all right

Of course there's an obvious complication to the bed angle, for the way I feel now, and have been feeling for some weeks, I would just have to kiss you and hold you tight, so tight that probably neither one of us could talk. My arms have been empty much too long my Bettsy, and will have so much to make up when we get the chance again. Even to think about it brings a stirring in my belly that is wonderful, even though I know it will start the elephants to walking again.

I never will forget, no matter what happens, how wonderful it is to feel your lips on mine, and to touch your smooth soft skin. And Betty if there was ever any doubt in your mind of my ability to withstand the animal urge you know I have, then throw it out now for not ever could <u>any</u> other woman be that to me. It's been a long time now, so that I should be about as desperate as I'll ever get, yet I found the approaches last weekend only a little amusing, and more than a little revolting. Whatever happens, darling, I've known you and had you in my arms, and no one else can enter there.

Don't know just what started that, but there it is and I can only hope you'll know it's as true as my love for you---- and yours for me.

There's no need to tell you that I'm awfully sorry to hear about Dad [Carl Dresser, Betty's father] but can't deny I've been expecting something of the sort, just as you have. In a sense, it's his own fault, for he's been warned and we have all pleaded with him to get the hell out of there, but I guess he was caught up in a web that just kept him from doing it. But maybe when he gets over this he will have seen the light and if he'll only get out <u>now</u> it's not too late. We'll have to wait and see what happens, and I do hope Mother or some one will take the time to keep you informed. If Dad should get very sick, I agree you ought to go, probably it would be best to take Fran with you but I think Buck and Sis would be all right at Somerset.

As to longer range plans, it seems best to me to let this ride for a little while we see what develops. If the worst should happen, it seems to me that the best solution might be for you and Mother to find an apartment in Somerset, and perhaps you could arrange it so that you could take some kind of job to supplement your $120. Knowing my darling, I'm confident you can swing it on your own; else I wouldn't have run away as fast as I did.

I think Bettsy dearest, that's about all that's in my head on the subject of living right now. And I suspect that, as usual, we're thinking pretty much along the same lines which isn't too odd, considering we've been doing that for some 14 years. Lordy our 9th anniversary is just around the corner and what a wonderful 9 years it has been. Not once, to the best of my recollection, have we had a squabble of even minor proportions, and while I know now I wasted too many opportunities we've had millions of glorious moments, any one of which would make a happy life for an average man. But I'm not average, for I want a million more, and mean to start on them one of these days.

Strange the things that come into my mind as I think back: Driving, just you and I, and stopping for a kiss; walking in the rain: the moonlight shining through the vines on those long, still nights we sat on Grandma's porch: the feel of your belly, big with child, as you snuggled against me in the night, and the never to be forgotten taste of your kisses - - and your breasts; the choking sensation and the blinding sting in my eyes that day you drove away over the hill to Allentown with your Dad, and how much it has hurt every time I've said goodbye since then. Not happy you say? Yes, there was happiness for looking back I know that every time I've said goodbye to you was just a prelude to a wonderful reunion.

The look on your face as I walked in that morning that was only seven weeks ago, and seems a million years: and how you sobbed, as though ashamed when you came up to me that morning, then got in bed and admitted you, too, couldn't wait.

I remember all those, dearest, and ever so many more, and I'm happy above everything else in the world that I love you and you love me. And one of these days - - if it's not so far away that we will lose one spark from the fire - - we'll start to live these things again. As surely as we've lived before, so will we live again, and as I always have and always will, I love you.

7-9-44 Sunday

It was only a couple of days ago that I was bragging about what a faithful correspondent I've been, and believe I let you down yesterday. Feel guilty, even though there was nothing much to tell you when I had time and was able to write.

Friday was a bad day, for just as I expected the majority of both sections flunked and I mean flunked—the recognition test. I didn't and even though my 76 was the poorest mark I've had by a good bit, I don't feel too badly. As for the gun, I think I'm okay for we had two more tests Friday, and I made 93 on each, and yesterday's test wasn't too hard.

We had the joint pretty well cleaned up yesterday morning, so there really wasn't really a whole lot to do when we got back at 11 except clean ourselves and then give the place a final polish. Inspection went off OK at 2 and then the other section kept things in a turmoil until they finally got I.D. cards and pulled out shortly after 3.That was the time I had planned to write my daily letter, but instead sat down in the poker game and won a couple of dollars before chow time.

Chow was OK, and I had a tremendous helping of a salad that included chopped radishes, onions, lettuce, etc. Gee it was good. But when I got back there was a real feed here. John Wunder, who owns a delicatessen in Cincinnati, had his wife send up a couple of packages, and what a feast. There was a whole 8 pound piece of thuringer, cheese, sardines, kippers, jelly, olives, pickles, potato chips, crackers - - everything imaginable. Of course I pitched right into it, and honestly I ate until I was stuffed so much that I couldn't move the rest of the night, I was so uncomfortable. And I couldn't even eat a piece of the cake he brought out to cap it.

Anyhow it was so much fun we all want to do it again, and I'm wondering what you could send me to help out a week from today. Would there be any possibility of a canned ham or perhaps one of those 5 pound cans of lunch meat? It would have to be something like that, to keep, and if you can arrange it send it parcel post on a Wednesday so it would get here Friday or Saturday. That would be for the week after next, should be mailed by the 20th to get here on the 23rd. If all of us get a little something like that it will make another feast, without one guy having to finance it all, for that must have cost at least $20.

I was even so full I couldn't sleep well but I got up OK today and went to 6:30 Mass and then came back and did my laundry so here I am on the ball again. When I finish this, I'm going to do some more writing.

Strangely, it's good to know that you're hungry (No, I'm <u>not</u> talking about food again.) as I am and only waiting for our real life to begin all over again. Suspect that it will be even better than being newly-weds again, for there are so many things we'll <u>really</u> appreciate again.

On the way back from chow this morning I stopped to see Red Sabin, who is back in O.G.U. waiting for yeoman school. Same old Red, he'll never change. He phoned me yesterday afternoon to report he was back here, and where he was. He was on guard when I dropped in this morning, but said he'd come over this afternoon, so I'm expecting him about 4 o'clock. If the poker game is going (it's stopped now but probably will be going again) I know what Red is going to do.

Stopping time now, Bettsy, for I'll have to be getting to chow. I'm sorry I let you down, and honestly I won't eat like that again.

I love you an awful lot darling, and always will.

7-10-44 Monday noon

I'm not promising, as I start this how long it will last for there isn't much time and I feel badly in need of a nap. We acting <u>petty</u> officers don't have to stand regular guard, but every now and then we get security watch, which means patrolling 5 barracks to keep the guards on their toes. I caught it this morning and had to get up at 3:15, so you can see why I'd like a little nap to carry over to midnight.

We were boxing this morning, and quite a session it was, mostly because the whole gang is getting a little more confident and sure of themselves. We had a session of calisthenics first, of course, then fought 7 tough rounds and we were really going to town. A punch bloodied my nose and made me see stars for a minute. All in all it was fun.

As usual it was wonderful to talk to you last night, and grand to hear Mom and the kids, too. I hadn't really planned to call, but I had been thinking about it and last night I decided I'd been a miser long enough so I might as well treat myself and all of you. Best investment I've made in a long time, too.

But you must get over being scared when you get an unexpected call or telegram. Now don't say you weren't for I could almost hear you gasp when the operator told you who was calling. And some time when I want to reach you I may not be able to get to a phone and will have to settle for a telegram, so please; please, please don't be a scairdy cat or I'll just cut it out all together.

Gosh, Fran sure is getting to be a talker, only wish I could be there to hear him perform in person. My only regret was that the line fuzzed up a couple times and I couldn't hear all Buck and Sis had to say. But tell them their Daddy thinks they're wonderful kids, and loves them very much.

After I hung up I came back in and gabbed with Red a little

while then he left and since I had nearly an hour I wrote to the Smiths which made me four letters for the day - - one to you know who - - and did some laundry. Ain't I wonderful?

I hope you'll forgive me for stopping here Bettsy, for I'm acutely in need of that nap and there isn't much time. But I do want to say I'm serious about the trip we talked about, if things work out right. You can come out the weekend before I get my 66 leave. You could take the 10:00 train out of Johnstown on Friday night, August 8, which would get you to Chicago Saturday morning. I'd meet you there and we could be together until 11 Sunday night. You'd be on your own for four days and we'd start home together Friday afternoon August 15. Food for thought!

This is the letter written by Jess James that was enclosed in a July 12, 1944 letter to Betty. Jess and his brother-in-law, Vone Jones, had just arrived at the Naval Hospital in San Diego, CA.

U.S. Naval Hospital Staff
General Delivery
San Diego, Calif.
July 4, 1944

Dear Chuck:

If by any chance you'd formed the opinion that Great Lakes managed to waste money and manpower while playing soldier, you should see this place. A properly organized civilian hospital could operate on this scale - - no one denies it is vast - - on no more than two-thirds the staff.

We arrived Saturday, after three days and four nights in one of those government-owned cattle cars. The Rock Island lost eight hours the first day out, and we never made it up. The Southern Pacific, which took over somewhere in New Mexico, held it's own until we reached L.A. From there we could have walked faster.

After we crossed Illinois, we dipped into Iowa for a healthy slice, cut part way across Missouri, the panhandle of Oklahoma, a tiny corner of Texas, the entire breadth of New Mexico and Arizona and into California in a blaze of hot boxes. Highest elevation: 6,666 feet. Highest temperature: 120 (in the desert).

Don't let anyone feed you any more Chamber of Commerce propaganda about the joys of sunny Southern California. When the sun isn't shining (and it never gets up earlier than 9 a.m.; one morning it was 11 a.m.) And after it goes down at night you freeze if you don't wear your pea coat.

Vone and I got pretty good shakes. After waiting around till 1 p.m. Monday for assignment, we were sent over to the emergency ward, where all cases coming into the hospital stop for assignment to wards. I'm to be moved into the office here (according to the petty officer in charge) as soon as one of the fellows who's expecting transfer moves on. Maybe it's more of the Army game, but a least I'm closer to a typewriter than I've ever been in the Navy, and that's something. I'm not crossing any creeks until I come to them, but I'm keeping my toes crossed. In addition, Vone and I both made Starboard watch - - which means our working hours and hours off jibe.

Chow here is good. Living quarters, terrible. In order to make room for what seems like thousands of Waves, corpsmen have been moved out of their barracks, and are living in tents. A sailor in a tent rivals one on a horse, doesn't it? I've got to get to work before I get fired from this cinch. Now that I've found this, you may hear from me oftener.

Jess

7-15-44 Saturday afternoon

The typewriter may surprise you and it happened this way. Liberty time arrived this afternoon and neither Reed nor I had any idea of where to go or what to do so we just walked out with the local party, took a trolley and wound up here in Waukegan, which is only about 8 miles from the station—total fare 14 cents per round trip.

From what we've seen of the place in the first hour or so it's OK, and we'll probably spend a very quiet weekend here just sitting around and doing as little as possible. The town is about the size of Johnstown from what I've seen of it and lacks Johnstown's dirt, with the additional advantage of a lake front. We've been walking around, after parking our bag at the USO, and discovered a bathing beach which we'll probably investigate further tomorrow.

We were wandering around a few minutes ago when a man standing outside a door marked Lutheran Servicemen's Center invited us in for something to eat and despite a reply that we weren't hungry repeated the invitation so there was little we could do but accept. Inside we found a very nice place, and there were a couple of mills [typewriters] sitting around and I asked permission to use one of them to write my daily missive.

It's been for some reason, a hectic day, because I didn't know what I was going to do and didn't care a helluva lot. We got the joint pretty well cleaned up (I thought) before breakfast, then took a reasonably easy test, and back to the barracks before noon to finish the job. Somehow or other I didn't get around to making my bag layout until time for chow, and was almost too late, but did manage to get it over with then went back and got into my whites for inspection.

As I said, I thought we had the joint pretty well cleaned up, but I must have been wrong for the inspecting officer found an awful lot of things that didn't suit him a little bit and we wound up with a 2.7 rating that was the lowest in that barracks in many years. Shortly thereafter, we all got our I.D. cards and left

This is a very nice place, much nicer fitted than regular USO, where we checked our bag shortly after arriving in town. I feel sort of like a fish out of water, or a man sailing under false colors, to be a mick in a protestant place, but know that is silly.

Meanwhile it feels good to be sitting back at a typewriter again, and it's a Royal, the kind of machine that I started out on and am used to operating. Which reminds me to tell you to put a home typewriter on our get-after-the-war list, for I'll be needing one to use at home, and I want the kids to learn as soon as they're big enough to spread their hands over the keys. See, there I go already; planning how to use up that tremendous stock of war bonds we've accumulated (?).

Anyhow darling, this should prove to you that I don't forget about my one and only even when I'm footloose and fancy free a thousand miles from home. And if you need any further proof that I love you, just ask me the next time I get a chance to put my arms around you. Bye, now, dearest and maybe won't miss my usual every-other-Sunday letter tomorrow, if I can wander back here and find this mill in working condition again.

Chapter 3
GUNNERY SCHOOL
GREAT LAKES, ILLINOIS
7/17/44 TO 9/4/44

7-17-44 Monday noon

Before I even get started with this report, I thought I might as well warn you that this weekend turned out very differently - - at least as to locale from what you might have been expecting after my Saturday evening report.

After I finished writing to you, I went downstairs to the canteen, where Reed and I had 2 or 3 cups of very fine coffee and a couple of ham sandwiches, then did some reading. About 8 o'clock we decided it was about time we located a hotel room, and right then and there we ran into difficulty. A checkup of Waukegan's six hotels showed nary a room to be had and for a while we debated the advisability of going back to the station for the night, then starting out again on Sunday but neither of us could stomach it, so we telephoned to Kenosha, next city up the line, and again no luck.

The second phone call, this time to Racine, which is almost to Milwaukee, brought results, although I confess I was dubious when the clerk said he had a double room for $2, it sounded too cheap to be any good. Nevertheless, we said we'd take it and climbed on the train and arrived in Racine about 10 p.m. There we told a taxi driver to take us to a good hotel, and we wound up at Hotel Racine, a really first class place, and got a huge room, with two double beds and a single, plus bath and shower, for $2.50 each. After sleeping jammed up in bunks for all these months, you can imagine how pleasant it was to wake up Sunday morning in a real bed. After checking in, we wandered around downtown Racine for two hours, found only the hotel's very luxurious cocktail lounge alive, and so we sat sipping beer until 12:30, then wandered up to bed.

I woke at 9 o'clock to find Reed still asleep quietly shaved and showered and by the time I was ready to shove off for Mass, Don was awake, so he wrote while I went to Mass. Afterwards we read the paper, then started out to find some breakfast. We wandered into a place called the Spanish Café, where we ate Polish sausage and scrambled eggs, cooked by a Greek and served by a blonde Danish girl to an Irisher and an Englisher. If that isn't international hash, I don't know what is.

From there we strolled up to the USO, just on the chance we might find a swimming party due for some time in the afternoon. The place was a pleasant big room, with a terrace outside overlooking the breakwater and lake, and we sort of settled down for a while, reading and talking, and when I got into a pool game with a couple more sailors, Don eventually wandered out to find a drink.

He didn't come back for some time, the pool game broke up, and after idling around for a while I saw a girl, one of the USO hostesses, sit down at one of the card tables and pick up a deck, so I stepped up and hinted that I'd enjoy a bridge game if one could be found. She was willing but couldn't locate any partners, so we sat and talked bridge for a little while. Her name was Martha Hawley and she was about to start a job as a stenographer with a Navy contract office that just opened up in Racine.

When Don returned we played Chinese rummy, and during the game Martha said something about having been swimming, and planning to go again when she was off duty. We rather timidly asked if she'd mind company to which she said she'd be delighted. So for most of the afternoon we sat out on the terrace and talked about where we've been and what we'd done.

Martha (she said she was 25) has never been out of the middle west, but has moved about a good bit out here, from Chicago to Detroit, to Sioux City, Milwaukee and now Racine. She's quite a tall girl, not beautiful but easy to look at, talks quietly and interestingly and listens very well. She didn't say much about her family except that she's an only child and her father "left" about 3 years ago. Didn't explain any further and of course we didn't ask, but she and her mother are great pals. Needless to say, we talked most about our own wives, but she didn't seem to mind.

About 5 Don and I walked over to the hotel and checked out, brought our handbag over to the USO, taking out our swim trunks. At 5:30 the three of us left, walked over to Martha's mother's very beautiful apartment in what seems to be Racine's finest residential district. There she gave Don and me a bottle of beer to drink while she changed to white shorts. Then she produced a beach robe, and we all climbed into a cab for the beach. It was a grand beach, with deep, very fine sand and just a little bit of a roll coming in from the blue horizon, where quite a few catboats, cabin cruisers and outboards were playing around.

I don't know how far out the beach runs, but it shelves very gently and at one time we are out nearly a quarter mile, and the water was only a foot or so over my head and the bottom was still sandy. And the water was grand, not a bit cold as I feared it would be. We paddled around for a while, then came back to lie on the beach and dry off and about dusk we dressed and went back downtown via bus, again to Mrs. Hawley's apartment, where Martha dressed again while we listened to the radio.

Mrs. Hawley came in then, a pleasant rather distinguished

looking woman whom I judged to be in her early 40's, and since we'd been planning to get a bite to eat, we sort of picked Mrs. Hawley up and took her right with us. They guided us to a place called "The Gourmet" five or six blocks away, and we all had a scotch and soda, and a super deluxe hamburger with real french fries and we were sitting there like ordinary civilians talking and listening to a man playing a Hammond organ when it occurred to me to ask about the time. We pretty nearly jumped out of our chairs when my question brought the answer. It was 10:10 and the train was due at 10:30!

Of course we ran from there, hunting a bus or taxi or anything to get us to the station 3 miles away in time to make the train. Fortunately a cab pulled up and we piled in. In the midst of all that we remembered our bag checked at the USO, but it was too late to do anything about it. All we cared about was catching the train and we said goodbye and thank you as we ran for the cab. We got to the station just at 10:30 and learned to our surprise and relief that the train wasn't due until 11:02 but even so we couldn't take a chance on going back for our abandoned bag, so we waited, rode back with the late-hour drunks and got in with a few minutes to spare.

A good night's sleep, a hike and a little laundry - - the whites and underwear I wore all weekend - - brings me up to now, along with the last hour and a half I've spent on this longest scribbling job I've undertaken in some time.

And so ends our big adventure for another two weeks, and it was a lot of fun, and I really do feel an awful lot better, more ready to go back to the grind. Racine is a swell town perched on a point jutting some miles out into the lake. It's an old town, with wide streets shaded by towering elm trees, clean and pretty as can be, reminds me much of Allentown, although its a little smaller (76,000). It's a town of small and medium industries and the people are quite friendly.

As for the Hawley's, the least that can be said is that they are fine people, the sort of folks it's a pleasure to know any place any time. They were kind enough to invite us to come back and we may have to do that if only to retrieve our abandoned bag, which contains for each of us a complete change of clothing, towel and shaving-tooth brushing gear.

So much for my side, I think I've covered the whole episode, if I remember any more I'll tuck it into a later letter. I'm waiting now to hear about Bucky's First Communion - - hope he was able to make it all right. I couldn't get to confession Sunday morning, and had no chance during my Saturday wandering, so will go next Sunday here.

Bye, now my only darling. I love you very, very much and despite the fact I did enjoy myself, I just couldn't help but wishing that you could have been there to make it a perfect weekend. But this school is past the halfway mark, and it won't be so terribly long until I can put my arms around you and tell you how long and how much I love you.

7-23-44 Sunday afternoon

It's only been a little more than 12 hours since I last wrote to you, and in a few hours more I'll be talking to you, but here I am at the table again, pen in hand, about to write to my one and only in between swats at some very annoying flies. I'm sitting here wearing only my swimming trunks and there's lots of epidermis available to them. This is one of those sunny summer Sundays that we used to spend walking and sitting in the back yard, and I suppose you're doing just that. Wish I were with you.

It's been a little different for me. I was up at 6, shaved and showered, then dashed off to early Mass and communion. I didn't get back in time to get to breakfast. Then at 10 I went back to Mass again, and this time served both Mass and benediction, the latter for the first in many, many years.

In between the two Masses I managed a letter to Jess. After

the second Mass I went straight to chow, which was swell; steak, sweet potatoes, green beans, a chopped vegetable salad and a bite of ice cream.

Since then I've been in the laundry business so that now, at 2:30, I'm proud to report it's all done except for what I'm wearing, and a few items that must be rolled. Outside, the guns are banging away again, and altogether it's a very ordinary Sunday at Great Lakes

Tonight we get the long sleep, and tomorrow we start into the 8th week, with boxing in the morning and a start on a new subject, ammunition, at night. As for recognition, I think we get British ships, but may be wrong for this is likely to be our last week of recognition.

One week from tomorrow we go on the antiaircraft range. This means a shift to day hours for the week, up at 5:30 a.m. and on the go all day. It should be fun, and a pleasant change from the sometimes humdrum routine of classes. But it will be school none the less, and very hard work too, so much so that we'll not have any physical hardening for the week.

The war news looks good, and I don't think it's unreasonable to expect Germany's collapse in the next few months, due largely to the Russian offensive, for our boys really haven't scratched the surface in France. As to Japan, I'm mystified about what is going on. I suspect that the Japs might reverse the present strategy of hiding their fleet in favor of a gamble on a successful major engagement. Such a Japanese gamble, if it fell in our favor, would be the turning point for we then would be able to go after the mainland bases we must have to win.

There's a lot of optimism here, with the wishful thinkers all ready to pack up and go home when they get their orders, fully expecting the fall of Germany in days or weeks, and the orders right after that. Me, I don't believe it until I see it.

To tell the truth, I don't feel much like writing now, for there's so darn little to say. I'm <u>NOT</u> giving up my idea that you may come out here. It would be a good chance to be together, all by ourselves, and (Yes, I'm selfish for this is secondary.) a chance for you to be free for a few days. I'm sure we can afford it financially. I'm really serious about this Betty, because it may be our last chance to be together for a long time since the next move for me will be to the West Coast

As I finish this, I'm sitting beside the squeaky old radio that Shorty brought back last weekend and a band is playing a tune both you and I should well remember.

"If I could be with you, one hour tonight ."

Which is a good place to stop, but I'll never stop thinking and wishing just for that. I love you very much, my Bettsy, and miss you like sin, as you should know by now. Give my little ones an extra hug and kiss from their daddy, and tell them I'll be seeing them before so awfully long. Yours as always, love.

8-4-44 Thursday Night

Well, as a further sign that we're nearing the end of our term here, we had our final recognition class and test last night and I surprised myself with 91 on the test, missing 3 of 30 Jap ships flashed for one second.

I think I've already answered your question about when I'll be home, but at the risk of repeating it will be about 8 a.m. on August 25, unless the Navy should change its mind. I've never heard of anything interfering with the 66, but anything is possible so I'll keep my fingers crossed.

Well, your husband is on the casualty list for the first time in 4 months (years?) in the Navy - - but it wasn't on the firing range and while it's darn painful I can see the whole herd of you on the floor before you finish this.

We had just come into the barracks after a hot, hard day working in the clipping room loading 20 mm. magazines. I was getting ready for a very welcome and badly needed shower. I had shed all of my clothes and had sat down on my bunk to take off my socks and put on my slippers. As I stood up I developed a very unpleasant pain in my personal spot. Ouch!

You see our bunks are a plain wire spring built right into the sideboards, covered with an inch-thick cotton mattress. I remember now noticing that when I sat down that the mattress was shoved aside slightly, but thought nothing of it then. But when I sat down - - naked, remember - - the spring stretched, and when I started to get up the spring came back, trapped my scrotum, and when I stood up I was minus about a square inch of skin. Double ouch!

Of course it bled a good bit, but I needed the shower badly so went ahead with it, then dressed again and went to sick bay where a corpsman put some salve and antiseptic on the rip then bandaged me up and here I am with a sizable bonfire in my pants but apparently no other ill effects. The doctor at sick bay looked me over but decided it wouldn't be necessary to stitch it, but I'll have to go back for a couple of days to make sure no infection sets in.

And - - I'm reliably informed - - the machinery is not damaged, just in case you're interested. Personally I don't care for I've about come to the conclusion that it's worn out anyway. Now laugh, darn you. I know someone else who'll be howling too when he hears about it, our friend Harley.

So much for my first real mishap.

This has been a terrifically hot day, but not a hard one, and our night firing session was cancelled for some reason or other, which is how I'm able to write. Actually nobody in either of our sections got to fire a shot today, and it looks like we'll not get to fire the 40's, durn it.

First thing after we arrived on the range today our section was detailed to clean up one of the barracks used by the permanent staff of the range. We spent most of the morning at that, loafed the rest of the time, then were sent back to finish up in the afternoon, which meant practically nothing to do.

As a result, most of the gang is full of pep and raising the devil now, so that it's too noisy down there and I had to come upstairs to an empty section to write this. I must go back down in a little while to do my nightly laundry, then off to bed. Tomorrow, we hope, will be an easy day on the 20's, and then Sunday we'll be through with the range.

And three weeks from right now I'll be on my way to you again. Hope the proposal I made to Dad in the extra letter last night works out OK, for those extra hours would mean an awful lot to me. Feel sure I'll be able to catch one of the two early trains, but if something should mess that up I'll still make the 5:30 out of Chicago that stops in Johnstown.

Which will end up the story for tonight, darling, but it shows the only thing I'm really caring about now. I can't wait to take all of you in my arms again and really have a family again even if it is only for a short time. And then Bettsy, I'll be able to really tell you I love you.

8-7-44 Monday morning.

The firing range is behind us and here we are back on the old schedule again, after by much the most hectic night I've spent in the Navy. And your husband is the only one of the petty officers not in some kind of trouble.

It all started shortly after I finished writing last night when the first of two drunks - - and I mean drunks - - arrived. And it kept up until nearly 2 a.m. One of the first two was all but out cold, so we gave him a shower and put him in bed. A little later two more arrived and had to be put through the same treatment, then things calmed until about midnight when the big bunch arrived. Out of 24, I judge 18 were drunk, two had been drinking and 4 were sober.

A little earlier, three guys from our section (This happened before 9:30 so it's out of chronological order.) had been talking to some Waukegan wench on the telephone, then went down to the gate to meet her, which isn't strictly legal, but might have been OK. But apparently she tried to hand them a couple of bottles of wine through the fence. An S.P. saw the transaction and when the guys ran he collared the girl and made her tell who they were. Then a couple of S.P.'s. came up and got the guys, took them before the officer of the day, and now they're prisoners-at-large, scheduled for mast tomorrow and charged with attempting to smuggle liquor on the base, a pretty serious offense. Suppose the girl's in trouble too, but she's just a tramp and nobody seems to know or care.

Well, at midnight the incoming gang dragged out the remnants of our feast, spread them all over the hall floor and proceeded to eat, plus tearing around and much loud talk and profanity. It wound up in a row, and the duty chiefs arrived on the scene and took about a dozen names of guys who were sitting around smoking, talking, etc. That was where our section leader and one or two other guys got caught.

The chiefs left then, and a couple of the drunks started pushing Shorty around, shouting and accusing him of calling the chiefs etc., which I don't believe he had done. And it was going strong, with at least one guy trying to beat Shorty up, when the chiefs returned, having gone out one door and ducked in another. That settled it, for they carted off three guys to the brig. After that (It was about 1:30.) things quieted pretty quickly, and I suppose I got to sleep about 2, but was awake long before 7:30, which is get-up time.

And so we go back on schedule. I loafed through half the boxing session this morning, getting a fresh dressing on my "wound" then ran the obstacle course and tumbled a while, all in good shape. (In case you're interested, my wound does <u>NOT</u> qualify me for a Purple Heart but is healing nicely.) Breakfast and my letter brings me up to now, and this afternoon we go to school, ready to spend a week studying the hydraulic gears which drive our gun mounts.

I'll have to shave before then, and help clean up the joint, but it all looks pretty tame after such a wild night. Sure glad I didn't get messed up in it, and keep wondering if that slight scalp itch is where my halo is rubbing. But I suppose not, it's probably just dandruff.

Bye darling, take care of yourself and I'll see you soon. Then I can tell you how much I love you up close and personal.

8-9-44 Wednesday morning

Your husband is writing with a red face, for I honestly haven't a shadow of an excuse for letting you down yesterday - - and then last evening I got three letters from you and that just heaped hot coals on my head, yet I was very glad to get them. And just now comes a card - - you rat - - . Just wait, I'll show you.

Anyhow, my failure yesterday was my own fault. When we came back from physical hardening, I put my daily laundry to soak and while I waited was inveigled into the first pinochle game I've played here. That pinochle game lasted until 2:30 when we had to quit to clean up, leaving me with my letter unwritten and my laundry still in the basket - - where it stayed until this evening. But it's a different story for here I am scribbling before I've even had a shower. I'm taking no chances today!

Going back to school hasn't been so difficult but we all got bad news in our marks for the week before last. My own fell to 84, which was one of only three that high, and they were the <u>best</u> in the class. And I don't doubt that the grades were generous, for I didn't even know that much about ammunition. We won't get any formal marks for last week, only recommendations from the instructors on our ability, willingness, etc. I don't know how I made out, but do know of one "excellent" rating. Nevertheless, my overall school average is still 89.8. And we got our marks for the lookout training test and my 94 was by four points the highest in both sections.

This week we're on hydraulics, spending half the school session studying a hydraulic ram that pushes the larger cannon shells into the guns, and the other half studying the hydraulic drive which powers cannon mounts, turning the guns and aiming them. So far it's been interesting and a lot of it is basic hydraulics and mathematics which has been easy for me and pretty confusing to some of the others. However we're not much more than started and the picture can change sharply before the week is over.

And we're back to physical hardening again, dad-blame it, but I loafed through most of the Monday session by getting a dressing on my wound, and got by all right yesterday and today on calisthenics, tumbling and the obstacle course. Tomorrow we swim, and I'm not sure what I'll do about that, and Friday we hike, which will wind up the week.

The wound, in case you're still interested is coming OK, and only slightly annoying by now, should be forgotten before we get home.

On our trip home, as nearly as I can find out, there's little or no chance of our catching the 1:30 train out of Chicago, but a good chance we'll make the 2:30, which gets into Pittsburgh at 12:10 a.m. And if we miss that, there's another at 3:10 that hits Pittsburgh at 12:29 and a 3:30 train that gets in at 1:01, so there's only a difference of an hour and 35 minutes in the four trains, which shouldn't be too long for you to wait there for me.

So, having run out of writing material, I'm going to stop now, shower and do some laundry. I do love you dearest, and I'm very sorry for having let you down yesterday. I will try to not do it again, and will try to apologize more fully, - - in two weeks and two days. Until then I love you.

This clipping was stapled to the 8-9-44 letter.

PORTRAITS
By James J. Metcalfe

I dreamed of you

I dreamed of you last night my love . . . I dreamed that you were here . . . And we were free of hours filled . . . With waiting and with fear . . . I dreamed the war was over and . . . the boys were back again . . . Not quite as eager now but not . . . Too much like older men . . . You had not changed so much yourself . . . Your kiss was just as sweet . . . And when you took me in your arms . . . My vision was complete . . . We walked along the garden path . . . Between the roses red . . . And out of all the days gone by . . . We planned the years ahead . . . I know it was a dream my love . . . Just one more thought of you . . . But have you never heard it said . . .

Sometimes a dream comes true!

8-15-44 Tuesday morning

Only 10 more days until I'll be on a train, traveling homeward at 90 miles an hour – and the train will seem like it's creeping. Which of course you know before I tell you, but dammit it's all I know and all I can think about these days, so it goes down on paper first, and probably last, too.

This is another boiling hot day, really too hot to do anything, but I've had my physical hardening and done my laundry, so here I am scribbling. And it will be a busy day too, which may mean a short letter for you, also may mean two letters, depending on how the schedule works out.

First of all I must take two pairs of white trousers to the tailor to have them taken in at the waist and fanny, for they're much too big to look half decent. And when I got them they were too tight and I was afraid just a little bit of shrinkage would keep me from wearing them.

From there I'll go to 12:15 Mass, since this is a Holy Day, then come back to the barracks and clean the joint a bit. At 2 o'clock the entire section is scheduled for classification interviews when we will be given a chance to ask for our future assignments.

I've already put in a bid for a ship - - on one of the many I helped launch - - but don't think there's a Chinaman's chance I'll get it. She's the battle cruiser Guam, a great big new one, which is being fitted at Philadelphia and should be ready for her shakedown cruise in September. I know a dozen or more gunners mates in ships' company here have been assigned to her, but unless a new draft comes up I'm out of luck.

I think that would be swell for it would be a big ship, which I'd like. It would probably mean a stay in Philadelphia until she's ready, and then a cruise to Bermuda and return to Philly for refitting, which might give me a chance to get home for a few days. Can't think of any all-around better deal than that.

I'll ask for her at the interview today, and as a second choice will ask for hydraulics school, about which you already know. Of course chances are I won't get either, will instead be assigned to amphibs, where most of the men are going, but at least I'll be trying. And too, the interviewer may be able to offer something better, so we shall see what we shall see.

School continues to go reasonably well and I'm confident I'll do well on the next round of tests. It hasn't been tough for me but some of the guys are floundering badly.

Anyhow, I will be coming home soon, about 8 days from the time you get this. All I'm interested in is getting to you as quickly as possible and staying with you as long as possible. So it looks like I'll get the 2:30 train out of Chicago one week from Friday, and be meeting you in Pittsburgh a few minutes after midnight - - and two hours after that I'll be waking up three sprouts and getting acquainted with them all over again. You know it has been so long since I've seen them I sometimes wonder if they will really know me again, and I'm terribly curious to see how they all have grown and changed. Wish we were leaving tomorrow, instead of a week from Friday; or better still to be leaving right now - - and never have to come back.

But of course I must come back and do my little bit to get this war over with. And we mustn't gripe or grieve darling, for somehow I feel we've got to do our part towards making this a decent world for our kids.

Must rush now, for it's 11:30, and I've things to do, maybe will get a chance to write a little more later. All my love, always

8-17-44 Thursday morning

Somehow your letter which came this morning has hit me right between the eyes, so much so that there isn't anything else I can do but sit down and write you - - although I don't know what good that will do either of us.

Gosh, I sure was sorry to hear about Bob McGough and Wally Bishop [Acquaintances from Somerset]. Seems just the other day they were little codgers going to Mass on Sunday and playing around. We've been lucky so far not to lose anyone close to us but this show isn't over yet and the chances are we'll have lost some good friends before the curtain goes down. Wonder if any of my old boot camp company are on the list yet? Could be, because a lot of them went out on general detail and probably have been out fighting for a couple of months.

Sure, I'm scared too, but down inside I still have the firm conviction that when it's all over I'll be coming back to you and ours at least a reasonable facsimile of the guy who left.

And poor Fran. Like you I had hoped he wouldn't realize what's going on, but it would seem he's wiser than his years. I'm awfully tempted to pick up the phone and call right now, but probably won't because I'm short on funds and anyway I'll be starting home just a week from tomorrow. But <u>that</u> day, which seemed almost upon us yesterday, looks pretty far away from right here. Anyhow the time is going past pretty quickly, and it won't be so horribly long now until I step off the train in Pittsburgh and go looking for the most wonderful girl in the world.

To get back to some old business, the assignment interview is of most interest at the moment, and I'm enclosing a sheet they gave each of us. How much it will mean remains to be seen. Anyhow, the guy who interviewed me was swell and after I told him of my request for the Guam, he put me down for 3 recommendations, something I don't believe anyone else got, for a good many only got one. The first was hydraulics school and the second advanced school on the 20 and 40 guns. Thirdly, he put me down for the proving ground assignment. We'll see what happens.

Last night was the best school session we've had this week, and although it was hard work I really enjoyed tearing down the breech mechanism and putting it together. The gun, despite its size, is fairly simple and much like the others we've had. But the pieces are heavy as hell, and awkward to handle, which accounts for the hard work. For instance the breech block, a solid piece of steel approximately twice as large as this sheet of paper and about 6 inches thick, weighs more than 100 pounds and must be lifted six feet off the floor to take it out or put it in the gun.

We had another terrific thunderstorm some time after last midnight, and it was so loud it even woke me up, which, if your memory is functioning, is somewhat of a feat. But, as you probably will discover, the Navy has changed my sleeping habits more than somewhat.

Anyhow, in the wake of the storm we have another dull, cool, foggy day and even the flies are lazy. So's your old man.

Which reminds me that I've a swell stroke of laundry business to do, and must get started on it as soon as I finish this. In addition I've a lot of rolling to do, all the stuff I washed Monday.

Seems like there's always a million things to do around here and never enough time to do them. For instance, I could do with a couple of hours of shuteye, but don't see any prospect of it.

We had our weekly swim this morning, and although it was quite a workout I did enjoy it. Not like last week, though, for there were 70 or 80 of us in at the same time which makes a pretty good crowd. And twice the instructors lined us all up, jammed would be a better word, at one end of the pool and gave the whole herd just 45 seconds to swim down and crawl out at the other end. You can figure out what a mess that was, with 150 arms and as many legs thrashing the water at one time in a final scramble to get out in time. Your husband made it fairly easily, but the workout, added to some stiffness remaining from yesterday, leaves me a little bit sore in several spots.

By the way, just in case you're interested, my wound continues to heal very nicely and apparently is going to be all right, though I'm still not convinced that the machinery isn't worn out. Certainly, it's very rusty, for it hasn't been <u>properly</u> lubricated for many, many moons. Wonder if I can find a little cosmaline next weekend? (Suggest you look up cosmaline and what it's used for. If you don't find it, ask me.)

At least - - if you're still interested - - the spirit is willing for even such thoughts cause my breathing to change from long drawers to short pants.

Think I'll go now, darling, and just leave you dangling there. Thanks very much for being my one and only sweetheart, for just to sit down and write to you has made me feel lots better, which is proof positive I love you.

8-21-44 Monday noon

Only four days from now I'll be shoving off to see you again, and it seems I just can't think or care about anything else. To tell the truth I wouldn't if I could.

Anyhow, will stand pat on our original plans, except I see <u>no</u> chance to make the 1: 30 train for we won't leave here in time. However I'm reasonably certain of catching the 2:30, which will put me in Pittsburgh at 12:25. Seems to me that since you're coming to Pittsburgh, Mother and Dad might like to spend a little time at Farrell's, and just in case I should get the earlier train I could fone you there when I arrive in Pittsburgh. I definitely am <u>not</u> thinking now about how or when I'll have to leave.

To get back to the more routine things of the moment, Don and I had a very pleasant weekend in Milwaukee with Leo and Ginny. Saturday night a fellow who works with Leo took us on a tour of a half dozen beer joints in his car and we wound up eating spaghetti at 2:30 a.m. Then the rest went home, Don and I went to our hotel, and I went to bed while Don went roaming on his own. It was broad daylight, maybe 7 a.m. when he came in, and I slept until 11, then went to Mass and we went back to Ginny's for dinner.

Don was so sleepy in the afternoon he couldn't hold his head up, so he slept on the couch while the three of us went to the zoo and wandered around. It was fun, but I couldn't help thinking how much more fun it would have been with you and the kids.

Then we ate again about 6, sat around drinking beer and talking until 9, when we climbed on the train, came back here and promptly went to bed. We were well ahead of the big gang but it was fairly peaceable, especially considering that both sections were out.

Woke at 7:30, had my boxing session, and now have once again completed all my laundry so I'll not have to be worrying about that when it comes time to go home. Now I must, when I finish this, clean the stripes on my blues, hang them up, shave and be ready for chow and school.

Now if there were only some way to control time, so these next four days would fly past - - whiz - - like that, and the next two days could be stretched out long enough to give me half a chance to tell you how much I love you, then everything would be wonderful. But it won't so we'll just have to take it as it comes.

Bye darling, and until Friday night I'll be most horribly hungry for the most wonderful woman in all the world.

8-23-44 Wednesday morning

This is by long odds the dreariest day I've ever known, and you'll have heard from me before you get this letter so you'll know at least part of the why. This should fill you in on the background.

The 66 liberty is all gone, changed right under our noses by an order that came out of nowhere yesterday. As of right now I don't know when or whether I'll be home again, and truthfully my heart is broken for I was counting on a little more than somewhat on seeing all of you the day after tomorrow. I'm still clinging to the hope I'll see you soon, but it's a hope and nothing more right now.

Scuttlebutt was running wild yesterday when I wrote you, but stubbornly I refused to believe it until it was official, which probably accounts for a screwy and altogether ambiguous letter, for I hadn't the nerve to tell you about it until I was <u>sure</u> our reunion was gone glimmering.

But we came back from school last evening, having puzzled through our final test with less than ten percent of our minds on the subject, to find notice on our bulletin board that the entire liberty plan for service school students, saying there will be no more overnight liberty except for men living within 50 miles of the base.

There was <u>no</u> specific mention of the 66 nor of the scuttlebutt - - reported substitution for it of a 5-day leave at the end of school. Of course we've been frantically trying to find out, and just a little while ago the regimental office told us <u>no</u> 66 and also <u>no</u> leave.

So here I am crying the blues to the one person in all the world I really want.

There remains a glimmer of a chance, for the Group 1 Officers are rumored to be still trying to get our status settled, but I've given up hope, as of now.

Of course it all fell on us like a ton of bricks, and I have never seen a bunch of servicemen so near mutiny. Our sections are not alone, although we, along with a dozen others also due for 66 on Friday, are hit the hardest. I shudder to think of how many thousands of boys planning to go home this weekend find their plans wrecked. And it wouldn't take much of a spark to start a real fire.

Strangely enough, the loudest bleats have come from the boys who have been going home every other weekend. Almost without exception the rest of the gang in the same fix as I have been keeping their mouths reasonably well shut, and their chins up. I think I can say that much for myself, even if I am letting my hair down now.

Scores, probably hundreds of others, have special plane and train reservations to go home. Of course they all must be cancelled. And since Milwaukee and Chicago are as far as anyone will be permitted to go to henceforth, you can imagine what will be happening there each weekend.

I'm not going to finish this now Bettsy, for we're about due to leave for our strength test. There'll be more later.

Later: The strength test is over, but so is our hope for a miracle dwindling away by the minute and the whole gang is sitting around in glum silence. Just to show you how bad it is, today was payday and no one has enough interest or energy to start a poker game. And here I sit with 3 nice crisp $20 bills in my pocket that I've saved and planned to spend with you. I might as well throw them out the window.

As I see it now, my only hope of getting home at any time in the visible future is by assignment to an eastern school or a ship on the Atlantic seaboard. So Bettsy dearest, the toughest job is as usual left to you to explain to the kids, and at the same time to keep your own chin up. Right now I don't even dare look at the pictures that I know are before me in the stationery pad for the apples are much too big even without that.

In spite of all the mean and wicked things that can happen to us, don't forget my Bettsy that I love you more than anything in all the world and some day, some how, will be coming back to tell you about it. And tell our little ones the same thing, so that they will believe it as you and I believe it. Their daddy misses them very much and some day will be coming back to tuck them in bed.

If nothing else happens, I'll telephone you tomorrow night to prevent a useless trip to Pittsburgh. And if I don't write sooner I will try hard to be in a slightly more cheerful frame of mind when I sit down tomorrow.

Bye, darling, and I do love you, always.

8-24-44 Thursday noon

Your husband has his chin up at least a little better today, so that I'm now almost ready to admit the whole world has not gone to hell, but still I must admit to being a pretty doleful sailor. Now that I've got my feet on the ground I think I'll be able to get by, but I surely am dreading having to make that call tonight. Some of the guys have already made theirs, and confessed afterwards that they would have rather undertaken a solid eight hours of physical hardening.

Of course I am, like all the rest, nourishing a last, flickering vestige of hope that <u>something</u> - - the Lord only knows what - - will happen to save us, but my reason tells me even that spark is dead. Nevertheless, I'm putting off the call as long as possible, will make it tonight when we leave school for chow. Don't expect I'll be wanting anything to eat, so there should be plenty of time.

And there has been no hint, not even via the scuttlebutt, of a leave when school is over, so all we can logically hope for is a break on reassignment from here, which fortunately is only 10 days or at the most two weeks away. I guess I can live that long - - and probably even keep on existing afterwards if things go wrong.

As it stands now, our section will have liberty (That's a laugh.) from 3:30 Saturday until 2 a.m. Sunday, but as far as I know now I'm not going to budge. There's nothing to do in that time except drink or raise hell, and I'm not even remotely interested in that so to hell with it. Two guys, who live in Chicago, and another who is meeting his wife there and has a hotel reservation, will get 32-hour liberties just as they did under the old plan. But there's no use in even trying that, for next week we'll only be entitled to liberty from noon to Sunday midnight.

So - -

To get back on more routine things, the final test was not too difficult, required only a little more than an hour although we were cooped up in the classroom from 5 to 7:30. I did all right, too, although I really don't care. And for last week I climbed back up to 90, the second best mark in the section. Don't know whether we get any more marks or not, but if we do I'll be all right, for I had 90 Monday, 85 Tuesday and 100 last night.

And I mentioned our final strength test yesterday, on which I improved just about as much as I expected. As an index, on our four tests, I chinned myself once the first time in boots; failed entirely the second time; made three the first time here and six yesterday. The others improved, but not quite so much, and while I tried reasonably hard the fact that I didn't overdo it is shown by an absence of stiff and sore muscles this morning.

Today we were swimming, but the pool was a bit too cool for much fun, and we had to work a bit too hard. I swam the length of the pool about a dozen times, besides getting a little practice in life saving methods; something else I haven't had in a good many years.

After breakfast John Wunder and I, just trying to get out of the rut, went to the movies and enjoyed it about as much as we could be expected to enjoy anything. The picture "A Guy Named Joe" with Spencer Tracy and Irene Dunne is one you'll really like if you get a chance to see it. Now we're back at the barracks, and I have a bit of laundry to do and need a shave, but don't feel a damm bit like doing either, and maybe won't. Think I'll go to bed.

What I dread most of all right now is mail call, for I know the letter I get today, and the one I may get tomorrow will be full of the one thing I'm trying hardest to crowd out of my mind right now. It was pretty rough yesterday for I'm so hungry for you I don't dare tear up your letter without reading it, and haven't guts enough to more than skim through it.

Which is what I hope you'll do to this letter, the one I wrote yesterday and as many more as it may take me to get leveled off again. Anyhow, I love you awfully, awfully much, and am still living for that moment when I can hold you in my arms again. Bye darling, and it's good to know you're waiting for me.

P.S. The bad news is official now. Only a little while ago (We've been to chow since I wrote the first of this.) the daily work sheet was posted on the bulletin board and it says: Attention Service School Students - - the 66-hour graduation special liberty has been discontinued. Despite all of which I love you with all my heart, and always will.

There was no mention in any letter but Betty came to Chicago on 8/25/44 for a weekend visit. Arrangements must have been made by telephone. Chuck's parents paid for her trip. They were joined by Chuck Svoboda and Chuck Walts and their wives.

8-28-44 Monday

I've just a few minutes to tell you that after the most wonderful weekend I have ever known, or ever will have, I'm ready for whatever lies ahead.

We can never forget it, my Bettsy, and while it hurts like hell to have missed seeing the kids and Mother and Dad I shouldn't have missed our second honeymoon for anything in the world. I still can taste your kisses and my eyes even now are full of the look of you, the most heavenly sight in all my imagination. These memories will stay with me so long as I live.

We were in good time getting back here, and I found two letters waiting for me as sort of a postscript to our adventure. Then I put my clothes away and slept for a little while and now I've had my dinner and am waiting to go to school.

As I write this I can (almost) see you riding alone somewhere in Indiana or Ohio, riding back to our children and the big job ahead. Somehow, and I think it isn't fair but can't help it; you always get the biggest and much the toughest job. Perhaps it's best, for I should hate to tackle what I know you'll be able to do.

So give them all my love, my Bettsy, and one of these days, perhaps real soon, I should come walking in to you again, to hold you in my arms for all eternity. God is very good to me, and I know he will not change. Nor will I, from loving you always, with all my heart.

8-31-44 Thursday morning

Yesterday was one of those days that you most like to forget, so much that I just couldn't bring myself to write. Then too I was nursing a flickering hope of getting home for a few hours, and managed to find somewhat of an alibi in that.

But now I know beyond all shadow of a doubt that there is no more chance of getting home from here, so am bucked up a little, getting my feet set under me so I won't be knocked over the next time I'm hit.

The big question now is what lies ahead, for this morning I moved into an entirely new phase ready to sit down and wait for the order that will send me somewhere else - - east I hope. However as I told you the probability is west, and in that connection be warned now that I may not have time or the opportunity to telephone you the news before I go. Therefore, do not be afraid of a telegram, for that's what I'll do if there isn't a chance to phone. I can always find a minute for a note, and give it to someone to send.

Of course we've two more nights of school ahead of us, but that's purely perfunctory, and too there's a little matter of graduation on Monday, but it means little to me for I feel sure I'll be advanced to S 1/c, and know there's no chance of petty officer. However I'm curious as to just how I finished in the section, know I'll be in the first four but it's a close race for the top and just for my own satisfaction I'd like to win it.

It appears now that I'll get - - how or why I don't know - - a 32-hour liberty this weekend but I don't have any idea what I'll do with it, if anything. Might go to Milwaukee if I get the urge to go out, but I'm short on dough as you know and may just decide to stay here. Had $9 when I left you Monday, have since spent nearly a dollar but was paid $5 by Uncle Sam and collected 4 more a guy owed me, and when Reed needed some dough today I lent him $10 which leaves me short until some arrives from you.

Anyhow, I'm very, very grateful for last weekend, a very wonderful time that I shall never, never forget, just in case you're worrying about me being broke. What money I spend when you're not around is unimportant, and I think I've proved that by the little I've spent since I left home.

Strangely, after such a time, I find it hard to write to you, because there's nothing solid or certain here to say or talk about. We're in another transitory stage, service school's version of O.G.U.

I was up at 6:15 this morning because I felt I needed to go to communion, and it helped a lot, something I can't explain but it is so. Then we started moving at 7:30, me with my gear on my shoulder lugging it from 614 barracks to 703, about a quarter mile but not too far for one who is physically hardened.

This barracks (703, one used by the transfer unit) was totally empty when I walked in today, but now is jammed to the gourds with other sections just like ours in the final phase of school. Once again we're crowded, sleeping in triple bunks with something over 200 men in the same size barracks our 50 have occupied for the past few months.

Seems very odd now, and all the faces except 23 of us from G 64, are strange and new. But we'll be here only 10 days at most and probably less than that so there will be small chance to get acquainted. Except for school tonight and tomorrow we'll be spending most of our time in here, waiting for the call to go. It may come at any hour of the day or night, and there'll be little notice before we shove off, which accounts for my previous warning to half-expect a telegram.

Then too, I've a lot of other correspondence I must catch up on, and I plan to do that over the weekend (if I stay in) or next week while I'm sitting around waiting.

Over the radio now comes Bing singing "I'll be seeing you----"and down inside me something is shaking. Perhaps it's the shaking that makes the apples fall off the tree and lodge in my throat, I wouldn't know. But I do know that every time I hear that song you'll be in my heart, just as "Stardust" brings back the memories of a decade ago. They're grand times, and I love them even tho they <u>hurt</u> - - I mean a real physical pain - - for they bring back to me just a little sharper picture of the most wonderful girl in the world. The only woman I ever have or ever will love.

And that, my own Betty is all I'm thinking or really caring about at any time. Remember it, Betty, and while one inch is too far to be away from you at any time still you are never gone from my heart because, I love you.

9-2-44 Saturday afternoon

The turmoil of inspection is over, the liberty parties are gone, and here I sit to write, one of only two men left in a barracks that is temporarily home to upwards of 900 men.

I have my I.D. card, and an out-of-bounds pass that gives me permission - - but not the time I need so badly - - to go to Somerset. But there's nowhere I want to go, nothing to do and nobody to see, so I'm staying behind to write my one and only, then do some laundry. Later I may go out, but I'm not promising anything.

If I do go out, it will be either Milwaukee or Racine tonight, in hopes I can at least find someone to talk to. It's a far cry from <u>Last Saturday</u>, and remembering helps stifle my loneliness. Frankly, I'd much prefer hearing the loudspeaker calling me on draft right now but know that won't happen until Monday at the earliest.

Surprisingly I'm not overly blue, just lonely and disgusted at someone's - - I hope some day I find out whose - - stupid bumbling. Last night there were just 14 of us left behind from our two sections, and every one a father - - and 33 kids back home somewhere. Except 4 of us, the rest will be able to get home for a few hours today or tomorrow. And I'm stranded as the <u>only one</u> of my section unable to get home since we started school, in May.

Yet there was no earthly reason why we couldn't have been released yesterday. We learned nothing last night, in fact were not expected to learn, merely required to go through the formality of standing around the gun shop one more night. How that helps to win the war I'll never be able to tell you.

But there's no griping, in fact I'm not really griping even to you, just trying to set down for our own record my feeble protest against what seems to be the crass stupidity that earmarks so much of the Navy. So much for that.

To be just a little more cheerful, the new ratings came out this afternoon, and as I expected I'm promoted to S1/C (the equivalent of Army corporal) - - you'll see it on the letter - - and get a $12 pay boost. Also as I expected there were <u>no</u> petty officer ratings, but I was surprised to find only 10 men of the 50 in our two sections advanced, would have been willing to bet there would have been 30 or more.

But while the advancement is nice, and the money will be welcome, it does nothing to settle my future, the big question of the moment. There's no use guessing, for we don't know and won't be told for a couple of days, but also we might as well accept fleet replacement or amphibs, for from what we hear there is little or no chance for any of us landing at an advanced school.

Isn't it amazing how the Allies are racing through France? From what I can see here there seems to be no definite German plan to stop these drives that must end the war over there before this month is out unless a successful defense is concocted. I'm expecting to hear any day of gas having been used, and I'll be surprised if the enemy doesn't have something else in the way of secret weapons up his sleeve, but the handwriting is on the wall, and will not be erased.

Things have been awfully quiet in the Pacific since Guam and Saipan, but the next indicated invasion should hit the Philippines island of Mindanao soon, and I'm still waiting for the strike from the west at Java or Sumatra.

Please tell my son and daughter I'm very grateful for their letters, and am very proud of their fine work in school, they must keep it up. I'll be writing to them next week, for we should have some free time.

Also, I plan a letter to Mother and Dad, too - - if nothing else - - to thank them for our wonderful weekend. And I'll be talking to all of you tomorrow, which is something else I'm really looking forward to.

Bye, Bettsy, and I do and always will love you very much.

9-4-44 Monday afternoon

I'm starting this now, even as I wait for what may be the news of when and where, because I suspect it will take quite a letter to describe my weekend wanderings.

But first of all I want to assure you I <u>really</u> am all right, and ready to whip anything that may come my way. Matter of fact, I feel about as good as I ever will without you. And I want to thank you for the money, too, for I suspect it will come in handy. However, I'll try to manage things so I'll not need to ask for help again because I know how many places you have to put your few bucks.

Guess the best thing to do is to take it chronologically from where I left off Saturday to do my laundry. Worked for nearly two hours, until 6 o'clock, then decided to shove off and when chow looked lousy I just walked out the gate and bought a beer, then climbed on the northbound train.

Got into Racine about 7:15, took a bus to the USO and got there in time for a swell supper topped off by a piece of apple pie. Sat around reading and talking with Mrs. (W???????) the lady in charge, and about 8 Martha Hawley came in and we played ping pong, pool, gabbed a while, ate a piece of cake and drank a bottle of milk, then got inveigled into a gin rummy game that broke up about midnight. Walked home with Martha, who wasn't feeling well because of a headache, and then climbed on a bus for the station, intending to come back here and sleep and let Sunday decide itself.

But at the station I found the last southbound train was gone, and a young service school student frantically trying to find a way back to the station by 2 a.m. when his liberty expired. Gave him some change and told him where to call in Milwaukee to see if there was a late train on the other railroad. Found one was due in 5 minutes but don't know whether he made it.

Hold tight - - here we go maybe. Nope no go. The draft

list included only Svec, and tells him only that he must move to another barracks. Leaves me as both MA and section leader. Nuts!!!

To go back to Racine, after the boy found there was a train we flagged the first taxi but he had two fares and said no until we told him how urgent it was. Then he said if it was OK with him if his passengers would agree, whereupon a gal in the front seat with him said no, she wanted to go home. So there was nothing else to do and as the driver pulled away I told her as nicely as I could "Thanks lady, we'll do you a favor sometime when the Japs are shooting." Hope it made her happy, the heel. Anyhow the kid caught another cab in a few minutes and I hope he made it.

While we were fussing around trying to find out about trains, a nice-looking red-headed gal, wearing a USO pin in her lapel, came in asking about a train to Chicago, and when the sailor caught his cab I told her, but she said she'd changed her mind and was going to Milwaukee.

That was where I was going, intending to get a hotel room and sleep for a while. Didn't see any more of the gal until we were getting off the train in Milwaukee at 2:30 a.m. when she was struggling with two handbags so I offered to help and she accepted. Obviously she was a stranger in the town, and when we got to talking she said she was en route to her home in Detroit, had been planning to go to Chicago for a train home.

One of Leo's friends who we (Don and I) had met is a night clerk at one of the good hotels, and I told her I was planning to call Riley to see if he could find a room for me, so I offered to see if he could put her up. But she said she didn't think she would, but instead thought she'd sit around the station until 6 a.m., then take the first train out.

Well, I wasn't sleepy either, and didn't feel much like spending 4 or 5 bucks for a room for a couple of hours, so I propositioned her that I'd stick around and we'd see what Milwaukee had to offer in the wee small hours, and maybe we'd get something to eat and a drink. Whereupon she said OK <u>if</u> I'd agree to go Dutch treat, and that was very much all right so off we went introducing ourselves. Turns out her name is Virginia Wells, she's 23, lives in Detroit and is a secretary to some Ph.D. who's an official of some kind of pharmaceutical firm. Said she'd been in Racine visiting friends, had checked out of the hotel there without checking up on trains, and felt a little too sheepish to go back.

Anyhow we had supper, and a bottle of beer each, then decided to go to a movie since the only theater still open was showing Bing's "Going My Way." And I here and now heartily endorse Mother and Dad's recommendation of a very fine picture. Not many good tunes - - "Tura Lura Loo" is much the best - - but it's very different and a swell show.

Afterwards we walked and window-shopped a while for the whole town was closed up tight, hardly a sailor in sight since nearly everybody had to be back here by 2 a.m. Then we had coffee and doughnuts and at 6 I put her on the train for Chicago, after first getting her address against the possibility I might be sent to school near Detroit. It was a swell evening, or rather morning, and I enjoyed it lots.

By that time I was getting sleepy, so I bought a paper, then went to Mass at Marquette University, where it seems many of the priests who teach at the university say their daily Masses. It's a big church, with a main altar and four side altars. And all the time I was there, a priest was saying Mass at each altar, so I guess I attended seven or eight masses in one hour, a new record for me.

Then I took a bus out to Leo and Ginny's, woke them up and bummed a couple of hours sleep on the couch while they went to church. Woke about noon, we ate dinner, and sat around for a while talking until a girl they know, her name is Margie something-or-other and she's engaged to a machinists mate first class now stationed in San Francisco, came over and we all went walking.

Finally took a bus to the lake front, where we wandered around watching men fishing for perch, stumbled onto a miniature auto race way, watched a big coal boat come in to dock, and drank a couple of beers.

We then went back to the house where I struggled quite a while to get my call through, and it wasn't very satisfactory for I could tell you folks couldn't hear me and I could barely make out what you all were saying because of the wire noise, However it was still a thrill to talk to my darlings, every one of you.

And please tell Mother and Dad not to worry about me for I am all right, and will stay that way. Gee they sound awfully worried and upset, and I'm not a little bit of either, honest. Sure, I wish I could get home but I'm resigned to it now and have tossed a big weight off my shoulders.

Anyhow, after the phone call we had some cheese and cold ham, etc. and when Margie said she had a date with another girl to go to a dance at 8 we all decided to go. So we took a shower, I had to borrow Leo's razor to shave for I went out Saturday without a thing, and at 8:30 we all arrived at the Eagles home where the dance was held.

Think I told you before about what an imposing place they have, well it's even nicer inside and the ballroom is much the biggest I've ever seen, as well as one of the prettiest. Margie turned out to be a good dancer, and while I was so rusty I wasn't doing very well (nor could it be I was missing my own particular dancing girl?). I really was having a swell time and didn't like a little bit having to leave at 9:45, but wanted to be sure of getting back on time. Anyhow I got back here about 11, ahead of the rush, and gabbed with Don for a while before hitting the sack at 1 a.m.

Before I left Milwaukee, Ginny and Leo had tentatively decided to come up here today as guests of Don and myself for commencement, but they didn't show up so Lord knows when we'll see them again. Gee they have been awfully good to us, don't know what we would have done without them

We were up at 5:30 this morning, dressed in whites and went to breakfast, then sat around until 9 when we marched to the auditorium for commencement which was just one of those routine things: A couple of talks, a little music, and we all marched up to get our diplomas, which I'll jam into this envelope if the letter doesn't get too fat.

Noon chow, since this is Labor Day, was turkey and very delicious but the serving was slow and I didn't get much so I'm not wildly enthusiastic about it. Now I'm back here in the barracks, with nothing to do except work on my gear and write letters. Except for mail and chow I've no intention of stirring outdoors until tomorrow.

How was that for a weekend, and isn't your bald-headed husband getting to be a wolf, tho? Imagine sedate old me out with a brunette (Martha) a red head (Virginia) and a blonde (Margie) all in the space of 24 hours! Woof! Woof! Woof! Somehow I thought the enclosed picture very apt, tho, I was not in the line, honest.

After graduation I'll be assigned to Transfer Unit. Here's how it works. Everyone is required to be in barracks at certain times and to stay until released. Meanwhile names of the men on the draft are read over the p.a. system, and they're told where to move to. In the new barracks they're told where they're going, and when, and I should know by the time I write again. Incidentally, it looks now like I'll have time to phone you. And if I don't call or wire, you can figure I'm still stuck here. All I can do is sit and wait.

Instead of sitting, think I'll do that work I planned to do yesterday. So bye darling, and take good care of yourself for I'll be seeing you some of these days, and loving you all days. Which is something very, very wonderful to have.

Chapter 4
TRANSFER UNIT
GREAT LAKES, ILLINOIS
9/5/44 to 9/13/44

9/5/44 Tuesday Noon

Once again as I start to write I don't know when or where, and while I know a little more about who, it appears I must wait at least until tomorrow to learn the rest, the all-important part.

Already our gang is split. This morning a huge draft cleared out all but 5 of us in my section, and four in the other section. I'm happy to report that Reed, Walts, Wunder, Svoboda and I are still together along with Prosser and Miller from the other section.

Of course we don't know anything, and can't make anything but wild guesses, but there would be some foundation for the idea that the seven of us may have been selected for more schooling or for some pretty good assignment. Nearly as I can tell we all were recommended for the advanced 20-40 school at Dearborn and that may be the answer, although it's only a guess. However we'll just have to sit and wait, and it's entirely likely we'll be split further before the final disposition is made.

Hang on again, here come more draft lists and my bunk has been assigned to someone else so something likely will be done with me.

Nope, nothing yet, but I expect to be called in a few minutes and assigned a new bunk, only hope I don't have to shift too far for this will be a wasted move on my part, merely to make space for someone else. Should find out in a couple of minutes.

It's fascinating to sit here and watch and listen while a draft is being called; everyone wondering what it means - - - -

It's an hour later now, had to back off rather suddenly. Anyhow I've run into really bad luck, for it seems, Reed and I are split, dammit, and I'm sure going to miss him.

In the middle of the above paragraph we were all called over to the office for reassignment since our own former bunks had been taken, and the five from our section were stuck into top bunks, but all together. And we were barely moved before the loud speaker boomed for Miller, Prosser, Reed and another guy who had been waiting here a week.

So far as we can see now - - I'll know more later - - they are drafted with our old gang. Probably they'll be shoving off tomorrow for wherever it may be, and I'm sure going to miss the big guy. Incidentally, to keep in touch with him until we both get our new addresses, I'm going to ask him to write to me in care of you, so you can forward any letter properly, and I'll do the same through his wife.

In direct contradiction to my previous guess - - that's all anything amounts to here, we're all up in the air - - I'm now convinced there will be no further schools, that the few of us who are left are being held only as a reserve pool to fill any holes in the main draft.

On that basis, unless enough are withdrawn from our old gang for some reason to allow the four of us to be called, we'll be stuck here doing nothing for at least another week, until a new group of gunners mates graduates. It would be bad enough to be stuck here a whole week doing absolutely nothing, and doubly bad to have to stay longer than that.

I think I've told you before that almost everything the Navy does is alphabetical, which to some extent explains our presence in this "held over" barracks - - <u>S</u>voboda, <u>W</u>alts, <u>W</u>elsh, <u>W</u>under.

The worst of it will be the deadly monotony of sitting around. We're told we'll be "secured" - - the Navy's pleasant way of saying "locked in" - - practically all day. Of course that's to make sure any man is instantly available should he be called. Of course we'll be allowed out for an hour or so at breakfast and lunch and I think we'll be released in the evening after 4, but it will be hard and unpleasant just sitting around for hours and hours every day, never knowing what may happen to you, or when.

Guess that's about all I can write today darling. It's hell trying to scribble when everything is so uncertain, and I just don't seem able to think very straight. So I'm going to sign off, but <u>not</u> seal the envelope for it's entirely possible the whole picture may be changed before I can get out to mail this.

Wish (Yeah, I know it's useless but a guy can wish can't he?) I could look forward to seeing you all - - and I mean <u>you</u> extra specially - - sometime in the foreseeable future, but know it can't be done so have to settle for a few backward looks, to that weekend in Chicago and our few days together.

Must have been a million years since you walked up that ramp in Chicago to lift me out of the cellar and set me on a cloud for a second or so. Doesn't seem possible that was only 10 days ago and that it lasted 48 hours, but my reason tells me it was and did, and I've enough memories to carry me a long time if I can't get any new ones.

That's 'cause I love you so very much, my Betty darling, and always will.

9-6-44 Wednesday morning

Dear Bucky:

Since it has been such a long time since I was home, and it

looks like it may be quite a while longer, I think it would be a good idea for us to sort of write regularly to keep in touch with each other. Suppose you could find time, say on Sunday mornings, to sit down and tell me what you have been doing all week? I think I'll have time enough to do the same for you.

Just now I'm in another of the changing places you seem to run into in the Navy. My old gang, all but four of us, has left or is about to leave for California and we must stay here until we are called to go with some later group. And it is probable we too will go to California when we leave, and since it is so very far from Somerset I'll not expect to be home for a long time, perhaps not until the war is over. You should ask Mother to get out one of the maps in the bookcase and show you where I am now, and where California is, so you'll understand a little better what is going on. A map is just a picture of a country or part of the world, and when you remember what a long trip it is from Philly to Somerset, and see what a little distance it is on the map, I know you'll understand how much farther it is to some of the places I'll be telling you about in these letters.

Hope you can read my writing as well as I read yours, for your first papers from school have been very good and make me quite proud of you. I'm sure you'll study extra hard and keep on improving.

Just now we've all come from swimming, these three friends of mine and about 100 other men I never saw before yesterday. Swimming is one of the forms of exercise the Navy gives us to prevent too much laziness while we're waiting to be transferred. I had quite a lot of fun diving and playing basketball in the water, something I'll try and teach you after we get back to a normal life again. It will be lots of fun for all of us to go swimming together, won't it?

One Sunday in Milwaukee we found a miniature auto race track that would have been a real thrill to you. The little cars are only about a foot long but they have real motors that roar like the dickens when they are started and the cars go so fast you can hardly see them. Of course they are too small to have drivers, so the track has steel grooves that guide the cars and keep them from colliding when four of them race round and round at one time. It's a thrilling race, and lots of fun.

Later we walked down along the lake front, and watched a big ship, big as those we used to see at Philly, come in with a load of coal. Coming in from the lake, the boat has to go up the river through the city to reach its dock, and almost every street crosses the river on a bridge which must be raised when a boat passes. Most of the bridges are drawbridges, the kind that split in the middle and are raised to let a ship pass, but we saw one, a railroad bridge, that looked a little like a seesaw and instead of raising it just pivoted around on a bearing in the middle until it was pointed up and down the river, instead of across. (Ask Mother to show you with a stick or pencil how the bridge would move on a pivot in the center). Of course when it was turned to let the ship pass, there were no tracks for a train to cross the river, but more came along just then.

I suppose you and Granddaddy will be going to all the football games this fall, just as he and I did when I was your size. That was lots of fun for me, and I know it will be for you too, but I'll bet Dad can holler louder than you can. And perhaps some of these days another Welsh will be playing football at Somerset. Me, I don't expect to see any games this fall, but right now I can look out the barracks window every afternoon and watch the Great Lakes team practicing. Kind of would like to be playing myself, but guess there's no chance.

One thing, son, I want you to be careful of is fighting. Remember long ago I told you not to run if someone started to pick on you, but somehow you seem to have thought that I meant for you to get into a fight every chance you get. That isn't it at all, for nobody loves a bully or a boy who's always fighting. Don't start a fight, ever, unless you have a reason that you think is good enough to satisfy me. And you needn't be afraid the fellows will think you are scared just because you are <u>not</u> in fights all the time. Fight hard when you have to, and <u>only</u> when you have to.

And above everything else, I'd rather have you take a licking from a bigger boy than to beat up someone smaller than yourself. You are big enough and old enough now to judge these things sensibly and I leave it to you to make your mother happy and me proud of you.

You know, Bucky, since I'm not home it's up to you to be the man of the family, and I'm counting on you to do a good job. Goodbye for now Son, take care of yourself, be a good boy, and write me all about what you are doing, until we can get together and talk about it. Much love from Your Daddy

9-6-44 Wednesday afternoon

Don't know at the moment whether two letters written to the kids went out or not but I'll soon find out and if there's more in me there are other letters to write before I finish this.

Truth to tell there's nothing to do here but write, read or sleep for we're confined to barracks against the remote possibility someone may be called on draft, but it seems fairly certain now that we are stuck here until next week. We are the "Last Battalion."

We are really alone, too, for all our old gang except six of us pulled out this morning for Shoemaker, California, destined either for amphibs or fleet replacement. I'm really sorry to see Don Reed go for we had become pretty close and he's a swell guy.

They were told last night where they were going, but also told they were forbidden to phone or wire home, which may mean that you'll not know until after I'm on my way. However, I plan to phone if there's any possible way to do it, but if I get through to you, you must keep it quiet until we arrive.

From what we were told they had quite a shindig during the

night, with everyone rather naturally excited at the prospect of a transcontinental trip. They were up at 4 to lash their gear, and all ready to go at 8 but didn't finally shove off until eleven. By now, 2:15, they're rolling somewhere south or west of Chicago, and here we sit.

We did nothing at all last night, except sweep down our section of the barracks, and aside from a pleasant swim this morning have done absolutely nothing today. In a little while I'm going to do a bit of laundry, but the thing to do here is wait until evening to wash so you won't be called out on draft unexpectedly with a bag full of wet clothes.

Wish - - without a chance of it coming true - - that I could have been permitted to go home instead of sitting around here wasting time, but know there's no hope. Still it's a good idea.

Suppose that if I stay here I'll get another weekend liberty, and if I do I'd kind of like to go back to Milwaukee and try to talk Leo and Ginny into going to another dance. That really was fun Sunday, and if I watch myself it won't be too expensive for it only costs 65 cents to get in. Just imagine that bald old husband of yours just woofing around and going to dances. Kind of wish - - just a little bit, you understand - - that my favorite partner were available but that's fruitless too, like most everything else around here.

However I guess the situation could be worse, so there's not much use in griping. Guess I can stand it here a little longer but sure would like to know a little more.

Bye now darling, and take good care of yourself. I want to come back some day, and find myself with enough wife to make an armful. All my love as always!

9-7-44 Thursday afternoon

Still here, still stalled, still wondering seems all I can report as of right now. Another day gone and no signs of a draft call, so that it now seems all but certain we'll be here at least until

Tuesday. All of our gang is gone now except the four of us and you can guess how closely we're sticking together among all those strange faces. We're hoping to go together when the time comes, but I'm keeping my fingers crossed.

Scribbled off a couple more notes yesterday after finishing your letter, and last night, for lack of nothing better to do, went to see a movie called "Cry Havoc," which wasn't very interesting. Didn't get a whole lot of sleep for I drew the 4 to 8 a.m. security watch for 3 barracks. But didn't mind it a bit for I've been loafing too long already. Snatched a little extra snooze this morning, however, and in between tried to read Jan Valtin's "Out of the Night." And that, my darling, is the sum total of what I've seen and done and know. In a way this place is worse than O.G.U., for here we're confined - - "secured" the Navy calls it - - so much of the time. When I get done with this there's the ever present laundry job. And beyond that I can see nothing to do until bedtime except to read and write.

By the way, I've lost Eleanor's address again, and want to write her, so will you please send it along. And in the probability I'll go west ask Mother for Joe's [Chuck's uncle] address in Los Angeles and I can at least drop them a note when I land out there. Don't suppose there would be any chance to see them, for Shoemaker is 300 miles or more from LA.

Judging from your letter today, I neglected to say so much as a thank you for the very useful $20 which arrived in good shape Monday. But I'm grateful, knowing how little you can spare it, and will try not to have to ask again. I've already spent $1, and it probably will be a long time until my next payday, for pay accounts are a little slow following when the Navy moves you.

Hope I get some in time, and have an opportunity to do a bit of Christmas shopping, since you're already "on the ball." And I know what a thrill it would be for an old-style shop-early-and-avoid-the-rush buyer like yourself. Christmas as usual seems a long way off, but more so than in other years because we haven't (at least I haven't) had any summer. Seems a LONG TIME BACK TO April when I was a civilian, yet the summer has flown past without my having seen it.

And that, Betty my only one, seems every drop of ink I can squeeze out right now, so I think I'll get to washing. I still - - and always will - - love you more than anything in the world, and am only existing for the day when I can come back to all of you and begin living again. As always, all my love.

9-8-44 Friday

A beautiful fall day: brilliant sunshine but still that snap to the air that spells football; everything peaceful and a lazy life; yet still I'm not contented.

All day I've been trying to escape from this joint to come home for a couple of days, since I know I'm stuck at least until Monday afternoon, yet all my pleas up to and including a talk with the lieutenant, have run into a stone wall. I can't get permission to go out early tomorrow, or to come back at 9 a.m. Monday instead of Sunday midnight and so I'm stuck unless I decide to do it and take whatever they want to dish out as a penalty.

To be honest I've even considered that, but much as I want to see all of you I just can't bring myself to do it that way. And I've considered, too, that we could fake an illness in the family, and with the help I'm sure we could get from Barch and Jane Freidline, get me an emergency leave. But that's cheating, something I'm not much good at, so just before I sat down to write this I put the idea aside for good.

As you may have guessed by now, I'm sick and tired of waiting around this hole, and unless it means a chance to get home to you I don't want to go anywhere else except somewhere I can do some fighting towards getting this war over with. I'm dammed good and mad, and somebody better get the hell out of my road.

Grr! Grr! Grr! Growled the big bald bear.

Once again I've nothing to report in the way of prospects or activity. After finishing your letter yesterday I went to the post office and drew a blank, ate and then came back to write a few notes. Then Walts and I went to the canteen, played gin rummy until 7:30, then came back to the barracks and dawdled around until bedtime (9:30).

Didn't get up this morning until 8, was drafted for a work detail. We goldbricked most of the time but after we got our work done the p.o. in charge tried to unload a lot of his on us. We stayed on that detail until 2:30. Ahead of me is chow - - and not a thing to do all evening, although I expect to write to the Smith's, and repack my sea bag again.

Just had a strange thing happen to me. I was sitting here writing, minding my own business, when the yeoman from Transfer Unit office walked in saying he wanted "a volunteer for a detail" adding the usual "it will only take a couple of minutes." You know me. There were only a few guys around, most of them due to leave on draft in a short while, so I stood up. "Go in my office," he told me, "Get that ice cream that's on top of the box, and eat it." And dammed if there wasn't ice cream there, and he meant what he said. That's by far the nicest practical joke I've found in the Navy.

So now - - to get back to me - - I'm left with another ordinary weekend, and probably will go to Milwaukee. Don't feel I can afford to spend much money, so it probably will be a pretty tame affair.

That was a good-sounding letter from your mother, especially the report on herself and Dad. Golly, I do hope this is the end of her long stretch, for she surely has been miserable.

How about you, are you getting any fatter - - or should I say less thin? Better eat heavy little one, for I really was dismayed at the way your illness trimmed you down until there wasn't much left.

But that little bit is all I want, or ever shall want, dammit, and right now you're much too far away from these empty arms of mine. Nevertheless I know that when we are together again I shall appreciate you all the more for having missed you so much so long, and will make our own lives together just a little brighter because of it.

Only I'm selfish enough to want you <u>now</u> and always for that's the only thing I can think of most of the time. And I do love you an awful lot.

9-11-44 Monday morning

Perhaps it's only sleepiness, but somehow I feel tired and let down this morning, despite a pleasant weekend. Betcha a letter from you will fix it, if I can manage to get one or several today - - and if I don't hear I rather think I'll be phoning this evening. However the sensible thing to do is hang in a little longer until I have something to report about when or where I'm going.

Lordy it's been a long time since I've heard from you; the last letter was written Tuesday. And I miss them more than I care to admit to the average stranger. But I suppose I might as well get used to doing without, for I don't believe it will be much longer before I start getting my mail in batches. Still feel sure it's all a postal mix-up that will be straightened out soon. Golly, seems like everything is mixed up, doesn't it?

Well, to report on my weekend which I said earlier was pleasant, but actually not quite so much fun as others. We shoved off from here, Walts and I, for Milwaukee shortly after inspection Saturday afternoon, got in there about 4:30 and went straight to the USO where they have a free tailor shop to get my new rating stripes sewed on. It took much longer than expected and I was stuck there until 7:30.

I then phoned Ginny and they had practically given me up and were eating dinner, so I grabbed a bus and went out, leaving

Walts at the USO waiting for a telegraph money order from his wife. He had no plans beyond that, and we arranged that if Ginny could find a partner for him I'd call him, and he could come out after his money order arrived.

However, Ginny couldn't find anyone else, and after Margie (her name I learned is Marjorie Franzene) arrived about 8:30 she couldn't think of anyone either but we decided to ask Charlie to go along on the probability that the girls would know someone at the dance, or he could find a partner on his own. But when I had him paged at the USO he was gone and I didn't see him again until this morning.

Anyhow, about 10 o'clock, we went to the dance and it seems that on Saturday night they have "old time" dances, with a lot of polkas, schatlisches etc., about which I know nothing, along with lots of waltzes, which, it seems, I can get by on. Nevertheless, the four of us had a lot of fun galloping around, stopping occasionally for a glass of beer, and gabbing in between times. The dance breaks up at 1, we found a little place nearby to eat, then took Margie home and I traipsed back to the apartment with Ginny and Leo, then they fixed up the couch for me and all went to sleep.

It was about 2:30 when we went to bed and after 10 when we woke up, although both Ginny and Leo accused me of waking them earlier by snoring. I wouldn't know about that. Anyhow we each had a shower, then a bite of breakfast, and I went to 12:15 Mass.

Ginny had invited one of two sisters who live in an upstairs apartment (The other one had gone to a picnic.) to have dinner with us and about 3:30 I went to the apartment where Margie lives with a Mrs. Hacker, and brought her up to Ginny's. We were going over to the park, but Mrs. Hacker didn't want to stop her jam making - - I filched a couple of plums while we talked. She has two sons in the service, one a navigator on a Flying Fortress now in England.

So just the four of us went wandering, visited the zoo, ate popcorn and wound up at the house of another couple Don Reed and I had met up there several times. Riley and Ann (I think their last name is Firth or something like that.) seem to be their (Ginny and Leo's) best friends. Riley has just gotten a license from the state board of physicians to practice hydro-therapy, a form of chiropractics, and has been working as a clerk in a hotel while studying and I guess he intends to continue until he gets his practice started. It was he who got Don and me a room the last time we were in Milwaukee together. Anyhow, they're very nice people, just about our age.

I had taken Leo's Sunday paper to the apartment for Mrs. Hacker to read while we were gone for she had been unable to get one, so we decided I'd take Margie home, bring the paper back to the others apartment and then Margie and I were going to go back for a couple of more dances before I had to leave.

Well, while I was waiting at Mrs. Hacker's house for Margie to powder her nose I developed an attack of cramps that made me unhappy and I just had to rush back to Ginny's for the bathroom. Meanwhile Margie decided she wanted a cup of coffee, but since I wasn't able to join her I grabbed a bus and beat it, leaving her in a restaurant next door.

When I got to Ginny's I made a mad scramble for the throne, in the midst of a barrage of questions about where was Margie, for they had phoned Mrs. Hacker right after we left to make sure Margie was coming back with me for they were fixing a bite to eat. And of course Mrs. Hacker had told them we had left, and not knowing my unhappy predicament thought we were going back out together.

Well, between the cramps and the questions I was in a dither for a few moments, but got rid of the cramps I drank a cup of coffee with them, said goodbye for the second time in as many Sundays, picked up and my gear and walked away and picked up Margie. That was about 8:30 and from then until 10 we danced and talked, she about her sailor boy friend and me about my wife and kids.

She gave me his address, and I surely will look him up if I get a chance, hope he's a nice guy for she's surely a nice girl. They have been going together for five years and are faced with the old wartime problem of whether or not to marry. He has been in California for most of the two years, is a machinist mate first class assigned to some kind of a training ship, but of course never knows when he may be sent out.

The girl doesn't talk much about herself, but she works in a defense plant, painting readings figures on dials used on navy range indicators. She's been in Milwaukee about two years, living with Mrs. Hacker who, I gather is a widow and very lonely with her sons gone. Don't know what descent Margie is, but she speaks with a decided accent which I was unable to identify. She's blonde, with quite a nap of real curly hair, not what I call pretty at all but a good, clean friendly girl. Doesn't smoke at all, and I suspect four or five glasses (very small ones) of beer she drank Saturday night represented an all-time alcoholic high for her. Think I did tell you she's 26.

Betty darling, I don't know exactly why I'm going into all this detail, for I suspect you'll think this whole letter is overcrowded with one gal, and may not be overly happy about it. But somehow I want to tell you about everything I do like that, and to go into detail so you'll know every little thing I've done against the possibility that I might omit something that would leave you wondering.

You see, my little one, there is only one girl in all the world who means a single solitary thing to me; only one girl whom I want to be with, all the time, any place. And since I can't be with you I like to find what little pleasures I can, while I can, where I can, wishing every second of the time that I could be with you. And I want you to know all about them, what I have done and who I have been with, so that never for one instant will you doubt that all of my love is for you.

I have just come back from chow and mail call, and am much relieved to find I'm on the letters list again, albeit a trifle (?) upset to learn that you have apparently been sick again. I got four letters, one from Mother and three from you, all written Friday, but I'm still receiving letters from Wednesday and Thursday in which you apparently admitted that you have been down with bronchitis again. Gee I hope you'll shake it off quickly, and won't have any more trouble. I'll be sore as hell if you let yourself get run down to the stage like Eleanor Brennan reached simply because you're worrying about me. Hell's fire, gal, I'm all right, and will be coming home to you and the kids for keeps just as soon as we can get this one over with.

You see, Bettsy, that's all I'm caring about now or any other time. I love you - - all of you - - more than all the rest of the world and not a single thing that happens can be of importance alongside that love. Please, my darling, believe that and don't worry about me. I assure you I'm most certainly not worrying about myself. I <u>know</u> I'll be all right, and you'd better be the same or I'll just turn you across my knee first chance I get and paddle your little pink bottom. Now then, I hope that's scolding enough - - and I hope it makes your belly tingle like it does mine, remembering how it feels to have my hands on you.

Hold on again, Bettsy, here at last comes another draft list and maybe I'll be on it. I have been dragging along trying to wait for this so I can report to you. - - - - - - - Nope, not this time but I think maybe there will be some more before the day is out.

Before it slips my somewhat (?) vacant mind, one of your letters mentions "running at both ends" which, I hope, means you have a visitor. If so I'm frankly relieved for I've been wondering if I hadn't turned out to be a whole lot more vigorous than I anticipated. Understand what improvement there was wonderful, if it wasn't an overdose. Agree?

Gee I'm glad your washer parts arrived and will take that

much more load off my darling's shoulders. I know you've had a helluva job with all that scrubbing - - which reminds me, I've quite a laundry job in front of me now.

The last draft call of the day has been made, and none for me, so I'm stuck again, probably will have no chance to get out of here sooner than Wednesday if then.

That my darling one is all I have for tonight. I love you more than anything or anyone in all the world, and want you with all my heart: to see you, to touch you, just to be near you. It's a very empty world when you're not with me, my Bettsy, and always will be. You see it must be that way because I love you.

9-11-44 Monday evening

I sit here drowsing and drooling, with a dozen things to be doing and 3 other letters I should write first, yet I can think of nothing but you and so - - for lack of anything better - - I'm scribbling again in hopes it will make me feel half decent.

Probably you've already guessed it from the long and disjointed letter I mailed a little while ago, but I've got me a dose of the blues at the moment and don't quite know what to do about it. If - - a fellow can't be stopped from dreaming - - I could only put my arms around you, and just bury my nose in your soft, sweet-smelling hair then the whole sky would change from gray to gay all in an instant.

Seems several million eons since I felt your arms around me and your lips on mine, yet I can remember the feel of you as only an instant ago. Looking back I can see so many times I could have taken you in my arms, yet didn't, that I'm utterly ashamed of myself for having wasted them. Would that I had just one of those lost opportunities back now, or even in sight for some reasonably near future

Yes darling, as you may have guessed I am hungry for you, but not in the fiery, lusty way of old. Now it is a smoldering blaze down inside this hollow shell of me, a fire that sends up smoke to sting my eyes and choke my breathing, and burns and hurts and burns yet I can do nothing about it without you.

It's true, of course, that I want you physically, I hope I always will. But worse than that, I want you, the comforting easy-going assuming presence of my own, very especially wonderful wife. At this very unpleasant moment when nothing is firm or assured it's good to have a solid memory of you and our children and our home, and believe me I'll appreciate these things at more nearly their real value when I come back to them.

Just why I'm crying on your shoulder like this is something I wouldn't be able to explain if I tried, nor could I tell you why it has made me feel better already, but it has and I do hope you won't mind too much. It's very nice to be able to do just that, even when I know it isn't fair for I've run out and left you with, as usual, much the toughest and most important job. But Bettsy you <u>must</u> take care of yourself physically, get yourself built up, your teeth checked and those x-rays taken so we'll know what the score is. There's no use in fooling with those things, and the longer you delay the more difficult the final solution can become.

Please darling, do these things for me, because I want to be sure while I'm gone that you take care of yourself, and are ready to live when I come back.

There, that's one thing off my mind and have just one more. Have you given any thought lately to becoming a Catholic? Probably you'll think it strange and perhaps crude that I should bring it up in this way and at this time, but I have been thinking about it, and if you haven't already guessed it then I might as well tell you.

As I say I have been thinking about it, but not quite in the way you might think: it's just that for some time past I've had the feeling that you have been thinking about it more than a little, and perhaps wondering about it too.

Long ago, before we were married, we talked this over and

I told you then that if and when you should decide you want to be a Catholic I would be happy to do everything to help; that I would never attempt to force you or persuade you. I mean that just as truly now as I did then, and nothing can change me on the matter. But if my guess is right then perhaps you do need help and after all what is a husband for.

Truly I meant to ask you about this when I came home, and it would have been so much easier to talk with my arms around you, but like so many other things it was forgotten in the glorious days of our honeymoon. So I bring it up now, and leave it just there.

Just as I am now, starting this letter blue as indigo, crying on your shoulder, then giving you a big order and asking a big question and at the end feeling almost like a human being again, although a little bit too lonely for my own comfort.

This may seem a strange sort of birthday present for you, my Bettsy, since it should reach you one day early. But in every word you should be able to read that I love you, always have, always will, as surely as the sun rises and sets. That, my darling is all there is in the world for me - - and all I want. You are the most beautiful, most thoughtful, most comforting and are the most glorious women in all the world and I never never shall stop being grateful for having been permitted to find you.

9-12-44 Tuesday

Well Betsy, this is it. Before I finish this letter, I should know where I'm going, and when, although tomorrow seems almost a certainty on the when, just as the West Coast seems to be where. And I am glad. Sitting here now in the midst of all the hullabaloo raised by 200 guys on the eve of a very important day in their lives, I feel as though a great weight is about to be lifted from my shoulders or like walking on a country road through a long, dark night and then you start to climb a hill and see just shining over the crest the lights of a town.

I didn't get very far with the above two paragraphs for we started through the mill quickly and now our next step is all outlined for us. Of course you'll know about it before you get this, for I'll be phoning tonight, and I'm glad of that too, although I know it will be hard to talk with all of you.

The answer is Shoemaker, California, leaving sometime tomorrow, and that means we'll probably arrive there about Sunday. What happens after that I have no way of knowing. It may be that we'll ship right from there to Pearl Harbor or somewhere beyond; or we may be held there for an indefinite time, perhaps for further specialized training or perhaps until our ships are ready. What kind or what size of ship it may be I don't know, but I think the chances are it will be a good one, for Shoemaker is the Pacific Fleet Replacement Center.

To go back a little in time - - somehow even last night seems to have been away back in ancient history - - after finishing my second letter to you I felt a very great deal better, and then proceeded to write to Red Sabin, helped clean up a little and went to bed feeling reasonably at peace with the world.

Woke this morning at 7:30, ate a little breakfast and then sat waiting for the call that I somehow sensed was coming. Come it did and it caught all four of us, Svoboda, Walts, Wunder and I, and again I'm glad to be with them. We were given our new billets in another barracks and told to be moved after chow. So we ate, got our mail, and then moved. Incidentally, all the letters that I missed last week caught up to me, filling me in on the background of your dual illness. I do hope you're better by now, and taking care so you can build your self up against the day that I'll be coming back.

After we moved we loafed a while, just waiting, until the chief came over with our orders, told us where we are going and when; how to pack our gear and a few other odds and ends incident to such a long trip. We don't know yet, of course, but we'll probably be going in troop sleepers, since there are nearly 100 sailors in the four graduating sections of gunners mates this week, along with a few of us holdovers.

Then we lined up to have our throats and peckers checked - - you walk past the men doing the checking without stopping - - and now most of the gang are digging into their final preparations. Mine are done, for the washing I did last night is all dried and rolled and it will take me only a few minutes in the morning to get mine all rolled and ready.

Strangely enough the weight isn't quite gone from my shoulders - - or more properly my insides. It's all very easy to say that I wouldn't be any further from you at Pearl Harbor than here, for there's no denying I haven't been able to get home, but dammit I could always hope, and out there I can't even do that.

But nothing and no one can stop me from thinking, and dreaming of you, and loving you always, with every fiber of me.

And so, my darling ends your birthday letter, and I regret it can't be a happier one for you. How I wish I could hold you in my arms, if only for a moment, and try to tell you how much I love you and miss you, but it hasn't worked out that way for this birthday. So let's both of us try to plan on doing it next time, and knuckle down to the job ahead. I'm going to be the best goddam fighting man in the whole Navy just as I know you'll be the best in the world at the big job asked of you.

Good bye, my darling, and I never meant anything so much in my life as I do now when I tell you I love you with all my heart, and always will.

9-13-44 Wednesday morning

It's hard to start this letter to you, sweetheart, for there's really nothing I want to say except the old, old things I've been saying over and over again these 14 years of ours. You see I do love you, always have loved you and always will love you with all my heart.

No matter how many miles come between us or what may happen to keep us apart.

Last night was so horribly hard to talk to you, and to try and act happy; although I'm afraid I didn't succeed at all in disguising my real feelings. As you can tell from the letter just ahead of this one I had known about it for some hours, and had at least a chance to prop my chin up, but somehow the first sound of your voice knocked out all the props, and then the kids - - I could all but see them, and know beyond any doubt what they were thinking and feeling - - just tramped all over me.

I had gone back to our old barracks, now half empty, to phone because I knew I'd need privacy, and tried to time the call so that everyone would be home. I'm glad now that failed. Anyhow, when we hung up I just sort of stumbled out of the place, and took a long walk through the gathering dusk. Finally I did, and came back to the barracks to write a few farewell notes.

At that time I intended not to call again, for I was afraid I wouldn't be able to talk at all and so I wrote just a brief note to Mother and Dad. But later, I had washed my underwear and showered and while the rather riotous gang was settling down to sleep I changed my mind again and decided I owed them at least that much. Now I'm glad I did and that I managed to get myself pretty well under control. It was wonderful to talk with the three of you and they sounded like their old cheery selves. Can't say the same for you, unfortunately, for I didn't like to hear you sounding so hoarse, and while I'm not too sure you've been telling me the truth about how sick you've been. Golly, darling, you've just got to take care of yourself now, because I can't boss you around and see that you do the right thing.

Sleeping was the toughest thing I've tried to do in a long time. Naturally, I was tense, and to complicate matters the bed was hard and the guy next to me sounded like a buzz saw all night. So I snoozed in fits and starts, yet was ready to get up at 5 a.m. reveille, had all my gear packed for shipment at 6 and then went to Mass and to communion. Afterward I ate breakfast (beans), shaved, and here I am writing so you could have at least something for your birthday.

I don't know yet, but my guess is that we'll not leave until some time this afternoon, which will give me a chance to get one more letter from you to carry me over until my mail starts coming again.

Don't know what the possibilities for writing will be on the train going west, but I will hope I'll be able to get off at least one letter a day for you between now and Sunday, when I expect we'll reach Shoemaker. Lord knows there will be plenty of time to write, and if I can't mail the letters I'll save them until I can. You'll have to do something of the same, until I can send you an address. Incidentally, depending on what I find there, I may decide to wire you rather than using air-mail.

And so, my darling, I'm all ready for the long ride, fortified in every way possible by your love and knowing that my love for you will be just as complete that wonderful day when I come back as it was the day I first saw you and has been ever since.

Goodbye, good luck and God be with you and guide you, for yours is the biggest and much the toughest job. Give all the little ones an extra special kiss from their daddy, who will be coming back some day - - soon I hope. All my love always.

This letter was found in a safe deposit box after Chuck's death. The date of receipt is unknown.

Somerset, PA September 8, 1944

My dear Charles:

Thank you so much for the lovely gift of towels. Not only do I appreciate them for their true purpose but I love to have them as souvenir of your stay at Great Lakes. And that is apparently what you are having now — a stay at Great Lakes. But don't worry my dear – I tell you as I tell Betty, that whatever is is for the best. I have that faith and that hope in prayer that wherever duty calls you, you will meet it splendidly and that our Blessed Mother will be with you guiding you and guarding you – of our love and prayers you know they are always with you. And I feel you have always made the right decisions although at times we may not have seen things as you did – And if you could hear Betty every night saying the prayers with your little children you would feel very guarded indeed. All three, even little Francis, finish up "God bless Daddy and bring him home safely to us." You haven't any idea how Francis is maturing. It is really strange because he was so little. Whenever anyone asks him something, he always responds "I'm Daddy's boy." Every play thing eventually turns into a telephone to talk to Daddy and clearly and distinctly he talks to you. He makes sentences like a much older child – trots back and forth through the house and yard and makes play things for himself out of everything. As you may guess he and his Grandfather are great pals. Today he told his mother "Grandma Mary came" when I came in. He had picked that Mary up from Daddy calling me Mary. I don't believe Charles or Elizabeth ever linked that thought together. All in all my son I'm just at my favorite pastime – bragging what smart grandchildren I have. Sister is proving to be just what I gathered two years ago when she went to Vacation School – one of those quiet youngsters who get it all and can retell just what she learned.

We had a letter from Eleanor today and she seems contented and is very happy with her two little darlings. I really think for all her worries – she is freeer of spirit than she has been for years because she does not have that other horrible personality on her mind all the time. Just the same we would love to have her home. The great distance between us really worries Daddy and me. Mary and Margaret are both coming home this weekend so we will have lots of laugh and talk. We have not heard from Dick for some time but Margaret has his address and I will send him some little thing for his birthday. Ed Morin told me today that Tom had been assigned to a new bomber crew (in England) and found his pilot to be a Somerset boy – Lynn Crouse. Guess Betty told you Pauline D'Amico Martz has a fine baby boy and her father is the proudest man in town – Also another bit of town gossip – the Blatts are going to have a baby early next spring – and they are thrilled. You know just before Christmas last year they adopted a baby girl and had intended adopting another child when this little girl was two years old. Well tomorrow, our registration opens for the blood bank the last week in September. So I sit in the postoffice from 8 to 12 to register the donors there. The Motor Corps is doing Fleet Week. There will be booths in eight places for registering. Did Betty tell you that Larry O'Neil is home and he and Mary will be married September 14 in the chapel (not inside the rail however as Nancy is not a Catholic) at St. Vincent's. The reception will be held afterward at Roy's house. The kids are having parties for her – Jean has had to shell out for a good many showers this year.

Well my dear, take care of yourself and be content that Daddy and I will take the best possible care of your beloved ones till you get back to take over again.

So goodnight and God Bless you and a world of love to you from

Daddy and Mother

Chapter 5
TRAIN TO SHOEMAKER, CALIFORNIA
9/13/44 to 9/17/44

9-13-44 Wednesday evening aboard Pullman about to leave Great Lakes

Having written early this morning, I've been in no hurry about starting this second letter which might be entitled the first chapter of "Gulliver's Travels." Wonder how many chapters there will be and where they will take me.

Anyhow, here we are about to shove off, on a journey that will last until some time Sunday. The li - - - - that streak is the jar of the first movement of the engine hooked on and starting us out of the siding and on our way. It's now just 6:35 p.m. This sentence started out to say that the lieutenant had just been in to give us our final instructions and tell us goodbye.

Now we're out on the siding where the liberty trains load, have stopped to get another engine on the front end and in a few seconds - - even now - - we're moving out onto the main line bound for Chicago and points south and west. Whoops, talking too fast for we've stopped again but probably only for a few minutes. Here we go for good, I hope, at 6:50

We were all set to leave when I signed off the last letter, but waited and waited for orders to load our gear which was all rolled and tied. Finally we were told to put it on a truck, then hauled it to the railroad siding, loaded it into a freight car and came back for chow and our mail. On the mail score, I think I'm all caught up now, including Bucky's letter, on which the spelling wasn't as good as usual. Needless to say I was glad to get every last one of them, and shall be rereading each as we move westward.

After chow we went back to the barracks expecting to be called to the train by one o'clock but no soap, and the whole 200 or so just lay around the barracks until 4. I snoozed on the bare springs of my bunk, and read a little.

Finally we were told we could go for mail and chow, and to hurry back, but Walts, Wunder and I seeing the long lines at the chow house, decided instead to blow ourselves to a meal at the hostess house. Returning we saw our special train had pulled in, so we raced off for the barracks and a few minutes later marched away. Luck was with us on the train, for we wound up on a genuine Pullman and the four of us are right together, Wunder and I on one side, Walts and Svoboda across the aisle. It should be a good trip.

We're starting into Chicago now, and I'm going to close this in a moment, in hopes I'll be able to get it mailed from here. I'll be writing as often as I can, although it's quite difficult sitting here with my pad propped on my knee. But you'll get your letters, and I'll try and get one to you every day.

And you'll know, too, letter or no letter that wherever I go or whatever I do I'll be loving you with all my heart, and thinking of you every moment. Goodnight, my darling, sleep tight and don't worry for I'll be loving you always. 'Nite my sweetheart and I do love you.

9-14-44 Thursday morning somewhere in Iowa, 9:15 a.m.

You are my darling, you know, even if you can't read this. It's a rather jarring train ride at the moment. This will be your strangest birthday, with your husband not even able to say hello, or deliver his customary kiss, but just mark it down on the log book as another I owe you, and I'll pay off some day.

I started this alleged letter in a little town named Waterloo, and we should be somewhere between Des Moines and Omaha when I finish. Hope the letter I wrote last night and threw off the train to a switchman in Chi reached you ok.

The four of us have just finished a stretch of KP, serving breakfast to about 300 men, half of them Negroes. We will have two more meals to serve today, then no more duty for the rest of the trip.

There isn't much to tell you so far. After reading your letter last night I stood up in the vestibule for an hour or so while we were shuttling through Chi, and about 10:30 I crawled into my bunk and slept well, waking momentarily several times to wonder where we were, then going promptly back to sleep. Was up and washed by 6:30 reveille, and we KP-ers ate our scrambled eggs, prunes, bread and butter and coffee before we started serving. We had volunteered for the job last night, so we could get our share over with early and enjoy the scenery of the west.

Looks like a smart guess here, for so far we haven't missed anything although I would have liked to have seen the Mississippi which we crossed last night. Ever since daylight we've been traveling - - not very fast - - across the rolling farmlands of Iowa, where they seem to grow nothing but corn, field after field of it, almost any where you look. Pasture lands are grazed clean, although we see little livestock. Houses are almost always nested in a clump of trees at the top of a knoll, apparently for shelter from the wind. Towns we go through are neat and clean, with wide lawns - - looks much like Somerset.

We're told the next city will be Omaha, Nebraska at 5 p.m. I hope to mail this before then. We seem to be following a freight route, bypassing the cities, and as you can see the roadbed is not smooth. Wunder, Svoboda and I are all trying to write, with about equal success.

The gang has been well-behaved so far, and I'm hoping will stay that way. Altogether, there are upwards of 400 men on this 19-car train, and some of the more fortunate ones have compartments, while the rest are in ordinary Pullmans. More than half of the gang are Negroes, including about half the boys in this car, but each color sticks to its own group while all are served from the dining car.

It's a regular Navy diner, and the cooks are colored sailors, preparing the usual Navy chow. When it's all ready, all the men in one end of the train walk to the diner at the other end then are served cafeteria style, on paper plates with wooden utensils, take their food back to their own cars and eat. Then the process is repeated with the other half of the train. No dishes to wash.

There are no real hills in this country, only little knolls that pop up here and there. Little clumps of trees dot the landscape, and line the banks of the many streams that meander sluggishly through the meadows, seemingly going nowhere. We don't see many people, except in the towns where old men and women seem to predominate. In Waverly, we saw quite a crowd of youngsters on their way to school, and they called to us and waved, and we waved back. Most of them were boys, just about Bucky's size.

Up to now none of us have left the train since we boarded last evening. Some time, perhaps later today, the train will stop somewhere and we'll all pile out for a bit of calisthenics. However it's going to be tough traveling four days without a bath.

So I guess I'll wind up this chapter two of Gulliver's Travels, perhaps can continue later today. All my love, my darlings, and I'll be thinking of you wherever I go.

9-14-44 Thursday 3 p.m. Nearing Omaha

Not much more to report except we're still rolling, quite fast now, towards Nebraska and the Missouri River crossing from

Council Bluffs to Omaha. The country has changed a bit, is slightly more rolling but still prairie corn continues to dominate the landscape, but there is more pasture land, and we're seeing more cattle and swine. It looks much like Pennsylvania except there are no blue hills in the distance.

Streams, and consequently bridges, are more numerous now. We crossed the Des Moines River at Fort Dodge on a great viaduct nearly 100 feet high and a half mile long. Since I missed the Mississippi I'm looking forward to seeing the Missouri.

One strange thing I've noted about these farms out here, big and rich-looking though they are. The barns are quite small and built almost against the houses, have very long gently sloping roofs - - never saw any quite like them.

This would be a marvelous trip for all of us, and I hope we can take it some day. The war seems very far away at the moment and we're all settling down to enjoy the ride.

At Carroll, a few miles back, we ran for a short distance beside a cement road marked U.S. Route 30. Seemed like meeting an old friend to be near the Lincoln Highway again.

We're served our meal - - steak, potatoes, peas, sliced peaches, bread and butter, and now have a little free time until we go back for supper. It was a long slow drag for the cooks weren't able to turn out steaks fast enough in a single galley, and it took more than two hours to feed all the men.

I'll lose a little sleep too, being on watch; yeah, we even have 'em on trains - - from 10 to midnight, but won't mind it a bit riding out into the night.

Bye now darlings and I love you all very, very much. Wish I could have a kiss.

9-14-44 Thursday, 8:00 p.m. Eastern Nebraska

My darlings: Note the plural salutation, which I've decided to adopt since this travelogue is being written for all of you, and besides you all are my darlings, even that grumpy pot-bellied one.

Southwest out of Omaha we rode for an hour into a raspberry sunset, and now it is just turning from dusk to dark as we chug up a little grade, the engine laboring valiantly up there in front. Outside the locusts are singing their harsh but homely song, and it's good to hear it for the first time in a couple of years. Peculiarly enough it makes me think of home, and other summer evenings and a little bit - - just a teeny bit, mind you - - of a certain girl.

We crossed the Missouri River on a high bridge linking Council Bluffs, and Omaha, just in the middle of our third chow line of the day. So I didn't get much of a look, but don't think I missed much for the "Big Muddy" looked low and peaceful.

Just a little while ago we crossed the famous Platte, a very different sort of river from any I've seen before. It wasn't really a bridge, just a long trestle 10 feet above a sandy wasteland that was a half-mile wide; then 100 yards of river and 50 yards of swamp, and all the surrounding countryside marked by the vicious floods.

This is the famed Indian Country, land of the Sioux and old Sitting Bull, where once millions of buffalo roamed the plains, but I've seen nothing to prove it. Just a few moments ago we passed through the outskirts of a peaceful little country town that looked clean and modern as any Philadelphia Main Line Suburb.

Soon we should be in Lincoln, seat of the University of Nebraska whose football teams have provided me with some very swell entertainment. And before I go to bed at midnight I should be able to guess whether we're going the northern route through Denver, or will swing southwest across Oklahoma, Texas and Arizona. Wouldn't Eleanor be surprised to get a letter from me postmarked Phoenix? Of course that would be the best I could do, for even if we stop there I would not be permitted to leave the train.

Note how much worse the scribbling has become. The train, which was going slowly when I started, is really rolling now.

The officers and petty officers in charge of our party seem to be making their first trip too, for they don't know much about the rules and regulations. First of all the lieutenant who is senior officer gave me permission to mail these letters yesterday, which I had not expected since mailing is specifically prohibited from military trains.

Then this afternoon, while we were crossing southwestern Iowa he discovered the train would be stopped in Omaha for servicing, and he decided to let us all go roaming for an hour. I didn't believe it when the fellows told me, but when the chief petty officer came around to tell us we'd all have to wear blues I had visions of a walk and a very delectable bottle of cold beer. Of course we all changed from the dungarees we've been wearing, and I even shaved.

Then he decided to feed the men quickly, and you should have seen us throw hot dogs, potatoes and kraut at that gang in nothing flat. But someone must have told the lieutenant that to let us go would be a direct infraction of accepted procedure, and besides some of the boys might be late or not get back at all, so he called it off and all we got was a 2-minute walk on the platform. It was a silly idea anyway, and he should have known better.

We're going through Lincoln now, and a pretty town it is, what we can see at night from the train. Here, as almost everywhere, men, women and kids stop to wave as we go by, and the gals who don't rate at least a couple of whistles or howls are homely indeed.

So endeth my chapter 4, my darlings, and I'll be writing tomorrow. A big hug and kiss to each of you, to be charged against my account until I come home.

9-15-44 Thursday 8:25 a.m. in Kansas

Through the night we rolled south and west onto the Great Plains, a land as different from the hills of home as any possibly could be.

It was a gorgeous night, clear and crisp; never have I seen so many stars. Riding alone out on the darkened platform through my 10 to midnight watch I was able to make out, for the first time in my life, the little Bear swinging from Polaris, the North Pole star, and to see the Milky Way, almost solid enough to walk on.

At a pleasant little town called Fairburg - - the name was blocked out in great brick letters on the station lawn - - we stopped to service the train at midnight and I got off to walk around, gave a letter to a civilian to mail, and stretched my legs a bit. A little later I woke Wunder, my relief man, and crawled into the sack, where I promptly conked off, snoozed beautifully until 7 a.m.

This morning we slept until 7, then loafed a while, ate breakfast (one egg, bread and butter, jam and figs) and here I am writing again while the train is stopped in some little town for servicing. We're not far from the Colorado border, and will be in mountain country before many more hours. I'm going to mail this now, I hope, and will start another letter.

9-15-44 Friday 9:10 p.m. nearing Colorado

We're rolling again after our stop at Goodland and an unfortunate incident. While we were stopped - - and as I was writing - - some of the boys decided to run a block or so to the business district for a bit of shopping.

So they did, and of course the lieutenant, who has been way too lenient with us in permitting us to be on the train platform and to move from car to car, rose up and raised hell! Now the guard must stay inside the car, no one may leave and the rest of the trip will be a little less pleasant, and what's worse, we may have a few less passengers for I didn't see as many come back as I saw run away.

I just found out we're taking the northern route. Our next stop will be Colorado Springs.

The country is changing now as we near the mountains,

becoming more like the rolling hills of Iowa and Nebraska, but I never have seen country such as we rolled through this morning. It was a single field, flat as a table top, stretching clear to the horizon on one side of the tracks, not a thing in view but stubble; no buildings, no trees, not even a bush to break the solid symmetry. A road that can be nothing but a lane to a single farm runs straight out to the skyline and on away to the invisible buildings somewhere down below the horizon.

Most of the fields are golden brown stubble; some have lain fallow through the summer, resting for another year. Here and there one is stacked thickly with shocks that may be only straw, or may be what's left to mold because there weren't enough men or machines to harvest it. Some fields are plowed and harrowed, ready for a new crop, and here and there you see a bright green patch in the ocean of brown that means winter wheat is already peeping through.

Just a moment ago, we crossed into Colorado - - we could see the state line marker on Route 24 which here parallels the track, and from the jerk of the train I judge we're climbing a slow but steady grade.

There are no rivers, or even streams, that I have seen in this great flat country, which seems to have been without rain for some time. Now and then we pass a dry wash, an ugly eroded scar in the earth where the water floods when it rains.

Again the farm buildings are close-knit little groups, as though huddled together for safety in the great loneliness. Every group of buildings has two or more, sometimes as many as five, windmills whirling frantically in the light breeze to suck up water from the subsoil level. Towns, when we come to them are dominated by great water towers perched high in the air, usually painted bright silver.

Memories of the "rootin" "tootin" "shootin" days: We've just passed through a town called Burlington and a sign says this is Kit Carson Country! Some time has gone by and we're deep into the Colorado range country now. The land has changed again - - great empty spaces, marked only by fences and a rare group of buildings. Lonely cattle graze in the distance, dwarfed by space until they seem only the size of the animals under a Christmas tree.

For more than an hour we could feel the engine chugging and hear a steady rapid chuff, chuff, chuff as we climbed an invisible but apparently a long and steady grade. A little bit ago we started down and the clumsiness of my scribbling increases in direct ratio to our speed. Now we've stopped, apparently in a yard, perhaps at a town called Limon.

Haven't done much reading on this long journey, and doesn't look like I'll get much done although I brought several books. In contrast I've done a lot more writing than I expected, but it's been fun.

Had a good chow just a little bit ago - - chili, potatoes, green beans, bread butter and jam, and two oranges. Traveling is making a pig of me, although I haven't yet expanded enough to fill my trousers.

This is another hazy but sunlit day, not hot but not cool either, just right for traveling. We've been very fortunate in weather so far, hope it keeps up. Strikes me I've been very lucky in all my seasons in the Navy so far, hitting it just right to get by all the way with a maximum of comfort and a minimum of washing. Which reminds me I've come this far and changed only one pair of sox; not much use cleaning up unless you can have a bath, but we'll probably be plenty filthy by Sunday.

I think we all are concentrating on enjoying the trip, which is something we're doing very thoroughly. It's a big thrill to see all the strange lands, and the war seems very far away. Haven't heard a man wonder out loud about what's ahead of us. Honestly, I don't think I'm even worried: I feel fit and clear, ready for anything.

The soil must be changing here, for we've just passed the first honest-to-gosh clump of trees in hundreds of miles. Almost everyone turned to look.

Anyhow, I'm looking forward to bringing you all out here some peaceful day.

9-16-44 Saturday 9 a.m. Western Colorado

Don't be alarmed if this letter is full to overflowing with superlatives. I am intoxicated with this beauty and grandeur of this country.

Just now we are coasting down the winding upper valley of the Colorado River. Orchards, farms, coal mines and the swift running green streams fill the level floor of the valley, which ranges from a couple hundred yards to a couple of miles wide. And where the green of the valley stops, as though chopped off by a mighty axe, rise the most awe-inspiring mountains imaginable.

Bleak, almost completely barren of trees and grass save for a few daring bushes that seem to cling to the sides by the merest of fingertips, the mountains tower 1,000, 2,000 feet, maybe more, above the level floor. They are not the comparatively gentle rising slopes of the hills of home.

At the top of each seems to be a level spot of unrecognizable size that runs out of the very tip then drops shear away for hundreds of feet. Then the eroded slope begins, a saw-toothed series of little ridges and valleys running up the slopes like rafters supporting a roof: ridges worn down and built up by the rains and snow, frosts and storms of uncounted millions of years.

Truly it is magnificent.

When I wrote you yesterday we were steaming toward the Rockies, over rolling land bleak and barren of all except a skimpy growth of grass, weeds and bushes.

At Limon, in Colorado, we hit "The Hill" and for 50 miles, with hardly a breathing spell, the one engine tugged our heavy train upwards. In Nebraska, our elevation couldn't have been more than 1,000 feet, but we climbed and climbed to a post along the railroad that said "Tiptop." Then on a sharp grade we dropped down at least 1,000 feet before rolling into Colorado Springs. A sign on the station said: Elevation 5,989 feet! We were all permitted to get out of the train and walk a few minutes there, and when we got back found a Denver and Rio Grande engine had replaced the Rock Island which brought us from Omaha.

As we came over the crest at Tiptop we had seen nothing that I would have called a mountain back home. Climbing all the way, all we could see was a gently rolling ridge ahead, some times unbelievably from far out here the finest details can be seen for miles and miles, the air is so clear and bright. But always when we crossed the ridge another higher still loomed ahead, and so we kept on climbing almost without noticing it until I was twice as high as I've ever been before.

But at Tiptop, as we looked down on the first easy grade in hours we were suddenly aware that the horizon was different - - over there, everyone pointed are mountains. Blue, almost purple in the evening sun, they dominated the valley as a tree does a blade of grass. Pike's Peak biggest of them all, was plainly a standout yet in the distance was the bluest hint of others even bigger.

They seemed so close, these mountains, that you wanted to reach out and touch them, yet they were half a hundred miles away. At Colorado Springs, where the mountains seemed to rise from the very back yards of the homes, we were told that it was 30 miles, more than an hour's drive, to the 14,000 feet summit of Pikes Peak.

In the evening we turned south, soon ran away from the mountains, speeding smoothly and swiftly through the sunset and the gloaming. I wanted to write then, but the purple fingers of night reaching across the land held my head turned to the window, awed me so that I sat in silence literally drinking in the scene.

At Pueblo we stopped again, and all of us were turned loose for 30 minutes to descend on the amazed bartenders like a swarm of locusts. Our gang split, and Walts and I went further than most of the boys to get our two bottles of beer (3.2 it was too!). It was a sight to behold 400 sailors scrambling for a moment's freedom that we hadn't expected.

And you should have the seen the looks and heard the groans from soldiers on a troop train eastbound who were there as long as we, but not permitted to get off!

We're coming into Grand Junction, and I may have a chance to mail this, will continue later.

9-16-44 Saturday 10:30 a.m.
nearing the Colorado-Utah border

We're riding again after a stop at Colorado Junction where our whole party took some of the travel kinks away. Surprisingly we have been really comfortable so far.

Last night it was dark when we left Pueblo after our brief and very pleasant liberty, from which everyone returned but a lot brought bottles and there were several drunks within a short time.

When we boarded the train we were told to watch for the highest bridge in the world, and so the four of us jammed into our two lower berths watching as the train wound and climbed up the gorge of the Arkansas River, past Canon City.

And about 11 o'clock we craned our necks out the window to see the bridge lined against the starlit sky like some freak spider web spun between the two pinnacles of rock. How far it was above us I don't know, but certainly it was 500 feet, and perhaps a thousand or more. But it was breath-taking I'll tell you.

A little later I slept, not well for it was cold in the mountains. We had only one blanket each and no heat in the car for our porter has loafed all the way. But I slept, and about 5:30 Svoboda woke me to relieve him on guard duty and the two of us sat in silence watching the miles roll by.

Through the night we had wandered in and out of the Rockies, like a tiny lighted worm seeking a passage through the hills, and some times at an altitude of 11,000 feet or better we crossed the divide and started winding down again.

The Colorado River was only a sizable trout stream, tossing and turning, leaping over and crawling under the boulders when I first saw it today in the purple dimness of dawn as it comes to the deep valleys in the mountains.

Gradually, as we came further west and south, the river grew wider and the mountains rimming it higher until we were rushing down the mighty gorge, desolate and lonely until the stream grew so wide it had cut a mighty valley out of the bare rock and carpeted it with the good earth carried perhaps from mountainsides hundreds of miles away, to be deposited when the floods of uncounted springs receded.

Then it was we came to houses, and peach and apple orchards, a prosperous-looking resort hotel surrounded by neat cottages, and finally to Colorado Junction, and our brief stop. Onward again we rolled down the growing valley, but again the soil turned rocky and barren and we could see no living thing except sparse clumps of grass and sagebrush.

A few minutes ago, just before crossing into Utah, we turned away from the gorge, climbed steeply for a little while and have emerged onto what seems a great plateau covered with brown grass and sagebrush but hemmed in no matter where you look by the forbidding cliffs that seem the trademark of this country. It is almost a desert.

On the near side, the cliffs rise so sharply as to block any further view, but in the opposite direction, in the dim blue distance beyond the cliffs rise rugged, ragged mountain peaks dwarfing everything close at hand. Somehow you have the feeling that other peaks even more mighty lie unseen beyond those visible.

For a long time we've seen no sign of civilization until just now we crossed a road black with fresh oil, a sign saying "Shady

Rest Cabins Just Ahead." Aha, I thought, an oasis for the weary traveler. We've seen no shade tree for a half hundred miles or any thing resembling shade. But Shady Rest Cabins turned out to be half a dozen boxlike wooden trailers parked out in the open, and I'll bet they were more than 20 degrees hotter inside than the average temperature of a blast furnace. And we rolled on across the endless mesa, eating on the way.

I do hope you are enjoying this account of a trip I should have hated to miss, for it's been fun trying to put down on paper just some of the things we've seen. It's a glorious country and I'm adding a No. 1 priority item to our postwar list. When I come back from all this I'll have a sizeable piece of money on hand, what with bonds and mustering out pay.

I'm going to spend a week or so at home getting acquainted with all of you again, and then we can take the car, kidnapping anyone who argues they can't come, and start out for six weeks or two months or whatever is needed to get a real look, at leisure, over this truly wonderful land. It will be time then for a vacation for all of us, and business or anything else can go hang until our looking is done. And all I ask of you is that you have the car, or a car, that will stand 10,000 miles or so.

That isn't only a dream family; it's both a threat and a promise. All my love darlings and take care of yourselves.

9-16-44 Saturday 4:00 p.m. Helper, Utah

I'm really beginning to realize this is a pretty large country.

On our maps, with which we've been trying to follow on our on our progress, it's only an inch or so from the Utah border to Salt Lake City, but for hours on end we've been riding through the wildest sort of country until a little bit ago we dropped down into a lovely green valley and finally stopped at this mining town which, except for its setting beneath the towering mountains that surround it might well be mistaken for a smaller Windber or oversize Jerome.

If this writing is even a little worse than usual, blame it on the mountains for we're being pulled by two huge engines, the most powerful setup we've had, and unless I'm much mistaken we are on the steepest of many grades we've climbed. Even the road which roughly parallels our course ducks through a couple of tunnels chewed into solid rock.

We still have nearly 200 miles to go until Salt Lake, which we were scheduled to reach about 8 a.m. It begins to look as though we'll not get to Shoemaker until late tomorrow or some time Monday, instead of Sunday afternoon. But we won't mind too much, if the food holds out.

Just to give you an idea of these hills out here, our two engines now have been dragging us up a grade for a half hour. The grade is the steepest I've ever seen on a railroad, yet we haven't even sighted the summit and on either side of us the mountains rise almost sheer to tower thousands of feet above our puny heads. I knew, of course, that these were real mountains out here, but until seeing them I had no idea of the sheer immensity.

And the badlands, beautiful at first and always awe inspiring, become downright frightening after a few hours of steady pounding across them, without a sight of homes or human beings or even a drop of water. How, you wonder, did men cross them before the railroads came? Honestly, it doesn't seem possible, yet you know they did, and we must pay homage to their truly wonderful and remarkable courage.

Since the above was written we've climbed the hill, eaten and started down the other side toward Salt Lake and Ogden. Here the grade is less steep, but the curves, which make our famous Horseshoe Curve in Altoona look like a straight line, come down through a great pass that reminds me of most of the pictures that I've seen of Chilcoat, where the '89 gold rush went through Alaska. We three times doubled back to within 50 yards of the tracks where we were going in the opposite direction.

Over here the mountains seem less harsh, much like some of our home hills but the scale is so much more grandiose. Trees, mostly evergreens, dot the slopes, and the whole contour is more rounded, giving the impression that erosion took place a long time ago and the rough edges have worn off.

And, aside from cattle, horses and swine we've seen no animals. Walts saw a rabbit, but none of the rest have seen a thing, although we hope for a grizzly bear, elk, deer, cougar or something equally startling. We've seen some marvelous-looking trout streams but nary fish or even fishermen.

It's 34 miles, we're told, down this grade which is dropping us cautiously toward Salt Lake, and looking out the windows we see the brakes smoking all along the train. However, they're steel, and I guess won't melt.

We're passing through now the greatest rock strata I've ever seen. The solid walls of rock, for miles along here, are studded with pebbles, large and small, the kind you find only along rivers. These pebbles are imbedded in and a part of the solid wall of rock towering far above us. The only explanation I can think of is that eons ago a river perhaps thousands of miles away rolled them to roundness and then deposited them in a bed of mud. Some great pressure and heat turned the mud to rock and another great upheaval brought them here where the wearing waters of the stream flowing agelessly down the valley exposed them to view.

Deep in the valley now, evening is coming on like a soft cloak around our shoulders. We run clickety clack through the shadows, for the sun touches now only the broadest parts of the valley and almost always our shining rails hug the hills, while the stream tumbles happily over rocks and riffles, singing a song we cannot hear.

Now and then a tree touched by frost splashes color on the hillside, and still the sun shines brightly on the peaks far overhead, where it will not be dusk until long after dark has shrouded the valley.

The scene is unforgettably lovely and peaceful and we have forgotten all about what brings us here. Everyone here is in uniform, which makes the uniforms themselves so commonplace as not to be noticed.

Now we debark into another of the great, prosperous valleys where the fields are golden with the left-behind stubble of the wheat harvest. The valley is flat, interlaced with irrigation canals. Trees are common along the lanes and around cozy farmhouses. Even the enormous backdrop of mountains is green and a little less forbidding. Peach trees bend their limbs laden with ripe fruit, and cattle munch contentedly on the clover. Life could be pleasant here.

The railroad station sign says Springville, and for a moment I am lonely. But the train rolls on. I love you all, and wish with all my heart I were with you or you with me.

9-17-44 Sunday 9:30 a.m. Rolling toward Reno

Our days of rambling seem to be coming to an end.

Since last midnight we've been beating the bell straight across the state of Nevada toward Reno (but I'm not having my divorce, thank you) and from there the map shows only (a purely comparative term) a hop, skip and a jump to Fries. We're due there shortly in the afternoon but probably will not arrive until some time after midnight.

Last evening the valley we entered after twisting down the pass from Helper, led to Provo, a scattered, pleasant-looking town nestled in the prosperous valley, past Utah Lake and Henry Kaiser's new steel mill and on to Salt Lake City - - much more modern than I expected. We stopped there for nearly an hour but were not permitted to leave the train which eventually headed up the hill toward Ogden.

Not being sleepy I had switched guard shifts so I could stay up and watch the country and at Ogden the lieutenant said we could go ashore for 15 minutes to the Red Cross canteen in the station so I routed the boys out and we all galloped over for coffee, sandwiches and cookies.

It was an hour later when we finally pulled out, and surprisingly the engine had been switched to the opposite end of the train and we went back down the hill again until somewhere we switched off to the west, slowed to pass a lonely girl in a dispatcher's shack and suddenly, in the darkness, discovered we had emerged from the land to a long causeway like a ribbon of rock stretched out across the lake.

The night was cloudy, dark and chill, but standing on the darkened platform we could see the froth-carrying rollers beating at the rocks from the north, and long evenly-spread strips of white spreading across the rocking waters to the south. The white, so spaced as to look like a permanent set of lines, running parallel all the way to infinity, mystified us until a porter explained it is always present there, a salty froth floating on the heavy water that when lifted away becomes crystals on your hands.

For a mile, or perhaps several, for it's difficult to judge speed or distance under such conditions, we chuffed cautiously along the rocky route until suddenly it changed and we could see the wooden handrails, hear the hollow echo of the steel wheels crossing to a trestle and, as we moved more slowly, listen to the water slapping against the pilings that held us up.

Off in the far distance, perched atop each low headland of the shore as though beacons for both ships and planes, three , four and sometimes more white lights whirled steadily, eerily on their towers. Some we could see only by the loam they cast on the clouds, others closer at hand we could watch through the full circle.

A steady wind whipped at us from the north, bringing with it the distinctive, unforgettable smell of dead water. I can only compare it to the times when as a barefoot boy I went fishing during a summer drought, ventured to walk out on a swampland that seemed caked and hard on top, only to break through the crust into gooey black muck beneath and stir up the gases of decaying vegetation.

Ten miles, we were told, the trestle stretches across the lake [The Great Salt Lake] but it seemed more than that as we crawled cautiously past the blinkers. Once the newness was over, I could easily have closed my eyes and imagined I was back on the Philadelphia EL heading home in the wee hours.

Then we slowed again to pass a very lonely girl in her shack alone far out on the inky water and a moment later the trestle changed again to causeway and we could feel the surging engine pick up speed. Faster and faster we roared into the night, away from the circling beacon lights, but for a long time, five miles or more, the lake splashed against the rocks beneath our wheels as the rollers kept charging against the eroding land.

Suddenly the water was gone from our feet. Choppy froth kept yielding place to glistening white and as far as the eye could see in the starlit night stretched the great salt beds. Here and there a rounded hill reared its head like a forgotten island, but a half hour later when I went to bed we were still steaming past salt, smoothly spread across the land glistening dully in the night.

When I woke this morning at 7 a.m. it was strange to think you all had been home an hour from 8 o'clock Mass, for now we are in the last American time belt, three hours behind you.

All this morning we have been speeding across the high waste-lands of what seems an almost sterile state. In three hours we have seen only a couple of tiny towns, among them Winnemucca which shows on the map, and between towns only a very very few trees or even spots of green.

Scattered sagebrush clumps, low and rounded, dot the hills and the almost level plains stretching away to forbidding barren brown mountains that are the horizon whichever way we look. Over, off to the southeast, a mysterious cloud of dust stretched across the plain for 10 miles or so, a dust storm like those raised by a farmer harrowing a very dry field.

Again it was an alkali plain, covering almost the entire visible area like a blanket of new-fallen snow. Not even the hardy sage can live on that.

Another time we went through a sandy desert waste, tabletop flat, reaching all the way to the mountains, and sculpted by the wind into little riffles and ridges.

Hardly a dozen buildings have we seen, and even the few are squat ugly-looking little one and two-room sheds that seem somehow to hug the earth as though for protection from the ever-blowing winds. Insofar as I have seen, not a soul lives in all these miles of wasteland. There has been no one to wave a friendly hand in passing.

Most of the morning our rails have been closely paralleled by the highway, old familiar U.S. 40. Now we see cars darting along it against the opposite hillside. In between us flows a greenish stream, lined by cottonwood and elder. Outside the rails and on the other side of the highway the wastelands, brown and lean, seem waiting to dash down and smother the lonely line of green intruding on their domain.

And we slide on down the valley toward Reno a somewhat less lively bunch after four days on wheels. I'll try to write again today, and will use my last airmail tomorrow to tell you where I am. All my love and I miss you all, lots!

Chapter 6
SHOEMAKER, CALIFORNIA
FLEET REPLACEMENT CENTER
9/18/44 to 10-13-44

9-18-44 Monday afternoon Chowhound's Heaven

The grand tour is ended now and I'm back in the Navy again much broadened (at least where I sit) by my travels. My new address is listed below.

Strangely enough, the trip already seems to have been something in the dim and distant past, although not quite as long ago as the time when I had a family and lived in a civilized fashion. Somehow this vast dusty base, overrun by thousands of sailors and building frantically to house the swelling flood, seems to have absorbed all my attention.

Of course there are some good reasons for that, especially since we're more than slightly interested in what this place is going to do to us - - and when. Then too there's a natural reaction due to the physical strain, for counting last night I've had only about 36 hours of sleep since last Monday night, and it isn't quite enough. However, I may be able to make up some of that here.

And in a somewhat parallel situation, the most beautiful and spectacular part of the whole long ride can rate only a few words from me now, perhaps I can expand later. That part came in our trip <u>across</u> and <u>through</u> the Sierra Nevada's, starting shortly after I mailed yesterday's letter at Sparks, a Western Pacific Railroad Division point just east of Reno.

We had stopped there to refuel, and also pick up some food ordered ahead from a nearby Army camp because our kitchen did not have enough food for the extra meal necessitated by the fact we were 12 hours behind schedule. Somehow the Army had gotten arrangements twisted and the truck was waiting in Reno where we stopped briefly and, from the train, got a quick glance at streets lined with bars and gambling joints.

Incidentally yesterday was the second Sunday in my life that I failed to get to Mass, but it couldn't be helped.

From Sparks we were taken in tow by a mountain engine, one of those weird looking things that seems to be running backwards with the engineer's cab clear out in front, and the tender just trailing along sort of aimlessly.

The reason for the big engine soon became apparent when we started to climb, following a rushing stream that wound up and up the valley that was totally different from any others we have seen. The Sierra's, unlike the Colorado Rockies or the Wasatch range of Utah, have clung through the wearing centuries to a thick blanket of topsoil and instead of barren brownness and ragged rocks they are green with grass and bushes and giant pine and spruce trees cover most of the slopes, rearing straight and tall 60 feet and more but their numbers make them seem smaller.

Anyhow, we wound and twisted up the valley for miles and miles until entering a corner we saw, some 500 feet below us, a deep blue splotch on the valley floor was our first look at Lake Tahoe, which I seem to remember, is about 8,000 feet above sea level. It was a lovely sight and we watched it intermittently for a half hour as the train climbed, clinging to the side of the hill and eventually making an almost complete circle around the lake.

On and on we climbed, circling, twisting, darting through

short tunnels and running for hundreds of yards through crude sheds to keep off the snows that fall many feet deep in the winter. At Donner Pass we slid over the hump, into a whole railroad yard complete with turntables and a huge snow shed, and then for 85 miles we rambled down the hill, the steel brakes smoking. The four of us sat glued to the windows watching the spectacular scene all the way. Once we darted out of a curving tunnel to find the train treading gingerly on the very peak of a ridge and on the right side of us the hill, too steep to climb, almost, sheered away 5,000 or more feet, enough to make you gasp. It was like that - - I mean I was gasping - - most of the way, but not from fright, only the sheer beauty of the place.

For hours we sat there watching, and gradually the mountains shrank until we were in sharply rolling country, a land of orchards all picked clean. Shiny cars spun along the road beside us, and here and there a palm tree or two, looking like something from another world, held its drooping clump of branches atop a tapering trunk.

Gradually we coasted down from the hills onto the flat and fertile plain of the Sacramento, criss-crossed by irrigation ditches, and at dusk came to Stockton and then on toward a new ridge of mountains looming on our left.

Through the darkness we could feel the train climbing again, then the sharp clickety-click as it raced along a level stretch. A light slowed us, and for endless miles we crept along, searching for our destination until we stopped at a long lighted siding and stepped off into ankle deep gravel. That was our first look at Shoemaker, and we shivered in the chill night.

As per our usual luck, we drew the most distant barracks on the station, and it was a good two mile hike before we were assigned to bunks, the four of us still holding together. Then we waited, in the unheated little barn, for our gear which didn't come until Svoboda and I hunted up a truck driver who hauled in the 140 bulky bundles, then took us to chow - - at 2:30 a.m. mind you - - in a Navy mess hall where we ate hot dog sandwiches, <u>REAL</u> coffee and good apples. Then, and we didn't mind the work, I assure you, we unrolled enough of our gear to make up our bunks; pulled on our sweaters and pulled up both blankets, then tumbled in.

I didn't wake until reveille at 6, finally got enough nerve to dash out at 7 and Walts and I, fearing filth more than the cold galloped over for a bath that was sheer heaven after four days of what Dad used to term - - with rather crude humor, I thought - - dry washes.

And while we were soaking I heard a familiar voice, yelled "Don" and in came the always investigative Svoboda with Reed in tow. Don and all the rest of the old gang still are here, and only 3 barracks away from ours. There's no hint as to when they may go, let alone us "Johnny come latelys."

So we had our personal reunion, and later we saw all or most of the rest. This morning we spent in a long interesting class on chemical warfare, and the afternoon I did some of my backlog of laundry, then started this, which is being concluded now as Don, Walts, Svoboda and I sit around a table in the telephone center which I guess is the only available writing place; there are no tables in our comparatively tiny barracks.

I said at the start this is chowhound heaven, and the mention of food at 2:30 a.m. - - something totally invisible at Great Lakes - - should be a tip off. The meals are swell, wonderfully prepared and you can have <u>all you want</u>, have to fight your way free from the line with only a little more than too much on your tray. I'll go into more detail on that later, as well as tell you about what this place, growing like a weed, looks like.

Don't worry about me and money, for it seems there is a real labor shortage out here, and sailors are permitted to work on their liberty days - - in the canneries and on the docks at Oakland and Frisco seem the most likely places. We're told we will be put on KP about Wednesday or Thursday, and then, for the duration of our stay will be on KP every other day, and on liberty the intervening days. So I'll be working at a civilian job some day this week, should be able to make $10 or so, and will be all right after that. I probably will try to earn as much as I can for a few times. Anyhow, if you've sent the money I asked for this morning I'll be OK and I'll repay it when you get the AP check.

Hadn't intended starting another sheet, but I wanted to add that if I'm working as much as I expect I'll not be able to write as often as I wish for a little while, but will do the best I can. Under any circumstances I should be able to write at least every third day, if not alternate days, but somewhat the letters will stop for a little while until I get to my next destination. There will be no chance this time to call you, for the call for me may come any hour of any day or night.

But you mustn't fret or worry, just keep on doing your job as I know you will, and as I know I will mine, and it will work out OK. And Betty mine, you'll know always that I love you with all my heart, and will forever.

9-19-44

Just to further complicate my writing problems here, there seems to be an almost total absence of chairs and tables, and it will probably work to shorten my letters so long as I stay at Shoemaker. Yesterday's letter was written in the telephone center but today we couldn't get near it so Wunder, Svoboda and I are scribbling at an improvised bench and table outside the barracks.

A glaring sun is beating down on us like midsummer, but I am _not_ happy about California's vaunted climate. From now until 6 p.m. it will get hotter and hotter, maybe over 80, and when the sun goes down it will change almost instantly to chilly. By 8 p.m. it's cold, and for the rest of the night and most of the morning I'm freezing. Draw your own conclusions when I tell you my two wool blankets are <u>not</u> enough to keep me even reasonably warm at night!

Of course there is no heat as yet in the crude little wooden coops that serve as barracks here. They're simply crude shacks, unpainted, about 30 x 80 feet, perched on pilings a foot or so above the ground. There are hundreds of them, each with one or two oil burning heaters, which are not in operation yet. In the mornings we must wear whites, so we put on our black sweaters to help a little; in the afternoon we discard the sweaters and roast anyway, and in the evening we change to blues, put on our sweaters, and keep on freezing. Phooey!

The base itself is about as barren and ugly-looking as possible. It covers miles of the level valley hemmed in on all sides by ragged brown mountains. There isn't a blade of grass in sight, nor a sidewalk. The streets are macadam, not nearly wide enough for all the pedestrians and surprisingly heavy auto and truck traffic.

Each barracks is set apart from its neighbors by a 100-foot square plot of black dirt that must be a horrible mess when it rains. Maybe I should say if it rains, for it's so dry there are cracks inches deep in the ground and I must be careful not to step in them or my ankles will cave in. Every where you look there is construction under way, huge wooden buildings springing up everywhere. To give you an idea of the size we saw a bulldozer, road scraper and steam roller leveling the dirt for a floor inside one of them on which only the walls have been erected.

Let's see, I was trying to tell you about this place. Well, there are two of the biggest mess halls in the world that do a marvelous job of feeding 17,000 men three times a day. You could stage a real football game inside either one although they're not quite high enough for a kick to travel properly.

The lines are quite long, but move steadily and the food continues to be marvelous, and far too much of it. At noon today, I had roast beef, mashed sweet potatoes, lettuce with bacon dressing, the best asparagus I've ever tasted, bread, butter, coffee and a huge piece of mince pie.

Anyway our gang goes on KP tomorrow, and I'm sort of looking forward to it, for it will be a little work and exercise, something regular to do for I'm loafing too much, and I don't believe it will be overly strenuous or unpleasant. However it will mean extra laundry, and I don't like that for the facilities here are far worse than at the Lakes. These tiny barracks are sleeping rooms only, with a separate building serving three or four barracks for toilets, shaving trays, showers and scrub rooms.

According to the schedule, we'll all be on KP for supper tomorrow, and breakfast and dinner Thursday then will have liberty from 2 p.m. Thursday to noon Friday. Me, I'm going to work in a cannery somewhere Thursday night, and again Saturday and maybe Monday then I'll have enough money to buy some little things I need, and maybe blow myself to a liberty in Oakland or Frisco. I'm not worrying much about sleep, the nights are too damm cold here to make it worth while anyway.

Our indoctrination period here seems to have been completed today with what is called our overseas physical examination which we marched through this morning. It was almost exactly the same sort of test I took at the induction center in Philly and again when we entered Great Lakes, and so far as I know I'm still hale and hearty. It sure would be a helluva jolt to get sent back at this stage of the game.

I'm still hoping to be assigned to a fighting ship, but of course there's always the chance I won't get it. Most of the men from here, I hear, are all lumped together on a transport and sent to Pearl Harbor, then forwarded from there to advanced bases where they stay, usually in laboring or repair jobs, for the duration or until the fighting area moves away and the base must be relocated.

The one thing that seems sure is that I'll be moving on and out of here soon, and golly how I'm hoping and praying you've got things under control and aren't going to fall apart on me. I'm not going to go into this all again, my darling, but you just mustn't let yourself get to worrying and be all upset. Honest, darling, I'm not one little bit worried myself, and I can only hope you'll have the same faith and keep right on plugging until I get back.

And maybe, it's the Pollyanna in me, but somehow I don't think it's going to take until the day after forever to get this war over with and me home. Really don't know why, but I'm beginning to believe the Pacific war isn't going to last so many years more after all.

One thing I do miss out here is my mail. It's been almost a week now since I've received any and there are no immediate prospects of any. I'll just have to twiddle my thumbs and wait. In the meantime, and always, I'll be thinking of you and loving you with all my heart and waiting for the reunion that will be along some of these days.

9-22-44 Friday afternoon

If this scribbling isn't even more wobbly than usual, you have a second-grade miracle on your hands, for here it is 4 p.m., exactly 34 hours since I last touched a bed. And there are a couple more hours to go before I do, but having gone this far I think I'll last.

Of course you know the answer, for I worked last night, and now am quite a wealthy man with somewhat over $5 in my pocket. So wealthy, in fact, that I passed up an opportunity to draw a $5 Navy pay this afternoon simply because I would have been forced to stand a half hour in the blazing sun to get it. Ain't it wonderful what independence is born of a little hard-earned cash?

However, and I'm very serious about this, I shall not work again unless there's some real money to be earned - - and it isn't to be had in canneries, ask Jean. We - - Walts, Svoboda and I - - worked (and we say <u>worked</u> in its fullest meaning) from 6 p.m. last night to 5:30 a.m. today in a big cannery at Hayward, near here, packing tomatoes. For that labor, I earned $10.35, less $1.10 withholding and 10 cents unemployment insurance, leaving me $9.15. And to get a true picture of my earnings, subtract my transportation and meals, the two glasses of beer I enjoyed so much, and you have - - rather I have - - $5!! Doesn't seem like much, does it?

I left you Wednesday afternoon saying my KP luck was holding up, and it still is but I'm afraid it's running low and I've had my share of narrow escapes. Wednesday afternoon Wunder and I were picked for a shovel-and-wheelbarrow job because we were supposed to be on the barracks detail and would not be going on KP.

The job kept us away from muster where our names were read on the KP list. Of course when we heard that sad news we grumblingly dropped our tools, changed to whites and reported to the mess hall, only to learn we'd been dropped from the list because we were working for the boatswain. And we reported to him yesterday morning and worked four hard hours pulling spikes out of waste lumber.

Today there was no muster because the "looey" who commands our battalion was all excited about a pending Admiral's Inspection by no less a personage than the chief of the Bureau of Personnel. Actually the admiral drove through our section at 20 miles per hour, did his "inspecting" from the window of his big Cadillac sedan.

Well, after our nail-pulling hitch yesterday we got dressed to go on our "liberty," taking our dungarees with us. Wunder, who's stronger financially than the rest of us said to hell with working and went to see the sights of Frisco.

So the three Charley's - - Svoboda, Walts and Welsh - - marched to the gate, found a bus waiting there to take would-be workers to Hayward free, and so climbed aboard. We signed up at the cannery, were told we'd go to work at 6, so went out and drank 2 beers, came back to change clothes and eat supper in the cannery cafeteria.

I had the easiest job of all, being teamed with a colored sailor feeding little cans, the size of small fruit cocktail cans, into a machine which filled them with tomato paste. I had the easiest assignment, as I said, but none the less it was work, and most mighty tiring to be on your feet all through the night. We must have handled hundreds of thousands of those shiny rattling cans. Anyhow we were through at 5:30, paid off and dressed at 6, and wandered up town to a restaurant where we ate bacon and eggs and debated our plans.

It seemed foolish to go back to the base, for we knew we would not be permitted to sleep in the barracks but instead would be put to work (horrid word!) getting the joint ready for "admiral's inspection." So, on the spur of the moment we decided to go to town, and climbed on a Greyhound bus for Oakland, just across the bay from Frisco. Arriving there at 8 a.m., we found we had 2 hours until time for a bus that would get us back safely, so we started to wander, eventually wound up walking along the docks - - I had my first look at the Pacific - - and our walk, just incidentally, carried us <u>more</u> than <u>40 blocks</u>. Supermen, huh?

There's not much to tell you about Oakland, a bustling city marked by California specialties; big lawns, weird if not to say grotesque architecture, and hundreds of flowers, shrubs and trees I've never seen before. Got back to the bus station at 9:30, and arrived on the base at 11, since then we've been wobbling around as best we could until a decent time to go to bed - - which is just about now. Boy, will <u>that feel good!</u>

We rate liberty again tomorrow night, but I'm not at all certain what I'll do with it. Certainly I'm not going to work. The other boys, spurred by Wunder's reports of a strange and lively Frisco probably will go there. If I'm recovered physically, I may take my five bucks and see how far I can stretch it, for I'd sure like to see the town and there may not be another chance.

And that will be all for now dearest, I'm off for dreamland in broad daylight, and the very nicest thing that could happen to me would be to dream of you and our little ones.

There are many, many miles between us, my darling, but no space nor time nor person can crowd you out of my heart. Nite, Bettsy, and I love you more than anything in all the world. Or did you hear that before?

9-23-44 Saturday night

Two, whole, gorgeous, wonderful lovely (Yeah, I know that's a feeble set of adjectives but it's the best I can do at the moment.) letters from you last night and I've actually devoured each of them half a dozen times. Thank you, dearest one, and if I could I'd love you an extra special lots. Anyhow, that's the way I feel after 10 days without mail. Sure is good to have a wife, even a long-distance one, again.

Well we dood it, and me and my five bucks are now in the process of scooting around the Golden Gate City as cheaply as possible. Decided - - after momentary fumbling and an unsuccessful try at hitch hiking - - to take the bus to Oakland, and there rode a high-speed trolley train across the Bay Bridge, quite an affair with two decks for traffic and no pedestrians.

Saw my first warship since entering the Navy, and simply dozens of cargo ships ugly and grim in the drab gray paint of war. The warship, a trim yet crowded looking destroyer of the Fletcher class, lay at anchor off Treasure Island, mid-point of the four mile pair of bridges.

Have walked on Market Street, climbed most of famed Nob Hill, and seen the funny little street cars, really cable cars, that slide up the hill, go around a loop and come back down again to Market Street and a dinky turntable, set spang in the center of the street. You can judge the size of the cars when I tell you the motorman drives them into the turntable, jumps off and pushes

- - yes pushes with his hands - - them around, then climbs aboard and drives away!

Blew me to a seafood platter - - lobster, oysters, crab meat and shrimp for dinner and so far have had one beer and one Tom Collins. Hope soon to waggle another beer for it's 9:30 and all this town shuts up and goes to bed at midnight we're told.

Never have I seen so many sailors, and especially so many officers. Philly and Chi were all civilian towns in contrast to this place. Yet there seem to be plenty of women around, although the only one I'm interested in, in any way and every way, most certainly is too too far away from me now.

But I still, and always will, love you with all my heart and wherever I go, whatever I do, you are and will be in my thoughts every moment.

This is a letter from Jess James that was enclosed in a letter dated September 25, 1944.

Saturday September 23, 1944

Dear Chuck:

I lost your address, and the only thing for me to do was to sit tight until you wrote again. Your letter arrived half an hour ago - - so you see the aridness of our correspondence was not due to any lack of desire to write.

Much has happened to Vone and me since we wrote you. They found out I was a newspaperman and put me on the staff of the paper here. (I don't think that had happened when I wrote you before, had it?) Dry Dock, it's called - - and it belies its name. It has nothing to recommend it except its circulation, 10,000, which is not bad for a service weekly in this part of the world.

Vone, until recently, was working in the legal office. And that leads naturally to the reason he's no longer there.

I don't think it would have been possible the last time I wrote, not to have complained bitterly about the waste, mismanagement and inefficiency of this hospital - - the largest in the Navy. We've between 8,000 and 10,000 patients. And, believe it or not, there's a staff member (nurse, corpsman, Wave, or doctor) for every three patients.

Of course, many are on details like mine, or working in offices, or in the commissary department, but even at that there are so many of us we're bulging at the seams.

You talk about being cold in unheated barracks. We sleep in unheated tents - - with our original two blankets. At first we did manage to snare a medical corps blanket each, but some kind-hearted, gold-braided, mother-beating bastard ordered them lifted. As a result, we drape our peacoats over our shoulders (between blankets so they don't slide off the bed) and freeze from the ass down.

Even the chance to cover the comings and goings and speakings and fumings of admirals and such illustrious civilians as the president of the American Medical Association doesn't offer compensation for that sort of living accommodations - - particularly when the strictly weekly, college-journalism type of routine in this office drives a man to overindulgence in hard liquor. (But that's another story; now I'm leading up to Vone's being fired from the legal office).

The combination of the muggy weather hearabouts (including Vone's sinus trouble) and my dissatisfaction with newspaper censorship a la Navy, well seasoned with our utter disgust with the New Deal methods of managing a hospital, led Vone and me to the decision we wanted to get out of here.

Furthermore, we both decided, since we were in the Navy, we wanted more experience aboard ship than a single crossing to North Island via ferry. So we began to scheme about getting to sea. In certain respects, this place is ultra G.I. (although because of the overpopulated conditions, and the fact that returning salutes would break the officers' arms, no one salutes anybody here). Unless you have an "in" at the detail office you don't get anywhere by asking for anything. In fact, it is well known that several people have got the opposite from what they wanted merely by voicing a desire.

Under the circumstances, we approached the lieutenant in charge of this department, Welfare and Recreation, and asked him to front for us in our request for sea duty. He agreed to speak for me, but said Vone would have to deal through his lieutenant. We explained we wanted to go together, and that separate requests would likely get us fouled up. He amended his stand, and agreed to go to bat for us if Vone's boss agreed. He said it would be suicide for him to meddle in the affairs of the legal department without a commitment on the part of Vone's officer. Vone spoke to him, and he said it was O.K. My boss verified the report we gave him. He then went to the head of the detail office, and reported back that the fellow said he thought it could be arranged, but he'd like to have a memo to that effect.

Before the memo could be submitted, Vone was transferred to the dirty surgery ward (piles, etc.) and my boss was appointed recorder on all summary courts-martial. Obviously this was the old-line Navy man's way of saying, "I'll teach you not to meddle in affairs which don't concern you"!

On top of all our troubles, I got picked up downtown by the shore patrol on a charge of drunkenness. I don't deny the charge, but I can't see why I should have been singled out among the thousands who were in the same shape. I pulled all the strings I could, but I had to stand captain's mast to answer the charge. I was sentenced to 10 hours of EPD (extra police duty - - meaning swabbing the shit houses, etc.)

As I was waiting to be dismissed after the captain's mast, the chief pharmacist in the hospital corps office (for whom I had written some stories) happened along and asked, "How the hell did you get yourself into this jam, James"? That was the opening I needed. I told him it was a long story, and that I would like to tell it to him.

I embroidered it a bit, in this vein. Vone and I, brothers-in-law, wanted to go to sea together. I had been encouraged by the preliminary report brought back by my lieutenant, and had indulged in a bit of premature celebrating. We still wanted to go to sea, and could he do anything to help us.

The old boy laughed like hell. He wrote out a memo immediately, commenting, "It's not often I get a chance to do anything like this: I'm bothered by people who mostly want me to keep them from going to sea. Take this over to Bing (the chief pharmacist in the detail office) and tell him I said to fix you up."

It was as easy as that. "Bing" (I never did learn his name) assured me it wouldn't be long until we were notified to ship out. (I don't know whether the special assignment business will snarl us up or not; I was careful to avoid all mention of our status, but I don't think the Navy's paying the slightest attention to it anyway.)

All of which could mean, given one chance out of 1,000, that Vone and you and I may be together again.

There's not the slightest possibility of us getting up to San Francisco. Do you realize, my boy, that that's 600 odd miles from here? We never get a longer liberty than Saturday noon to Monday at 7:30 a.m. And to go outside a 50-mile radius we must have special permission. I can't see them giving me any privileges the week after a captain's mast.

However, you may put in here after you're assigned to a ship. If you do, try to get in touch with us. We may not be here, but try anyway. If and when we're moved, I'll speed off our new address. And don't neglect to let us know where you go and how to get in touch with you. Write to this address, and it'll be forwarded, if we've left - - although that'll probably take a month or more.

I've got to run to the printers. We had to go to press this afternoon.

9-26-44 Tuesday evening

Hot, Lordy but it's hot here today, and as I sit down in the phone center to begin my daily scribble little rivulets are running down my back, yet it's only 6 p.m. and I know that when I finish this in a couple of hours - - it's likely to be a long letter, I'll be freezing when I walk back to the barracks. What a country!

Damm but I'm sorry to hear about Wally Bishop, for I'd convinced myself he was a prisoner and somehow news of his death hit me pretty hard. I'd like to write a note to the Bishop's, and may if I can think of anything to say.

And I was sorry, too, to learn of your strained finances, and feel like paddling your bottom for running yourself too low. Knowing you, I know what happened to the dough, too big a bank payment in addition to the 20 you sent me, and it makes me damm good and mad.

I don't give a damm about myself, for I'll always get along somehow, but you have <u>no damm business</u> running yourself that low. You never can tell when you'll need a couple of bucks, and I don't want you to make any more bank payments until you have a reserve of <u>at least</u> $25 for emergencies, a fund you can carry over untouched from month to month. Then it will be time to go to work on the note, but not before then, or I'll warm your bottom when I get home. <u>Don't you dare</u> let that silly debt problem run you in the hole again!!!

There, I guess that's enough scolding.

So, just back at noon from another very interesting trip to Frisco, we're planning to go back again tomorrow. We're back on KP, which turns out to be a cinch, and have served our evening meal. Wunder and I are here writing, and the other two are back at the barracks, where we'll be going when we finish for I've a spot of laundry to do and want to hit the hay for 4:30 comes awfully early in the a.m.

Our journey yesterday was swell. We managed to get out a

little earlier, about 3, and just as we got to the gate with the intentions of trying to hitch a ride we found a sailor needing a push to start his car. We supplied the push, and he took all three of us and two other guys straight into Frisco. He was an aviation ordinance man first class, and had driven here a few days ago from Jacksonville, Florida.

He started out slowly enough, but by the time he got us to Oakland he must have decided he was late for he drove like a bat out of h_____, twisting and squirming through traffic and racing like mad across the bridge. But he gets us there at 4:10 p.m., and we promptly arranged our 50 cents bunks at the Pepsi-Cola place, then started to tour the town.

Hadn't walked far until we came to the dinky little streetcar on the turntable, and decided to try our first ride on the cable cars, to see where it went. So on we piled with 50 others, all clinging to every possible foothold, and away we went up the very steep hill.

Gee it was fun. Svoboda and I, hanging on the back platform, were sort of assistants to the lady conductor, a rather nice-looking Negro girl, helping people on and off and generally having a helluva time. Nob Hill goes up about as steep as the Johnstown Incline and then goes down almost as sharply.

All stops are made on street intersections, which are almost level, so the hill seems to go up in regular steps. Going down is much the same, with the girl conductor cranking away for dear life, and the Negro motorman, Wunder told us, was doing the same thing up front, as well as having a helluva time with the bell, which he clangety-clang-clanged almost continuously. Most of the people were going to their homes, so there was a constant flow of passengers on and off the car, but it was just like a big family on the roller coaster, everyone having lots of fun. As John said later, anyone who didn't think that ride was seven cents worth of fun was just plain nuts.

Up one side and down the other, we unloaded at another end-of-the-line turntable to see a sign pointing to Fishermen's Wharf, and of course we had to go. Saw the crabbing boats at anchor, walked through the strange bazaar of a myriad of fish. We had already eaten so when we walked past a dozen places where beautiful fresh shrimp were cooking in strange oven right out on the sidewalk I never ate a one.

Bet that makes Dad mad for he'd love it. We walked past Joe DiMaggio's place which would have been a thrill for Bucky, but couldn't go in for it was closed. So many places close Mondays out here. We also saw the Bal Tabarin and a half dozen other of the world famous places on Frisco's waterfront.

Then we decided to see Golden Gate Bridge and a friendly gas station attendant said he was closing soon and would take us there since he was going that way. The three of us climbed into his coupe, rode past the huge Palace of Fine Arts built for the 1915 World's Fair and now taken over by the Army, and past the famous old Presidio fortress, first built by the Spanish in the 17th century.

He dropped us out at the entrance to the bridge and we walked into the setting sun towards the huge and beautiful bridge. It was only 6:30, but already evening in this queer country and as we walked up the curving drive, beautifully landscaped, with four lanes of traffic whizzing past us, a lonely little cloud drifted in from the Pacific and just seemed to wrap itself around the towers that support the mile-long span, so that we could see 250 feet of the massive structure reaching up from bed rock at the gate, then the spot of white, and projecting above it another 50 or so feet of the 472-foot towers.

We paid a dime each, the usual pedestrian fare, and walked out onto the bridge in the teeth of a rising wind. Far down below us, on the landward side, were the remains of an old fort, and off a couple miles across a curving arm of the bay the white buildings of Frisco, packed together so tightly on the steep hills, looked in the bright light of the setting sun like a miniature make-believe city under some movie-maker's spotlight.

In the bay we could see the tuna fleet, the 40-foot diesel cruisers with long slim masts which carry a lookout box like a cutaway barrel at the top to better spot the schools of fish. The fleet was making ready to put out for the night; we could see a gray Coast Guard boat shuttling from ship to ship and now and then some of the white fishing ships calmly lifted anchor, bobbing and dancing in the heavy surf.

As we walked the wind blew even harder, and more cold, and we began to see wisps of fog drifting in, then a solid wall of fog riding the wind from the Pacific to us. Suddenly the sunlight was gone, and in the west a yellow ball, looking much more like a full moon behind a cloud, poked feeble rays at us. Less than half way across we were chilled to the bone, could see very little, and so crossed the bridge to come back the other side.

There was a sight I'll remember a long time. The fog, for some reason, was perhaps 50 or so feet above the water, and the bobbing white tuna boats moved in stately procession straight down the golden pathway to the sun just setting across the Pacific. I stood there in the fog on the spider web bridge just drinking it in until the curtain of white closed down. It was dusk, we were cold, yet we hated to leave. But leave we did, running, skylarking like boys past the grim gun placements and barbed wire put down two years ago to shield the bay against invaders, and on to the toll gate where a man picked us up, took us to a carline going downtown.

Back in the city we wandered a bit more, then drifted into the Stage Door Canteen which we had visited for a few minutes on Saturday. We stayed there until midnight, in a horde of sailors and soldiers all trying to dance with a handful of girl hostesses on a postage stamp floor. It was fun though and we enjoyed it a lot. All the dancing was tag-in, and you rarely danced more than a minute before someone tapped your shoulder, took the gal, and sent you back to the stag line.

The hostesses are hand-picked volunteers, work regularly assigned 3-hour shifts one night a week. The rules are very strict. They may only use their first names, are barred from making dates during duty hours and a lot of other things. We learned this because I asked a lonely-looking sailor to join us, and he fell quite hard for one of the girls - - and she wouldn't let him take her home.

At midnight, the place closed and we wandered out, intending to get a bite to eat and then turn in but we passed a movie I couldn't resist, so I dragged the other two, protesting, in with me. It was a double feature, and we sat through "Sweater Girl" (can't remember when or where you and I saw that) but "It Happened One Night" took me right back to Johnstown, and 1934, and some wonderful, wonderful dreams.

Anyhow it was 4 a.m. when we got out. We walked 3 blocks to our bunks, slept until 8, had breakfast and came back via bus. I found your letters, and a very good one from Bucky, waiting for me, read them and then snoozed until muster and time for KP, which brings me right up to now, when I've got to gallop off to my laundry and bed. Bye, Bettsy, and I'll be dreaming tonight of the one I love with all my heart.

9/28/44 Thursday 5 a.m.

Woe is me.

Having spent one hitch in the "Lost Battalion," the "Three C's" now seem about to volunteer for the "Loster Battalion" for the big draft I told you was scuttlebutt yesterday has been posted now. It includes all of our old outfit and we're left out.

The boys don't know yet when or where they're going, but Saturday is the guess for when, and there's at least a hint of where on the draft list which carries the significant words (To be equipped) - - usually that means an island base crew or amphibs. We may know more when we see what kind of equipment is issued, possibly today.

Anyhow we're lost again, and don't like it. Probably the same thing will happen as at the Lakes - - we'll lie around here doing nothing for a week or a month, then be shipped out with a new bunch and find the old gang waiting at Pearl Harbor or some such place.

I feel worst about John Wunder and sorry for him too. He's an odd sort of fellow who doesn't really open up until he's known you quite a while, and we were all getting along so well together. Of course we'll stick together so long as we're in camp here, but there will be no more liberties together for once you are on draft all liberty automatically is cancelled.

When I finished writing before noon yesterday we served lunch, and when we went back to the barracks to shower and clean up for liberty the word was passed that everyone must report for the 2 p.m. muster in whites. That was a tipoff something was in the wind, and at muster the lieutenant announced all liberty cancelled, and all men must return for KP at 3:30.

We've been working alternate days, with half the battalion on duty and half on liberty. So we lost our liberty, served supper and the four of us went to the movies. Don't know what it was or who was in it - - yes I do the name was "Seven Days Ashore" - - but we laughed and enjoyed it. About 8 o'clock we went back to the barracks and all the gang was gobbling about a new draft list that had just been posted, so we galloped right over to the bulletin board.

Wunder had stopped somewhere along the road, and of course each of us looked for our own names, didn't find them and then looked for John's, found it and swore. Then we checked the list more closely, found all of our friends and swore some more. Then the three of us hiked to the barracks where the G 6-4 is billeted, gabbed and gassed with the boys for a while and went back to our own joint about 9 because we figured a little sleep would be useful by 4 a.m.

Today we were all changed from the CPO mess to door guards, directing traffic in the chow lines, and I drew the even easier job of gear locker, just handing out soap and other stuff as it's needed. It's loafing pure and simple and I've scribbled all this, standing up, while the rest of the gang was serving chow.

What happens next I don't know. Might be the three of us will rate liberty this afternoon, but to tell the truth I don't much care, and will hate to leave John behind and just might walk out. Or maybe we'll be on draft ourselves; you never can tell in this screwy place, just sit and wait. It's better than Transfer Unit only because the scene is a little different, and strange.

Just now John brings me, unsolicited, a couple doughnuts and a cup of coffee. He's like that, dammit, not always thinking of himself. Bet Walts and Svoboda bring me more (I don't want 'em!) just because I'm stuck in here while they're free to wander a bit since the doors are closed and cleanup under way. Yep, Walts is here already. Whatta gang! Here's Svoboda now and I don't know what to do with all the stuff! But it's nice to have in the ordinarily selfish way.

It's nearly noon now, and we're back in the mess hall waiting to check in, eat and go to work. Since I wrote the first of this I've been back to the barracks, threw a basketball around for a while to get some exercise, and devoured a letter from you in the morning mail. It's good to get letters, and I'm sorry about you having been blanked out for I thought I'd kept writing regular mail often enough between the air mail letters so you'd have at least one a day.

It hurts especially because I know you're blue and lonesome and I'd do <u>anything</u> to end it if I only could. But my darling so long as we're apart we must both be like that, it's the way we're made so that neither can be complete unless the other is near. And no matter how much it hurts, I would not change that for the world, my darling, because some day we <u>will</u> be together again and I couldn't ask for anything more.

You see my Bettsy, I love you with my whole heart and soul, with all I am or ever hope to be. Nothing will ever change that.

9/29/44 Friday afternoon

I'm in an unhappy frame of mind now as I start this, for we came back from liberty this morning to find I'm an alternate on a draft, and while I feel pretty sure I won't be called I don't like it for neither Walts or Svoboda are on it and it looks like another breakup for most anything can happen.

The draft itself is a dandy, just 8 men, two of them gunners mates, which is an almost certain sign that the men who go on it will be replacements on a fighting ship. Since the draft is called for tomorrow it means I must get all my gear packed up tonight, get up early in the morning to roll it, carry it (160 pounds) a half mile to the draft field. There I'll sit in the sun for Lord knows how many hours, then pick it up again, carry it back here and resume waiting. Phooey!

By the way, our old gang, including Wunder, got their new equipment yesterday - - heavy duty high shoes, a mess kit and water canteen like the Army uses, raincoat, shelter half, and free-protecting mosquito netting, all obviously designed for land use in the tropics. It looks like island bases for them and not a ship.

There isn't much to tell you about last night. We three, Walts, Svoboda and I, were released about 4 p.m. and hiked out sort of half-heartedly; ashamed to be leaving without Wunder but there was nothing we could do about it. A sailor gave us a ride to Walnut Grove (the name fits for the town is surrounded by miles and miles of English walnut groves, the trees planted in beautifully even rows) from where we got rides into Oakland, then took the train to Frisco arriving about 9 p.m.

Wandered around a while, ate a hamburger and drank a beer, then wound up at the Stage Door Canteen. There was a jam-packed crowd, and we arrived just in time for the main show. On the program were the Jack Saunders Orchestra, Bonita Granville, a movie star who sang a couple of tunes, and Rufe Davis, a movie comedian who stole the show.

There was some other minor entertainment intermittently throughout the evening, and we all danced a couple of minutes. Left shortly before 11:30 in order to get 2 drinks each before the bars closed at midnight. Then we walked a couple blocks on Market Street, returned to the Pepsi-Cola place and crawled onto our 50-cent bunks about 1, slept until 7.

Had toast and coffee for breakfast, took the train back to Oakland and hitched back to the base in 2 rides, arriving about 9:30, as I said to find me on draft. Since then I've done a little laundry, eaten chow, stood muster and had another pecker check (you always get one before you ship out) and here I am scribbling.

I think, my darling, I'm going to stop this now, and mail it, then write again tonight. I'm hoping for a letter in the evening mail for I've had none since yesterday morning, and any kind of note from you will brighten the whole day for me, any day. That, my darling, is because I love you, just in case you hadn't heard.

10/1/44 Sunday evening

As I start this I'm planning only a note to you, for I want to write to the kids and what little has happened to me will fit nicely into their letters.

The meat of the matter is that I didn't get on the last draft. I'm back at Shoemaker, settled down for another wait of the Lord knows how long. One good thing about it is that I'll no longer have to work on KP for the three of us have been appointed battalion messengers, a very easy job.

Anyhow, we returned this morning from our most economical - - but least pleasant - - liberty. I think we all were a little depressed because Wunder and the gang were gone, leaving us behind, and that added to the tiredness from the heat and sun and wind of a long hard day sort of dampened our spirits.

We arrived in Frisco about 7 p.m., after our late start, and after writing our letters we all went for a walk, through Chinatown and the International Settlement, the latter a single block lined with clip joints that might have been interesting with a wad of money in your pocket. Chinatown, blocks and blocks of it perched on the side of Telegraph Hill, was very interesting and just thronged with sightseers, most of them window shopping. You'll enjoy it a lot - - don't laugh - - when you see it.

Then about 10:30 we went back to the Stage Door Canteen, where we sat for an hour but the entertainment was far below the usual level since most stage people have no free time Saturdays. The place was jammed, and none of us felt like dancing so we pulled out early, had our second and last drink of the evening, then went to bed - - in a firehouse.

Svoboda (I think I told you he was a city fireman in Chicago.) had been itching to go somewhere and talk shop for a long time, so when we found all the servicemen's dormitories in Frisco filled on our late arrival, he suggested we go around to this fire hall we'd seen, and maybe there might be some spare bunks in the dormitory.

Well, we walked over, introduced ourselves to the lieutenant in charge of the night shift, a brogue-speaking Irisher named Duffy. He and Svoboda chatted a while, and we wound up by Duffy inviting us to come back after 11 and he'd find bunks for us which we did, and he did, and we had a clean place to sleep, free. I got up and went to 7 o'clock Mass at nearby Saint Patrick's, then back to the fire hall where we had coffee and a roll with Duffy - - free breakfast.

Then we took a bus across the bridge, hitched back to the station in good time, had a swell noon chow, waited until 2 for muster, went to the football game, ate again and here I am.

I said the liberty was my cheapest: well including 42 cents for bus fare, I spent just $1.15, and if that isn't a new low for a sailor on 24-hour liberty it will do until a better one comes along.

I do hope you didn't let yourself get upset over my draft

letters, but I can hardly blame you if you were, for I don't even remember what I wrote, it all happened so fast and there were such unpleasant possibilities and so many things to be done. However I shall be better prepared next time, and hope I can at least have time to phone you and do whatever else needs to be done in a more orderly fashion.

Speaking of phones, I'd love to call you right now, for it would be wonderful to hear your voice, but I hesitate to do it for it's so expensive and I probably wouldn't be lucky enough to find you all at home. It's really difficult to believe that right now, the sunset of a beautiful hot day, it's 10 p. m. back home, the kids have been in bed asleep for hours, and things are so vastly different.

But we will, after a fashion, get used to it and someday it will all be over. Then, my darling, it will be a real job to get me so far from you that I can't pick up a phone at 7 p.m., and know that you'll be answering it at 7 p.m.

'Bye now, darling, and I love you with all my heart. Do you still love me as I love you?

10-1-44 Sunday night

Dear Son (Bucky):

Your letter came yesterday, and I enjoyed it very much, was glad to hear you got to go the football game. Hope you will go to all of them and take your Granddaddy with you.

Did Grandpa go to Pittsburgh yesterday to see Notre Dame? Golly I hope he did, for he would have had a lot of fun watching those Irish (that's the nickname for Notre Dame) run up such a big score.

However you are not the only ones to see football, for while I had not expected any this fall, I was able this afternoon to see a game on the base here. The Fleet City Bluejackets, a team of sailors on this base, beat St. Mary's Pre-Flight, a team of sailors learning how to fly airplanes, stationed at St. Mary's College, near here. The score was 12 to 0, and since it includes every possible kind of score in a football game I'll try to tell you about it.

A touchdown counts <u>six points</u>, and is scored when a player <u>carries</u> the ball over the goal line, or catches a pass in the end zone, which is a space as wide as the football field but only 10 yards deep. If a pass is caught outside the end zone it does <u>not</u> count a touchdown. The Bluejackets, scored today on a wide run around left end after two completed passes and a 15 yard penalty gave them a first down on the St. Mary's 3-yard line.

After every touchdown the team that scored the touchdown gets a chance, only one chance, to make <u>one more point</u>, called the point after touchdown. The ball is put on the 2-yard line, and the point can be made by running or passing across the goal, or by a placekick or dropkick that goes <u>between</u> the goal post and <u>over</u> the crossbar. The Bluejackets tried a placement and big Joe Stydahar, whom Grandpa and I saw play football for West Virginia years ago, kicked the ball squarely between the posts.

Another score is the field goal, which counts <u>three points</u>, and is made whenever the ball is either dropkicked or placekicked through the posts and over the crossbar. It can be kicked from anywhere on the field, and if it does not go between the posts and over the bar it is considered just the same as a punt, and may not be caught by anyone playing on the same team as the kicker unless someone on the other team touches the ball first. Stydahar kicked the field goal today, from St. Mary's 20-yard line, when the Bluejackets were close to the goal but afraid they couldn't make a touchdown.

The other score, one you rarely see in football, was a safety which counts <u>two points</u>. The one today was made by the Bluejackets when a guard blocked a punt by one of the St. Mary's boys, and the ball took a great big bounce off his chest and out of the end zone. A safety also is made when any ball carrier is tackled and downed in the end zone, or when a forward pass is grounded in the end zone. But you don't see this score very often, nor do you see many field goals except in professional games.

That's all for now. Be a good boy!

Dad

10-1-44 Sunday evening:

Dearest Chubbin:

I was so glad and so proud to get my first letter from you, and I shall be looking for a lot of them now that my big girl has learned to write so well so quickly.

And it's just a wee bit difficult for me to picture you losing teeth, for that's a sure sign that your baby days are over and soon you'll be a grown up young lady. Sorry I couldn't be there to help you spend your dime, but maybe I'll have a dime when I come home and we'll go out and have a party on it.

Remembering how you, as a tiny girl when we lived in the White House, used to love to sit on the fire truck when we went past the fire house, I thought you'd like to hear something about how and where I slept last night in a San Francisco Fire Station.

You see in cities they have paid firemen, not volunteers like Somerset, and because the men work long hours and are permitted to sleep when they don't have to go to fires or do other work, each station has a dormitory, a big room with lots of beds in it.

Last night we slept in one of those dormitories with 6 or 8 firemen, and we had only been in bed a few minutes when a bell started to ring and all the lights went on. There was a fire alarm from somewhere in the neighborhood.

Very quickly all the firemen jumped out of bed and into their clothes, which they can put on very fast, and then as they dressed they ran over to a shiny brass pole in a corner of the room where there was a hole in the floor. Because it's faster than running down the stairs, the men grab hold of the pole and just slide down it to the first floor where the fire trucks are. And in what seemed like seconds from the time the lights went on, we could hear the motors roaring, the bells ringing and the screaming sirens as the trucks rolled away to find the fire.

That happened three times during the night but the trucks were not gone long and the fires were only little ones that were put out very quickly. And each time the men came back and went to bed. I would have gone out, too, if any big fire had been reported, just because I'm used to going as a reporter. But I stayed in bed and slept pretty well.

This morning when I got up to go to Mass some of the men were still sleeping, but they were up when I came back and we all had coffee and sweet rolls in the kitchen where the firemen cook and eat their meals. They wash their own dishes, too!

Which reminds me that I hope you are helping Mother with the dishes these days, for she'll be needing a lot of help and that's one place where you can pitch in. Don't let your mother read this but I hope you'll be careful not to break so many dishes, and especially glasses and cups, as some people.

Have you had any pictures taken lately, Chubbin? You might tell Mother I should like some new ones, to see how my family is growing, and one of these days I'll have some taken of me to send you.

Goodnight, sweetheart, sleep tight, work hard and be a good girl until I come home. Lots of love.

Your Daddy

10-1-44 Sunday evening

Dear Fran:

It's time for your Dad to be off to bed, for it seems this grown-up family of mine has me scribbling far into the night, yet I can't stop without at least a couple of words to the fellow I hear is "Daddy's Boy." Just you keep on claiming that sonny, and one of these days I'll be back there and give you a chance to prove it.

Back home by this time I suppose the leaves are turning

brown and red and yellow and the rest of the colors that make those hills of home so beautiful in the fall, yet here all we have is brown hills and brown grass under a blazing sun that glares at you all day - - then hides at night when you could use some of the heat.

Just today, riding through Oakland, I saw red roses blooming on a porch trellis, and thousands of other flowers in the lawns and around the houses. Nonetheless although it's not like home, this is pretty country and I intend that all of us - - your mother may say no, but I say go - - shall see it one of these days.

Perhaps it's because I haven't been around the residential sections much, but I seem to notice a striking absence of children in the west. This makes me, if possible, a little more lonesome for my own, yet proud and happy that I have such grand kids.

You must try hard to do as Mother tells you, sonny, especially about staying in the yard, for she's far too busy now to be running off searching for a wandering boy. And since I haven't heard anything about it, I presume you are eating your spinach and carrots and other vegetables that will help you grow up big and strong, so we can have a lot of fun together.

Goodnite, Son, and God bless you and keep you.

Your Daddy

This letter from Jess James was enclosed in a 10-3-44 letter.

Dear Chuck: Friday Sept. 29, 1944

Knox ships out tomorrow to the Naval Auxiliary Air Station at Holtville, CA, 130 miles east of here and 40 miles west of Yuma, AZ., in the Imperial Valley south of Salton Sea. His name was posted on a draft of 5 at suppertime. Lamond, scheduled to go also, says he got out of it. Lamond, by the way, came down with us from the Lakes; I guess you didn't know him. George knows none of the others. An ideal winter climate seems to be all Holtville has to offer. It's in the middle of the desert, and the only green around is that achieved by irrigation in the Imperial Valley.

Vone met Vic Barrison (company clerk) in downtown San Diego the other night. He's stationed at a Marine base near here. Rotten duty, he reports. About six weeks ago we ran into a couple of the 762 boys downtown: Thoma's friend (the little boy from Detroit; George something I think it was) and the kid who was the drummer - - not XYZ; and one of the Tennessee boys - - the one who worked in the newspaper circulation department. They're on a destroyer, and at that time were on coastal patrol, but expected to move into the battle zone as soon as a few of the kinks had been ironed out. They had a new ship. They reported that Jewish guy from Detroit (the butcher who was MA in the barracks proper) had been discharged because of emotional instability; Harry something or other, wasn't that his name?

Vone and I haven't heard a thing more about sea duty. I've begun to suspect they looked us up, found we were S.A., and ruled us out. It would be strictly the Navy way not to let us know, if that actually had been done.

Vone has won his Navy E. I told you didn't I, piles were a specialty in his ward? Well he's been detailed to the enema department - - gave 28 last night, four each to seven patients.

In rereading your letter, I just came across your query on Herbert, Wilson and Waller. Don't know a thing about them. George Knox's wife was up here for a couple of weeks about a month ago and she had seen Herbert's wife. He was in school at that time, and Mrs. Knox joked about her husband having a rate and Herbert, former ACPO, having none. West, by the way, got an emergency leave from Corona to go back home to try a case - - something involving a suit against his wife over provisions of a will.

Janie and the three (!) are O.K. She hasn't been able to get any help to sit in so that she can go out for an evening now and then, and it does tie her up more than I like to think about. She's even had difficulty finding kids to mow the lawn, and do routine masculine duties around the house. The kids are growing, of course, and I'm missing the middle of fatherhood, damm it. I'll be more than glad when this thing's over.

Give my regards to Reed and Clark and save a place on that ship of yours for Vone and me.

Best regards,

Jess

10/5/44 Thursday 5 a.m.

It's a lovely starlit, moon-bright morning, much too early to be up but here I am in the mess hall, wearing my dungarees and rubbers, ready to eat and go back to the scullery. The only thing I mind about the deal is having to get up so early, for despite the fact I was in bed before 9 I didn't get enough sleep. ("Yeah", she says," that's my husband".)

Still find it hard to realize that while it's so dark and still here and most of my world is fast asleep, you are probably scurrying around right now to get our two students ready for school. Gee I wish I could be helping you, and maybe sneaking a kiss all around now and then. I hope you don't know how wonderful that would be.

It must be a million years since I saw you and held you in my arms, sweetheart, and a century or so longer than that since I saw the kids. I miss every one of you every minute of every day. and always will no matter how long I am away.

I reread all five of your letters again last night after I crawled into my bunk , and they were very, very comforting my darling, helped me a whole lot towards making me a little more sensible and less lonely. Don't know how I'm going to get along out there where mail doesn't arrive every day, or even every week or month, although I suppose I will, somehow. Anyhow, that part of it, at least, will not be fun.

One phrase in one of the letters keeps running through my head and I can't seem to get rid of it even if I wanted to. You said you dashed up to Pucci's for bread "(minus pants)" and then came back to jump into bed and honestly darling I have to force myself to stop thinking of it so much. Even as I sit here in this great mess hall empty even though there are 2 or 3 hundred of us here ready to work, it starts something boiling down inside of me. Just to remember - - even at this distance in time and in miles - - the touch of you, the feel of you, the way you smell, and how you seem always to nestle into my arms does things to me no other woman could or will.

And do you remember those times when we lay naked together in bed, and you would ask why I wanted to leave the lights turned on? My answer always was "So I can look at you my darling," and although it sometimes sounded queer even as I said it, I wouldn't sell that mental picture of you for all the gold on earth.

They are just a few of the many wonderful memories you have given me, my Bettsy, to carry me through my part in whatever is ahead. It's good to have them darling, for if I had not been so fortunate as to find you I should never have lived. Our life has been very, very wonderful.

And isn't it grand that when all we have to rest our heads on is our memories, but <u>every single one of them</u> is happy and clear and lovely? Of course I know that we have had some unhappy moments, there must have been some in 14 years, yet whatever they were they have faded into the dim forgotten past while a million happy moments keep crowding back into my mind in the strangest places at the strangest times.

I don't know exactly what got me started in this vein, my dearest, for I confess it strikes me as odd that I should be thinking such things just now when all my surroundings are as foreign to me as if I were in Baghdad. Perhaps it's because I'm not fully awake yet, and am scribbling down the stuff of which my dreams are woven. Anyhow I hope you won't mind. And maybe some day you'll be moved the same way too, for I think I should like such a letter from you.

Bye now darling and I love you with all my heart.

10-7-44 - - Frisco Saturday night

I hope another letter from The Pepsi-Cola Center For Service Men and Women won't be as much of a surprise to you as it was to me, for when I was told that I could come back you could have knocked me over with a feather, and I'm afraid even that would be too much for you in your frail and weakened condition.

Anyhow, I'm here, and far more happy about it than last night, for by a stroke of luck the three "musketeers" are together again and I for one am a lot less lonely. And that is how come I'm here in Frisco tonight, and very possibly will be back again tomorrow! "Liberty Hounds" they call 'em in the Navy.

As I told you last night, Walts rated liberty today, and I guess he's somewhere here in town although we (Svoboda and I) haven't been able to find him and he doesn't know of the changes yet. He left this afternoon just before the whole thing happened.

When I got back to the camp this morning I found quite a big draft gone from the battalion, and decided this was the time to move together if we could wangle it, so I talked to one of the ship's company men who said he would see what could be done. Walts and I were given permission to move into Svoboda's barracks, which would put us all together.

Well, as I said, Walts was already gone, and when I started to move myself I found Svoboda and his bunch getting ready to go out, for they rated the <u>weekend</u> this week. Of course having come back from liberty only a few hours earlier I never expected to get out again but thought there would be no harm in trying and lo and behold the lieutenant said OK - - and here we are Svoboda and I. Nothing in sight to do, of course, but we'll find something and at least it's good to be away from Shoemaker for as long as we can. However it's not quite a full weekend for we must be back at noon tomorrow, against the ever-present possibility of a draft, and then if we're not called we'll be released at one. What a life!

There isn't much to tell you about last night. Spent most of the night in the AP office, and when I got tired of that about 10 I went to the Stage Door, where one of the senior hostesses, a Mrs. Henstadt, sat and talked with me for quite a while and we ended up eating hamburgers and French fries at a restaurant across the street after the canteen closed, and I took her home via trolley.

Curiously she never mentioned her husband, and somehow I didn't feel free to ask. She was wearing black, and I had a hunch she might be a war widow. She seemed about our age, perhaps a year or two older or younger. I couldn't tell and as I said she didn't talk much about herself, just let me ramble on in my usual mien.

Slept here at Pepsi-Cola until 7, then went to church before starting back to camp, but even so arrived back there at 9:30, via the hitch-hike which now is my standard method of travel. It's not always as good as it was this morning, but it's fairly typical. I got off the bus in East Oakland and the second car to pass in my direction picked me up and took me halfway to camp. And the first car behind us picked me up and carried me the rest of the way! Folks out here are wonderful about giving service men a ride, and I think it's pretty swell. Tonight we came all the way into Frisco in two rides, thus saving even the 21 cent bridge fare.

Had a grand crop of mail this morning, two letters and some clippings from you, Service Chatter and a letter each from Pump [a friend from Somerset] and Harley Smith. Pump, by the way, says he's working, and seems fairly happy. He promises to come see you. I'll send the mail along tomorrow or as soon as I've digested it.

And that, my dearest, seems the Saturday night crop. If my thinking on the mail is right you'll get this letter and another

Thursday, a rather special day for both of us. But we'll let that go until tomorrow, when I'll try to write sort of a special letter. Meanwhile you know I love you with all my heart, and am thinking of you and our loved ones every moment of every day.

10/8/44 Sunday morning

Somehow I'm finding it more than a little difficult to start this letter which I'm hoping will reach you Thursday. I know you're far better than me at remembering dates, but just in case you've forgotten that's Columbus Day, October 12, and a very important day for us.

Seems a long time - - much more than nine years - - since that fall morning we stood before Father Manning and my knees shook so. They shook their hardest, Bettsy, when you said you would be mine forever because up to then I couldn't believe that I could be so fortunate.

Even now it's hard to believe, almost too wonderful to be true, that even when we have been apart so long you are back there with our little ones, waiting for me and loving me no matter how much longer it must be until I can return to you. I don't deserve any such good fortune, yet it's mine and I am so humbly grateful.

Nine years is a long time, my darling: I should be sick if I thought for one moment I must remain away even a third that long. Yet our nine years have been much too short; have passed so quickly they seem hardly longer than as many weeks. Yet so many things have happened, every one of them wonderful to remember.

You have been told before, several times at least, that I love you and yet try as I will I can't seem to find the right words to tell you how deep and enduring that love really is. Like a fire that burns down inside of me, never so much as flickering for even an instant day or night, it lights and warms my every thought and deed. No matter where I go, or what I do, it shall be that way so long as I live, my darling, and I'm glad and proud that it is that way.

It is good to be that way. Especially so just now when 3,000 miles separate us and it is likely that mileage will be doubled or tripled.

But no matter where I go, or how long it takes, I shall some day be coming back to you and we can all live again. Be sure of that my darling, and in the days to come when I will not be able to tell you about it by letter you will know that I am thinking of you and loving you with all my heart.

Right at this moment I want more than anything else in the world to take you in my arms and kiss you and hold you tight. That is as close to heaven as I shall ever come, my darling, but even though I'm denied that joy, now nothing can take away from me my memories of the past when I have done just that.

Even to think about it makes my breathing difficult, and brings that old sensation of apples in my throat, so much so that it really hurts. My arms feel empty, helpless without you, and my lips are dry and hard, useless without you to kiss.

Always, Betty, it will be that way until we are together again.

So we will wait together for that moment, my darling, and I pray that it will not be many more months. Then, and not until then, will life be worth living.

Goodnight, my dearest one, and may we never again be so far apart on our wedding anniversary. I love you.

10/10/44 Tuesday afternoon

This very probably will be a broken-up letter, for I'm starting it now at 3 o'clock, just before mail call and we're expecting to go out on liberty at 4, so if I don't get said all I need to say now I'll wind this up in Frisco tonight.

Right now I need to get to work on my answer to your letter, which, it goes without saying, was a pretty rough one. Perhaps it's just as well I was on draft, else I might have written a hurried answer that I'd be regretting now.

Perhaps strangely to you, I didn't especially resent the bawling-out for my chin-up scolding. Matter of fact that suits me all right, for if I can make you mad enough so that you're determined to show me how well you can get along without me, then I'll know you're all right, and any kind of scolding I may get will be all right.

I don't think there was any general or special cause for my original letter except two things: (1) you're a chronic worrier, and (2) I've heard and seen too much of how other strong women have folded up under the identical circumstances. Your letter today in which you already accept my departure as a fait accompli suits me swell if it's time, and it might as well be for I couldn't, to all practical purposes, be farther away. So please, my darling, write me as much of your thoughts as you can, and above all don't try to deceive me, for such a letter could be worse than none.

But I was mad, hopping mad, about your interpretation of Joe Brennan's letter to me which I sent to you. I feel it was dammed downright unfair, especially when you said I "evidently did a bit of bragging about my 'women companions'." You know every-thing about my "women companions", and even if I were a braggart on such subjects, which I never was, I've done nothing to brag about.

Matter of fact I can't recall having mentioned women in any way in my letters to Joe, except that I may have said in the letter I wrote while in Transfer Unit at Great Lakes that I had been to a couple of dances in Milwaukee.

To the best of my knowledge, Joe was only mentioning it in a very casual way a subject that is often brought up when sailors talk. I don't think I'm bragging very much when I say that not many men made bachelors by the Navy are content to stay on the open road, especially when there are so many inviting sidetracks.

One thing more: when I come to the stage where I do things I "wouldn't tell anyone about" - - I'll stop doing them.

There, darling, that gets a load off my chest, and I can only hope that it makes sense now that I've cooled down a lot. And no matter how you scold me or anything else I still and always will love you with all my heart - - and <u>only</u> you.

Another of your letters yesterday contained another $10 bill and I was shocked and a little ashamed when it came, for I've enough money now when I know you'll need all you can get. I haven't decided yet what, if anything, I'll do with it. If and when I do I'll let you know. But I do thank you for it, my darling; you're too good to me.

And I guess that's the finish for this, Bettsy dearest, for it's nearly time to go and there's nothing very pressing remaining to be said. Anyhow you know I love you with all my heart, and I always will.

10/11/44 Wednesday morning

Just a few minutes ago I was talking to all of you for the first time in centuries, and while all of us - - yes, me too - - were shaking down inside. It was wonderful to hear you again. Leaves the nicest warm feeling down beside that very empty spot where my heart used to be.

Maybe this is the big step, maybe it isn't, but at any rate it must be a little closer to what I came into this Navy for. And honestly I am glad for I have a feeling somehow that the sooner I get out there and into it, the sooner I'll be home.

Up to right now I don't know a darn thing more than I told you - - that I'm on draft for tomorrow. As I said the chances are I'll still be in the States a while, perhaps for weeks or months, but I won't mind that if I'm certain of what I'm waiting for. It's the everlasting sitting around and uncertainty that gets me down in places like this.

However, indications are that we'll wear undress blues, and if we do our probable destinations, in order of likelihood are: Treasure Island, Frisco, San Bruno??? Almost always the far-traveling drafts, to Bremerton, San Diego, etc., go out in dress blues and travel by train.

Right after I talked to you I talked to someone else who has occasion to remember October 12, 1935, he was there too. Yes it was Duckie [An old friend from Somerset who was best man at their wedding] and he sounded just the same as always. Your letter with his address came yesterday, and last night I figured out you probably misunderstood San Bruno for Camp Bruno. So all the time I've been here he's been only 40 miles away - - and we find it out the day before I'm to ship out, and he can't even run out here tonight because he has the duty!

I had to take a chance reaching him by person-to-person call, but it worked out OK. Was swell to talk to talk to him, too, after so long, and it's at least reasonable to expect we'll be able to get together before I leave. He said he's in charge of outgoing drafts at San Bruno, which is a destroyer or destroyer escort base, and if we land there it will be swell.

Hold on to your hat - - and I suspect it's very confidential up to now - - they're expecting in April! I told him he and Lib must hurry like h_____ to catch us.

Wish I had figured out where he was last night, so I could have gone over there instead of Frisco. Walts and I hitched in, Svoboda staying here because he was sleepy and low on dough, and we got there at 7. Lolled around a bit, had a bite to eat and a few drinks, then spent the remainder of a very dull evening at the Stage Door, just sitting around.

About 11 we left, had another drink and hamburger and French fries, then hitched a ride back with a sailor, arrived here at 2:30 and went to bed. Slept in the morning until 7:30, missing breakfast and the lightning struck at muster. It was sort of funny in a way. Yet I was quite unhappy for a few minutes because I was afraid it was too early for my card to be back in the files after another draft, and I'd be left here alone.

We three were standing there together in line and Svoboda was called first. He was sort of stunned, for he didn't answer until I slapped him on the back. Then Walts, and I had to hit him too, and then me, and I went to sleep too, then woke up with a whoop.

All three of us are together on the draft, which calls for 63 men. The draft seems certainly to be a ship, and I think a warship, should know before we leave tomorrow and perhaps can even write you a workable address. Included with us on the draft are 15 basic engineers, a couple of radiomen, shipfitters, signalmen and quartermasters. Anyhow, I'm suited.

I think that will be about all for now, my darling, but there will be more tonight. I want to get this away as soon as possible, and will follow up with air mail for a few days or for so long as I can. Bye sweetheart and I'll love you always with all that's in me.

10/11/44 Wednesday nite

It is now nearly nine o'clock of the night before I go, the night before our anniversary, and my thoughts are turned to you and to you alone.

What I want more than anything else in the world is to take you in my arms and hold you tight, to try if I only could tell you how much I love you, how long I have loved you and that I will go on loving you with all that is in me so long as time endures. But someone or something - - just who or what I don't care right now - - has prevented me from doing just that so the only thing I can do is sit down here in this base barracks, take up my pen and try to put something of the thoughts crowding my mind and heart onto this cold paper.

When I mail this letter in a little while it will have no air stamp as have the others I've sent lately. This is your own letter darling and there's no hurry for it. What I have to say I've said before, and it will be as true five days from now as three, and as true five centuries from now - - and even longer. And perhaps coming late it may fill in a hole if I'm unable to write for a few days or perhaps longer.

This is the first time in ten October 11ths we have been apart, my dearest one, and while it is distinctly unpleasant still I am more thankful than I can tell you that we have had those other nine and it will be so wonderful when we can resume our lives together. If I never were to draw another breath I still would have had more of life, because of you, than any other man who ever lived. But we have so much of life in front of us Bettsy, and it will be so much the better because we have been apart, and understand better how much we mean to each other.

As you probably can tell by now, I'm just a little bit on the serious side this evening, which is natural enough for I still do not know what's going to happen to me, or where I'll go, tomorrow. And since what does happen undoubtedly will directly affect our reunion, as to when and where, so it's natural enough I should be serious.

But serious or no my thoughts are of you and they are happy thoughts - - the way you smile, how you laugh, the feel of you in my arms - - a million things come crowding through my head like the proverbial sheep jumping a stile in endless procession.

The moon, how you chattered on our first night; racing across the state to be with you for a few hours; rains, the way we walked together through them; a certain night when you put my hand on your breast doing something I was afraid to risk; how three times I waited outside a hospital room door for that first piteous wail of our newborn child and the way you smiled at me when I went into you after it was all over and I was so helpless.

That doesn't sound happy does it? But deep underneath the surface there was a joy for both of us, joys that will continue and grow to make our life even more beautiful, more wonderful when we live again.

I'm going now, my Bettsy, out where only your prayers and love can stay with me, but I feel them even now like a protecting shield around me, an invulnerable armor of love that I am so sure will bring me back to you safe and sound and soon. And no matter where I go, what I do, I know they will go with me and I shall be a better man because of them and you. Pray too, my darling, that I and the millions of others like me shall do our job so well this time it will not need redoing by our sons a few years hence.

And so, my sweetest, dearest one I am going to stop now and walk with this to the post office. In the starry skies I shall be looking for you tonight and as many nights as I must remain away. So long as those stars shine, even when they are hidden behind the clouds, I shall love you with all my heart

10-12-44 Thursday morning [Their 9th anniversary]

I'm starting to scribble this as I sit here in the loading shed awaiting further orders. Probably I'll be able to write more outside when (if) we're released for chow, but it's possible too I may not finish it or get this mailed for days.

As I write I'm grinning like a Chessy Cat, for the dice have come up seven, at least as far as my orders are concerned, for I've just wangled the information we're heading for our ship - - a first line fighting ship - - the cruiser San Francisco. [Some anniversary present!] And it's closer than I dared to hope I'd come to what I want.

I'm not sure whether she's a heavy cruiser (designated CA) or a light cruiser (CL) but think it's the latter and believe she's the Brooklyn class. Perhaps the library will have something that you can read about your husband's ship.

Have been released now (9:30) for chow and anything else until 1:30, so I'm in the telephone center waiting for a call to Duck, again for I <u>think</u> I can tell what's what without getting cut off, and maybe he can pull some strings so we can get together. I hope so.

Would like very much to call you, but I know that such outgoing calls are monitored and the only new thing I can tell you would get our connection broken pretty quickly. Perhaps, just maybe, I'll be calling you again tonight, but we'll have to wait for a more favorable time.

At the moment I don't know exactly where our ship is, except that she's in dock somewhere in Frisco, has been there for a couple of weeks and may be there quite a while longer - - or may have steam up even now and be ready to sail as soon as we get there. Life in the Navy, you know is like that.

Anyhow the whole thing is a much nicer anniversary present than I had any cause to expect, and I am very grateful. Of course I could - - and did - - wish for much more - - you, but that was and is reaching for the moon and I know my arms aren't long enough.

Strange how I'm carried back today in my thoughts to another October nine years ago when you and I started to live. It is the same sort of day, a cool morning that even now has changed to brilliant sunshine. Beans for breakfast weren't quite (?) like the chicken we ate then - - if we ate.

Remember sweeping the ice out of the car when we stopped for gas? And have you forgotten Hagerstown. Gee that was funny even though it didn't seem so at first. Yes and I know you're reminded of Washington and hotels, and I shouldn't even mind that if only we could laugh together about it. There I go again reaching for the moon.

Wonder what you and the kids and the family are doing and thinking now. It's about time for the two of them to be rushing off to school and how I wish - - more moon reaching - - I could be there to help you get them ready and kiss them goodbye.

Have you ever told them about the day we were married? I think they should like to hear of it.

Strange how slowly the words flow today. Somehow I have the feeling I'm all written out, that there's nothing more to be said. Right now my mind (?) is crowded with memories of moments we've shared and they run so fast there are so many of them, that I barely start to write one down and another pops up.

Anyhow, my darling, they're wonderful memories that will warm and comfort me for so long as it takes until we are together again and can start coining new ones.

I will love you always, my Bettsy, and I am eternally grateful for that day of days nine years ago.

Shoemaker! ! # ! ! 10/12/44 Thursday evening

Confusion piled on confusion! All signals are off - - only for the moment we hope.

We waited all day as we expected to do, confident always we would go, and very happy in the prospect. At 2:30 this afternoon the officer in charge told us to load our gear and, almost singing we picked up those 150 pound bundles, toted them out and stacked them neatly on the truck. We stood there waiting for a while, then were ordered inside, told to line up in draft number order and waited some more.

Then the axe fell.

"Now hear this," the loudspeaker roared. "All you men on draft 7565. Draft 7565 has been deferred. Go out and unload your gear and go back to your battalions." Period!

You never saw such a crestfallen bunch as we dragged our stuff off and wondered what to do. Inquiries as to our status ran into a blank wall. Finally the three of us left our heavy gear, took our handbags and came back up to the dear old fifth battalion where we learned to our disgust that new incoming drafts had filled the whole place. "Guess you'll have to sleep on the floor," the man shrugged. So we went back out, went to Wolfe's barracks and found bunks there, decided to move our gear in.

While we were collecting our stuff, very dejectedly, I got to talking to a lieutenant and wormed from him (Lieutenants do not like to talk to nosey sailors.) the information we would probably go tomorrow, and somewhere else we were told the delay was only because of transportation, that another big draft was called hurriedly for this afternoon and there weren't enough buses to go around.

So we are downhearted, but not without hope

It is such a lovely draft. I've found. I've found that the San Francisco (Frisco) is a heavy cruiser, that she is at Pier 31 in the Mare Island Navy Yard, and we were supposed to go directly aboard now, although there are some indications she may be here quite a while.

So here I am contemplating a very cold sleep, just about as different from the same night nine years ago as could be imagined. You see I miss <u>my</u> Armstrong heater too!

10/13/44 Friday noon

Back once more, for the last time I hope, writing in the telephone center just so you shall have some kind of a letter, though it can't be much. Once more it looks like we're on our way, but all of us are keeping fingers crossed against the possibility of the same bad break as yesterday, or an even worse one that the draft might be cancelled. There are a couple of unfavorable signs, but we all hope and believe we'll go.

Gee, I sure hope the mail business will improve after we get on our ship, at least so long as we're in port. I had two letters from you this morning, one of them by airmail postmarked the 7th, although some airmail has reached me in three days. And I guess my outgoing stuff has been just as erratic, although the mixed uses of air mail and regular mail undoubtedly contributes to that.

Slept, fairly well, last night without unpacking my gear so there was nothing to getting ready for today. We were able to draw only one blanket, no mattress, from the stores department so I decided to appropriate the bunk of one of the guys in Wolfe's barracks who was out on liberty.

That worked all right until 2:30 a.m. when the owner came back and I woke to find him searching sort of dazedly for his own bunk which should have been empty. Explained our predicament which he accepted very nicely, then I moved across the aisle to another bunk still empty and slept there sort of restlessly for the remainder of the night. The owner of that bunk never appeared and I don't even know who my so generous host was.

I awoke quite early, got the others up by 6:30 and we went to breakfast, then reported to our own battalion and I shaved and cleaned up a bit before we carted our gear over to the shed once again. There we sat for an hour or two until at 9:30 we were dismissed until 1:30. Since then we've been loafing, waiting for mail and eating more to kill the time than anything else.

Soon now we should be on our way, and as I say I think the ship will be around San Francisco for some time yet, so you should be hearing more from me. By the way, in case you have to use the tentative address I gave you in the letter yesterday, you can delete the line "Shoemaker Draft" for it will be complete enough without that.

And so once again, my dearest one, I come to the end of what may be my last letter to you in a long time.

No matter, Betty dearest, how long that time may be, or where I may go or what I may do, you can be eternally sure you and all of ours are eternally in my thoughts and in my heart. I shall love you always, my dearest, and I ask only that I can come back to you soon and go on proving my love through all our lives.

Chapter 7
ON BOARD THE U.S.S. SAN FRANCISCO
GETTING TO KNOW HER
10/14/44 to 10/30/44

10/14/44 Saturday 2:30 p.m.

Aboard U.S.S. San Francisco at Mare Island Navy Yard
Well it's happened and here I am.

Ever since I walked aboard last night I've felt like cheering, for at last I'm sure that I'm on my way to the thing I came into the Navy for. Not that I have any anticipation of a pleasant or peaceful cruise ahead for I know that I am going to work like h--- and there won't be anything peaceful on this ship. But soon, possibly before you read this, we'll be on our way to the war, and I'll be one step closer to coming home to you.

As yet, all is confusion; I've no idea what my assignment will be, or even where I'll sleep. But it will be worked out in due time.

It was nearly 3 yesterday afternoon, when, after a long, long wait we boarded the bus to come here. The division leading our party got lost en route, and we wandered for quite a while before we reached the yard. When we came to our dock the ship was gone, and our hearts sank for a moment, until we learned she was out on a test run, due back in an hour. Sure enough, while we sat on the bus at the end of the dock, in she came, sleek and trim, not shiny or modern as the others in adjoining berths but very, very businesslike. And it was real thrill to lend a hand on the lines as the tugs nosed her smoothly into the berth.

We stood there on the dock while the liberty party - - first officers then seemingly hundreds of men - - poured ashore over the gangplank. Then gear on my shoulder we went aboard and for the first time set feet on what will be our home probably for the duration. A little later we had chow, then mustered out on the dock where the executive officer, a commander, welcomed us aboard in a brief talk.

Then back we went to the ship, and for want of a better place until we are assigned to one of the many divisions, spread our gear on the steel deck of a mess hall where we spent the night. It was a hard bed but I dropped off to sleep soon after 9 p.m. lights out, and woke only a couple times before 6 a.m. reveille.

With time out for breakfast and lunch I have spent the day so far poking into a few of the million odd nooks and crannies of the ship. It is an amazing maze, and I very much doubt that I shall ever know much about where I am.

Of course the guns were high on our list of interests, and we've already been inside two of the three large turrets from each of which projects 3 eight inch rifles. And we've seen, too, the more familiar 5 inch, 40 mm and 20 mm guns that literally ring the ship.

Then we went down into the active fire room where roaring oil flames turn water into steam with the power of thousands of hoses; along the deck from the peak of the bow to the broad fan-tail stern and finally up and down steep ladder-like steps and into the aircraft hanger. We haven't seen any of the guns fired, missed that while the ship was on her trial run, but we did see the plane catapult fired twice, and it's quite a bang.

Up until now we're still awaiting assignment, with fingers

crossed that we may stay together, hope to know shortly so we'll at least have berths tonight. As soon as I find out what's what, I expect to phone Duckie and maybe he'll be able to come up here for me. It would be swell to see him before we go.

As for your writing, I suggest you use airmail for a week or so after you get this, for it seems logical that our first stop after we leave here will be Pearl Harbor, and it will be swell to find some letters waiting. As for me, I'll do the best I can, but I don't expect much time; most of what there is to say will be censorable, and I doubt if there will be much chance to get mail off the ship.

But whether you hear from me or not, you'll never for a minute doubt that I love you, and always will. Give the kids a special big kiss for me, darling, and tell them their dad misses them very much.

10/16/44 Monday morning

Seems so very, very odd to be sitting down writing to you when I know that this letter can't reach you until I'm gone, and there are so many things I want to say. Yet all of them have been said before and no matter how long it is until another letter reaches you. You will never doubt for a minute that I love you with all my heart. Forever.

There was no chance to write yesterday, for it was a long, long hard day of getting ready, and I really worked all the way. Surprisingly I'm not stiff or sore, except that my hands are some scraped and bruised. Guess I'll be getting used to that.

And the day ended surprisingly in our first and likely last liberty here, which provided a really good occasion to spend your anniversary present. Not that we did anything spectacular or exciting, but the other boys were broke and I just <u>had</u> to get to see Duckie. Walts and I were still working about 6:30 when we were told we could go ashore until 8 a.m. and of course we rushed, grabbing the first bus for Frisco.

When we got there I called Duckie and finally a sleepy voice answered, and it was our pal, in bed and asleep (he very carefully explained) at 9:30. But I got him awake and because he was typically out of gasoline and low on dough we figured we'd meet at San Bruno, so we three climbed on another jam-packed bus and rode down to the base. When we got there the duty chief was more than a little skeptical about an ordinary seaman expecting to meet a lieutenant but we finally convinced him and Duck showed up a few minutes later.

He looks much the same as always, a little older and pretty thin on top, but I was glad to find him solid and chunky - - he weighs 190 - -instead of flabby fat as I might have expected from family stories. As always he's solid and assured, but not overly happy about his prospects for he says he may get overseas administrative duty, but no combat. Lib didn't come along, but he says she's well and happy.

They may be coming up here tonight and it will be swell to see him again, but if not I'm surely happy to have seen him and I thank you very much for a lovely anniversary present. There wasn't much else to the night. We four (including Duck) had a couple drinks in the two hours we were together gabbing, then Duck started his nearly-gasless car back to Sharp Park and the rest of us climbed on the bus back to Frisco. There we had a bite to eat, took a 2:15 bus back here, and bunked down on the deck for 2 ½ hours sleep.

So far today we haven't had much to do and again I've spent most of my time wandering over the ship. I started this after breakfast, had to break off for muster, and am now writing high up on the after bridge, almost against the radar projector.

All of us were assigned to divisions yesterday, and the 6 GM's all landed in Division 6. Our quarters will be aft, and since our division mans and maintains the aft anti-aircraft batteries my battle station will probably be on a familiar 40 or 20, which will (or should) help me keep my feet on deck. And by the way, my complete address is on the envelope. Some address, huh darlings? Unfortunately I've had no mail since we left Shoemaker, and have no prospect of getting any until and unless we reach Pearl Harbor.

Of course we ordinary gobs don't know a thing about it but it does seem logical we'll reach Hawaii next week, and stop there for more food, fuel and ammo before we shove off to where this war is going on. By the papers, there must be quite a bit of it just now at Formosa and two possibilities strike me:

1 -- that the next landing may be imminent there to save Foochow, the last Chinese port. Recent Chinese criticism of the U.S., and the Donald Nelson visit, may have forced the decision. Or

2 -- the whole thing - - raids, criticism, Nelson et al. - - may be a gigantic feint preceding a new major operation designed to catch the Japanese asleep at some distant and totally different place.

There goes the strategist in me. I'd better get a tight grip on my mop to keep me from soaring off the deck.

There really isn't much I can add to my previous description of our ship. A little bit of her history is contained in a pamphlet handed us today. I'm sending it along to you via regular mail.

And somehow, my dearest one, I seem to have written out everything that's in me. All that's left is a queer all-gone feeling down inside for here I am on the very eve of departure, and yet I've been gone so long from everything in life that is worthwhile. But being away has not and never will - - diminish by one iota my love for you; has on the contrary made it stronger, more firm and enduring. I know, darling, it will be that way always.

Perhaps this will be your last letter for a long time, although I may have a chance to try again tomorrow. But if you do not hear anything more - - for no matter how long, because we may not even touch at Pearl Harbor - - never doubt that I am thinking about you and loving you every hour of every day ; as I have from that moment I first saw you 14 years ago and will forever and a day.

Tell our little ones and Mother and Dad I will write as soon as I can, and God bless them and keep them all for me.

Tuesday evening 10/17/44

I hadn't expected to be able to write again for a long time, but here I am in that familiar pen-in-hand pose, seated on a bench in the mess hall.

Up to now I've had my first voyage - - on salt water at that - - and enjoyed it very much. The voyage wasn't long, for we pulled out of Mare Island this afternoon and cruised cautiously down the bay to San Francisco where we're riding calmly at anchor for the night. Liberty parties are going ashore now, Wolfe and Svoboda are gone already, but Walts and I were ashore last night in Vallejo and so must stay aboard tonight.

Scuttlebutt has it we sail in the morning, and it may be in convoy for anyone driving across the Bay Bridge this evening can see riding at anchor our cruiser, at least 5 destroyers, a couple of transports and a flock of merchant ships. Further scuttlebutt says I may have a reunion with some more of our old friends because we may be bound for a stopover in San Diego. If so I'll be seeing Joe Brennan and Jess James, and you'll hear more about it. I can only guess this is the last of the line for a while.

Yesterday Chuck and I decided to go to Vallejo. Spent an hour in an unsuccessful attempt to phone Duckie and about 9 o'clock we crossed the San Joaquin River on the ferry and landed in Vallejo. Took a quick look around the bar-room district jammed with sailors and girls (?) then we went for quite a long walk through a very nice residential district. Finally we found a nice bar where we had a couple of cold bottles of beer and from there we went to a hamburg joint then back aboard the Frisco by midnight.

Up early this morning, and spent the entire a.m. slaving down in the magazines in the very bottom of the ship shifting ammunition. Most of the way down the bay this afternoon we were doing the same thing on deck, and as a result I'm more than a little tired tonight. But hard work will keep me from thinking of you too much, and so I like it.

Our ship moves beautifully, sliding almost silently through the water at low speeds and the more I see of her the more proud of her I am, and happy to be on her. Of course I'm not altogether happy, for always without you I'm lonely, but then that's been going on more than half a year now and I guess I can keep going for however much longer it takes until I can come back.

That's all for now dearest I'm going to get this off for shore, and if it's the last remember I love you with all my heart, now and forever.

10/18/44 Wednesday Evening

Yes, I'm still in these more or less United States.

How long it will last I don't know, but at any rate I'm ashore again, until 8 a.m. tomorrow. I've just tried to call Duckie at his office, but he's left for home for the evening and I'll try there in a little while - - so another letter for you.

Scuttlebutt - - quite a talker that guy - - continues to say we're going to San Diego from here, but we haven't been told a thing about when or where so it's still a guess. At any rate we'll likely not leave before tomorrow afternoon, and I think it's about a 24-hour run down to Dago.

However it's still a good bet we'll go out in convoy, too, for the bay is simply lousy with destroyers, and there are two more cruisers now, plus a couple of submarines. The Baltimore, which was berthed beside us at Mare Island, came in this morning and this afternoon the Montpelier (named for the capital of Smith's home state Vermont) came sliding past. She too had been at Mare

Island, as was the Astoria, which I saw being built in Philadelphia last year. Astoria, I guess, is still up there.

As seems to be the case, these recent days there's not much to tell you about me. After writing to you yesterday, and eating chow, I managed a note to the Smith's and another to Rusty [Rusty Russell from the AP office in Philadelphia], then rolled into my bunk for a 10-hour sleep. Spent most of today scrubbing paint and splicing ropes, but didn't work too hard, as usual. Now I'm free for the night after an enjoyable ride to the pier on the liberty boat.

They're quite large, these boats, and we had 50 or more men aboard coming in, but there was a fairly heavy swell running in through the Golden Gate. And we were tossed around like a cork. Even got showered with spray, and I'm wondering "Does that make me salty"?

Anyhow, I'm still enjoying myself, and beginning to feel at home on the ship as I find my way around a little better. Gradually we're getting her a little cleaner, and while she'll never be spick, span and shiny again she looks pretty good. And, too, I'm beginning to get acquainted with some of the crew which helps. They're mostly a hard-bitten lot, which is natural enough considering where they've been and what they've done, but we'll get along ok.

But I still and always will miss all of you more than mere words can tell you, and wherever we go I'll be thinking of you always. I do love you, my Bettsy, with all my heart, and the only day that can really be important in my life is the one that brings us together again.

10/20/44 Friday night

Something has happened to me, I don't know just what, but the writing spark is gone and I have had to just browbeat myself into sitting down to write to you. It may be that censorship is the thing that prevents me from taking pen in hand.

This despite the fact that I had <u>seven</u> - - that's right, seven - - whole wonderful letters from you yesterday, one of them mailed on the 17th, which is unbelievable service especially so when I tell you that they were delivered to me at sea, and I sat on the stern (fantail) of the ship with the wake foaming greenly beneath my feet as I read them.

Anyhow we've had our first taste of the sea, and I seem to have passed it although my stomach was a bit queasy for a while. Now it's been 48 hours since I set foot on land and I begin to believe I'll be OK, at least until we get into some rough going. Although I can't tell you where we've been or are, I can say that the trip was fascinating to a landlubber; to be out there where all is water is something new and wonderful to me although undoubtedly it will become boring soon.

The water is such a solid grayish blue out from the ship, tossing uncounted little peaks and splashes out to the horizon on every side. The ship rocks gently to the long Pacific swells, which I seem to recall amazed Magellan by their difference from the Atlantic, yet our big fighter slides smoothly through. Along the sides the turbulent water changes to a lighter green, and the bow wave curves away like a rope stretched across a stream yet left in the water so it's bent by the current.

Under the fantail the water literally boils under the thrust of the screw, comes to the surface a brilliant amethyst color that is beautifully phosphorescent at night. And the zigging wake stretches all the way back to the horizon, a strangely still path through the water like a skier's trail through new-fallen snow.

Aboard the ship life and work drops into routine before land is out of sight and we're sweeping decks, splicing ropes, cleaning guns and the million and one things that must be done.

Sleep is easy, even in our crowded compartment where I sleep on the bottom of a four-rack bunk. You'll believe it's crowded when I tell you the top bunk is only 5 feet off the deck!

So far I've been able to determine so far there isn't a soul on board from our part of Pennsylvania, let alone anyone I know. As a result we three Chucks [Svoboda, Walts and Welsh] are sticking as close together as possible despite the fact we're in different watches and on different stations.

Golly, I sure wish I could see the kids. It's been a helluva long time since May and as Jess said "We're missing the middle of fatherhood." dammit. Hope you answered Jane's letter, and will go to see her as soon as you get to Johnstown.

Which will be about all for now, darling, for I must run down and change to blues for morning quarters (I started the letter last night but had to stop at taps). Anyhow, I love you all with all my heart, and will forever.

10/23/44 Monday morning

This is my first "letter from a foxhole" although undoubtedly there will be many more of them in the days to come. My foxhole, however doesn't quite meet the Websterian definition for I'm perched at my battle station, high amidships where I'm a very minor - - very, very minor - - cog in a machinegun crew.

All the morning the guns have been roaring in my ears and very literally belching fire in my face. Try as I can, I still am unable to prevent flinching when the big ones let go, but I suppose that will come in time. Besides this is only practice, not shooting for keeps, and when that time comes I probably will be too busy to notice any thing but my own job. It's an awesome and fascinating sight to watch these big guns go, especially at night, when a gigantic stream of orange flame blinds you momentarily if you happen to be looking the wrong way.

Noise is not too bad. Most of us stuff our ears with cotton that takes away the sharp edge, leaving a dull, heavy WHOOM that hits like a not-too-well padded boxing glove. I still think the most bothersome noise in gunnery is the nasty snap of a 50 caliber.

I don't suppose there is much I can tell you about where I am or what I've been doing but since sailing and shooting are to be expected of any warship at any time I suppose it will be all right to say that I haven't set foot on land for nearly a week (My, what a salty citizen!) and much of that time we've been engaged in gunnery practice.

Lord, Bettsy, you ought to see how this ship hurls 8 inch shells at a target nearly 10 miles away! I don't know how big the target is, but it's towed by another ship (at a safe distance). Shells splashed all around it, with what seemed to me very remarkable accuracy, but since none of the old crew was cheering I took it that we usually do even better. Anyhow, bad shooting or good, I would <u>not</u> have moved voluntarily from the shooting ship to the one shot at.

The whole cruise of course is a brand new experiment to me, and as such it's fascinating even though I work pretty hard and can sleep only irregularly, what with night watches, etc. I'm still a deck hand and see no immediate prospect of a more interesting assignment although it does seem to me there's work on the guns I could be doing.

And today I got my first look at the daily ship news sheet, and after looking it over rather critically am inclined to hope I may find some work in my own sphere there. Lord knows some editing and timely writing would make it more readable and more newsy. As nearly as I can tell, some yeoman takes the news shorthand from commercial specialized radio broadcasts, then types it to fill two mimeographed sheets.

I'm still hoping to see Jess and Joe before too long, and by the way I think my last letter was broken off before I had a chance to tell you that I had seen Duck and Lib. Remember I wrote that I was going to phone him from Frisco. Well I did and it just happened that the two of them were coming into the city that night and we arranged to meet over in Chinatown.

They blew me to a very deluxe (and reasonably edible)

Chinese dinner at the Cathay something-or other, one of the famous restaurants there, and then the three of us went over to old St. Mary's Church to hear a lecture on the origins and meanings of the Mass. Duck remarked it was rather odd for two old altar boys to be going to such a lecture, and that wasn't the only odd thing about it for it's a bit unusual to say the least, for a lieutenant and his wife to be touring the city with an ordinary seaman. Lib, I suspect, is considering becoming a Catholic which would account for their having planned to attend the lecture. She looks well, acts well and says she's happy, and blushed very prettily when Duck (in his usual clumsy way!) made some half-jocular remark about the fact she's "eating for two you know."

After the lecture we went over to the Hotel Stewart for a drink, and about 10:30 they left for home after arranging that I should come down there for dinner Friday night if we were still in port. Of course we weren't so that's just another date on my post-war calendar. I spent an hour or so wandering around the town, met Walts and the two of us rode the midnight liberty boat out to our anchored ship.

By carefully checking my pocket calendar, because one day is much like any other out here, I was able to determine that yesterday was Sunday, the third in a row I've been unable to get to Mass and since we do not have a Catholic chaplain aboard there probably will be several more.

However at St. Mary's I collected a missal which contains the complete Mass, and for so long as it's necessary I propose to do the best I can each Sunday by reading the old familiar prayers alone. My first spare moments came yesterday afternoon about 1 when I was on watch at one of the aft (rear) guns. And while it was more than a little odd to be sitting there cross-legged on the sun-washed deck rolling with the waves, somehow reading through the Mass seemed to bring me closer to home and closer to you than I've been in too many days.

With which the writing spark, which has seemed to glow at

least a little for the last hour or so, goes out. I'll stop now Bettsy, and perhaps resume when I get another chance, or mail this as is. Either way, my darling, you can be very sure you're in my mind and in my heart every moment of every day. Give Bucky and Chubbin and Fran a great big kiss from their daddy, who will be home one of these days to deliver others in person, and perhaps can even spare a little one for their mother.

'Bye my darling, and I'll love you always.

10/24/44 Tuesday noon

There's little or nothing I can think of at the moment to tell you, but since I'm waiting here in my "foxhole" for general quarters to be sounded for the afternoon firing I should have at least a moment to tell you that I love you and am - - as always - - thinking of you.

It's a hazy day, with the bright sunshine only partly breaking through the gray overcast. It has been a busy day too, for the ship is being readied for Admiral's Inspection Thursday. Of course that means a lot of work and we all have been scrubbing, painting, cleaning up. There is always a lot of that to be done aboard a big ship, but gradually, here and there, the results are showing and Frisco will be spick, span and shiny when the big man comes aboard. It will be my first look at an admiral since I've been in the Navy.

To add to the confusion this was payday, and your husband drew $25 which is a very comfortable financial reinforcement. So don't you go sending me any dough unless I ask for it, and if you find any extra just sock it into the bank or buy war bonds. However with three kids to clothe (plus yourself), I'll be very much surprised if you have surplus.

My main problem at the moment is laundry for I haven't done any since I came aboard and there's a mountainous accumulation of underwear, sox and hats. Hope I can get some of it done this evening when I should have some spare time. Naturally enough washing facilities are crude and crowded, which at least partially accounts for my neglect. But I must get started sometime.

That's about all for now, dearest, for G.Q. is imminent, but I can't sign off without telling you that somehow the stars last night made you seem much closer than you have been to me in much too long a time.

I went on watch at 4 a.m. out on the fantail, and until daylight I lay there watching the clouds float across the sky and imagining what you were doing. Of course that was 7 a.m. to you, and I could see you scurrying to get Buck and Sis up and dressed and almost hear the bunch of you chattering at the breakfast table. Breakfast with you is something I've wasted much too often, but be sure that I'll be there each morning after I come back. That will be <u>good</u>.

'Bye, my Bettsy, and I love you with all my heart.

10/25/44 Wednesday evening

I've decided now to send, if I can, my rather meager collection of letters via direct airmail tomorrow, when I should go on liberty in San Diego, so I'll not have to send them through the slower censorship. And if I don't get in to Dago, or ashore, I'll have to tear this one up for it would never be passed. The others, of course, were written to be censored and are necessarily ambiguous.

But since I feel you're a reasonably safe repository for vital naval secrets I think I can tell you now that we left San Francisco last Thursday morning, steamed down the coast to San Diego and anchored in the bay there. That's where I broke off to run to my battle station last night. Now it's Thursday noon and we'll soon be heading in to Dago.

All that time, most of every day and a good many nights, we've been drilling for combat, firing all the guns and learning our battle stations. Mine is a 20 millimeter high amidships between the smokestacks on a searchlight platform. Suits me very well for it's a gun I know and like, and as safe a place as any on the ship. Walts is a first loader on one of the boat deck 40's, also pretty high, and Svoboda is a trainer on the 40 on the fantail.

What happens next I don't know, but there's scuttlebutt aboard now that we may be going into port for another stretch perhaps a week or more, but as always we'll find out when it happens. Anyhow, all I'm really looking forward to at the moment is seeing Jess and Joe tonight, and I'll feel pretty badly if anything turns up to spoil it. And if it works out OK I should be able to tell you about it tomorrow.

Oh yes, I'll be sending some of my clothes home, too, things I won't be needing like blues, winter underwear, and towels, to sort of lighten my load. I expect to take them ashore and ask Joe or Jess to handle the mailing when they have a free moment.

Which, my Bettsy, is about as far as I can go for now. It's too difficult to write out here on the fantail, and I can't go anywhere else for I'm on watch.

Bye, my dearest, and I love you with all my heart.

10-26 Thursday Nite

Damm what a life! We had a slight accident coming in so we anchor here, near Dago for an hour and then go to San Pedro, so no Joe or Jess.

Anyhow I love you, and that will never change.

10-28-44 Saturday morning   1:15 a.m. Los Angeles

Seems funny after so many months to get my hand on a typewriter, but here I am in the LA AP bureau with a few moments to kill and a mill in front of me so here goes to make up for the negligence during the day.

As you can see by this and the hurried postscript to the letter I mailed last night, from San Diego, I've missed out so far on my reunion with Joe and Jess, and I'm about ready to give up hope. Just a little while ago I wired both of them that I'll be here at least until Monday, and asked them to come up or arrange some way that I can be in touch with them by phone.

What happened, and I didn't have time to tell you about it before shoving the letters over the side last night, was that as we were coming into Dago yesterday afternoon we were testing a new method of refueling with a destroyer at sea, with both ships making 25 knots or better and a heavy sea running. I don't know exactly what caused it, but I was standing on the fantail when the destroyer came swinging over towards us, hooked an anchor in the side of the Frisco then suddenly began dropping back, with the huge chain literally being pulled out by the roots.

My first thought was of a second collision, right near me, with a good chance it would strike a gun shield full of ammunition and set it off, so I jumped into the best available hole. Then when the destroyer slid past our stern without striking again, the next danger was of the chain snapping, and just wiping the whole deck of our ship clean so I hid behind a turret, the safest place I could find. But the chain ran out for 200 yards, then broke of its own weight, and dropped across two of our four propellers. No one on either ship was scratched.

The damage didn't look serious on the surface, but eventually we limped slowly into Dago and anchored in the bay, and just when we were hoping to go ashore on liberty the captain announced we were going to limp into San Pedro, which is 25 miles from LA, and 150 from Dago. That shot liberty there, so the best I could do was get off a brief note to Jess and Joe, and yours, and then send them ashore with a couple guys leaving the ship.

It took us all night and until noon today to make the 150 miles, largely crawling because of the damage and a thick fog, and when we arrived at San Pedro we found another cruiser in the only drydock big enough to take Frisco, and we must wait until at least Monday. How much longer it may be I don't know. Perhaps only a couple of hours, and perhaps a couple of weeks, with even a possibility that we may have to go back to the larger Mare Island Navy Yard to have the work done. Anyhow I doubt very much that we will see Dago again, and unless we stay in Pedro a week until a week from today I'll have no chance to go down there.

After we were docked this afternoon we had to start carrying ammunition aboard again before we could go out on liberty, but about 5:30 Walts and I left the ship and hitchhiked in here. We split before coming downtown, arranged to meet at a hotel at 1, but after waiting until midnight I gave up and will have to get his accounting tomorrow.

However, the wreck did enable me to see Mother's brother and sister-in-law, Joe and Jose, and we had a swell visit for about three hours. I had written them from Shoemaker, so they weren't surprised when I showed up, and we spent the time gabbing about the family

Both are well, and bright and happy as always. Joe seems much smaller than I remember him from the last time I saw him (circa 1918), but he surely looks like a Kearney. Just about Mother's size, with a slightly more pronounced jutting jaw and a larger nose, but a distinct family resemblance. He's quite thin, but looks well and hearty. He has been working for quite a number of years in a laundry, a very big one, nearby.

And I think I should have known Jose had I met her on the street. Her hair is graying a little, and she's heavier, about 160, but the same bluff, hearty laughing person I remembered. She had been working in a nearby restaurant for about 10 months until it closed recently, which made Joe happy for he thought she was working too hard and too long.

The three of us sat there chattering, and smoking cigarettes a mile a minute, and Joe, who said he hasn't had a drink of whisky in 10 years, decided it was occasion enough to break out a bottle he'd been saving, and the three of us each had a nip. Then Jose flipped me a couple of eggs, since I hadn't eaten, and we drank some coffee and then gabbed some more until I had to go, promising I'd come back if at all possible. They wanted me to stay tonight, but I had arranged to meet Walts, and wanted to be sure of getting back to San Pedro, which is a bit difficult, tonight.

They live in a comfortable little three-room cottage in the eastern section of the city, off the main streets, a homey cheery place that would be just the kind you would expect them to have. They've many friends out here apparently, go visiting quite a bit, and are completely contented. Both say they never have any desire to go back East.

I left them my pea coat, a set of blues, and a couple towels to be mailed to you when they get a chance (DAMM! I just now realize I should have had the decency to pay for the mailing, and didn't.) so don't be surprised when the package arrives, and it should bring Mother a letter.

Joe saw me to the trolley, and I found my way downtown easily enough, wasted the remainder of the evening waiting for Walts and since then have sent my wires, bought a couple of stamps and here I am, about to leave to catch my bus.

So goeth another odyssey, Bettsy my dearest, and I guess you can expect a couple more letters if they don't work me too hard (which is possible since there's a helluva lot of ammunition to be taken aboard). We shall see what we shall see about the staying or going, but no matter about that, I still love you with all my heart, and always will, my darling. 'Nite my beautiful one.

10/28/44 Saturday noon

There is little or nothing to write about now and above anything in the world I would like right now to sit down and talk to you but since that's impossible this letter will have to be a poor second best. I've also given up on seeing Joe and Jess.

We were told a little while ago the ship is going into drydock this afternoon and repairs will be completed in a few hours so that we probably will be shoving off on Monday - - for where we don't know but the likely answer is Pearl Harbor. There's a possibility we may go back to Mare Island, but unless we go there I think it will be Pearl - - and on west.

Somehow I've the impression we're being rushed and the answer may be written in the Battle of the Philippines where it's my guess we had considerably more losses than have been reported. If those losses - - not necessarily ships sunk but so badly damaged they need major repairs - - were cruisers then Frisco would be a badly-needed replacement.

As I write here on the aft gun platform the riveters are chattering away stitching a new-steel plate over the hole in our hanger where the anchor struck, a repair job that will be done shortly, I assume. And I assume the skipper doesn't expect to find much wrong with our propellers or he wouldn't be counting on such a quick repair. And apparently we've taken aboard all the munitions, food and other supplies we consumed at sea. So that all we need is to replace the fuel we burned and the ship will be loaded.

To be honest, now that the day's so close, I'm not one bit anxious about going. In fact I'm afraid that if I could I would cut loose and run for home to hide behind your skirts for the duration.

Right now I'm more than a little tired and sleepy. Right after I finished writing to you last night I galloped down to the terminal, rode a trolley to San Pedro, a ferry across the channel and a taxi to the ship where I arrived at 4:30. Got me just three hours sleep and have been working easily most of the morning. I'll send this off with Svoboda when he goes on liberty, and maybe write again tonight if I don't get too sleepy.

Football games are blaring over the radio, (I still find it hard to accustom myself to the fact that noon here is 3 p.m. back home.)

but somehow I can't seem to work up much interest in the game. Wonder what Dad's listening to - - probably Notre Dame.

Your letter which came today - - did I tell you I got 6 from you Thursday, plus one each from Joe and Pump? - - gives me Ensign Moglever's [a shipmate from Somerset County] name and I surely will look him up at the first chance. A couple of the older guys here say they don't know the name. I don't know the ensign but have known his dad for years. Said dad runs a barroom in Central City. I sold him liquor when I was working in Windber and Somerset, and also knew him in politics for he's a power among the foreign population of the sector. Dad probably will know him too; his name is Paul Moglever, a short, stocky Slav or Polish Jew who talks very fast, with a decided accent and many gestures.

By the way, I'd like to have the address of Tubby Braucher, Dutch Critchfield (Critchfield Electric), John Luteri, Dick Pitzer and any of the others from home that you run across. I'd like to have Tubby's real quickly for he's an ensign at Pearl Harbor and we'll undoubtedly stay there at least a couple days.

Wonder what you and the kids are doing right now? Just setting that sentence down on paper brings a lump in my throat but there's no use in sitting here wishing I could take you all in my arms and hold you tight for the miles are too many and the distance too great.

But I do and always will love all of you with all my heart, which I wouldn't change even if I could although it really hurts right now.

Bye, my dearest ones, and May God bless you and keep you safe until I come back.

10/29/44 Sunday morning

The big news of the moment is that I shall be going to Mass this afternoon - - serving, in fact - - aboard the Frisco and it's quite a story.

To make it short, we went into dry dock last evening, and about 8 o'clock I went off to start a series of still-fruitless attempts to telephone Joe and Jess. When I came back about an hour later I naturally walked back along the stern to see what I could see of any damage from our bang-up.

While I was there I saw a familiar figure also standing on the dock. It was Father Holland, the priest I served at Great Lakes and the one who knew Father Manning. It was a nice reunion for both of us, for he said he'd been here, assigned to a transport, since August and I was the first man he had met from the Lakes.

I told him that I had been inquiring about permission to go to Mass Sunday morning when he told me there would be no need for that, because he was coming aboard to say Mass at 2 in the afternoon. At the time he was with the Protestant chaplain from the Frisco, who had made the arrangements for Father Holland to say Mass aboard. I guess it will be the first Mass on this ship in a long time, and of course I'll be going to communion, for it likely will be my last chance in a long time.

There was no chance for me to write again yesterday, for I worked - - and darned hard, too - - all the afternoon painting. I was a downright laboring man during the three hours it took us to be tugged away from our first pier out into the channel and then up a short distance and into the drydock. I was really tired, what with no sleep, etc.

There's no indication yet as to how long we'll be here, but I think Tuesday is a fair guess although the liberty party going ashore this afternoon is due back at 6 a.m. At least the daily routine sheet for Monday contains no reference to departure or to sea watches. Scuttlebutt persists that when we leave here we'll go to Frisco, but I doubt that very much, won't believe it until I see it.

Somehow that seems to be all there is to write, darling; at least nothing more wants to come out of this pen although my head is, as always, full of thoughts of you and the kids. Right now you may be starting on another Sunday afternoon ride and I think you'll believe me when I say I'd surely love to be going along.

And so the kids are going to the Halloween parties and all dressed up too! Until your letters came I had completely forgotten about Halloween, for I've seen no signs of it out here, perhaps because the West Coast autumn is a different sort of season. Gee it would be good to smell the burning leaves and walk hand in hand with you in the crisply cold moonlight night.

There have been some such nights for us, very wonderful nights, my darling, and one of these days there will be more.

Walts just now comes in with the report we're pulling out of drydock tomorrow morning, which might explain the unusually early expiration of liberty. If that's so, and it may well be, I guess we're on our way.

It must be tough on you Bettsy to get so many of these "last" letters but I just can't seem to help it. When I feel we're ready to go something down inside me whispers there ought to be something extra special to say that might comfort you at least a little bit for however long it takes until you hear from me.

But I can't find anything special darling, or anything that says more clearly and fully what I mean than those same words you've been hearing the past 14 years. I love you with all my heart and always will!

10/30/44 Monday noon

Once again it looks like the finish but I believe now it's the real thing: there may or may not be one more letter, then a blank space for the Lord knows how long.

As I write this the drydock where we've lain since Friday is being flooded and in a short time we'll be out and moored to a pier to take on oil while we carry aboard a huge stock of foodstuffs. Tomorrow we sail, and we're told, we'll make a test run to see if the propellers are OK; if they are we keep on going - - to ???????

So far as I know Walts and I will be going ashore tonight on the last liberty party, and I rather think we'll go to Hollywood, just to see what that fabled town looks like. There's nothing special we want to do, but we might consent to buying a drink each for a couple of movie actresses - - if they ask us.

All this morning I've been on the pier waiting and trying to reach Joe and Jess. I did finally get Joe, and talked to him for 3 minutes, but that wasn't much consolation for having been so close yet not to have been able to get together. Jess I never did reach, although I tried all morning. He was apparently hopping about from one office to another and I couldn't quite catch up. Will try again when I go ashore, but I'm prepared to fail on that, too.

Mass yesterday was a real treat for me, for I served again and received communion. There were only about 40 men present for half the crew had gone on liberty. Presuming that we'll not have another chance to receive communion again for a long time, Father Holland gave a general absolution to all those who had not been able to go to confession or who were not fasting , and every man at Mass got to go to communion. Afterwards I helped him pack his things, took a long walk about the yard and then went to bed quite early for I had the midnight watch.

And so my dearest one, I come again to the end of the last letter, and can only find to say what I've said so many times before. I love you all with all my heart and may God watch over you for me until I return.

The Welsh men in Somerset. Charles Sr., Francis, Charles Jr., and Charles III (Bucky). This was taken in mid-May 1944 in the back yard when Dad was on leave after completing Boot Camp.

Mom and Dad in the back yard at Somerset
in mid-May of 1944. A very happy couple
on a sunny day during Dad's Boot Camp leave.

The *San Francisco* at anchor in San Francisco Bay in October, 1944. It was here that Dad boarded the ship which was on its way to Ulithi atoll in the Carolines.

The *San Francisco* taking on ammunition at Mare Island in October, 1944. Dad's battle station was located at the top circle and the bottom right circle is where he often slept at night. The cruiser *Baltimore* is alongside and this is the ship that Dad took from Pearl Harbor to the states after his father passed away.

The men of the *San Francisco's* Division 6. Dad is fifth from the right on the top row. Note his "salty sailor" visage as evidence by the severely cocked hat.

Bucky, Fran and Elizabeth on the front porch in Somerset. This was
the "Tenement Picture" referred to in the December 4, 1944 letter.

"The Picture" as it was termed In Dad's January 27, 1945 letter.
Elizabeth, Francis, Betty (Mom) and Bucky. This was the only
war-time picture of Betty and the children that could be located
and the only "family picture" ever taken professionally.

"'Frisco" the dog, although Dad suggested that it be named "Shanghai" in his May 19, 1945 letter. The dog became the *San Francisco's* "mascot" after it was appropriated from his master on a previously Japanese-held island.

Discharge, November 2, 1945 in Philadelphia, PA.
The official end of Dad's World War II odyssey.

Chapter 8
FRISCO AT WAR - PART ONE
PEARL HARBOR AND LIBERTY ON A CORAL ISLE
11/1/44 to 12/12/44

11/1/44 Wednesday Morning

The land is gone and all about us the tossing sea stretches to the horizon. I wonder how long it must be before I shall see that land again.

On a gray misty Monday I sat all alone on the high gun platform and watched the last rocky shoreline slide down over the watery hill. Strange, almost foreign to me, it was nonetheless a part of our land and I'm not ashamed to say I was sorry to see it go.

Once we were clear of the dock I had no immediate work assignment and so was glad for it gave me a chance to drink in that long last look. So far as I could see there were few others who cared about it, which somehow made me feel even a little more alone with my thoughts and memories - - of you and ours.

It's hard to write now, not only because my thoughts are not too clear or easily worded, for the ship is rolling and pitching more steeply than at any time on our previous cruises. My stomach is more than a little queasy just now, but I'm hoping to settle it with some food shortly. That feeling is further complicated by a mild attack of grippe that caught up to me yesterday and if I don't shake it soon I think I shall go to sick bay for a check up tomorrow.

My last night ashore was rather a disappointment for Walts and I roamed Long Beach like a couple of lost souls. It was too late when we left the ship to go to Hollywood and so had to settle for the nearest town where we could find nothing to do but walk around, sort of shuttling from bar to bar. Chuck managed to get pretty much high for a little while but it wore off after we blew ourselves to a couple of steaks. Then we stumbled across a bowling alley where I rolled just one game (152) and eventually we took a taxi back to the ship about 3 a.m.

----- Time marches on, on the double.

It's now nearly 48 hours since I wrote the above, and I've spent the goodly part of the interval in bed. Went to sick bay yesterday (Thursday) morning, was handed a flock of sulpha pills and told to go to bed and stay there. Without specifically saying, the doctors confirmed my diagnosis of grippe. The sulpha kept me dozing dazedly most of the day and night, and today I felt considerably better, have gone back to work and am writing this while squatted out on the fantail, where I must be on watch at 4 a.m. tomorrow.

In case you can't recognize it from this stupid scrambled letter, I'd better warn you that writing on shipboard is going to be very difficult. First of all we're on watch, even now, eight hours out of 24, and I assume when we get into the combat areas it will mean considerably more time. Then there is always the ship's work to be done, cleaning, painting and a thousand and one other things to keep us occupied.

But worst of all is the actual physical difficulty of a flimsy pad propped on your knee while you sit on the rolling deck. The only tables available are in the mess hall and they are put away during the day, are usable after the evening meal but then not for long because all lights on deck and below decks, are extinguished from sunset to sunrise.

We're plowing steadily through the endless sea that is bluer than any blue I've ever seen before. The waters have calmed, so that my unpracticed eye sees only the little ripples beyond the waves of our passing but the ship is never still, rolling from side to side with a gentle but very firm rocking motion I have <u>not</u> learned to like. However I haven't yet really been seasick, and once again have hopes of avoiding that unpleasantness until and unless we hit some really rough going. Svoboda was pretty sick two days ago, but now seems to have made a complete recovery.

There is the strangest optical illusion I must tell you about. We seem to be sailing always in the center of a vast blue bowl, with the water on the horizon all around us seeming higher than the deck of the ship. Looking back now over our own wake we seem to be going down a long-long hill sloping evenly back to the meeting place of the sky and sea. And looking ahead from the bow you have the sensation of climbing an identical hill. Yes, I know that by all the laws of science and mathematics the deck of our ship is higher than any water, yet the illusion is a very real one.

It is so difficult to keep up with the world out here - - I'd very much like to have the overseas edition of Time Magazine. We have radio speakers going most of the time in various parts of the ship, but you have to be lucky to hear a newscast at all, and even then it's jumbled and garbled. Then too we have a daily press radio news sheet which many of the men devour hungrily, but it is so badly in need of editing and organizing, leaves so many questions unanswered. Wish I could get my fingers in it, but so far my rather tentative inquiries have brought little results.

I used to say back at Great Lakes, when all the rest were going home and I couldn't, that I couldn't possibly be any farther from you but I'm beginning to realize now how very foolish that was. Even now, there are so many thousands of miles and so many obstacles between us I find it almost difficult to conjure up the little memories of you and the kids that used to make life away from you a little bit livable.

But now, my darling, and always I love you with all my heart something time nor miles nor events can change.

11/5/44 Sunday

Brilliant sunshine, so hot too much makes me dizzy, has driven me to the shady shelter of a gun mount to write this letter. It is a spectacularly beautiful day; the sky is a hazy powder blue, the sea almost purple splashed with whitecaps, silvery flying fish, much smaller than I had expected, skimming through the air, sun glistening from their sides, then disappearing into a wall of water.

The world and the war seem very far away, but if I needed a reminder the snub-nosed gray guns above me now could furnish quick proof that no ordinary errand has taken me so far from all I love.

But gradually I am becoming accustomed to this strange life, and I begin to believe I'll be able to get along - - at least exist - - until this chore is ended. I've shaken off the grippe, feel physically good, and even have become accustomed to the roll of the ship. Gradually I'm learning to do my part of the ship's work, and to feel not too much like a stranger in a strange land. Of course the ultimate test in battle is yet to come but I'm confident I can do what little bit falls to me then.

I was surprised to receive some mail yesterday; Bucky's letter written the Sunday Mary was home, and three envelopes full of clippings from you. All had been awaiting classification in the ship's post office for they had no division address. They were as awesome as a sight of land.

All of the ship, you may be interested to know, is divided into divisions, with the six deck divisions identified by numbers and perhaps a score of other big letters. Each division, in addition to maintaining and keeping its living quarters, has certain specific daily work to do; ours, for instance, is the boat deck, which is actually the roof of the plane hanger. It must be swept and scrubbed, painted occasionally, and there is always work to be done. And each division has certain assignments, such as manning gun mounts etc. in the ordinary preparedness watches which are maintained every moment of the day and night while we are at sea.

Also each division has certain specific assignments for general quarters, or battle stations, and the division officers (we have 6 - - a lieutenant, a JG and four ensigns) make the selection as to which men have which duties. Did I tell you I have a new battle station? Instead of my 20 mm "foxhole" amidships I'm now a "talker" manning a set of telephones and relaying information at one of the stations where officers direct our gunnery. Like it first-rate too.

Our food continues to be a little less than good, and I guess it's logical enough to expect it will get worse as time goes on. Too much starch, too much cooking, too little greens and too little imagination in making up the menus seem the main difficulties. Some of the boys have discovered some very delicious onions in an accessible place, with the result that quite a few sailors appear in the chow line with this "piece de resistance" in their pockets. I've never seen a simple onion devoured with such gusto, but golly they do taste good.

Today is payday - - again - - and I'll draw $15 which should be more than enough to get me by. From now on I expect to let the money accumulate until I've a hundred or so in the kitty, and maybe then I'll add that second bond. I don't expect to need much money, for cigarettes are only 50 cents a carton (no Raleighs, dammit so I'm smoking Camels, Luckies or Chesterfields whichever I grab) and there's little else to spend money for aboard ship.

Guess that's about all for now, darling, for it's nearly time for chow, and besides this knee-scribbling is most uncomfortable.

Take good care of yourself and our kids, Bettsy, and one of these days I'll be seeing the sun rise, instead of set, over the bow and then I'll know I'm on my way home. All my love always.

11-6-44 Monday

Out of the fog of morning a pinnacle of red rock took shape in the brightening sunlight; so we came to Diamond Head and the place where December 7 will never be forgotten.

Along the coast rocky ridges rise to towering heights inland, reminiscent in a way of the Rockies, until you see a fertile valley unbelievably green; greener even than winter wheat in our home hills. Then Honolulu, perched wherever space could be found for a house, the apparently small coastal plain crowded with buildings that dwindle to winding rows down the valleys and climbing the notches in the hills.

Clouds wreath the island peaks, but some of the rounded volcanic cones can be seen, though I looked in vain for Kilauea. In the haze we saw Molakai, the home of Father Damien's leper colony and (I was told) a bit of the island of Hilo. All the names of course are familiar, but I must find me a map tomorrow and try to learn a little more of this storied land.

I know of course Pearl Harbor must be a huge and busy place, but I don't think I was prepared for even the little bit I've seen. Like Johnstown three years after the flood, all visible scars of the attack seem to have been removed entirely, and of course there has been anything but stagnation and decay since the first repair was begun.

Striking without a warning, it's easy to see how an attack could have been so devastating, yet I don't think it's any military secret now that many here would like to see the same thing attempted again. An attempt it would be, no more.

Even amid the pulsing of the Pacific War's heartbeat, Pearl Harbor is a lovely place to see. Coming in, the blue water of the

Pacific changes to a bright jade, rimmed by Waikiki's whitest of white sands. For a mile from the beach the water is almost as white as the shore. Beyond are the villas of the resort, a couple of big hotels nestled in palm groves, and behind them the green foothills against the rugged mountains. A blazing sun, white dots of clouds floating breezily in the blue sky, and the wind blowing salty spray in my face complete a picture I will remember for a long time.

I'm hoping to get ashore some day soon for there's a bit of shopping I want to do, really had planned to do in Los Angeles but never got the chance. Some of the men say we'll get day-time liberties (if any) while we're here, which would be grand for shopping and would also give me a chance to see some folks. I think especially of Tubby Braucher [a friend from Somerset now located in Honolulu] and also I very much want to look into our Honolulu Bureau which is the operating center for all Pacific War coverage.

Speaking of coverage reminds me that there may be a chance I'll get into the shipboard news I told you about. Lieutenant Barrett, one of our division officers, told me today that the officer in charge had said he wanted to talk to me, so I'm still hoping. However if I do get the chance I'd like if possible to keep my present battle station. For it's a good one and one I'm sure I can handle well.

One thing you surely would like about this place (in peacetime, I mean) is the climate. We've left behind us even the thought of winter and today, while you may have been wading through snow, I lay on the deck for an hour soaking in the sunshine that was almost too hot to stand. I've been taking it sort of easy, to avoid a burn, but when I come back I should be brown as a frost-bitten chestnut burr.

But one thing I dislike very much is the long spell without any letters. Even rereading those I've saved doesn't help a whole lot for I think I know most of them by heart.

I think I'll be stopping now darling, for I've another letter to write to go with this one and I'm needing a bit of sleep since I got very little last night. Anyhow, I do miss you terribly, and love you with all that I ever shall be. Sadly, it grows harder and harder to bring up a mental image of you and the kids and what you're doing - - some mail might help that. 'Nite my Bettsy, sweet dreams and God keep you safe until I can hold you in my arms again.

P.S. The second letter is for Chubbin's birthday, and if you haven't already opened it by this time, perhaps you can save it until then - - just in case I have no present, or it doesn't arrive on time.

11-8-44 Wednesday

Your husband is tired - - very tired - - tonight and it's some-what doubtful how long this attempt at a letter will, last but after receiving five letters from you today I just <u>must</u> write something.

But besides that there's something to tell you, and I hope you won't mind my bragging a little for this is the first time in history I've beaten you to the punch. All my shopping is done, what little there is of it, and bright and early tomorrow I'll take my package up for censoring, then send it off to you.

As I said, there isn't much, just the simple little things you could buy at home for we're not permitted to send anything that will even hint where we are - - despite the fact that any school child would be able to guess. Nor will there be any gaudy wrappings nor even tags to show you which is which but those answers will be obvi-ous Christmas Eve when you open the box for the only double-wrapped one is yours, and the rest can't go astray. But unseen in the package will be all the love and good wishes of my heart and I can only hope the little trinkets can speak for me.

Oh yes, and there will be a little one ahead of it, for I shall send the package I promised Chubbin by air if it's at all possible.

The stores are strange here; a myriad of little shops and nothing ever approaching Penn Traffic, let alone Strawbridge's or Wanamaker's, but the goods are about the same as we see at home, and the same things are missing from the empty shelves. One noticeable difference, cigarettes of all brands are plentiful. Whiskey and good beer, I'm told, are unattainable, but I can't guarantee that for the only thing I drank was a glass of milk.

But when my tour was ended I climbed on the bus that took me back to the liberty launch and so back to Frisco earlier than necessary but glad to be on the safe side and aboard ship. I found work needing to be done so changed from my whites back to dungarees. Now that job is done for this time; rain has driven most of the gang away from the well deck and the movie, and here I am scribbling. Soon I'll be in bed, and Morpheus will be a welcome visitor.

My mail today also included a very much belated letter from Jess and another from Joe Brennan which had me cheering even before I opened it for he's at last made his rating, and once more I'll have to catch up. But he would sooner be on a ship, rate or no. Jess's letter wasn't much, just a set of directions on how to reach him had I been able to get ashore in ****** [Censored]. And Joe's was a report on his end of the telephone tangle we had before I finally got in touch with him. Must answer both soon, and I've a half dozen other letters I should write but I'm too tired tonight.

Is that last phrase a memory-shaker?

To get back to the family, I thought both the letters on the kids' progress in school were fairly stupid, but I wouldn't be overly excited about them; matter of fact that sort of reporting is to my mind asinine from the start. Of course I hope you'll go back to school, make it your business to do it every month or two, and I think you'll get a lot more real satisfaction besides discovering just how you can help. And don't be too hard on the teachers for they simply <u>must</u> walk the fence in such letters, which probably are read by the principal before they're sent out. Work with Bucky on his math; make up your own homework if necessary (Mother can help.). And of course we've always know he's a talker-out-of-turn (like Pappy) and more than a little rambunctious (ditto).

Now it's bedtime girl friend, and I'm hoping my dreams will be of you. It would be very, very wonderful to be with you my darling, but since that can't be I'll dream the best I can and go on loving you with all my heart, forever. 'Nite sweetheart, and a big big hug for our kids who will, some of these days have a Daddy again, home to stay.

11/9/44 Thursday

Dear Bucky:

Another letter from you arrived today, and while I haven't done very well on my end of the suggestion that we write every week, you're doing a good job on yours and I hope you'll keep it up. The letters are swell, interesting always, and they help me to know how you are growing and progressing. I'd like lots better, of course, to be there watching the process, but since I can't we'll have to ask Uncle Sam's postal service to help keep us in touch with one another.

No, I didn't get to hear the Navy-Notre Dame game, but I was very much surprised at the score for I hadn't thought Navy was that good. However the team this year is the same as the one Granddad and I saw whip Pennsylvania last fall and they were plenty good then. Watch now for the Army-Navy game which ought to be the real football highlight of the year. Of course, Notre Dame might turn around and beat Army, the Irish have a habit of doing that, but Army looks (from way out here) much too strong this year.

I'm glad you're telling me about the football, for as I said, I don't get much chance to listen to the radio and even when we see a newspaper it's not up to the standard to which I've become accustomed.

As for Somerset, they've been doing very well, and I'm hoping that you've been able to see all the home games. Wish I could be there to go with you. Remember the games we saw last fall? That was fun. Incidentally, beating Windber was something Somerset hasn't done since 1927, and I played in that game.

One thing that makes it hard for us to listen to the football games out here is the time difference. You see time is not the same all the way around the world, for the sun shines on only half the earth at a time so that when it is daytime in Somerset it's night on the opposite side of the globe. And as you go farther away from any one place, the time changes according to the position (note to Betty: That should be relative position but I'm afraid I'm in too deep to explain that; look in the Compton's Encyclopedia or the Book of Knowledge for I seem to recall one of them has a pretty lucid explanation and some diagrams that would help.) of the sun. Thus if you go west, as I did, it becomes earlier so that while it is noon in Somerset it was only 11 in the morning at Great Lakes, and at Aunt Eleanor's home in Phoenix, it's only 10 a.m. Away out here it's 6:30 a.m., which should give you an idea how far away I am.

Being far away means a long time to get back, Son, and so I'm afraid there's no chance I'll be able to come back to be with all of you this Christmas. It will be strange for all of us, and must take some of the fun out of the day, but it's one of the things war does to people and so we must accept it even though we don't like it.

Let's all hope and pray it will be over soon, and by next Christmas we can all be together again as all good families should be. I promise you that when I get back from this job I won't miss any more Christmases.

But wherever I am or whatever I'm doing I'll be thinking of you that day, Son, as I do every day. And until I do come back you must be the man of the family, and act for me when Christmas comes.

Bye Buck, write often and I'll do the best I can. Lots of love from Your Dad

11-13-44 Monday afternoon

Time marches on, so does our ship, yet my conscience remains with me so strongly that I have once again succumbed to the insistent urgings that I pick up my pen.

It's a lovely day, a brilliant sun shining through the cloud-specked sky. But for the breeze of our movement it would be blistering hot. Even so the shady spots are sought by all hands whenever possible. The blue sea splotched by white-crested waves tossing snowy spray into the air looks as inviting as a Tom Collins but of course this is not the time or the place for swimming. Perhaps some of these days I shall get a chance for a pleasure dip in the briny (and it is salty as I shall relate later).

For two days now I have seen no living thing except men - - and an occasional flying fish. The birds which followed us for days on other cruises and often appeared when it seemed we were much too far from land for them, either are not with us now or I have simply failed to see them.

We do have rats aboard, I'm told. This morning's daily routine sheet, which each day lists in advance what we'll do and when we'll do it, includes a footnote calling for the help of the men in ridding the ship of rodents. A reward- - and a very attractive one I might add - - of one quart of ice cream is offered for "each bona fide dead rat."

Yes, we do get ice cream once or twice a week, made in our own mixers from powdered preparations and it's quite good. Once or twice ice cream, we call it gedunk, has been available at the ship's soda fountain, but so far the fountain has not been open for business much of the time and I have yet to spend my first nickel there

And you may be interested to know that the milk we get each

morning with our cereal is made from powdered milk since it would be obviously impossible to carry sufficient whole milk for even a few days. The stuff has a strange taste, resembling coconut milk a bit, but gradually I'm becoming used to it - - along with a lot of other things.

A bit ago I spoke of salt; well I never before realized just how really salty the sea is. Yesterday afternoon I sat for a while on the prow of the ship, where the guns we work on are located, and occasionally a bit of spray, pleasantly cool, came splashing over. After a bit I was surprised to discover I was literally coated with fine white crystals, as though someone had upended a salt shaker over my body.

But hot as the days may be, the nights remain pleasantly, if not a little too much so, cool on the upper decks. Last night I had the 8 p.m. to midnight watch, and about 10:30 when my turn on lookout was ended, I lay down on a cot and went to sleep. Two hours later I was so chilly I woke up, and since I had been relieved in the meantime, I went below, took a shower and shaved, and spent the rest of the night in my bunk. You see you're not the only one missing an Armstrong heater just now, even though your winter may make the absence a little more noticeable.

For the past half hour, I've been sitting here looking out across the empty sea and daydreaming - - of you of course. Sometimes, so far away out here and so long away from you, I can't help wondering if all those lovely minutes and days of the past 14 years weren't just a wonderful dream, much too lovely to be true. You of course never were and pray God never will be a part of this strange life except in my heart and in my mind. Yes, if things were different, it would be nice to sit by your side here and look out across the truly beautiful waters; anything and any place can be heaven if only you are near me.

But when this is all over, and our job is done and <u>done right</u>, then give me our home, a comfortable chair and a bit of grass where we can romp with the kids or just sit and loaf and live; I shan't want anything more than that, ever, and I shall never be satisfied or truly happy until I get it.

And that starts me off on another train of thought: where shall we go and what shall we do after I get back? Yes, I know my AP job is waiting for me in Philly, and I know also that Jess would be more than glad to find a place for me on the Democrat; make one if necessary.

But I'm wondering very seriously whether I want to go back to the hurly burly scramble of newspaper life; all sorts of weird hours, your kids growing up without seeing them sometimes for days at a time. No, Somerset looks and sounds vastly more inviting just now if I could find some way to earn a respectable living there.

Now probably this is all very silly, for there's no denying that printers' ink has seeped into my veins and it's much harder to eradicate than anything I can think of at the moment. But don't say you weren't warned if the idea persists. One thing is certain. When I do get back from all this journeying I'm going to sit down there for a good long stay; just eat and sleep and live until I get to know all of you again.

So far we've steamed along westward without any sign of any action, past present or to come. But as one chief gunners mate puts it very succinctly, "We're getting into Indian territory," and of course our precautionary measures are increasingly more stringent. We have been told, too, where we're going but not why, but censorship prevents me from revealing anything to you.

Don't think I've mentioned this before, but the youth of the crew amazes me. I've been told that the average age of the enlisted men is 21, and this despite the fact the vast majority of them have been out here fighting for 2 years and more. They don't look it, and most of the time they don't act it, but by and large they're kids. Of approximately 100 men in my division, only 3 are older than I; at least five of our division officers have seen at least 5, and in a couple of cases 10 or more, less years than my 32.

So its natural enough, I guess, for the guys who don't know

my name to have labeled me "old man." Perhaps as they get to know me it will change. I hope so for inwardly I'm inclined to resent it. But if not there's nothing to do but let it ride.

Might be, too, that I can find a moment or so to take you in my arms to see if we can recapture some of our lost romance. I may by that time have forgotten how to make love to you, but we learned once and there's nothing in the book that says we cannot learn again.

And I think, my darling, your kisses will be sweeter than ever before, for I'm learning the hard way what life (?) is like without you. That's it for now my "green eyes." Hug our little ones and give them a big kiss from their Dad!

11/19/44 Sunday afternoon

Sorry Bettsy, but it was just too damm breezy to keep on writing last evening, so I stopped very abruptly, somewhat in disgust for I felt like writing then and now may not be able to recapture the mood.

This is the sunbathing period, and right now I'm seated up on the boat deck, wearing only my swim trunks and my clacks - - oh yes there's a cigarette sticking out of my face, too. We worked quite hard this hot morning, had a good chow (the meals seem to be quite a bit better the last couple of days or maybe it's just that I'm getting used to the food) and after that I showered, hung up some washing and here I am. To go back to yesterday: (wish we could go back to physically repeat that swim).

At swimming call, sounded after the ship is anchored, a big cargo net is draped over the side from the fantail, and our crane lifts a big life raft, made of many blocks of wood tied together, over the side. Then crew and officers alike dive over the side (12 or 15 feet) and swim around as they choose, or hang onto the raft. A couple of small boats are kept on patrol nearby just in case anyone should get too ambitious, catch a cramp or have something else go wrong.

Our first swim was about an hour before the noon meal, and we were in again for another hour before supper. The water was quite choppy, but just the right temperature and I had a grand time. So would you and the kids.

I was surprised to find only a comparatively small percentage of the crew taking advantage of the swim; why they didn't I don't know but I got the impression from some that they thought it a bit silly and juvenile. Why they feel that way I don't know - - it's still fun as well as good training to me and I'll go every chance I get.

On the other hand, I thought most of the officers went in, among them the captain who seemed to enjoy his two splashes very much. I suspect it's highly unusual for the skipper to join in such a party, but he dove right in and with him went several other of the top-rankers.

The sea has changed today from the choppy water that we've been seeing to an almost glossy smoothness, the look I guess, which gave this big body of water its name. It's a strange sight, not a dot of white anywhere between us and the horizon except the splotches of our own wake. Not that the sea is perfectly level, for the rollers are plainly visible hills and valleys, and our ship is rocked from side to side.

Do you know, Bettsy that, if it weren't for grim mission we're on this cruise could be in many ways pleasant. Of course that must be further qualified by the fact that nothing I can do that does not intimately involve you and the kids can be truly happy. But to go on with the original thought.

Primarily of course it's all new and strange to me and that in itself makes almost anything interesting to someone of my natural inquisitiveness; and much that we see is truly beautiful. For instance during the past half hour I've been watching what I think is the most beautiful cloud I've ever seen. It's a tremendous thing, a solid white tower against the powder blue sky, and it must be all of 15,000 feet high and half that wide.

The sea is beautiful to watch (if you don't get too much of it) and stately ships move across it with no apparent effort, leaving only the frothy effervescent wake where they've been.

Coral atolls are just about as I mentally pictured them, a white sand beach before a lower spit of land that is all but covered by palm trees and green underbrush. Beyond the islands the surf breaks frothily at the reef in an unending although rarely successful struggle to get in at the lagoon. The place is pretty, no doubt about it, but no sane man would want to risk his life to own the whole damm thing.

So far the life aboard has been fairly easy, albeit not a sufficiently comfortable one. We work pretty hard at times, especially taking on stores or munitions but so far it hasn't hurt me a bit. But as a first-class passenger on a good liner this cruise would be a grand vacation. Of course that necessarily must include all of you, for I already have been too much alone, and know that situation must get worse before it gets any better.

But Betty dearest, when I do come home I shall have a so much better understanding of what home <u>really</u> is and what you all mean to me that I shall understand and appreciate a great deal more than I have.

Golly that was a funny feeling the other evening when I realized that our daughter's birthday had come and gone almost unnoticed by me. Brought a lump to my throat, I can tell you, and some lovely memories, too, even if they did hurt. I'm so glad I sent her letter before, and the package too although that was probably late and certainly very little. But any way she knows her far-away Dad hasn't forgotten.

Bettsy, I want you to know that I have loved you a long time and shall love you a lot longer. But never was that feeling more real or tangible than right now, when I'm further from you than ever before, and have been away longer than at any time in our 14 years. 'Nite, my darling.

11/26/44 Sunday afternoon

Honest I don't feel one damm bit like writing now, for I'm sleepy, (lazy of course) and the wind whipping the paper makes it difficult to scribble but since the mailman brought me five letters from you and two from Bucky today I just haven't the nerve to go snooze somewhere.

It's so very difficult for me - - and I assume you, too - - to keep any chronological track of things because the letters arrive so mixed-up as to dates. So for some time I've been turning over the idea of numbering my air mail letters, 1-2-3 and as many as it takes until I come back, so it will be easy for you to sort of fit the jigsaw puzzle together. I'll start with this one, and suggest you do it too after you receive this.

Mail from you wasn't the only nice thing that happened to me today for once again I had a chance to serve Mass and receive communion. The priest, who came aboard from another ship while our chaplain went over there to hold the Protestant services, was quite nice, a Father Smith of the Redemptionist Order, from St. Louis. He said Mass in the hanger, and the wind made it quite difficult, we couldn't keep the candles lit among other things, but we got by all right. There was quite a crowd too, I think the largest I've seen at Mass on the ship despite the fact that nearly ½ of crew either was on watch or on the beach.

Which brings me to my story of my first liberty on a coral isle. Listen, my family, and you shall hear.

First of all I ought to explain we're at anchor within one of the myriad coral atolls that dot the Pacific. Generally atolls are roughly circular in shape with a few or many little dots of land around the circle, the dots being connected by an underwater coral reef which provides for the lagoon or water inside the circle, protection from the waves of the open sea.

Yesterday morning, after inspection, Walts and I along with a horde of others from Frisco piled into an LCI (Landing Craft

Infantry) which came alongside to take us to the beach. It took us to the beach, and we jumped off the ship onto a crude quay of logs and sand and coral jutting out into the water. Along with us went a couple of crates of sandwiches, prepared by the Frisco's cooks for our lunch, and we straggled over to the depot where the officers in charge of our party collected our quota of beer.

Eventually we all rallied around and it was distributed, and Walts and I stuck with the Sixth Division group which gathered under a big strange tree that must have had 20 or more trunks running into the ground; not at all like any tree I've ever seen before. There we had the strangest of strange picnics, with enough beer to satisfy almost anyone, and plenty of sandwiches, too. The beer was free, all bought by the Navy and shipped thousands of miles out here to give sailors a respite from their ordinary routine, and believe me I think we all appreciated it: I know I did.

We chattered and laughed, drank our beer and ate the sandwiches, then a half dozen of us walked down to the beach for a swim in the surf that came pounding in at times flipping us head over heels. It was lots of fun although the coral sand was rough, and the coral rocks sharp and painful as the devil when I stepped on them. A half mile out from shore we could see waves that appeared 15-feet high piling up against the reef, and it was beautiful to watch.

Then after the swim I wandered around a bit, ate some fresh coconut some of the boys climbed trees to get, and was sitting in the sand, my back against a palm tree, writing a letter to Jess when it was time to go.

The island itself is only a pimple on the surface of the sea, less than 120 feet above water level at any point. It's almost covered with coconut palms that grow right down the sharply shelving beach, and the central part is swampy and dank, with green and dead vegetation of a myriad sorts I've never seen. There are a few brownish thatched huts that were built by the natives but I saw none of the people and assume they have been moved to one of the other isles.

On the island the Navy has built a recreation field, where a dozen assorted baseball, softball and football games were going on, all tangled up with each other. There were crap games - - bearded kids waving fistfuls of money - - in a shady grove, and over it all the ravenous loudspeaker calling men from the ships to start back aboard. I only saw a few birds, none very close or spectacularly colorful, and no animal life except a few tiny black lizards running up and down tree trunks.

Back to beer for a moment, we were told the ration was to be 3 bottles of beer or 3 bottles of coke for each man, but I guess some of the kids didn't drink their share for all in our gang had more - - I got 5 bottles and my it tasted good. It was all good old USA beer too, from breweries all over the country. I saw some Duquesne and Iron City bottles (aside to Dad: Maybe that's why you can't get your favorite brew.) and it was almost like meeting someone from home.

Anyhow, it was a lot of fun, and I enjoyed myself a great deal.

I didn't get to finish Jess's letter there, but did manage it when I got back to the ship, along with a note for Jane. It was sweltering hot and I sweat bucketfuls writing, which accounts for my not writing another letter to you and one for Peg too. Now I've done nothing all day except this one measly little scribble, and doubt very much if I'll do any more for I must get to bed quite early.

Anyway, my darling, it was very grand to hear from you, that you're all well and miss me even as I miss you, and the letters shall be saved for some future rereading when no new ones are coming. Somehow, it would seem, I love you more than a whole lot, and never can be truly happy until and unless we're together. Bye, my Bettsy, and may God in his goodness watch over you for me. I love you.

This was in an envelope postmarked 11-27-44 along with a letter from his wife Jane James.

Dear Chuck: Nov. 11, 1944

I get faint-hearted, too, sometimes, and feel as though submitting to a psychiatric examination to determine, if possible, why I let myself in for this, but fortunately it doesn't last long. What I'm getting at is this: We may feel now, when both of us are hankering after our families, that we made fools of ourselves by sticking our necks out, but it doesn't require too much rationalization to bring oneself around to the position of seeing the wisdom of our move from the long-range standpoint.

I, too, am sorry we didn't get together two weeks ago. I was unable to get downtown either Thursday or Friday nights you expected you might put into Dago. Thursday I was sent down to the printers with copy at the last minute. It was a rush errand and I didn't get a chance to go back to the tent to change into my dress blues. I would have been picked up for sure in undress blues if I had stayed as I planned. Friday we didn't finish putting the paper the paper to bed until 6. Usually it's about 4, and ordinarily I would have had plenty of time to slip back up here and change, getting out the gate in plenty of time. I stayed at the phone here both nights, however, till 9, waiting for you to call. A week or two later, your letter came back for more postage, and I realized you hadn't got my letter after all.

You're right, I'm strictly a reporter here - - and that's all I want to be. Being editor's too much of an ass-kissing job to suit me. I'd pop off at the wrong time and get myself clamped into the brig. The editor's a college journalism student, and he runs the paper true to form, collegiate form, I mean. He's about to be given a medical survey. It's too long a story to bother you with, since you don't know him, but there's a lot of stink about it.

I had occasion to talk with the chief pharmacist who's pretty much in charge of filling sea drafts here. (When I say pretty much, you'll know what I mean, knowing as well as I that the Navy can't stand giving one man a job and not cluttering him with a lot of restraints and dual responsibility.) An order had come out from BuPers ordering the Hospital to send to sea all personnel, enlisted that is, who'd been ashore more than two years. (The editor of Dry Dock fell into that category, and his discharge has something to do with not wanting sea duty.) I wanted the local angle. He said there was only one man who would fall into that category (the Dry Dock editor) and that they were getting rid of him. I complained that I had been after sea duty for two months and had gotten nowhere. He said "If you weren't PhM3/c I would ship you out tomorrow, but we haven't had any calls for a third mate since you talked with me about it, and I don't know when we will have." Which makes it look as though Vone and I will be twiddling our thumbs for the duration, if not longer.

Vone's been transferred again. He's on SOQ (Sick Officers' Quarters) now, and says it's a swell deal, eating officers' food, and fucking off in a strictly official manner. Ben Faunce's son, Dave, is a patient there. He's recuperating, and has been given liberty privileges, so he's invited Vone and me to his house for dinner some night next week. I hope he isn't as bad as his father.

I hope you make your news job, but I'm warning you, from first-hand experience of dealing with Navy newspapering, that you'll be amazed at the number of things you can't print. If I ever get to sea I'm going to stay as far as possible away from this business. In fact, I'm considering wangling a transfer off the staff right now. However, first I'd want to know where I'd land after jumping out of the frying pan.

Janie hasn't said anything about a visit from Betty, and I'm sure she'd have mentioned it if Betty had been down. She asked for your at-sea address, and I expect you'll be hearing from her shortly. You're quite a fan of hers.

Here's a quote from Vone: "Tell Chuck the blue Pacific is much better than the blue Dago. The color's internal here." I asked him (He's sitting beside me waiting for me to knock off for the afternoon.) "Anything more"? I asked. He replied "I'm very terse. My thoughts about the Navy are largely unprintable."

In your next letter tell me as much as you know about a corpsman's life aboard ship. How many? What kind of quarters? Any better chow than run-of-mill? How you were treated in sick bay? How are the medics? Etc.

If I don't get over to the post office to get this mailed, it won't go out till Monday, since I don't have any six cent stamps. So I'll quit for this time, and promise to answer your next letter just as promptly as I did this one. I received your letter only an hour ago.

Gobs of luck, you gob, and may we be cracking a bottle together soon - - although not with you in the role of patient. God forbid! I know Navy medicine.

Your friend Jess

11/29/44 Wednesday morning

Burns sure was right when he made that crack about the best laid plans, for I had to break off last night to go to supper and never was able to resume again. It's been raining most of the night and morning but now seems to have stopped momentarily so here goes.

This is off the record so far as the kids and family are concerned - - here is what I sent so you won't be duplicating. Fran, a little shirt and a little toy dog; Chubbin a pink wool sweater; Bucky a pair of cowboy type overall pants that should be good for Saturday play; Mother a luncheon cloth set and Dad a necktie (how original!). But honest Bettsy there wasn't much time, or much to choose from, and I had to worry too about durability in transport. Of course we were not permitted to send anything that would ever indicate where we were.

I concur heartily in your opinion that if Chubbin's wish comes true her Daddy will be surprised. On the other hand, are you <u>sure</u> you're <u>not</u> holding out on me?

Glad you have decided to take Bucky to the dentist, hope you'll take all three and then rally enough nerve to take yourself.

And I'm <u>very</u> glad that Mother and Dad have taken my advice to use the car and get around a little. There's <u>plenty</u> of gas and no reason why they shouldn't use what is allotted to them. Tell them to keep it up - - although by now Pappy's probably snow bound for the winter.

In case you haven't found out about the frig, the gas in ours is non-poisonous though it will make you cough and blink. If it ever should break down that way, <u>turn the motor off</u>, open the doors until the gas is gone, and yell like hell for a repairman.

The Time magazine will be swell when it comes, and thank you very much. As for sending anything else, the only things in the world that I really want are you and the kids and home - - but I don't think the U.S. Mail carries such packages.

Which seems to cover at least some of the points you raised in your letters. Funny I never have written answers to letters; just go prattling on in my own peculiar way. But at this distance I realize I must be leaving some awfully big holes for you and so I'll try to fill in the gaps as best I can. And as you know there are so many things that can't be written. I have to catch myself all the time. It's not so difficult when a letter is turned back by the censor (only the one of mine to you has been) but we never know whether parts are clipped or blotted out, and if they were what parts so I may be going on making the same mistakes time after time. However I try to be careful, and rapidly am overcoming that censor-peering-over-the-shoulders feeling, which takes the psychological check off my scribblings.

Along with your letters yesterday came another from Jess, whose speed and response is vastly better now that I'm out here. He sent me, too, clippings from the Democrat with all the election results

Golly, one little thing I've been meaning to write and don't want to forget: when it comes to the family party Christmas Eve, (in case my package is there) please ask Bucky to pinch-hit for me in distributing them, will you? After all he is the titular head of the family for the time being, and that should be one of his jobs.

And so, my darling, here's the end of another letter. I wonder how many thousands we've written each other over the years. And how many more (I hope we can count it in dozens.) there must be until we are together again. I remember the shortest one. Just a picture and on the back "Have you forgotten so soon"? Bet you'll remember that, too.

Always they must end the same way, and so my Betty I send you all my love and prayers until I can hold you in my arms again and tell you all about it.

11/29/44 Wednesday afternoon

Dear Bucky:

It has been a long time since I sat down to write to you but I hope you know the delay has been caused only by the lack of opportunity. Every time one of your letters arrives I want to sit right down and answer it but my time often is not my own so I must wait until I have the opportunity as I do now.

Meantime I haven't forgotten about you, for never a day passes that you and all of our family are not in my thoughts many times. One morning a couple of weeks ago we sailed right through a big school (that means a big bunch of fish) of flying fish and one of them sailed right out of the water and landed on the deck of our ship.

Since it was the first time I had seen one at close range, I was very much interested in this fish. And thinking that you would be too, I made a drawing, in fact two of them, which I'm enclosing with this letter. It will show you just how big that particular fish was, for I traced the outline. I guess most of the flying fish I've seen are about that size, maybe a little smaller.

The fish's back is blue-back, with quite large scales, and the belly silvery white. Aside from the "wing" fins it looks very much like a kind of fish I used to catch in the Juniata River near Mann's Choice - - I'll take you there some day and we'll see if we can't catch some.

Your letters and those from Mother too, tell me you are having lots of fun with your new sled. You're very lucky Grandmother and Grandfather were able to find such a sled for you, because they haven't been made for several years. Once when I was your size, I had a Flexible Flyer, too. As I remember it, I broke a runner going over a big jump. After that I had several others, all Lightning Guiders, I think, but I always seem to remember that Flexible Flyer as my best and fastest sled.

Do you think we could take a ride together on yours next winter, if I can be home by then? Maybe we can talk Mother into trying it: she used to enjoy coasting when she was young, but I bet she didn't walk up hills very often. That's the tough part about being a boy, you must always walk up to ride down; I suppose you have noticed the <u>pretty</u> girls usually can find some boys who will pull them up a hill.

I was very sorry to hear that your teeth needed filling, but Mother has told me how brave you were and it made me very proud of you. We'll try and see to it that you get to the dentist more frequently for a while, so we can catch any trouble before it develops too far.

What of your school work, Son, what are you doing and how are you progressing? Your letters always are full of what you do in playtime, but I should like to hear what kind of school work you are doing, too. Do you miss St. Lawrence and the nuns? I know I do, and for a long time I have wanted to write a letter to Mother Incarnata, perhaps will be able to do it in the next few days.

Wouldn't it be grand to be back there now, all together?

But we aren't and can't be for a little while; let's just hope and pray that we will be soon. Until then I'll be thinking of you and missing you very much.

Always, Your Dad

P.S. Just in case you don't get another letter from me before your birthday, I haven't forgotten Son. May there be many more of them and may we spend the next one together.

11/30/44 Thursday afternoon

A belated - - and a very strange - - Turkey Day arrived for us at noon with the Thanksgiving Bird and all the trimmings on the table. I passed up the soup but had a big piece of turkey, mashed potatoes and stuffing with gravy, peas, asparagus, olives, apple sauce, pumpkin pie, chocolate ice cream, bread and butter and a cigar to top it off. Quite a feast, and quite good too, but there was none of the old Thanksgiving aura.

After finishing your letter yesterday morning I drew two more from you at mail call and spent most of the afternoon scribbling - - but not to you. I got off 5 letters (of a sort) and feel right proud of myself but still owe or should write a half a dozen more and I'm not optimistic about whether or not I'll have enough time or energy to even get a letter off to my sisters in time for Christmas. But I hope you and Mother are keeping them posted until I get a chance. You can tell them I haven't forgotten, and will write when I get a chance.

Today was payday, another $15 for me, and probably the last I shall draw for some time because we just don't use money out here. It has taken a little to buy new dungarees, etc. but I'm all stocked up now and have $20 in reserve so I shall let the pay account accumulate. I think I told you I plan to allow my pay account to grow until there's enough to fly me home when we hit the states. I might as well take out the other bond and meanwhile one a month will be counting toward our post war fund. By the way, I would be interested in a report on our bank status, especially the note.

Spent the morning painting the base of our four gun mounts, and despite all the work we've done here there's plenty more in prospect, scraping decks and lockers, painting them and general tune up work. As you probably know by now, a prospective gunners mate does many things besides work on his guns.

Just as you mentioned in one of your recent letters that I would enjoy the snow, so does it occur to me now that you would really be enjoying this weather. The sun is hot, but when you find a breeze not too much so, and the showers are the kind we used to walk in, pleasantly warm and refreshing.

Yes Bettsy, I should very much like to walk with you right now, shower or shine, I wouldn't care nor probably even know. But it seems we're destined to be apart for a while and so must content ourselves with memories of the past and dreams for the future.

In all of those dreams of mine you're in my arms, my darling, and until that dream comes true nothing can matter very much, really. 'Bye my dearest, and remind me sometime to tell you I love you.

12/3/44 Sunday morning

Sorry to confess it, but I've let you down for two days on letters that you might have had before this one, but honestly there was so little to write, so little time and I just wasn't able to make the grade.

As it is, I'm afraid I'll be scratching for copy before I can finish one sheet. Let's see, I left off Thursday morning. That afternoon I spent painting, getting myself as well as the mounts pretty well darkened up, and Thursday night I slept very little since we had the midnight to 4 watch.

Consequently I was dopey (more so than usual) all day Friday and that combined with a very hard rainstorm and the roughest sea I've encountered left me no ambition to write. I spent most of the day when I was not on watch, dozing in my bunk or just anywhere I could find space to curl up a little. That, by the way, is a sailor's trait I'm gradually acquiring; being able to sleep almost any place at any time. But, oh, how grand a soft bed will be - - especially a certain bed which is equipped with an Armstrong heater for cold nights.

Strange, isn't it, how often my thoughts stray back to that, and by such devious routes! There I was in all innocence relating a bit of shipboard life I thought would interest you, and look where I wound up - - postwar planning again.

Anyhow to get back in the channel as we mariners say, I got fairly well caught up on my sleep Friday, got up at 3:30 a.m. yesterday to go on watch and then spent the morning wire-brushing the steel deck around one of our gun mounts where Friday's rain had brought the rust through Thursday's paint. Knocked off at 11 for a swim, and if I do say it myself I find I'm rapidly becoming a better salt water splasher. Now find I'm able to swim around for 15 minutes or so without a rest, or becoming very tired, although it's often difficult to make any real progress against the tide and the chop.

Spent an hour or so after lunch at division instruction, and then decided to go to the beach when a recreation party was announced for I've been on land less than a dozen hours in the last month. So Walts and I climbed into the LCI which shoved off for the island, but before we got there a very heavy rainstorm, accompanied by terrific thunder and lightning, swept down on us, and I guess the control officer on the beach declined permission to land and we headed back to Frisco, barely crawling through the blinding rain.

Well, let's see. That brings me up to last evening, and supper and the 6 to 8 watch followed. We've been having movies every night, showing a night of a miscellaneous assortment of pictures, but I haven't bothered to go even once for most of the time I much prefer to sleep or just sit around and talk.

Last night I attempted to sleep on the boat deck on a cot I've found, but a shower came about 9 o'clock and it wasn't too hot below so I snoozed very soundly. Which makes me think that I can't understand how some of these guys sleep on deck through heavy rains, but some can and do do it. The first drops always awaken me. As a result I'm about ready to give up trying until and unless the weather improves although it's often mighty hot below decks and pleasantly cool up here.

I'll bet Bucky is really into football and loyally rooting for Navy just and rooting against Notor (his spelling) Dame. Has he started to read the newspapers of his own volition? Surely he should be reading his own funnies now, and perhaps if you show him the sports section and explain that all the football and base-ball stories are there he'll want to read that.

And something else I've been wondering about, is Chubbin still writing with her left hand, and is her teacher trying to change that? Don't let them force the change Betty, let the child write with or use whichever hand she chooses. Of course I still prefer that she (or all of them) be ambidextrous but don't let some un-thinking teacher upset the balance.

There, guess that's all the writing that's in me this morning, darling. At that it's better than I expected but I guess when I get right down to thinking about you and home I can always find some kind of words.

And thinking of you and home is something I do very often, my dearest, as you may suspect by now. I miss you all an awfully lot, and am only living for the day when this is all over and I can come back to stay. 'Bye, my dearest, and I'll love you forever with all my heart.

12/4/44 Monday afternoon

Even as I sit here starting to write, I'm grinning like the cat that ate the cream; reason: we got a little mail aboard today and I drew more than my share, what with two letters from you, one from Bucky and one from Joe Brennan.

It's good to know you're all right, and that my letters were coming through to you at good speed from our first stop. Wonder how we're doing now? Seems that I neglected to thank you for the picture of the kids which you sent me some time ago, among them the "tenement" shot. Sorry to have been so neglectful darling, for I did and do appreciate them and have added them to my often inspected collection.

I'm continuing this somewhat later, for I had to break off to go on lookout, then got into some work and discussion on one of the 40 mounts which I hope will get Walts back soon as a gun striker. Some of the gunners mates got to examining a part of the mount that seldom or never is disassembled and Chuck and I happened to be the only ones who had done it before so we pitched in. It was fun too.

Later, I had a swim, then chow, now have rigged my cot on deck and will be going there to sleep after I finish this. Slept topside last night, and very soundly too, although I was forced to take cover by two brief showers. Strangely, for this part of the world, it hasn't rained today and so it probably will pour all night.

I spent all of this morning working like the very deuce on our guns and mounts, after loafing and playing cards all yesterday afternoon. Must work hard again tomorrow painting and scraping, after which we should have things pretty much under control.

Shortly after I finished writing yesterday a priest from another ship came aboard, and since I was able to find someone to fill in for me on watch I had another chance to go to Mass and receive communion. So far I've done better than I anticipated on my religious obligations out here, but my fingers are crossed for I'm afraid we've just been lucky.

By the way, has anything been done towards starting to train Bucky as an altar boy? Surely he's big enough and old enough now and it's a privilege and an honor he would not want to miss.

I think your Christmas shopping job was a dandy, darling, and gee how I wish I could be there to see the kids' eyes shine when they see what Santa brought. There will be many miles between us then, my darling, but I'll be there in spirit and the happier you all are the better it will please me for that's what we're out here for - - to see that the life we've known and loved isn't taken away from us.

And imagine Mother and Dad finding real sleds for the kids! I thought they were as extinct as the dodo. Betcha I can take a better bellywhacker than you. We must try it some night some winter - - or are you too old and sedate?

Rereading your letter with the Yule list I'm more and more impressed by the job you've done, and very very proud of the way you're pinch hitting for us. And Bettsy you are 100 % right about the money end and I'm very happy to hear (a figurative term) you talk that way. Don't tell me I had to run off half 'way' round the world to cure you of that nasty old money-worrying habit!

As for money for Mother and Dad, you shouldn't worry too much about that, for they don't really need it, and probably would have to pay it out in income tax anyway. If they won't take it, you go ahead and buy what you see and what you want for the house, and we can discharge a little bit of our obligations that way.

Also, I assume you have never received the income tax refund due us for 1943, and I'd like to know the amount since I'll need it when I make out my 1944 return, which should bring us a couple <u>hundred</u> dollars refund. You can find the amount of the 1943 refund on the duplicate blank which I filled in and kept with my valuable (?) papers.

Which brings me around to another bed-time Bettsy, and I must get me a little sleep for we have the 12 to 4 watch tonight. Goodbye, my darlings. I send you all my love, and promise to come back home and <u>stay</u> home just as soon as possible.

When I get there, Bettsy, remind me to tell you — I love you!

12/7/44 Thursday morning

This is an ungodly early (8 a.m.) hour for your husband to be taking pen in hand but the inner voice is heckling most unpleasantly because of my failure to write yesterday so here goes now. Maybe, if all goes well, I can write twice today, to sort of atone for my error of omission.

There really wasn't any good excuse for letting you down except that I was unaccountably very sleepy after our visit to the isle - - and so I slept.

We left the ship quite early, about 9 a.m. and had more time on the island than our previous excursion but somehow it was less interesting; perhaps because I'm calloused to strange sights and places. Each of us was given three bottles of beer, but either there weren't enough sandwiches or someone beat us to the punch for we wangled only one each.

Then I wandered off to the beach, where I splashed and hunted seashells (no luck with pretty ones) for an hour or two, after which I traipsed about the island, watched a couple of the craps games for a while, then back to the ship via the LCI.

I spent a goodly part of my swimming time under water, prowling around the coral reef which is very lovely. I've learned (rather become accustomed) to keeping my eyes open in salt water without too much sting, so it was fun down there where the strangest little colored fishes play; pink and blue and yellow ones come swimming slowly past you then scurry for cover when you move.

It was about 2 p.m. when we got back to the ship, and I was so dopey when I came back aboard that I just dropped into my bunk and dreamed for about two hours. Woke at four, took a shower, and found four letters from you had come aboard. One letter was the Sunday night jobbie which you regretted, but Bettsy I must confess to a real thrill reading it, which I shall do many more times. You see Betty, away out here a fellow gets to sometimes feeling sorry for himself and sort of half convinces himself he's the loneliest person in all the world, etc. And then when the gal he loves gets honest enough to tell him how lonely she is he sort of forgets about being sorry for himself.

Admittedly a queer piece of psychology, something I can't understand myself let alone explain. But what I'm trying to get at is this. When you feel that way, write that way without regrets not only is it a real pleasure to read such a letter, it's <u>good</u> for me. And probably I should do the same, but I haven't yet shaken the subconscious looking-over-the-shoulder business and until I do I just find myself jamming the gears every time I really try to write.

Does the date on this letter strike you, Bettsy, or did you slip over it without noticing as I did until someone reminded me? [Pearl Harbor attack] Seems a long, long time ago when I look back to that Sunday afternoon in Johnstown when I heard the first radio flash, found Jess and John Sheridan and then lit out for the office where the three of us and Pat put out a very respectable extra in a couple hours.

So very many things have happened since that day when Fran was just a not too noticeable bump. The tide rolled in and when the truth is told we'll find we were all but engulfed, and now it's ebbing out again, surely but not nearly as swiftly as we all wish. And I can't help but wonder how much longer this must go on, for the one and the only thing I really want now or even shall in the future is to be back with you and the kids, living our own lives in our own quiet way.

Yes, my darling, I am homesick, have been since the moment I left you and will be until the moment I come back to stay. That isn't just words, either, for homesickness hurts and you know it as well or better than I. But still down inside me something says this is a job that must be done, not only for us and our kids but theirs too. And while I hate the job like sin I'm afraid that I should have to undertake it all over again if I had the chance. I'll hold no grudge against the men who could have come, perhaps should have come, and didn't. But at least I'll be able to hold up my own head.

What a dolorous letter but if nothing else this should tell you I love you so much it hurts, and always will. And maybe tonite I can find something cheery and chattery to talk about. 'Bye for now, my sweetheart, and remember to save me a kiss.

12/8/44 Friday afternoon

This is one of those times when I feel completely helpless and hapless as I sit down to write to you for there is so very little to tell you of me that's worth putting on paper, and nothing in my thoughts that hasn't been said or written a million or so times that it just doesn't seem possible I can scrape together even enough words to make a letter. But here goes, with the hope the resultant missive will be better than the preliminary outline.

It has been another blistering hot day, perhaps the hottest sun I've ever encountered despite a few sprinkling showers. Only a steady breeze keeps us from roasting - - perhaps frying would be a better word since we're on steel decks most of the time.

Perhaps because of the heat we didn't get much work done this morning, but I'm not worried for our mounts are in pretty good shape and all our major jobs should be completed tomorrow. From then on our work should be much easier.

All this afternoon I've been on watch, and because of that and a tracking drill was unable to get to Mass. A priest from another ship came aboard since this was a holy day: hope he'll be able to come back Sunday.

So much for today. After writing yesterday morning I worked through the afternoon and last evening when I thought I might pen a second letter to you, I wrote four others to pretty much clean up my correspondence backlog.

Slept again last night in the open, my cot nestled beneath the skimmer and expect that's where I'll snooze until and unless we get into colder weather. Can you imagine sleeping outdoors in December, without even a blanket?

And that, my darling, are the very small events of another day in my life. Understand it's not quite as drab as all that for I enjoy most of these men , and as would seem natural enough we spend a good deal of time gabbing, mostly about home and the war; where they've been and what they've done and had done to them, and what's going to happen next.

Believe me these boys who have been on here three years and more, through Pearl Harbor, the Solomons, Kwajelain, Truck, Polau, etc. can spin some tall yarns. And there are quite a few men aboard who have swum away or been taken off a sinking warship, notably the Chicago sunk nearly two years ago. They don't talk much about that.

This talk of home is interesting, too, and I find a number of surprising factors.

One of them is the surprisingly (to me at least, for I had suspected much worse) good morals of the boys. This possibly can be attributed in large part to their youth, for I seem to notice the older men are the more ribald. Now don't get me wrong, you can't find a set of incipient wings in the entire crew (possibly ex-cepting myself!!), but as I say I had expected much worse.

Surprise, too, is the postwar planning for there seems to be big percentage who want to stay on the sea. However most of them are thinking of the Merchant Marine and I believe they've been influenced by stories of the fat pay merchant sailors are reported to get.

Some, however, want to stay in the Navy, and with many I think it's because they feel they've dropped behind the rest of the world and see in the Navy a safe and relatively easy and certain living until their 20-years service is up; and beyond that a pension and then freedom. And a few want to see the rest of the world.

Through the lonely hours of my night watches - - and often in the daytime too - - I find my thoughts turning back across the sea, across the mountains and the plains to a quiet little town where I know you and the little ones are waiting for me.

I can sit here looking out across the restless sea and up at the star-filled skies with my mind filled with pictures of all of you. And memories of our moments and hours together that make living out here a whole lot easier to bear. With these thoughts I live a good deal of the time by myself, and some of the boys think me a bit queer because of it. But the memories are so much more wonderful than the present that I don't think you'll scold me overly much for preferring them.

As seems rational enough, I'm changing out here in this totally strange environment. One shift is that I'm slowly turning away from the garrulity that has always been one of my earmarks. I find myself more and more content to be a listener, keeping my own thoughts to myself instead of blurting them out. There are other changes too, possibly more noticeable to an outsider than the one I've mentioned, but the range is too close for me to see them.

However I believe some of my physical habits will be altered permanently, for a real benefit to me. My appetite has changed and I doubt if I'll ever be the trencherman I once was. Nor shall I allow myself to backslide into such miserable physical condition as I was when I came in. And whether it's a cause or a result of my improved condition, I'm not nearly such a sleepyhead any more, could in fact kick myself for having snoozed away so many hours we might have spent together.

All of which boils down, my Betty, to the simple truth that my heart is now and always filled with you; that my thoughts are only of and for you, and I am waiting only for our reunion, when I can be living again.

That, my dearest, is because I love you with all my heart. And

I always have -- And I always will.

12/12/44 Tuesday afternoon

It has been two whole days since last I wrote, but since I haven't the faintest idea when you'll get this, I'm hoping you won't mind the lapse too much. As usual there was and is little to be said besides which we've been sailing through quite the roughest seas I've encountered and that discomfort made more acute my laziness, or whatever you wish to call it.

I mentioned rough seas, and believe me they really are; waves 30 feet and more high and the whole ocean flecked with white caps every way you look. I doubt if you can imagine what such seas do to a big ship like this, but to a seagoing civilian it's a little less than pleasant. Most of the time you feel like you are on a see-saw as a wave slides under the ship hoisting first the bow, then teetering at the fulcrum, then sliding back to the stern until you begin to wonder if you didn't get into the submarine service after all for sometimes the whole bow is under water.

Add to that an almost constant sideways roll, usually through an arc of about 20 degrees but often more than that when we're turning and you can begin to understand why the poets sing of the "bounding main" and "rolling deep." Phooey on that from me.

Now don't get me wrong, I have not been seasick - - yet. But all the motion and commotion causes a mild upset and lassitude that makes me want to sleep and do nothing else. I don't want or even care about eating, but haven't missed a meal for I'd hate to miss one and then have several more miss me.

Whew, such writing. Hope you can make it out though for it's the best I can do. Larry Plume, my teammate in the director crew, and I are on watch up in the director, a roughly circular steel tub about five feet in diameter, high on the after superstructure. There isn't much room, to start with, and of course the ship is far from steady. But I'm squatting to write between tracking drills, while he wears the phones. He's a nice guy, one of Frisco's veterans; 24 years old but looks 30.

Walts remains, and is very likely to stay my best friend aboard ship. He's still unhappy as a deckhand, and his chance for gun striking seems to have faded for the moment, but he'll get on eventually and be a good one, too. Incidentally, we see less and less of Svoboda, who is in another section; on another gun, and stands watches at a different time in a different place than Walts and I. Svoboda seems to be drifting out of our orbit just as he drifted into it while we were Shoemaker.

It would seem I'm just not fated to sit down and write a letter to you without interruptions. Three times since this was started I've had to put it aside temporarily for drills and each time it becomes more difficult to resume.

Worst of it is that I'm afraid all my recent letters have been more than slightly on the lugubrious side and they may give you a picture of a weak old man wasting away of sheer loneliness. Dammit of course I'm lonely but not to the point of depreciation for I know the only way I can help myself get home soon is by staying "on the ball" out here and doing whatever I'm told to the best of my ability. And I'm doing that, Bettsy, and will continue to do it so long as necessary, thinking all the time of course of my one and only desire and objective.

The other day I was squatted in the mess hall, trying to scribble when the radio played that old familiar "Smoke Gets In Your Eyes" from Roberta. Does that take you, too, back to 1934 and York? Remember how I drove there to see you one Saturday and we sat through the picture twice, enjoying very moment of it. We were young then and the world a very much different and wonderfully pleasant one. Please God we can recapture those days soon.

Somehow tonight you and our little ones seem even more near and dear to me than usual, if that's possible. No, I don't mean I can see the end of this thing, not by too much, but you have been in my thoughts so constantly, the little things we both love so much keep coming back to warm me in my loneliness.

With which your husband runs plumb out of words, hence this missive stops abruptly. There are lots of words down inside me, darling, that would come out if I could whisper in your ear but I'll just have to save those special ones for the time being.

But I do love you, my dearest, with all my heart and I'll tell you about it some day. Give the little ones an extra special hug and kiss from their Daddy to start the New Year right, and mark another debt for me to pay you when I come home. 'Bye, my Bettsy, for now and I'll try to be a little more faithful with the letters until that happy day when we no longer need to write.

Chapter 9
FRISCO AT WAR - PART TWO
TYPHOON, FIRST BATTLE, MAN OVERBOARD, FEAR
12/19/44 to 1/31/45

12/19/44 Tuesday morning

As usual, my best intentions of writing every day have "gone south," as Bobby Burns put it, but this time through no fault of mine for it has been physically impossible to write during the past two days.

I mean impossible too, for even now with the sea comparatively calm it's difficult to scribble, and it simply couldn't be done while we pitched and rolled through the wildest storm I have ever seen. It has been a terrifying experience for me; for it just didn't seem possible the ship could hold together or be prevented from turning over. But she did come through nobly, and we didn't lose a man which to me speaks volumes for the way we were handled and guided.

Through the peak of the storm no man ventured onto the main decks, and even below decks in the compartment and mess halls we had to hang on pretty firmly. No attempt was made to set up tables or serve meals yesterday; sandwiches were made up and distributed and my total for lunch and dinner was two sandwiches, a cup of broth and an apple!

Ropes were strung about the mess halls as hand rails, and quite a few of the crew spent most of their time there; drinking cup after cup of mud. Me, I still can't like the stuff, so let it alone, but doing so leaves me out of some of the friendly little circles where 3 to 6 or 8 guys squat in a ring, passing the mud mug from hand to hand until it's empty. Then there's a debate about whose turn it is to "make the run" until someone gets up, ambles over to the urn and sugar bowl and comes back with a full cup to start the cycle again.

It was even difficult to remain in our bunks, but that's where I spent most of my time alternately praying, thinking of you and dozing. Looking back now I don't know which of those endeavors consumed most of the time, but I'm not ashamed to confess that I was afraid. I doubt if I shall be afraid again in a storm, now that I know what this sturdy ship can take and yet come through unscathed.

Yet with it all the sight from topside, where we stood our watches on the boat deck, was so awesome it was fascinating. Great green waves, some of them must have been 100 feet from trough to peak, surging at us endlessly, one after another like rows of marching giants. Some broke and collapsed in foaming spindrift before reaching us. Others picked the ship up and tossed it like a match so that we rolled first to one side and then the other until it seemed we never regain an even keel. And still others just surged in over us, burying the bow and the fantail under feet and tons of water.

With it all a terrific wind that flung spray and rain like shotgun pellets so that no one could face into it, and over all lowering clouds that completely blotted out the sun. At times we could not see 50 yards in any direction.

Altogether it was for many hours the most spectacular sight I've ever seen, and even at times when I was not on watch something dragged me up here as a spectator. Yet while it is something I shall never forget, I am perfectly willing to let it remain the only storm I shall have to remember. Incidentally, I was not at any time even a little bit seasick, so that I'm ready to say now I'm not susceptible to mal-de-mer.

"Huh" she says, "There he goes bragging."

And that my darling is how come no letters. Think you can forgive me if I promise not to let anything else interfere?

One thing troubles me: I'm beginning to lose a clear mental picture of our kids, especially Fran, for I know they must have grown and changed amazingly since last May. Was it only that long ago since I saw them? Seems at least a million years.

Perhaps the loss is due to the fact that I've been quite a spell without any mail, but I'm afraid it goes deeper than that. Of course I can conjure memories of how they looked and what they said and did in Philly, but the only clear picture I can bring from Somerset is the way they looked as we tucked them into bed the night before I left. Wonder if they aren't having the same trouble with me.

As for you, praise be, it's different for I shall always be able to paint an imaginative picture of my girl friend in any setting I choose, and the one that I found easiest was of you and the snowy night. I can see you right now, almost as well with my eyes, curled up in bed with a few ancient letters scattered around while you write your nightly missive. Outside I could all but hear the blizzard howling, and I suspected too you might be a little happier if you had your Armstrong heater.

Well, my darling, some day we shall have all the things we want together again, and believe me it's going to take a mighty powerful lever to pry us apart after that. I think I was a reasonably home-loving husband and father before I left, but believe me when this is over I'm going to stick so close you'll think you have another kid on your apron strings.

That, Bettsy, would be because I have learned how really essential you are to my life, and also because I love you.

12/22/44 Friday evening

And so it seems I have again reneged on my promise of a daily letter, and so I'm forced to the conclusion said promise never should have been made. In its place I can only substitute to write every possible chance, and make a special effort to see there are one or more letters in every outgoing mail.

I've had mail today - - five whole gorgeous wonderful letters from you plus one from our son. Thank you Bettsy for the grandest Christmas present you could have sent me. I've devoured them all and will hit them again tonight.

There's a lot to comment about them but I will confine my remarks to our three sprouts. Bucky's letter was much the best he has written, both as to script and continuity. Your tale about Chubbin and her birthday gift really choked me up. I could just hear her saying sleepily from her bed in that darkened room "Thank you berry much." I 'm glad to hear that Fran will get a big boy haircut and that he has been a good boy at Mass.

There isn't a whole lot to report of the last few days except that I've been kept pretty busy working and standing watches. But while I should have found writing time somehow, I didn't and can only say I'm sorry.

Did sneak off into a corner for a couple of hours last night to play poker with a couple of the guys, and enjoyed it very much. Gambling, you know, is strictly forbidden by the Navy, but the guys do take a chance and like stolen fruit it's that much sweeter. I came out - - this is the truth, so help me - - exactly even except that I exchanged my last $5 in cash for an equal amount owed to me but out here money means little and I'll get along ok until payday.

The sea is always dangerous as I saw yesterday when, as two of us were washing up for lunch, my companion looked out the porthole and exclaimed "Hell's fire there goes a man overboard"! I looked out, too, and saw the man floating past, followed by a string of life jackets thrown towards him by other men on the main deck as he passed them. For some time we could see him bobbing in the wake, and of course our escort put on full steam toward the spot. But the sea is unbelievably huge, and a lone man in the water infinitesimal, and as far as I know he was never found. I was told later he was standing on the forward part of the ship when the bow dipped into a wave; tons of water rushing across the deck carried him off like wind-blown chaff.

Some time has elapsed, about 18 hours to be exact and it's now Saturday morning - - last shopping day before Christmas back home and I'll bet it's a frantic one. Never a guy to enjoy shopping in crowds, I'd nevertheless be a little more than slightly enjoyed to have the opportunity today. Yes, my darling, that's just another of the many little joys of home I shall appreciate when I get back there. Weird thing to wish for isn't it?

Despite the time passage, there doesn't seem to be a whole lot more to write, so I'll stop now and maybe be able to restart this afternoon. Bye my Bettsy. Remind me some time to tell you I love you, and to tell the same thing to our little ones first chance I get.

12/25/44 Monday (Christmas afternoon)

And so it came to pass that at the very hour all of you were trudging through the midnight snows to Mass, I was kneeling on the rusty steel hanger deck before an improvised altar assisting at the same sacrifice. An odd coincidence, to be sure, yet one that brought me a whole lot closer to all of you.

In a large measure because of that I have had the best possible Christmas out here although I must admit it still wasn't good enough to chase the blues and loneliness that seem to have become a part of my life - - and must of necessity stay a part until this whole damnable business is over.

Of course there was another factor in making my Christmas

merry (a <u>very</u> relative term), for as you can judge from the fact we had Mass aboard we're back in port again and soon after we arrived a veritable deluge of mail descended on us, which is one of the finest presents a guy out here can get! Blue and lonely, I had no taste for the movie last night so crawled into my bunk where I was lying restlessly when the first mail call brought me a letter from you and some cards. After reading your letter I returned to my bunk and peacefully dropped off to sleep.

This morning there was more, lots more, for along with 4 letters from you, one from Buck, a letter from Harley Smith and a couple of envelopes full of clippings. So I spent almost all of my four-hour watch reading and now must settle down to some heavy-duty writing in my spare time.

Please tell Bucky his letter was a grand Christmas present, much the best be has written and I'm so proud of his improvement and so glad he's not taking writing as a chore. Honest, Sonny, I'll answer just as soon as I can, within the next few days, and will try to be a little more faithful although I know he'll understand that my writing time and opportunities are restricted.

And our daughter is doing very well in school, too, from the sample of the work you sent me. And Fran being a good boy in Church is swell news, too.

From all of which you can correctly assume I'm downright proud of our offspring and more than ever convinced they're the world's most wonderful young ones. Of course, being the children of the grandest girl in the world they could hardly miss being tops, but then they had to assume quite a handicap on the paternal side.

Your storm sounds wonderfully interesting; wish I could have been there for just to read about it takes me back to the old days. I guess I'll never forget one winter when I was about 10 years old that the heavy snow came early and never melted so that all through the winter there were great piles of packed snow, higher than my head, along all the sidewalks. We kids going to school got a big thrill out of running along the tops of the piles; I suppose Bucky is doing the same thing now, more power to him.

Out here, of course is by far the strangest Christmas I've ever spent for only a swift breeze keeps it from being a roasting hot day; brilliant sunshine, white clouds against the blue sky; boats skipping about among the anchored ships for all the world like those funny little bugs we called water skippers. In the distance green palm trees and the white sand beach of our coral isle and beyond that the rolling surf surging and breaking in white froth against the barrier reef.

Spent all morning lounging about the guns, for even in such a protected harbor, the Navy does not relax its vigilance. Any visitor would receive a more-than-warm welcome, believe me.

Christmas dinner was good, the cooks, et al really having extended themselves to do a job. Turkey, of course, and roast pork too; mashed potatoes, filling and gravy; corn and cranberries; celery, olives and mixed pickles; all topped of by apple pie-a-la-mode, an apple, a cigar and some hard candy. It was good, too, much the best meal I've eaten aboard ship. But I'd trade the whole thing for a cheese sandwich if we could be together to share it.

But the strangest - - in some ways the most painful and yet the nicest - - coincidence was our Mass at 2 p.m. For as I figure it we're just 14 hours ahead of you in time so that 2 p.m. Christmas Day to us is at the same instant midnight Christmas Eve to you. The priest, coming aboard again from another ship, was the same one for whom I served once before, a Chicago native, quite young. He gave us all general absolution, and 106 men went to communion. I went to confession after Mass, since he had not had opportunity to hear us all earlier.

Afterwards, though, there was none of the walk home through the snowy night that has always meant so much to me, nor any family party such as I hope all of you had and enjoyed. And did the kids' eyes pop when they saw what Santa brought and did you all have fun and chatter like magpies as we always used to do?

I find myself now trying not to think of it for my eyes are sweating (must be the smoke from the stacks) and an apple (probably the one I ate at noon) is sticking in my throat but do want to hear about every little thing that went on. Felt much the same way at Mass too, especially while the priest was reading the old familiar gospel that has been a <u>part</u> of every Christmas in my life.

Time out for a bit, I'm going to supper.

There, that didn't take too long and here I am back on the boat deck to write again - - still feel in sort of a chatty mood; it's a lovely evening.

A lot of the guys chose last night to get drunk on the liquor they've been hoarding since we left the states - - or whatever else sailors find alcoholic out here. Anyway there were several parties, a couple of them lasting through the night, and I've seen some gorgeous hangovers today. Of course we're all wishing out here, just as you are at home, that by another Christmas this will be all over and all of us can go back to living again. Let's look ahead a bit.

First of all I can't for the life of me see how it's possible for this to be over by then, let alone to have demobilization well under way. The Nazi theater is proving to be a long-lived, hand fighting war but I still believe the end over there is only months away. The new drive is strongly reminiscent on Ludendorff's last smash in June, 1918, that was stopped at the Second Battle of the Marne. Seems to me history is very likely to repeat over there, perhaps even a quicker ending for if Russia lets go a Sunday punch soon the weight should be too heavy.

But there's still a helluva lot of war to be fought out here and even after the Europe war is ended there must be an interval of months before any substantial portion of our fighting men, equipment and supplies can be brought to bear against Japan. Me, I'm highly dubious that Russia will throw any great weight there, although it's reasonable to expect she'll be willing to open some bases to us if she can gain sufficiently thereby. Perhaps those bases may be the balancing weight in some Polish or Balkan deal. Obviously Stalin's principal interest is there, and the recent Soviet-French pact seems to me a Stalin maneuver to get peace-talkers on his side; at the same time DeGaulle is trying to hoist France's now-worthless name back to the old position of rivalry with Britain by hooking on the Soviet bandwagon.

And France, of little or no aid in Europe now, will be worthless out here while I'll be surprised if the British so much as regain Burma and Singapore which leaves the big job to your Uncle Sam, who can do it but will require a little time. Australia will help, of course, and Canada may, but their share will be only fractious.

From all of which I don't see how we can win in '45. I pray I'm wrong, but as an old reporter must present the facts as I get them.

Even if the war continues, there's at least a fair chance I'll be home within the next year or so. And that, again, is provided all goes reasonably well and we don't get banged up too badly. You see, darling, cruisers are after all machines, and can stand only a certain amount of wear before they pass their peak of efficiency and begin to deteriorate. And when deterioration reaches a certain stage then major repairs must be undertaken and there just aren't facilities out here for everything that must be done.

And so I dare to hope that this New Year which is almost upon us will bring you and I and our family back together again even if only for a little while. And always praying, too, that the end which I cannot now see will come about and we will be together again for always.

So, this Christmas evening (I am glad it's over.), I say good-night and may the Babe of Bethlehem watch over and keep all my darlings safe for me until I come home. I'll not need a reminder, either, to tell you - - all of you - - I love you.

12-26-44 Tuesday evening

Well Christmas has come and gone and for the first time in 32 years I can say honestly I'm glad to see it over. It really wasn't so bad as I feared it would be for your letters - - I read them all three times - - were the grandest thing that ever could have come to me out here. And the Mass meant a lot, too, so that all in all, the day wasn't too bad.

Your husband is more than a little tired tonight for it's been a long day of hard work. The storms jammed up one of our mounts so that it wouldn't turn freely, and we had to tear the whole thing down, make repairs and then put it back together again. and cleaned the gun, too. Now tomorrow we must get our other three guns cleaned up and then, if all goes well, I shall go back to our coral isle nest for a couple of bottles of beer. As nearly as I can figure it, I've been on land less than 60 hours in the past 60 days, and it's likely to get worse before it gets better

Anyhow, my first combat operation is over, and from it I've learned two real lessons:

1. I'm very sure I made the right choice between the Army and the Navy, and 2. I fully realize what Churchill meant when he said "Never did so many owe so much to so few."

As to the first, my original guess that the Navy would be better living and eating conditions has come out 100 percent correct, and it seems to me there is an added advantage in fighting conditions, for we never will have to fight day and night without stopping for days and weeks on end as the boys in France must be doing now. They are the ones who are really fighting this war taking a gamble with life every time they go out against the enemy in terrible weather with machines that can and do break down. My hat's off to them - - they do a great job!

I've come to the conclusion that this is not the place for a settled old married man like me. These kids are so much more adjustable, can fit themselves into almost any life so that it must be admitted they do in many ways make better fighting men. Me, I have so many wonderful moments to look back on that many of them never will be fortunate enough to know, yet they only make me wish all the more that I were back there adding new moments to my memories.

I had thought last night I might write or at least start another letter to you, but instead got to re-reading my mail and even collected another letter from the final sorting, which made me a total of 16 for the day, not tooo bad. Then I decided since one of the lot was a Christmas card from Martha Hawley, the girl I met in Racine, to drop her a line since the card was for both Don Reed and I, and was forwarded from Great Lakes. We haven't heard anything from or about Reed, Wunder or any of the old gang.

Somehow the writing spark has left me. Now if I only could sit down and talk to you I know I'd babble on for hours without stopping. But stop now I must. However, if I were to talk to you, most of my hours-long babbling would be likely to sound like a broken record, repeating itself over and over again, and I can put that much of it down here, just for the record. I love you - - and always will.

12/27/44 Wednesday night

Dear Bucky:

Been a long time since I sat down to write to you but I hope you'll understand that I haven't written more often only because there is so little time or opportunity out here.

On the other hand you have been very faithful with your letters and I want you to know that each one of them is a big thrill to me. They show me, too, better than words from someone else could tell, how you are growing and advancing, something I would very much prefer to see at close range but I'm out of luck on that score for the present so keep the letters coming.

By the way, ask Mother to measure you, and Chubbin and

Fran, then all three of you get weighed and you can give me the results in your next letter. **(Whoops! Out of ink so I'm shifting colors in the middle of the letter.)**

Back a good many years ago when I was a little boy in that same house we kids would get together occasionally in the kitchen and measure each other against the board at the foot of the back stairs. I think your grandmother will remember, and perhaps some of the marks are there yet if they're not too deeply buried by successive paintings.

Your snow back there sounds very interesting, and I wonder if Santa was able to dig deep enough into his stock to find a sled for you. Those hills are grand fun in the wintertime; perhaps next winter we all can enjoy them together - - Mother, Chubbin, Fran and you and I.

And some day I'll be teaching you to ski, too. I'll leave the ice skating to your mother, whose ankles probably are stronger than mine. (Aside to Betty: I was going to add something about being better-padded in an essential place, but guess I'd better not.)

I'm looking forward to a long Christmas letter telling me all about what Santa brought, what the tree looked like, and most of all about the family party, for that's the most fun of all.

That will be my real Christmas, for out here we didn't and couldn't have much. Matter of fact there isn't much Christmas anywhere without you young ones around.

From all of which you can judge I'm more than a little interested in hearing from you. Letters are always the best thing that can happen to a guy out here but I'll forgive you for losing the one Mother wrote if you'll be more careful with them in the future, and write as often as you can yourself.

Tell Chubbin and Fran I'll write to them the first moment I get. I can't do it tonight though, for I'm due to go on

watch shortly.

All my love, Sonny, and be a good boy, for you must be the man of the family until I come back.

Your Dad

12/28/44 Thursday night

As always it would be heaven to sit down and <u>talk</u> with you tonight, but at this long range I don't feel particularly chatty so that this is not apt to be much of a letter. However much of it there is will at least tell you I'm thinking of you and loving you as I always will.

Just why I'm tired and dispirited tonight I can't quite figure out, for it's been an easy do-nothing day. Perhaps it's because I have been a bit short on sleep the past two nights for last night I completely forgot about having the midnight-to-four watch until I was writing Bucky's letter (?). Which was one reason I broke off so abruptly, for it was then 9:30 and I had to get up at 11:30.

Took my blanket with me and slept on the deck for an hour until it was my turn to go on lookout for an hour. Afterwards I climbed up to the forward director, highest part of the ship, where I sat for an hour in the wind-washed moonlight talking post-war plans with a young fire controlman. Then I went back to the mount, slept for another hour until the watch was relieved whereupon I took my blanket, went back to my battle station and curled up for a couple hours more snoozing.

After breakfast, the liberty party shoved off for the coral isle, where Walts and I got four cans of beer but I drank only three and then went swimming for an hour or so, spent part of the time hunting seashells. I'm going to pack them some way and mail them separately to you.From the beach I wandered a while past a couple crude native cemeteries - - they built a sort of sarcophagus over the graves, big flat stones much like the ancient Saxtons used in England and can now be seen at Stonehenge - - and eventually

I drifted back to the grove where the crap games were going full blast.

One fellow at one of the tables had a roll of bills in his hand that must have totaled $1,000, and he was betting on anything and everything, often he had more than $150 riding on a single roll. He was doing right well, too, for when I left the fistful was still increasing. I get a kick out of watching that kind of gambling even though I have no urge to step in myself - - nor have I the money.

We came back to our ship about two o'clock, found chow waiting for us, and after I ate I worked until 4:30 on the guns, sat around listening to some of the guys chatter for an hour, took a shower and that brings me up to the start of this letter. Which, I'm proud to note, is at least a little more long-winded than I expected.

Apropos of nothing at all, I meant to tell you in the paragraph where I mentioned I'd had a shower that the crew's nickname for shower is "douche" and the ever-crowded shower room is of course the "douche room." Just thought you might be interested.

There are many such names in the ship's lingo, most of them bawdy or worse. For instance, two of our fairly regular (about once a week) breakfasts are a peculiarly watery concoction of boiled hamburger (grains) and tomatoes which is spooned onto toast, and small link sausages usually deep-fried quite hard. The former is "sh_t on the shingle" and the latter, more obviously, "dog sh_t." But a man has to eat something and often I don't bother!

By the way, I hope you've learned by now to obtain almost as much information from my letters by those things left unsaid as by what I can tell you directly. Naturally much of what we do out here cannot be reported, such as when we enter or leave port, or expect to do so. Incidentally, censorship out here differs sharply, and in many ways from censorship as I knew it under the newspaper code.

That slurping noise you've been hearing is the pump draining the last drops from my well of information for the night, my dearest, so here this epistle ends. But I've done more - - if not better - - than I expected. And as I said at the start, at least you can tell I'm thinking of you and loving you as I always will.

This is a letter to Jess James, who was just given an editor's job as his Navy assignment. It was initially rejected by the censors. It is not known when it was received in Somerset.

12-28-44 Thursday night

Dear Editor:

And weren't you the guy I somewhat jocularly labeled leg-man a few weeks back? Betty, as you may have guessed, sent me The Democrat clipping of your promotion (?) so herewith my congratulations or condolences as you choose. I suspect the latter to be more appropriate. Do you get another stripe on that crow?

Anyhow, I've been trying for some time to get around to this, and have tried, too, to bum a typewriter on the theory my thoughts (?) might flow more freely with a mill under my fingers. But no soap on that and conscience is whipping me so here goes.

I think, John, I've seen enough of what goes on out here to begin to have some definite conclusions about the whole thing, and I begin to suspect for the first time in my 8-month Navy career, that if I had known then what I know now I might have at least debated a little longer before jumping in. Yet a man must live with himself, and down inside me I know that at some future date we would have found it hard to look our sons in the eye had we stayed home.

Here is some background on what has been happening to me. I've been through my first operation, plus a real storm at sea, a man overboard and my feet have been on dry land about twice in 60 days. I've heard the bugle squeal "ta-ta, ta-ta" - - etc. for A.A.

defense more than once, and I've had the pleasant privilege of seeing the fiery glow that I know was a Jap plane going down in flames.

That, I think is as much as I can tell you of what's happening, but what I think you will be more interested in is what its done to me.

First and foremost I've been afraid - - a cold, very real fear that grips your guts beyond all imagination - - for the first time in my life. I'm afraid that I had thought or at least hoped the heat and excitement of action would save me that, but it isn't so. The first notes of that bugle call send chills up and down my spine even as I scramble to my battle station, and they stay there until the same bugle blows "secure."

But happily, even while it hurts, I can keep control, and my only reaction is to want to start fighting back. Some of the guys say (we're very frank out here; fear is no shame so long as a man does his job) their first reaction is to want to hunt a safe hole to hide in. That hasn't happened to me, and I hope it won't.

Strangely, though, my worst fright came from the sea, and not the enemy, for the storm that hit us was a whopper and for hours on end my un-nautical brain couldn't believe the ship possibly could shake off those huge waves and come back right-side up against the tearing wind. That, my friend, was the bottom of the abyss, for I was absolutely helpless to aid in that fight and thereby aid myself. And I knew that if the ship didn't come back up from any one of those rolls that had me hanging on to keep my feet my chances were somewhat less than those of the proverbial snowball.

And long after the storm had subsided, a wave reached up to snatch a man off our forecastle. I happened to be looking out a porthole when he went floating, screaming, past, followed by a string of life jackets tossed after him by other men. For a mile or more I could see him bobbing in the wake. Of course our escort started for him immediately, but he never was found.

But this sturdy ship did come through, beautifully, and I doubt very much that I shall again be afraid that way. Even while the storm frightened me it fascinated me so that I couldn't take my eyes off the scene. Looking back, it was an awesome and brutally magnificent spectacle; one that since I'm safely through I should not have wanted to miss even though I can get along nicely without another.

Another thing I've learned is the real truth of Churchill's 1940 crack about "never did so many owe so much to so few." They're fighting this war, Jess, far more than I ever realized and taking the biggest gamble in the world every time they go out, while they do their job and they come back. I find myself, watching a laden plane trying to climb, wanting to put my shoulder under a plane and lift. And when they come back I'm mentally on tiptoe as though that might help ease them down safely. The loveliest sight I can think of (away from home, I mean) is a flock of Hell Cats heading out to head off trouble.

With it all, I'm more than ever convinced we made the right choice between the armed services. Food (still bad but always better than K-rations) and living quarters (crowded but not muddy) are superior, and while we may have to fight dammed hard at times, there can't possibly be any of the day and night for days unending stuff that the boys in France are getting now.

And I'm proud and happy to be on this ship, for she's sturdy, ably handled and plenty powerful. All things being relative (as you and I always insisted) this is a good deal.

On the other side of the ledger, I find myself frequently regretting the fact - - as you must be too - - that I didn't try Washington on that long-ago commission application. Out here, just as back there, this is an officers' Navy and their advantages are many. But above and beyond that, the officers as a whole are the kind of people you and I have been used to associating with and you can't help wishing that at least you could have brought some of these associations to this out of the way place.

Now don't get me wrong, the crew as a whole is a <u>good</u> bunch of <u>youngsters</u> and they've treated me swell. But there is such a vast difference in background and experience and more often than not, find myself sort of an outsider. They call me "Pop" and "Old Man," for to most of them my 33 years seem like a century. And almost to a man they think me a queer old duffer who should have stayed home.

As a matter of fact, I'm ready to admit now it seems unlikely that I can or will do anything out here that wouldn't have been done probably as effectively or perhaps more so had I remained a civilian. But a man must live with himself, and at least our consciences will be clear.

And so I would suggest that you and Vone stop butting your heads against the stone wall of sea duty and stay where you are, doing what you can, until this damm thing is over. Believe me, you are not needed out here unless you have some very real skill for war, and I don't believe you have that any more than I, who am not indispensable to the conduct of this war.

It's been more than half a year since we were home, and it looks like a much longer stretch before we get there again, which it seems to me is a sufficient sacrifice. Meanwhile, make all preparations to get the hell back to your own editor's chair at the earliest possible moment. There you'll have a <u>real</u> job to do.

Is this thing as lugubrious as I'm afraid it is? I don't dare re-read it for if I do you're apt to have no letter at all, but I've been trying to give you a sort of impression as honest as possible and it just may be that my current mood looks to the darker side and so weights the scale.

Don't get the idea I've become morbid, any more than I've become joyful. This is a tough job out here and the only part any sane man relishes is anticipation of the moment he can mark it finished and start for home. That's the thought uppermost in all our minds all the time.

You'll note I refer to you and Vone, although your reference to his _____, hospital confinement and imminent "discharge" was a bit ambiguous. Hope there's a letter on the way from you clarifying that and filling me in on your latest comings and goings. If not pls do SAP.

Happy New Year, John, and I know you'll understand that only in one event can it be <u>happy</u>.

As ever
Chuck

12/31/44 Sunday night

A new year is almost upon us out here in the watery world where a golden moon paves a path to our ship over the gently rolling waters. Here it is 9 p.m. but at the moment you probably are sitting in Church and New Year's Eve is still some hours away. Me, I've just come off watch and have what we sailors call "all night in," the one night in four during which rotation of the watches enables us to sleep through from 8 p.m. until reveille for we need not go on watch until 8 a.m.

This is a strange ending, my dearest for the strangest and in one way the most unhappy year we've known. I wonder what the New Year will bring us? All I - - and millions of others ask for is peace and home but at this distance they would seem to be only things to pray for, without any concrete hope of attaining.

Unlike some of the others here I have no hankering for a celebration, a party - - most of them think of it only as a good opportunity to get uproariously drunk going to waste. I suspect there will be some partying aboard, but not nearly so much as there was Christmas Eve when we were in port. Out here life takes on a much more serious aspect.

One year ago tonight we were together, and if memory serves me right over at the Smiths enjoying a pleasant evening with no thought that the approaching year would keep us apart ¾ of its time and in the end find half a world of water and mountains and plains separating me from those I love. Wherever we were that last December 31, we were together and I must admit now that I did not really realize then how happy and how fortunate I was - - being with you.

Looking back, I know now that I must have been taking it all too much for granted, as I have most of the good things of life. But that, among other things, will be changed when I come home. Looking ahead, I can't help wondering how 1945 will turn out for us. I suppose you and millions of others like you and I are doing the same thing and there's no need to name the universal wish, but as yet we can only pray and hope for the end is not yet visible. What that end will be there is no longer is any reasonable doubt: but when it will come, aye there's the rub.

As you can see from the date, I didn't write yesterday, principally because I had little or nothing to say, hadn't the urge to write, nor any necessity for it would have gotten to you no sooner than this. So I spent a lazy day dozing and reading the first book I've picked up in months aside from gunnery texts. It was some rootin', tootin' shootin' western which I enjoyed although I've forgotten the name if indeed I ever noted it.

Today I went to church - - we Catholics sang a couple of hymns, said the rosary and listened to our Protestant chaplain read the epistle and gospel when no priest was able to come aboard to say Mass. An ironic touch - - our chaplain carries a sheath knife strapped to his belt as do many of the officers and men and sometimes apparently forgets to take it off while he's conducting services. Afterwards I worked a bit, then "secured" for the day as we say when we quit. And I played a bit of poker in the afternoon, losing the net sum of $2.

And the letter I told you I wrote to Jess came back rejected, so must be saved until some future date, and I'll have to write another. I'm sorry about it, too, for on rereading it I still think it's a good letter, and that he and you too would be much interested in. And the queerest part is that all of the information has already been written to you and passed by the censors - - unless you've been getting some severely clipped letters. But I'll send it along with the one to you that was turned back, and add them to our archives when this is all done.

Wonder how many letters we've written in the past nine months? Must be a couple of hundred each, and I know your total is greater than mine. Did I ever remember to thank you for them, my darling? Remind me some time.

And, as a special favor to me, would you give our little ones an extra big hug and each a kiss each as a New Years present from their Daddy. And let us all hope and pray that 1945 will bring us all to where I'll not need a letter, only a whisper, to tell you I love you with all my heart, and will forever.

1/6/45

Not a very good start for the New Year, is it, I mean my failure to write regularly? My apologies, dear. I did try to write yesterday, but honestly just couldn't find the time. But even though I haven't been writing my thoughts seem to have been of you and with you more than usual, if that's possible. Half a world away a guy needs something pretty solid to hang onto, and naturally I find myself leafing back through my memories to moments we've known, and trying to imagine, too, just where you are and what you're doing and saying at any particular moment.

However I do have a happy side as yesterday's mail call brought me two very swell letters from you and caused me to spend a whole four-hour watch last night just setting and dreaming; wishing and remembering too. Would it seem strange my darling, if I told you I am more than a little hungry for you? But there isn't much use thinking of that, though it's wonderful to remember.

Your letters brought me up to four days before Christmas and I'm hoping the next mail call - - when it comes - - will bring me your accounting of the big day. Now that it's in the past I don't mind thinking about it, and I'm downright anxious to hear all that happened.

Along with those two most important letters came a very swell note from Mary and a Christmas note from Jess supporting his ascendancy (or descent) to the editorship of Drydock. There wasn't much to the letter, but I think you'll be interested in these excerpts;

"I have my own idea of the proper kind of punishment for Herr Hitler: bring him over here and demand that he please each of the 14 captains in putting out this weekly navy propaganda sheet." x x x x.

"I'm going to get drunk on Christmas (we have a 72-hour liberty) but I assure you between drinks now and then Vone and I will raise our glasses and think Merry Christmas, Chuck, you old son of a gun and may we spend the next one with our families."

I want to make a point about censorship: anytime you get a clipped up letter don't fail to mention it, and perhaps you can make some reference that may enable me to identify the letter and guess at the excised parts. Thereby I could save myself some writing time, and the censors some trouble by not repeatedly making the same error since the only way we have of knowing something is not permitted is when a whole letter is rejected. I suspect that some of my recent letters have been very sharply censored.

In one letter you say you think we'll reverse roles, with you becoming the sleepyhead after I get back? We'll just have to see about that!

The same letter speaks of doing two weeks' washing and starting on the ironing, and I can't help remembering how (the way, I mean) I sometimes used to tease you while you were ironing. Remember? It wasn't always teasing, and sometimes ended very pleasantly, which perhaps is why I like to remember it, and why I'm thinking of it now. Wonder if your heart skips a beat or two, too?

And that, my Bettsy, is as far as I'm going just now. I know you'll know how I'm thinking and feeling and I'm just mean enough to hope that this will do the same thing to you. Is it necessary to tell you I love you, and miss you, more than anything or anyone in all the world? I think not, for you'll have read it unwritten before you get into this but just in case you haven't. I do love you my darling with all my heart and soul and body and will always.

1/12/45 Friday evening

Time flies past so fast out here I can't recall just how long it's been since last I wrote; however I know it's been at least two days, perhaps three and maybe even four. Which isn't right, I know, but I just haven't been able to do better for all my hours seem to be full.

I'm writing in the mess hall, sitting on a huge valve wheel with my pad propped on my knees which I keep bracing first to one side then the other against the roll of the ship. One feeble light bulb lights the big room, where a couple of guys are writing, and a score more are sprawled on the deck, reading, playing cards and just chattering. A couple of guys have spread their bedding on the deck where they'll be going to sleep in a little bit when the light goes out. They sleep there too, quite soundly, while all through the night others step over and around them going to and from the ever-changing watches or drinking a cup of the always present "mud."

There's been a big event - - the biggest we can have out here, mail call - - since I last wrote and it brought me three letters from you, one from Bucky, and two from my AP compatriots. Your letters brought me up to the night before Christmas, and I must confess there were apples all over the ocean when I read the letter you wrote that lonely night. Truth to tell, I haven't even had the nerve to reread it as I do all the others, though I shall tomorrow.

And even while it hurt to see so plainly what was in your mind and heart then, it somehow warmed me to know that despite all the miles between us we were thinking and feeling alike as we have so many times. I know that for me that night was by long odds the bluest and most lonely of all my life, and I know too that it must have been the identical thing for you.

And golly I hope you bounced back as quickly as I did, for once over that night it wasn't too bad. I'll know when I next hear from you.

And it seems that Bucky must have been feeling much as you and I, as indicated by the tone of his letter. I'm sorry for that, for I had hoped he would stay young enough to escape most of the pangs of our separation. But it's plain he's growing up and Lordy knows how I hate to miss it.

Another of your letters contained the snapshot of you, Chubbin and Fran and it becomes a treasured item in my collection - - the first picture to tell me the baby I left has become a boy and our lissome lass is fast growing to girlhood. I doubt very much if you can see it at close range and day by day the tremendous changes the picture brings me, and Betty I need pictures like that for studying them tells me more than many words.

As for you, I'll always be delighted with any picture, but your image is so burned in my brain that I would never need a photograph to refresh it. And you'll not be changing overly much, probably less than I.

To turn, as it were, from the abstract to the more concrete realities, the one new excuse I can offer for failing to write the past two days is that what little free time I've had has been devoted to completing my Gunners Mate progress course. I've been studying and will take the test tomorrow.

There should be more to this letter, I know, but where, what and how are verboten, and I don't think you need to be told that my nights and my days are full of thoughts and dreams of you and ours. I've seen your face in a million stars that are glittering company as we sit looking out across the sea. And every one of them knows I am always yours.

Anyhow, Green Eyes, (I haven't called you that in a long time, have I?) I do think of you almost every hour of every day and always I love you with all my heart.

1/18/45 Thursday afternoon

This scribbling is apt to be even worse than usual, for the ship is heaving so that even a salty (?) character like your husband finds it not only difficult to walk, but even to sit: I'm beginning to feel like the pendulum for an eight-day clock. But a guy has to write sometime, and this is the best moment I've found in some several days. I've just come off watch and have nearly an hour before chow.

We had our first mail call in a week which brought your very special Christmas Day letter and some clippings. I was napping in my bunk when mail call was sounded, scurried out to grab my share and settled back to read it like a miser counting his hoarded gold. And I was glad I did too, for somehow when I read of things I had wanted so much to be a part of, it got a little bit dampish around the edges and the breakfast apple bothered me no little. But I got over it quickly enough, and since have reread the letter a couple of times, just drinking in the picture you drew me; next best thing to being there.

I see Bucky becomes more like his father every day and I confess I got quite a chuckle out of him sending Sis downstairs to tell him where the hands were on the clock, so he'd know whether it was time to get up. The lazy lout!

Seems to me I remember Dad pulling some other sprouts about the house on a new sled on another Christmas that seems an awfully long time ago. But he was much too dignified <u>then</u> to go belly flopping down and wait for someone to pull him. But it was a grand letter, my darling, and one I'll be keeping for a while to cheer me up when I get blue.

Since I wrote you the other day, I have been given the dope on my progress test, which was to me disappointing although I was told my mark was very good, 3.25 out of the Navy score of 4.0 as perfect. However, I'm not permitted to take the final test at this time.

In the clippings yesterday was one about Jay and Ray, the Hauger twins, whom I'll always remember for their boxing but one day when they were about six Jay (or maybe it was Ray) socked Ray (or Jay) on the nose, broke up the bout when sockee turned into socker and asked plaintively "Is the blood coming out"? Tell Dad to ask Charlie Hauger what ship his boys are on and let me know, for it's entirely possible we've been galavanting together, and I might be able to look them up.

She asks "What about my husband?" and dammit darling I've written 600 or so words and not a line about me for there just isn't anything to say. We sailed, stood watch, sailed, ate, sailed etc. and that seems to be not only the sum but the substance of our life out here for lo these many moons. And the only part of that you could possibly be interested in is where, which of course is forbidden, leaving me without a story before I start to write. Isn't that a helluva fix for an ex-reporter?

But some day, my Bettsy, I shall be able to tell you all about it, and I guess it will keep 'til then. Meanwhile be very sure I think of you more often than is good for strict attention to the business at hand, and as I have from the first moment I saw you, I love you with all my heart.

1/24/45 Wednesday afternoon

Strangely, after so long an interval, I find myself totally without the words to start this which I hope will be the first of a new series of daily letters. Part of my reluctance is a heavy heart for not having been able to be more faithful, and a humble gratitude for the fact you are all that I'm not.

I honestly don't know how many days it has been since I last wrote; seems ages ago, and yet I think it was less than a week although I can't be sure. And yesterday brought me 15 - - that's right, fifteen! - - deliriously-wonderful letters from you.

Your letters, every one of them, were wonderful, did more to me and for me than anything except actually being with you possibly could have done. Every word had to be devoured at the earliest possible moment, and now that it's done I feel so warm and tingly and satisfied down inside I remind myself of nothing except the cat that ate the cream.

And just as the sun is shining in my heart again after a long bleak siege of few letters, so is Old Sol shining down on us all again, an old friend we're more than glad to welcome back. The sea is the bluest of blue; our wake a green path glistening in the sunlight and the whole world seems altogether a vastly more livable place.

Now I ask you, isn't that a meaningless jumble of words to come from a guy who has for fifteen years earned his living as a writer! But I don't think I ever before tried to set down on paper something I was feeling so deeply and I guess my feelings are like an ice jam blocking the stream. Let's hope it will flow better now, and I think maybe it will.

This morning, though, we had the 4 to 8 watch, and at the first moment there was light enough I began reading again and now I've been through the whole haul once, and will begin re-reading as soon as I finish this. Makes me feel good just to anticipate.

Of all the days when I failed to write there's little I can say. I wouldn't claim it's been monstrous, but my days and nights have been more than full. Looking back it's hard to reconstruct those days which in passing seemed so slow-moving, yet in retrospect they must have been short. Some day I'll tell you of them, but not here for I'm planning to lean over backwards so these next few letters at least will be cleared expeditiously through the censorship.

Here are my reactions to some of the points raised in your letters.

Strangely, I've begun again to lose touch and interest in the news, just as I did for a while at Great Lakes. Out here of course our only source is the daily mimeographed press news, and it's often difficult if not impossible to find a copy. When I do, it isn't overly helpful.

On the Russian Front, I'm convinced the new Red winter offensive in Poland will break the Nazi's back before June -- but this has been either sadly neglected or omitted entirely from the afore-mentioned news. The other day I learned of the capture of Warsaw only through a single paragraph under a London dateline that said the victory seemed a surprise to almost everyone!

But still and nonetheless I am managing to get along reasonably well, reasonably happy, physically sound. It's good, (a weak word) though to have you and the kids to hang on to mentally; to know you are thinking about me, and missing me even as I do you. It goes without saying, that days and nights are full of thoughts of all of you: where you are, what you are doing and thinking, what you look like.

I try not to spend too much time wondering how much longer we must be apart, for even if I knew right now it would be only 30 seconds I'd think that too long. But I confess I'm not quite so pessimistic as a few months ago, for it does seem obvious we've moved ahead a long ways in a little time.

But there are many hours I do spend planning what we'll do WHEN, and afterwards, and I've added one new item to my projected couple of months in idleness to really get to know all of you. That project, my darling, is a third honeymoon for us and I've been dreaming very pleasantly of retracing our first. No, I did not say reenacting! But you say you count on me to make you young again, my ancient sweetheart, and I promise to do my best so perhaps those familiar scenes will help.

Which dream, (it will come true) should be proof enough, Bettsy, that I do love you, and will always.

1/26/45 Friday evening

For the first time in a long time the ship is still beneath us, and so the evening shadows find me seated on the boat deck writing a letter I'd hoped to pen earlier in the day. But as always in (censored) port there were too many things that had to be done first and so your share of the day was shoved back to now. Night falls quickly out here, so quickly that even though it's not quite time for the sunset colors ceremony I'll not have many more minutes to write here. But the movie will be starting then, leaving me lots of room and light though it's hot and uncomfortable in the mess hall.

Everything seems so peaceful and quiet now; dark gray clouds skid across the dull sky, and a myriad of blinking lights stutter their mysterious messages. It's even good to smoke on deck, and I feel all dressed up in a new suit of dungarees and new shoes, after my bath.

Time out for a minute until I go below ----------------Below being where I am now, in the big mess hall that's all but deserted, the radio is blaring, always too loud here for any kind of reason.

Another mail call today, and while I confess it didn't have the "kick" of my jackpot a few days back I was nevertheless more than happy to get two letters from you, my first from our daughter, and one from Joe Brennan.

I was glad to hear that you finally made a trip to the dentist which was long overdue I'm proud that Bucky and Sis were so brave although it's too bad that Buck needed so many fillings

See by your letter that Mother and Dad have wrangled out the income tax return, and expect Dad was quite touchy for a couple of days; he usually is about that time. Maybe ours is coming soon, huh? And oh boy I can't wait to get at our "44" return!

In one of your letters you skipped rather lightly over my <u>order</u> to get your ring fixed. Now with the AP check and the money order I sent you, let's have no more shilly-shallying, my stubborn one, or I'll plant a solid whack on your pink you-know-what first chance I get. Matter of fact, I'll probably do it anyway, 'twould be a <u>real</u> pleasure right now. "Sadist," says she.

I'm looking forward to Sunday when, I hope, I'll be able to go to Mass and communion again. I've never been away so long before in my life and it bothers me even when I know it can't be helped.

Chubbin's letter delighted me no end, please tell her, and I thought it <u>very</u> well done so much so that it doesn't look even a little like a first letter. It was a real thrill, my Blondie, and your Daddy will be looking forward to the next one; will do his best to answer.

Whereupon I am plumb out of words and even a turn about the deck doesn't restore the flow. It's a warm, murky moonlit night, albeit a cool and pleasant breeze is sliding past us. The moon and the radio ("Long Ago and Far Away" and "Carolina Moon") bring me dreams and memories of you that seem too wonderful to be true, yet I would so much prefer to be back there sharing the winter with you.

To me you will always be the pretty girl I fell in love with one summer day - - the one I laughed and played with who almost broke my heart and then mended it forever. <u>And</u> the <u>one</u> with whom I shall laugh and play and make love forever.

1/27/44 Saturday night

Not until I wrote the second line above did I realize why I'm more than usually blue and mopey tonight, but the explanation is there now for you and I to see because this is <u>our night</u> and once again we're apart. Which explains my mental status despite the most wonderful windfall I've had since Chicago.

But to my windfall. This was <u>my</u> Christmas doubled in spades - - bit late but none the less wonderful! And once again I feel like a very ingrate for having done so poorly by all of you when all of you have been thinking of me and doing so much for me. I hope you'll never know how grand it is when you're <u>all</u> alone, to know that away off at that distant yet wonderful place called home there are people (that's a helluva weak word) like all of you, thinking and waiting and wishing for me.

To make the whole thing chronological, though, I must go back to last night when mail call was sounded at 10:30, just after I'd been ordered out on a work party. Well, I told you that I had gotten your 15 letters two days before, 2 more yesterday, and dammed if I didn't draw <u>11</u> more, and had time only to read the last one while I was working until 1 a.m.

So I slept on the loveliest pillow I've had since August and this morning before breakfast Walts brought me <u>4</u> more, plus a letter from your mom, a note from the AP office, a Service Chatter and a card from Martha Hawley, the girl I met in Racine.

Of course I wanted nothing else but to read, so pitched in right away, forgot all about breakfast and wasn't half way through until I had to back to work! So ended my reading for the morning and when we broke off for lunch I found some second class mail aboard and <u>three </u>packages, my Christmas, for me. You'll be delighted (as I was), to know they <u>all</u> reached me in <u>fine </u>shape, but alas and alack Mother's wonderful candy was spoiled, the butter in it rancid, and the treat I'd hoped for the gang shrank a lot.

Betty dearest I haven't the words to begin to tell you what I was thinking and feeling as I opened each of those boxes and unwrapped each separate package. But it's a dammed wonder I wasn't blubbering like a baby long before I was done. Every single thing, starting from the Christmas tree which now decorates our compartment, was wonderful

But then it was time to go back to work and my tough, dirty job of paint scraping was like climbing down a ladder from heaven into a coal mine, but it had to be done so I stowed my things as best I could. Finally the afternoon dragged to a close and back I rushed for my shower, more Christmas and more reading.

Your letters and the others I finished by chowtime and now I'm spending the last hour of my watch writing, and probably will, when I'm relieved, have to go back to the mess hall to finish. Perhaps it's in contrast with my guilty conscience of a few days ago, but one of the most pleasant sensations of the very wonderful past 24 hours, was the feeling of self-satisfaction that came to me last night when grabbing your letters, I knew I had just sent one back to you. Do as you would be done by, The Good Book says.

And of course, I want to say thank you, yet I know that doesn't fit, and don't know how else to say it. So I can only say once again that I love you and all of you and in the years to come after I come home I shall do nothing except attempt to show you how much I mean that.

So much for my day; tomorrow I hope to go a-beering with Walts on our island, despite the fact we've much work to do. But the hell with the work, for this time, I feel I need and am entitled to a little relaxation.

Your letters, as I read through them, opened a score of things I want to talk about, but there are so darn many. I'm very sure I can't remember all of them so I'll do what I can now, and then go on tomorrow.

First and foremost I'm amazed and delighted by your progress at the bank, and suspect that by now it's all over and done with, the note paid in full. You've done a great job!

And hours over the War Bond pile? You should have one a month starting from July, which would be $150 to add to the handful we had, though you haven't mentioned any arriving for some time.

While I'm on finances, don't let that bank balance get below $100 now; and I hope to be able to write a note to Ann Wunder asking about John, and checking with her about the $15.

Hell, it just occurred to me tomorrow is Sunday, when I hope to be able to go to Mass - - and if there's to be Mass I probably won't be able to go ashore. Oh well, it's much more important and maybe I can go ashore another time.

It goes without saying that the highlight of all my Christmas was the picture, which I've already displayed to most of my friends and shall spend many hours admiring until <u>that</u> day when I no longer need a picture but can look at the real thing. The changes (except you, you'll never change) all but floored me. And have you noticed how much Fran resembles Mother? Look some time at the old pictures of her and Dad, in case you haven't noticed the likeness.

It seems a bit strange to me that you haven't guessed more accurately about my whereabouts but I suppose it's easier for me to read things into my letters that you would never be able to expect. So guess you'll just have to stay in the dark and keep on guessing my darling.

Whereupon, your husband, having hacked out his longest letter in a long time, decides to call it off for the rest of the night, while promising more tomorrow. It's been a hard working day, with little sleep last night, and some shut-eye will be more than usually welcome. Remind me some time to tell you I love you, even though you're a wench who sends rocking elephants to me. That my darling, would be because I love you.

1/30/45 Tuesday night

Don't expect much of a letter tonight for it's hot as hell and I'm dirty and stinky, not having had my bath yet - - but I shall before I turn in. This has been much the easiest day in some time, for we worked only a little while this morning then were stymied by another group of workers and can do nothing until they're done. However our work is in good shape and we can afford to coast if it's not too long.

To bring you up-to-date about the sick bay visit; well it seems there was another answer than sinus to the headache I told you of the other night. After I went to bed I had a curious holes-burned-in-a-blanket feeling about my eyes, like I used to get after a too-salubrious night out, and when I awoke in the morning it was still there.

About that time I remembered there was some electric welding going on near where I was working the previous day, and apparently I had not kept my eyes away well enough, so I went to sick bay and told my little story. The doctor put a couple of drops of something in them, advised me to wear dark glasses all day and then come back for more drops. The glasses, a Christmas present from Dad, and drops did the trick and I'm fine now.

And along the same line, whom should I thank for my toothbrush? The day before my packages came I had dropped my old brush where I didn't care to recover it. Thank you again, my darlings for the very opportune gift

So taking advantage of the free afternoon I managed - - wonder of wonders! - - to wangle a typewriter and banged out my long-promised letter to Jess. Glad I had the mill, too, for it was long, probably 3,000 words and would have taken a year in longhand. Jess' letter, I hope, will clear the censors this time for I've studiously avoided anything I thought might be objectionable, while still trying to give him the clearest picture possible.

Yes, you're right, the thought <u>has</u> entered my head that instead of going back to AP in Philly or New York or somewhere I might be coaxed into pitching in with Jess to do a real job of waking up that smoky town. Just a thought as yet, although I know I can always get a <u>pretty good</u> job there, and maybe a <u>real good one</u>. Time will tell.

Another letter from you today, telling of the unfortunate incident preceding Bob's [Betty's brother] embarkation. Your mother hadn't mentioned that part in her letter. Probably he'll get busted down a couple of ranks but since he didn't miss the ship I doubt if under the circumstances he'll be brigged or otherwise penalized. And if he has a good record, no previous similar offenses and the C.O. is in a good mood, he may get off with no more than a lecture.

The same letter gives me your slant on Min's [Betty's sister] status and I agree with you 100 percent. I can't see how she can be now or in the future physically be able to support herself, and if Carl wants to discard his playthings he should be made to pay. Phooie, what a mess.

By the way, Francis Garrett is on my correspondence list and it occurred to me you might know how old he'll be next birthday which I seem to recall pretty closely follows mine. Just curious about him, for he's the little fellow I don't really know.

In the midst of my correspondence today, I've found a little time to start reading the short book "And Then There Was One" by Gene Burns, an AP war correspondent. It's a swell book on the earlier dark days of the Pacific war, and Frisco is mentioned in it a couple of times. Some of the guys who sailed her then are still doing so today.

Funny how I lost, some years ago, the knack for reading and now find I can only get back to it in hit-or-miss fashion. Some men out here do a lot of it, and there are some pretty fair books aboard but all I do is grab one at random, gobble it down and toss it aside. One of these days when we get back to a civilized life we must try to recapture that lost art. That is if I can spare any time for it from love-making, which is something I don't propose to forget no matter how long I must be out here. Chicago convinced me that the spark survives very stubbornly, my dearest, and needs only you to fan it into flame.

Wish I could start now, Betty mine, but know I can't. Nevertheless, I'll go on loving you with all my heart so long as we must be apart; and after that.

1/31/45 Wednesday afternoon

Dear Fran:

Even though you can't write yet, I guess it's only fair that you should have your own letter when Bucky and Sis get one, so here goes even if I can think of nothing to tell you except that there are few things in this world I should enjoy more than hearing you talk.

Seems an awfully long time to last May when I left a little boy just learning to say "Da-Da." But now I guess you're talking a blue streak, sort of taking the place of your gabby pappy. Don't mind admitting I envy you all the hours you are spending with your Mother.

I guess that like Bucky and Sis you are a real snow fan by now, enjoying yourself outdoors whenever you can get there. Tell Mother that Daddy said to let you go out as much as possible, for a little bit of even very cold weather shouldn't hurt <u>my</u> son even if it is too much for <u>my</u> wife. Has Bucky taken you for a ride on his sled yet? I hope so, and if he hasn't, tell him I'd like him to do it even though I know the "kid brother" business seems to take some of the fun away from coasting.

Your first real Christmas that you could understand and appreciate must have been a big thrill for you as it would have been for me could I have been there to see your face at the big moment. However I had to miss out this time so I'll have to settle for hoping I'll be there next year.

Meanwhile, be a good boy, especially at Mass, and I'll be waiting for the day we can get started on really knowing each other.

Love from Your Daddy

Chapter 10
FRISCO AT WAR - PART THREE
ANATOMY OF A CARRIER STRIKE,
TOKYO RAID, IWO JIMA BATTLE
2/2/45 to 3/31/45

2/2/45 Friday night

Not a very good start for a new month, is it, when I miss out on the first day - -and probably won't do too well on the second. It wasn't because I had forgotten, or wasn't thinking about you; I just wasn't able to write.

You see we were unable to get to the coral isle in the morning because there was no transportation and so I worked all morning. Then just after lunch we were told an LCI would be available so Walts and I climbed aboard and away we went. A very quiet trip, but a pleasant one, for we simply sat in the shade drinking our five cans of beer, then wandered around for a bit listening to a negro (sailors') band, watching the crap games and talking until it was time to go back to the ship.

Not altogether strangely after such a long dry spell, the beer provided me with a pleasant glow, but somewhere along the LCI ride back to Frisco I lost the glow and acquired a dammed unpleasant headache, so bad I crawled into my bunk, ignoring supper. After a bit I dozed off, then awoke at 8, debated a moment about writing and maybe seeing the second movie, and you lost for I shucked my clothes and went straight to bed - - which is what I shall do when I finish this. Felt especially bad about letting you down, too, for just before I left for the isle yesterday I got three letters from you and another came today.

I'm so sorry darling, and will do my absolute best to see that it doesn't happen again. But if it does, you are not to worry, for the letters will be coming to you as often as I can write and just as fast as possible for the mail to move so many thousands of miles under war conditions.

Let me tell you of our latest gripe: water hours. The machines which convert salt water to fresh water for us are being overhauled and for two days now fresh water has been turned on in the washrooms during only three 45-minute periods daily - - and no showers are permitted. However, we have all the cold drinking water we want.

As a result of the no-showers I'm beginning to feel positively crawly and if it continues tomorrow I shall try a salt water bath although I know it won't be overly successful. However I guess I shouldn't complain too much for the guys say that last year while they were in the tropics the durned machines broke down entirely and they had to live for a long time under the circumstances we face now temporarily. But it ain't fun.

To back to your letters for a moment, it's grand to hear our son is doing so well in school. Hard enough to believe we have a son in the third grade, let alone that he may be skipped to fifth. Hellsfire, at that rate he'll likely be in college when I get home.

And the letter today brought me three new pictures of the sprouts and Lordy how they're changing, Elizabeth especially. Just can't seem to believe what the pictures tell me; that the little blond child I left with you has grown into a very pretty schoolgirl. Fran and Buck, of course, are changed too, but not so much as or perhaps I had anticipated it more, I don't know which. At any rate it was swell to get the pictures and they gave me my first and possibly only look at snow this winter. Damm, how I hate to be missing all of this!

Well Bettsy, it's about time for me to hit the hay for I'll be on watch in four hours and I need some shuteye. Wish - - silly word isn't it - - my sleep were not destined to be so physically lonely, but I'll see you in my dreams and one of these days will be coming home to hold you in my arms

2-8-45 Thursday evening

This letter will probably shock your frugal soul, so I give you warning now, then go on to the routine things of life before getting down to what I'm sure will be the worrisome part (for you). Hold it, I <u>need to</u> hear this newscast - -

Whee! 47 miles from Berlin and patrols in the outskirts of Manila! Never would have believed the Reds could go so far so fast, but still think my analysis of last week will prove correct, with the knockout blow coming on the western front. What will happen to Hitler?

After finishing last night's letter I sat down to gab with a couple of guys until the end of the first show. And the more I gabbed the sleepier I got until finally I decided to hell with the movies, shucked my clothes and climbed into bed about 8 p.m. Rolled out again at 7 a.m., ate breakfast, and then loafed the rest of the morning. Was on watch all afternoon (will be again from midnight to 4), showered, ate and here I am on the boat deck at sunset winding up the busiest scribbling session in a long time.

Have had my mattress and pillow up on deck all day for airing and in a few minutes when it gets dark I must take them below, make up my bed (my very lonely bed) for the night and then finish this. Also during the afternoon I've dried and folded all the clothes I sent to the laundry this week, so you can see it's been a busy but not burdensome day.

So much for that. Now to take my stuff below, fix my bed and then continue with the "shocking" part.

Continued: 15 minutes later.

Now to the shocking part Bettsy and the best way I know to shock you is financially, and that's what it is this time. As I told you, I went to bed quite early last night, and must have been with you through my dreams for when reveille woke me at 6 I came wide awake - - snap, like that! - - with my ordinarily empty head filled with thoughts of you and ours and us. Technically I'm required to get up at reveille, but actually there was no need for it (there rarely is) and so I lay there for an hour or more.

And then it happened! I got to planning our postwar home, not what it will be like but what we'll <u>need</u>, and I came to the astonishing total of $1,300 before I decided it was time for me to get the hell out of there before I impoverished us for all time. Whoee, what a spending spree! I think you'd like to hear about it so here goes, as best I can remember, room by room, what we'll need and what it will cost:

Living room - - Counting on our suite being OK. we still must buy a rug ($100), a radio ($100) the little one to go into our bedroom or Buck's, a good medium sized table ($50) and another easy chair and footstool ($75).

Dining room suite ($200) - - I would like Early American or Chippendale walnut - - rug ($75) and extra chairs and server may run the total up, say $300.

Kitchen - - Our stove and frig will do, but we'll need <u>good</u> china ($50) and an every day set (fiesta ware?) ($20), silver service ($75) and glassware set ($20). Total $165.

Bedroom 1- - Ours - - Rug ($50), phone stand ($10), 2 comfortable chairs and indirect lights ($100). Total $160.

Bedroom 2- - Buck and Fran - - Two maple dressers ($50), Rug ($50) and desks ($30). Total $130.

Bedroom 3- - Sis - - Twin-bed white oak suite ($150), rug ($50) and desk ($15). Total $215.

Bedroom 4 - - spare - - Our bed OK and studio couch to go there, but we'll need a rug ($40) and a dresser ($20) and if we're to use the room as a second living room, which would depend on the house etc., there would be chairs, lights, etc. Minimum total ($60).

Let's see; that's $1,355! Whew!

Then there are such items as new linens, bed and table, and new blankets, quilts and bedspreads. And I want indirect lights for the living room, and just dozens of little odds and ends, not to mention we'll need curtains and drapes. Say $400 more.

Still With me Bettsy? That's $1,755 I've spent already, and we still need a car, and one helluva lot of other things. Didn't I warn you I'd shock you? Bet I've succeeded - - or had you been doing some similar dreaming and been afraid to tell me?

Looking at this list, I'm inclined to wonder what sort of a house we lived in before, and where all that money went we've spent over the past 10 years. But I guess the answer is our house has been <u>lived</u> in and a lot of the things we did have are just plumb worn out.

But surprisingly as it may seem, I did some thinking, too, on the other side of the ledger about where all this money is going to come from, and there's a bit of encouragement there.

Let's see: Suppose I should come home, the war being over, next February without having come home on leave in the meantime. That's my most optimistic guess at the moment but of course the chances are it will be longer than that, or perhaps not as long as that. O.K., let's say February, just as a talking point. That would mean 20 months at a war bond a month, or a total (face value) of $500 from my allotment.

In addition, it seems reasonable I should save $20 a month of my $35 cash pay, starting from November 1 of last year, for as I told you I already have (or will next week) $80 on the books. Again supposing I do not advance, that's 16 months or another $320. Add to that my discharge pay of $300, (I think I'll be eligible for the maximum although I'm not sure.) and a wild guess says I should have a $200 refund from our 1944 income tax payments, which would give us a starting capital of $1,320. If I ever make GM3/C it will add $15 to our monthly accumulation.

Furthermore, if I know anything about you (and I <u>think</u> I do) you'll be hoarding a bit of a nest egg from your allotment checks, although it can't be as big as you want it to be; not with all the stuff you must buy for the kids. But you have by this time paid off the bank note, perhaps have $100 in the checking account, and that's somewhere upwards of $200 saved since April. That's something like $25 a month, and if you should be able to keep it up, which I doubt, would mean something like $500 a year from now.

So you put all these imaginary figures together and get:
Needed expenditure $1,755
Cash on hand $1,820

Now wait a minute; I am <u>not</u> challenging you or asking you to try to squeeze the few pennies you get. It's different with me for I'm out where I need not, and actually <u>can't</u> without being downright wasteful, spend any money. I should and possibly will do better than $20 a month, but I'm giving myself lots of leeway. And I want you to do the same. There are so many things you and the kids need and must have, and I don't want you to stint on a single one of them. I will in truth feel badly if you do.

I guess that covers it all Bettsy, and it's time for me to be hitting the hay for a little while, until I must get up at 11:30. Anyhow it's been grand fun dreaming with you and of you; perhaps I'll get some more of it tonight, who knows? 'Nite sweetheart and sleep 'tite.

2/9/45 Friday afternoon

Dear Bucky:
Yours and Mother's letters about the school reports letters arrived today, and while I'll admit I was a bit disappointed still one

A and 3 B's isn't such an awfully bad report card. I'll bet there were lots of other boys in your room who didn't do as well.

But what Mother and Grandmother found so disappointing was that you <u>should</u> have had a <u>better</u> card. I think so, too, and while I don't want you to feel badly about the marks you got, I want you to make up your mind that they will be better next time. And I want you to try extra hard with your arithmetic, for in studying that you are not only learning to add, subtract, divide and multiply but to <u>think</u> straight; that is to set each figure down in its proper place in relation to all the others. Ask Mother to help you every night with your homework; if you don't have any ask her to give you some problems. Soon you'll find it's <u>easy</u> to do. And I hope some day soon you'll discover that arithmetic and all mathematics are good fun. Yes, it's a different sort of fun than sled riding and building snow forts, but you can only do those things in the winter and you can play with mathematics any time.

Please tell Elizabeth I thought her report card very good and want her to have the next one just as good or better. And when I come home I'll try to find some special reward for both of you, and Francis too, for being the very nicest children in the entire world.

'Bye for now Sonny, and do a good job of being the man of the family until I can come home to all of you.

Love always, Your Dad

2-14-45 Wednesday evening at sea

It isn't entirely my own fault I'm so late starting, but it seems I managed only a couple of v-mail notes while on watch this morning and then proceeded to sleep away the entire afternoon.

So 6:30 finds me in the crowded mess hall where a couple of dozen stragglers are bolting the last bites of supper and a couple of others are clustered mothlike around one of the few lighted spaces in the ship. Some are like me, writing; others reading and many more just sit and talk or think. Most of them clutch the inevitable cup of mud that shuttles from hand to hand until it's empty when a debate arises within the circle as to whose turn it is to "make the run" - - refill it. Someone always does.

It's quite a noisy place; the buzz of voices backgrounds an obbligato of tinkling silverware and clanging trays en route to the scullery; and the whole is dominated by the blare of the radio speaker carrying a most catholic mixture of jive, hillbilly and now and then a semi-classic.

A jive record booms and Vale Pena, a shock headed little Mexican gunners mate who at 20 has been through all the war on Frisco, goes jitterbugging past me. His face wears an odd grin; the step was for me to see. He was showing off, and loves it. Funny kid, always chattering about his "squaws."

A white-uniformed mess cook shuffles around the tables brushing particles of food onto the floor. Others follow him collapsing the benches onto the tables, then hoisting the whole assembly to the racks overhead where they will sway with the gentle roll of the ship until breakfast time tomorrow. They're making sort of a game of it tonight; one boy calls signals like a football quarterback and on the last "Ho" up it goes to the cradle.

Now the brooms come out to sweep the debris, and a boy with a bucket splashes soapy water on the deck. Others come behind him swinging swabs (mops, to you) in a rhythmic line that leaves dim "uuuu-shaped" water streaks. Ten minutes more and the job will be done, the deck dry and the evening influx of loafers will begin. Some wait already at the entrance hatches, to pounce like vultures on their favorite spots at the earliest moment.

As I said, the men cluster here like moths around a lantern in a summer camp, for there are few other places where, at night, they can be together in a lighted room, without being in the way of the work that must go on. Every evening at sunset - - although it is quite light then and remains so for a half hour - - the ship is "darkened." That means that all lights that show directly or might show indirectly above decks, are extinguished. No match or cigarette is permitted to be lighted where it would be visible and none ever is. No officer is needed to enforce that rule; the men are too acutely conscious that their own safety depends on its being kept to the letter.

Half an hour ago the crew was eating in this room. Now a couple of men have brought their bed-rolls in, spread them beneath the blowers that bring cool fresh air from the outside; shortly they'll be asleep there, oblivious of the radio, the chatter, men walking past and sometimes over them.

Life goes on - - sometime strangely, but nonetheless it goes. Wonder if it isn't much the same on Jap ships - - when and if they muster the courage to venture out to sea? Suppose so.

Rather a windy description of a brief and unimportant moment in my life away from you, Bettsy, but I thought you might like a look at it. There isn't anything more to tell about my day, for as I said, I slept away a large part of it.

By the way I have an up-to-now secret that is just a little too good to keep - - plus a request. The secret is that I've already started a fund for our third honeymoon, and you'd be surprised if I told you how healthy it is already.

I'm working it this way - - whatever change I get my hands on goes into the treasury, all of it, and while I normally don't handle much money still every time I buy a 10-cent ice cream, 90 cents goes into the fund. At that rate I'll not need to eat as many ice creams as I should like to have a roll that should finance us beautifully. Would you like to go to Hagerstown?

But there is just one thing in connection with said trip that I want you to promise me you'll do. And I ask the promise blindly, for I do not propose to tell you now or later - - until the proper times comes - - what it is that I'm asking. I will, however, give you one little hint, then expect your promise via return mail. My idea stems from our Chicago interlude; plus something you wrote about that and which you wish; plus an embellishment of my own. Just teasing, my darling, for you <u>could</u> never guess, and even may think it silly when I tell you, but it will be something very wonderful to me, something I shall be looking forward to and dreaming about.

Strangely enough, I dreamt last night and again today of homecoming, and both times went further than I've ever gone before, even to the reunion with Dad and Mother and the kids swarming around and over me. Yet in these dreams, as in all my others both waking and sleeping, I couldn't or at least didn't reach the point where I could put my arms around you and begin telling you how much I love you.

I think that is so very odd, but can only guess that even in dreams one can seldom find such joy and so to experience it I must keep on waiting for that day. Until then, and forever afterward my Betty, I love you.

2/18/45 Sunday evening

For the moment I seem to have overcome the time obstacle, for I now have the better part of three hours to spend writing to you, but as usual I'm facing that other old handicap, what to write. Seems odd that such a talkative character as your husband should find himself without any words for you so often, but guess it has to be that way sometimes.

After opening my stationery, I found the one letter of yours that I've saved after I've finished reading. It's the note you penned Christmas Eve and whenever I'm jumpy or out of sorts it perks me up no little just to read and know again that all of you back home are missing me and praying that I'll be home soon. You'll never know how comforting that reassurance can be - - that's why I keep the letter.

So 4 p.m. finds me slick and clean, smelling (to borrow your own words) like a Polish _ _ _ _ _house. I've just folded and put away the laundry which has been waiting since Wednesday, then managed my first shave and shower in three days and slipped into a complete clean uniform. All of which, topped off by a touch of my new (thanks to Dad and you) shaving lotion, a cigarette and a stick of gum, leaves me feeling quite pert, I can tell you.

Now if I could only pick up the telephone call up some gal and make me a date for tonight I'd really be all set - - except there's no place to go. Might be I could wangle one of our whale-boats, to take her for a make-believe canoe ride in the moonlight. Want to try it with me?

Must tell you something odd that I meant to include in my letter last night. I was up in my tub on watch during the afternoon, paying attention to my job, too, when somehow suddenly I was reminded of one night long ago, before we were married, when I came to see you in Allentown. Very distinctly I could see you as you looked then wearing a white shirtwaist and a darkish skirt, sitting on the couch in the living room at 19 ½ [Lafayette Street]. It was a moonlight night, and one I think you will remember too. What brought that particular night to mind at that particular moment I am not able to say. But it was a lovely memory, one that I confess distracted my lookout for a bit, and there was one very minor incident that came back to me most clearly. Ask me about it some time - - perhaps during our projected trip.

Once again I'm writing in the mess hall, quite full with the usual pre-supper crowd. This bunch waits for meals like so many starved wolves. For a change the radio is not going, but some of the men are standing around it in hopes it will start up. Maybe it will bring a Tokyo newscast, which is always good for a big crowd standing around hooting and laughing at the stories we know are not true.

Have you ever heard or seen anything about Father Manning? I often wonder about him, rather wish he were still in Somerset if for no other reason than that he would have started training Bucky to be an altar boy.

And I often think of Mother Incarnata, too, and one of these days soon when I have a chance I mean to write at least a note to her. Gosh I wish we were back there - - but there's no sense in wishing that now, although it does seem it may not be so eternally long until we can start making some of these wishes and dreams come true.

Which will be very very wonderful for every one of my wishes and dreams is built around you, and if any one of them comes true the central one must be completed first - - the one in which I again hold you in my arms.

=2x22=44 (5) Thursday evening _ _ _

Well, my anticipated busy day materialized very thoroughly yesterday, as you can tell from the absence of a letter, and today is almost as bad so you may get only a few lines - - but at least there will be that much and you will not only know I still (and always will) love you but also that my resolution retains a firm grip on me.

I'm looking forward to receiving the Time magazine that you ordered. As I told you we lose almost completely all contact with the news except what we are told or what we can see about what we're doing aboard ship. For instance: our alleged press news for yesterday and again today failed to carry a line on the European situation; gave only the texts of a couple of Pacific communiqués.

About me there's little to be said at the moment. Just a little while ago, before supper, I managed a shower, shave and change of clothes, which always helps and especially so when you have slept in the duds you shucked.

I've been meaning to tell you that I have been sensing and noticing among my shipmates a new attitude in the last few weeks. Probably it stems from our military successes on all [censored] fronts within that time. And if it is a general feeling as it may well be growing and spreading throughout the services, it is bad news for our enemies.

I've told you before that the majority of the crew of the Frisco is a hard-bitten, war-wise bunch of kids who have been battle tested many times. When I came aboard a few months ago I was amazed to find so many vocally bitter against the Navy and the skipper, especially because they felt they were being hurried back to the fighting zones. It was of course my first real closeup look at the morale of a gang of fighting men, and it was startling.

But soon I saw it was mostly just the everlasting griping that seems to infest any body of military men, and it subsided as we neared the war zones. Until now I haven't heard such a squawk in quite some time; matter of fact, I think even the loudest squallers would now, if they were able to talk honestly, admit our skipper is a damm good one - - while insisting in the same breath "Well, he could have let us stay in the States a little longer"!

Amazingly, replacing that reluctance is the new spirit that that's just the opposite. Ken Swanson, a boy in my division, put it rather succinctly the other day, when, during our interminable discussions about war, strategy, what has happened and what might, he remarked. "Hell, it looks like now we're fighting this war on our own time! Let's get on with it, get it over and go home." He's not alone in that sentiment; I would almost be willing to say it is the belief of every man who stops to think what's ahead and what it's all about. Look out, Tojo!

Yesterday was a most gosh-awfully long day, for I went on watch at 3:30 a.m. and didn't really have a minute of my own until I went back to bed 18 hours later. Couldn't believe the night had slipped away so fast when reveille roused me at 6, and I had to hurry and eat and get back on watch. However there was a welcome chance to snooze this afternoon - - I was debating whether to get up or to take another nap when the bugle made up my mind quick-like - - and now feel reasonably rested for the 8 to midnight watch which will start soon.

You asked about my hair (?) cut, and I guess I must confess

that I sort of lost my nerve at the critical moment and settled for just an ordinary very close trim rather than a complete head shave. But I think next time I'll be able to muster enough courage for the dastardly deed and then we'll see whether such a desperate resort will restore my (sic) fallen glory.

Time out - - the radio, from which comes many strange sounds, is bringing us Gounod's "Ave Maria." Always one of my favorites among the world's beautiful music, it has an extra thrill now for it takes me back to those long ago days when we were little kids listening to the Victrola and those old, well-remembered red seal records. Don't suppose there is one of them left now, is there? Remind me some time that the new radio on our postwar list must include a record player.

Seems I'm getting more time to write tonight than I had anticipated - - for which I'm glad and grateful but must remember in the future to lay in a reserve stock of words against other such occasions. Yeah, I know before you say it, it's difficult to imagine me running out of words, but let me hasten to add that I mean <u>writing</u> words, the kind I can put down here. I've quite a reservoir saved for the day when I again hold you in my arms; and while every sentence begins with "I love you." and ends the same way. I'm hoping there will be enough variation in between to keep you interested and listening for it's going to take me a <u>long</u> time to say half that's in my heart.

Just rereading your letters for inspiration, and am reminded to tell you that I consider it very unfair of you to stop in the middle of a letter, take yourself a bath and then come back and write me about it. Or is your memory failing?

By the way, the shredded wheat picture interests me, and if it <u>is</u> a heavy cruiser it is very likely one of this (New Orleans) class. Save one and I'll tell you some day.

That brings me to the end of this missive and so goodnite, my darling. Give Fran and Chubbin and Bucky a special kiss from their Dad who misses them very much.

2/26/45 Monday evening at sea

My bed is most inviting at the moment but I just couldn't let myself roll into it without writing at least a few lines. Truthfully the few lines - - or a lot of them - - should have been written long before this for it's been an easy, lazy day.

Whoa, there's one of our old songs on the radio "Ain't Misbehavin." Remember it? And how apt the line "I'm saving my love for you."

Anyhow, to recount my adventures, I slept quite securely last night, got up this morning to eat breakfast and go on watch, spending four easy hours on deck, reading part of the time and the remainder just listening to the boys gab. Mostly they talk about (1) past liberties, usually drunks and dames, in the States and a couple of ports (2) battles they've been in and who did what that may not have been so funny then as now and (3) the future course of the war, both short and long-range, and when they will be free again.

Just now some of them are much upset over a report (true or false, I don't know) that a bill is before Congress to keep all reserves in the Navy four years after the war is over. My vehement assurances that no Congress would dare enact such a bill seems to give them little consolation.

Chuck Walts remains about the best friend I have aboard, although the difference in our working assignments keeps us apart, and conversely, throws me in more and more with Sam Dooley and Will Fairbanks, with whom I work on the guns. The latter are a pair of rough and ready young huskies - - both are 20 - - whom I have discovered to be a little more than all-right guys and we work well together., They've been fast friends for quite a long time, tell some weird tales of roistering liberties together. The two of them, once wound up in the Honolulu hoosegow after a spree that wound up with them lifting a manhole cover from the street and bowling it through the door of a bank!

Before I started this letter I got out my family pictures. Gee, it's hard to believe those are our kids, they obviously are <u>so</u> grown up, so different from the little ones I left behind 10 months ago. But there's one girl in the pictures who changes little, or not at all, except perhaps to become more beautiful. I have in my possession one picture taken of her last fall standing on the sidewalk in front of a house and another of the same girl 15 years ago.

And curiously a song pops into my head from nowhere - - "lovely to look at, delightful to know x x x thrilling to hold you terribly tight."

Hey- what goes on here - - me writing love letters again? My, My!

Anyhow, it's a sample of what I'm thinking now and always, Betty mine, whether we are in each other's arms or a dozen thousand miles apart. And there is so much more of it to tell you about that I'm going to have to talk fast as hell from the day I get back until the day after forever in order to get half of it said.

And with the light seems to have gone my inspiration and so once again I must tell my darlings good night at long range. But one of these days I will be back to stay where I can hear Bucky and Chubbin and Fran say their prayers and can tuck them in and kiss them goodnight as a daddy should.

2/26/45 Monday evening at sea

Dear Bucky:

When I finished your mother's letter a few moments ago I thought I was through writing for the night. But then I remembered there's a big day coming in less than two weeks and if there's any hope at all that you shall have a birthday letter from your Dad then it must be written tonight.

Eight years! Lordy it just doesn't seem possible it has been that long since the wintry night you arrived. I'll never forget that night, or the first sight of you, a wrinkled red-faced squaller.

Some day I'll tell you more about it, but just now ask Grandma what I said when, as I was telling her the big news by telephone when Adeline brought you in for me to see.

And do you know the seven years we had together seem in retrospect to have flown past so much more quickly than this last year we have been apart. I pray that the rest of our separation will pass more quickly for you and I - - and all of our family - - can begin to discover some of the so many good things of life we're missing now. All sorts of odd things like going to Mass together; the tug of a fish on the line; snowballs and snowmen and the joy of walking in a summer rain; of talking and thinking and reading and just <u>living</u> all together. That may sound like a lot of mixed up words just now, but you shall learn some day what I mean.

The bottom of it is, of course, that I miss you and all of you more than I could miss anything else in the world. And I wait and pray only for the day when we can be together again for good.

Until then, my son, you have a big job, even for an eight-year old man, for you must take my place in every way you can. Be obedient and helpful to your mother, helpful and the <u>best</u> friend always to Chubbin and Fran. You must go faithfully to Mass and communion, and be just as faithful and persevering in your school work. Be kind to your friends, not always fighting with them but willing always to stand by what you think is right.

And make your life be <u>fun</u> no matter where you go or what you do. Guess that's a pretty big load for your shoulders, but I'm sure <u>my</u> son can carry it. And so I send you eight big hugs, plus one to grow on, and I pray I'll be able to deliver them in person next March 10.

All the love in the world from Your Dad

3/5/45 Monday night in port

I begin this letter to tell you that a new censorship policy in effect today permits us to tell something of what seems the dim and distant past. We were given the enclosed mimeo sheet as a suggested outline of what we may write, so I send it to you intact. As I understand it, others will be issued from time to time when security permits revelation of our past stories - - or part of them.

I was able to get to Mass yesterday. Got up for good (?) at 8, had breakfast and loafed until 9 when it was announced a priest was aboard to hear confessions. So I went and stood in line and afterwards served the Mass for a Father Kosky, an odd little duffer who seemed more interested in hurrying through - - and conserving his sacramental wine - - than anything else. He wouldn't let me pour the wine into the chalice, explaining that it was "precious" since some of the boys on his ship had broken into his reserve stock. Nor would he accept my offer to help pack his vestments stating "Nobody but me seems to be able to put them away right."

My sleep last night was interrupted by the 12-6-4 watch, but I didn't mind that overly much, went back to bed later and stayed there until 7 a.m. Spent the first two hours of the morning reading a flock of Tribunes and then it was liberty call and my day on the coral isle. There I drank four cans of beer, ate a couple of sandwiches and gabbed away the afternoon. Then it was back to the ship for a lousy supper and a bath.

I took time out for an examination of our third honeymoon prospects. Interested? Well, as I think I warned you once before, there'll be a package one of these days that should convince you I'm not fooling - - and at the same time further pique your curiosity.

That's my day so far; now the movie is being shown on the well deck and afterwards there probably will be a poker game. If so I think I'll sit in for a couple of hours; might improve my disposition.

Up to now I still am not in the mood to go into all the passages of your recent letters that I want to answer, but I note a general trend of increased worry which although I understand I had hoped you would avoid.

Sure this is no Sunday school picnic, and I don't ever want to try to deceive you about that. But honestly, my darling, to the best of my actual ability to see and know, I have been in far less danger than I anticipated, and certainly only a fraction of what you are imagining. I've given you in the past, some hints and pointers on that, among them several references to my reaction - - now that I <u>know</u> the difference - - to my choice of the Navy over the Army.

Don't get me wrong, I have been scared but never so much by the enemy as the typhoon. Every time the bugle calls us to battle stations - - even for routine scheduled morning and evening alerts - - there's a tingle that honesty compels me to call fear.

I felt it first when we were skirting past the once formidable bastion of Truk en route from Eniwetok to Ulithi. Your map will show you how close we must have been to the place that a year ago was (or seemed) the ultimate symbol of Jap power in the Pacific. And I've felt it many more times - - with more reason - - since and I suppose always will.

As you know from the papers the Jap fleet has been conspicuous by its absence, so obviously there have been no recent really personal threats to me from that direction. And the censorship sheet I sent you said of our first operation something about we saw little action. Perhaps you'd like to know of my first sight of the enemy.

It came one morning during the dawn alert when we knew enemy planes were somewhere seeking us. Suddenly, off on the horizon, a ball of fire burst in the sky and went plummeting downward. Leroy saw it first, and I think our report was the first on the ship. And minutes later the loudspeaker boomed "Splash one enemy" and we knew one of <u>our</u> fighters had scored; knew the comet-like trail of a son of heaven going to join his ancestors in an even warmer place.

Another day the enemy sought us, and for an hour a swirling dogfight raged up and down beyond the horizon as those gallant kids with wings fought them off. How many Japs came out on that hunt, I never knew - - I never saw a one. But I can promise you a lot less went back whence they came.

Does that help any, Bettsy? I fervently hope it will make it easier for you to believe me when I say that now I feel very sure I have just about as safe - - the word is relative; all words are to me - - a berth as there is in the front line of this war.

Those kids in the planes - - no matter whether they fly at Hitler or Tojo - - and those equally gallant ones on the front-line - - no matter whether they slog through the bitter snows of Europe or climb the rocky face of a cliff out here to rout out the madmen - - they need your prayers more than I. Believe me, they have mine.

It's a glorious sight to watch the planes go off of a flat top on a strike. From a solid mass on the after end of the flight deck a little bug moves out, crawling at first then faster, faster as he nears the bow to lift and soar away: circling, waiting for his teammates taking off behind him in a procession like ants carrying winter food to their storeroom. Sometimes a laden bomber slides over the end of the flight deck without having gained enough speed to climb. There's a tense, breathtaking moment as he seems to drop nearer, nearer the water, and an audible sigh of relief as the plane visibly gains flying speed, lifts his wheels and begins to climb away from the grasping waves.

And when they come back! One minute the ships are alone on the vast ocean. The sun is shining; white clouds drift across the blue field of the sky. In the distance a speck appears, a look-out spots it and we all watch. Is it ours or - ? We watch and the speck becomes three or four planes, in a V, and powerful binoculars confirm our own eyesight: "Friendlies returning" the control officer says over the phones. Still on watch, and behind the speck grown to a formation come other specks that swell into other formations, and more are coming. Seemingly slow but amazingly quickly, they come toward us until the whole sky above us seems crowded.

Carefully, almost mathematically, they swing into formation above the carrier. No acrobatics, no "victory rolls" mark the return. It reminds me more of miners trooping out of the pit at the end of the day. Out ahead of us they fly then one by one bank away until a group becomes a long, circling line of widely spaced planes while other groups hover. Each plane of the circling line has his try at the carrier, either lands or is waved away to try again, taking last place in the circle. As the line thins other groups come down to fill the vacant places and wing-folded planes crowd the forward end of the carrier.

As each plane lands we watch -- - and pray, too, for it's no cinch - - the approach, the nose-over down to the flight deck and a short, bouncing roll until the arrester device snubs to a stop the thing that seconds ago was traveling hundreds of miles an hour. With each stop we breathe a sigh of relief as the carrier crew rushes out and the halted plane, freed again, trundles forward to its parking place. Finally they all come down. We feel like cheering - - and wonder how their mission succeeded.

Such was life on that first (for me) operation my darling. It gave me many hours to think of you and dream of the day we'll be together again. And always it warmed me down inside to know that you love me and I love you.

3/7/45 Wednesday night in port

Strange, it seems to me, how unattractive an endeavor is writing this time in. For another day has passed, I've made no start on reducing the mountain of correspondence and must in fact push myself to do this little bit. My letters are probably stiff, wordy things that tell you nothing except I know I must keep on writing.

After writing your letter last night I did manage to get off the income tax return - - which after figuring it over - - I'm forced to conclude must be pretty nearly correct, dammit. I thought we'd have a larger refund.

That was as far as I could go with the pen last night, so I wandered up to see the last ¾ of the movie. It was one of the Abbot and Costello things: good slapstick but much of it smothered in gingerbread - - rather boring

There's little more to say of the intervening 24 hours; a bit of sleep and up to work, lunch, work, shower and a little reading; there you have my rather drab day. Some mail would have made a very bright spot, but I expected none, got twice that much. Perhaps tomorrow.

Stuck already - - and long cogitation provides only one topic in which you might be interested - - the package. Well, I can tell you now my original plan was to send you my beer-can bank intact, but it developed today there's an acute shortage of change aboard the ship and so I opened my can and surrendered my hoard. Nope, I'm not going to tell you how much there was. Nor will you know or be able to find out until the package arrives.

Which sent me into a ten-minute blank spell during which I must have been grinning like a chessy cat? Just dreaming and remembering and dreaming some more, my Bettsy. Gee, it's lovely to be able to do that - - with you.

Remember the song
"No one else it seems
Even shares my dreams - -"

Wonder what you and the kids are doing right now. It would be about 7:30 a.m. Wednesday, just about the right time for all of you to be assembled in the kitchen for breakfast. I can almost hear the babble, the crinkling of the newspapers, the warming thump of the toaster delivering two slices of golden bread. And swell coffee - - REAL coffee. MMMM!

Shush, mustn't waken the animals. They might be hungry

- - and there's no hay in the house.

Anyhow, my darlings, silly as that may sound I do love you all and miss so much those days and moments that I once accepted so casually. I'll live each one of them to the full when this job is done. 'Nite my dearest ones. I love you.

3/9/45 Friday evening in port

Your husband is still tired and sunburned this evening after yesterday's hard physical labor on one of the gun mounts. Unfortunately I shed my shirt when we started and forgot to put it back on so my back is red and tingling, not painful but not pleasant, either.

At least I can start with a slightly different day, and a big event, and perhaps I can go on from there. The big event, of course, was mail - - five swell letters from you, all were very tasty though 3 were three months old. They were dated 12/11-11-12, numbered 2, 3 and 5 and apparently had been in a batch of mail that went astray somewhere. No matter, though, for they were just a delectable as if they had been written 2/28 with the other two.

A distant radio brings me faintly an organ playing a song called "Stormy Weather." Ever hear it? It's quite a nice melody, but lonely, though. Now follows "Make Believe" - - I wouldn't have to. - -

Well I said our day was a bit different. It began ordinarily enough when I had to get up at 6 to go on watch, and after breakfast Sam, Will and I started in on our painting job. Worked hard for a while, got most of it done, then stopped short when we needed one color of paint and were told there was no more aboard. So, perforce, we stopped and will have some more to do next week. Then, since we rated liberty today but had intended to stay aboard and keep on working, I asked and received permission to go and spent a pleasant afternoon on the coral isle.

Drank my four cans of beer, then somehow got separated

from Walts and the rest and wound up making an exploratory tour of the isle - - not much to see but most of it was new and strange so I enjoyed it all alone. Its rough walking: huge hunks of sharp-edged coral everywhere you go; palm trees, underbrush, and a dark green swamp, the whole surrounded by a white sand beach. The open sea is on one side, the harbor on the other.

The interior of the island is literally overrun with lizards, tiny-little things (2 to 4 inches) that scuttle out of your way much faster than you would think their stubby legs could carry them. Quite a few are really pretty - - brilliant blue tails, yellow stripes running along their backs.

Saw only two kinds of birds. A fairly large snow white kind that flies over the water, sweeping and turning like some kind of gull; and a large bird looking much like an oversize starling except for a brown-mottled breast, that sat on a limb a few feet over my head, then flew away after a minute.

Getting back to the recreation area (technically, I guess I was "out of bounds" during most of my walk) I ran into a guy wearing the SP brassard who was posted at the rear of the beer depot to shoo away any guys who might try to swipe a couple of cases. He turned out to be a Philadelphian, and we talked quite a while about the old town, mostly its football and baseball.

Finally our party was called to the corral to await our boat, and I promptly went to sleep prone on the sand in the midst of a milling mob! Someone recognized and woke me when the boat docked, and so I got back to the ship; ate a lousy meal; collected and read your letters, bathed, shaved and changed clothes and here I am writing.

Incidentally, gambling on the island has been stopped and the lush crap games have passed out of the picture. I'm a bit sorry about it, for there's little there in the way of entertainment and while I didn't play myself I know a lot of the guys got a big thrill out of it. Money means little out here, anyway, so I don't see that angle as wholly evil.

Tomorrow we break out our whites for the first time since we left Pearl. It's captain's inspection and the ship is shined as best we can do it. Guess I still have some whites (yellows probably would be more descriptive) and if necessary I'll dig 'em out and wear 'em. We will be on watch so I'm hopeful of escaping.

Had hoped to write to the kids tonight, but here it is 9:30 and your old man hears his bed a callin'. Wish it weren't such a lonely, cramped little thing. I know of one that meets all of my requirements for what a bed should be, but haven't seen it in some time so that I'm beginning to wonder whether I know or just dream. However if it is real I hope you're taking good care of it for me.

Wish too, I could take a certain girl in my arms and tell her how much I love her, but haven't done that in a long: <u>much</u> too long time and she too may be a dream.

Hmmm. Perhaps if I go to bed I can recapture those dreams. I'll be seeing you in my dreams darling and loving you.

3/12/45 Monday evening in port

Sunset, it seems is my writing time, at least the part I've set aside for you. Matter of fact it's becoming downright habitual for me to be pen-in hand at colors and you won't have to remember very much to recall that true habits - - regular ones, that is - - were the one thing I had least most of.

However, habit or don't habit, to pun poorly, here I am enjoying the evening breeze all slicked up and clean. Worked quite hard today, mostly painting, and it was a relief to get a shower and shave. After which I promptly crawled into bed and napped for an hour until Svoboda woke me at supper time.

News to report about him: He's our, (Sam's and mine), new working companion. Yep, the big shakeup happened today, five strikers back on deck force, five new men on the guns. I'm glad to be with Svoboda but dammit Walts had the evil luck to miss out and I'm afraid now it looks like he never will make the gun gang.

I didn't make the movie last night That didn't happen because a card game started and I joined in. I played - - with one interruption - - until 3 a.m., and as a result you'll have a surprise as soon as I can get to the postoffice. It was no night to sleep and I was more than happy to turn it to profit.

Before you start worrying about me and these games, and the possibility I may become an "addict" let me tell you a little about them. Firstly there are two kinds, penny ante which is almost solely for pleasure and in which a shift of $10 up or down for any one player is considered large. That was what I played yesterday morning, and from which I think I told you a couple of dollars went into our postwar fund. Almost anyone can and does play, and it is pretty much sociable.

Secondly there are the so-called "big games," in which a chip is a quarter, and the limit on a bet is two bucks. Quite a lot of money can change hands pretty quickly in that game, and most of the players are the older fellows, quite a few of them rated men. It's a friendly game, basically, but you play each hand for what you can make out of it.

And as must be obvious by now, I've been more than a little lucky. For instance, I hadn't played before mid-December when I was invited for the first time. I then had $16 to my name. Since then I've drawn $10 in pay, a total of $26. The next installment will make $150 I've sent you - - plus the package amount which I'm not going to tell you. And I now have in my pocket $18, am owed $16, plus an undisclosed amount in my second bank.

But the point I want to make clear to you is this - - when and if my luck goes bad I'm not going to get over my head in debt, or lose all the money I have in the pay account. That's to get me home some day. So - - I have been and expect to continue to keep a working capital of 15-20 dollars. Any time I'm lucky enough to build it up to where I can send you a money order, I'll do it and that money will be safely away before I get a chance to lose it back. When I lose - - I have a couple of times - - I will not borrow but wait until I draw enough pay to start a nest egg again. Meanwhile, I'll always have on hand an ample stock of cigs, etc, so I'll not want for anything, and have on the books enough money to get me home when and if the chance comes.

Meanwhile I'm getting a big kick out of it, getting to know more and more of the guys here better and better, and it's the only real fun I've found! So much for the gambling. I await your reaction with interest.

While I'm on the subject of recreation, tomorrow should be our day to go for beer, and I'm planning on going even though we still have work to do. We'll get the painting done some day, and those couple of beers look good to me now, wish I had one right now.

And for more in the line of what might very properly be called recreation, I'm heading now for some sleep. It's hot as hell in this hole; I'm sweating jellybeans as you used to say. So goodnight, my darling, I love you so very much and am living and waiting for the day when I can take you in my arms and tell you all about it and how I have missed you.

3/16/45 Friday evening in port

I'm writing to you now while I'm on watch. When I finish there will be mail for each of the kids. Then tomorrow, when I expect to go ashore, I must do some writing. After that I should be able to get to Mass on Sunday and also clean up the rest of the correspondence backlog.

I received two jam-packed letters from you yesterday and am still ruminating on them for they're lovely to read. I want to address a few of the points you made.

So all of you have been walking. Yes my darlings, well do I remember those walks that made so many of our days in Philly pleasant. Miss them, too, for there's no such thing here, let alone no such company. Don't be too hard on Bucky for seeming bored by them; boys of his age have <u>so</u> many <u>important</u> things they want to do. Mother will tell you it wasn't so terribly long ago another Charles decided he couldn't spare the time to go on Sunday afternoon auto rides. - - and how that Charles wishes he could have one of those rides now! Must remember, though, to talk to Bucky about fighting when I write again in a day or so. Was it anything really serious? I don't mind too much so long as he stays in his own class.

As for Mother and Fran being pals, it seems to me that Bucky possibly has more of my traits, but of course I'm not one to judge. And that reminds me of a remark you made in a recent letter to the effect that I never have been as close to Fran as the other two. He'll be three in June, by which time I will have seen him in only 19 of his 36 months. It was a vastly happier story with the other two. Does that explain anything? Anyhow I'm hoping to start making up the deficit soon.

Golly I hope Chubbin's eye is all right long before now. I don't know how the teacher could have missed her condition.

To get back to me, Svoboda and I worked quite hard today putting the finishing touches on the guns. Wiped all of them clean, and oiled them and cleaned all the barrels. They look quite spic and shiny, too, thank you. It's been another of those blazing hot days, too, and I've a bit of new sunburn tingling on my back.

A slight interruption: had to go below for a drink of water and en route Lieut. Barnett, one of our division officers, and a very swell guy, stopped me to say that he wanted me to see another officer tomorrow about some writing. I doubt very much that it will mean anything to me but I'll see.

And also he told me censorship is clearing our second operation, so I can tell you Bucky's flying fish picture came from the South China Sea. That operation, also with a fast carrier task force, had us covering with air strikes the invasion of Luzon, working over that island, Formosa and Okinawa and Iwo Jima to shut off the enemy air supply route. Of course you don't need to be told that the Jap fleet didn't dare stir into that hornet's nest, even to try and save the Philippines.

Our cruise took us through the strait between Formosa and Luzon down into the China Sea, and believe me it was cold there; many a night that that I wished I'd been a little less hasty in disposing of my boot camp "longies." All the way down to Hong Kong and Saigon we went, just about as far away as I can get from you without crossing the equator or sailing into the Indian Ocean.

Once again we were in comparatively little action, much of it due to those gallant kids in those Hellcat planes. It wasn't quite as peaceful as the Mindanao coverage; a couple of times we saw that lovely ball of fire a Jap plane makes before the last splash. And the weather, although cold and damm rough at times was nothing like the typhoon. The night we came back out into the Pacific the little yellow boys were all fixed for a party, but spoiled it themselves by picking the wrong time and place to start.

It was for me and I guess for all of us, a long and grueling operation. I know I spent so many hours in our little tub that I began to believe I lived there. After it was over, Admiral Halsey, in a message to all the fleet, told us it had been a job well done, a material contribution to victory. Not surprisingly, that made me feel good even though I knew my part alone was nothing.

Guess that about covers that trip. Of more timely interest there's little or nothing to be said except that the coral isle prospects are pleasant. Lordy imagine it, I've been on land exactly three times this year, each time for something like three hours! Anyhow, I'll tell you more about it tomorrow.

And tomorrow, I hope, also will bring me a letter saying you've had an armful of mail from me for it grieves me you've had such a long dry spell. Nite my darling; even when the letters don't come, don't ever doubt for a minute that I'm thinking of you and loving you with all heart.

My own Bettsy: 3/17/45

Having written the daily letter for all of you, I'm starting this as sort of a post script for you only, and I don't want you to feel badly about not sharing it as you do the others; after all even an old (ten years, almost!) married couple is entitled to a moment alone occasionally. I've been meaning to do something like this for some time, and probably will again.

Firstly there's the sad news from your family you asked me not to mention in the family letter, and I can't tell you how sorry I am to hear about it. They certainly have had all the lousy breaks. You didn't say what was wrong with Kay but I assume it was some post-maternal difficulty. Gee, it's tough about Wilb, too; seems to me he's done his fair share over there, and I'll be dammed if I can see anything resembling a manpower shortage.

Yes, my darling, I know how it must hurt you to sense that they feel you have deserted them by going to Somerset, especially because you always were the rock they anchored to. And I agree you can't explain it so that they could understand. Therefore it's best left unsaid.

But Betty darling when we made the decision where to go we made it solely on the basis of what would be <u>best</u> for our little ones, knowing (but not fully, then) that they (the kids) must lose a lot of life every child should have, rightfully. I know I tried to disregard any possible resulting resentment from either family in making the choice, for there's no doubting that the same re-action would have come from my family had the decision been reversed.

And can you not say, honestly in your own heart, that our kids are better off in Somerset than in Allentown - - physically, mentally, in every way?

That is the only salve I can offer you for your conscience. And while I know it can't heal, or remove the regrets from what might have been, still I hope it will take away much of the sting.

For our children, no one can honestly blame us for being selfish. Nor should we blame ourselves.

Which is enough preaching from the guy who ran away and left you with all the job to do. But Bettsy, when you need a shoulder to cry on, mine is always waiting for you no matter how many thousands of miles lie between us, just as it would be if I could take you in my arms and hold you so very tight. Don't ever forget that, nor neglect it, dearest.

To hold you in my arms - - what lovely words and marvelous memories - - the husky sound of your voice, the feel of your lips, your satin-smooth skin. Those things my green eyes, I am horribly hungry for yet starved as I am and must be, no other can take your place or fill even the smallest part of my need. Seven months I have been away from you, yet not once have I ever wished for anyone but my own darling. Nor ever will. Of this I'm glad.

I love you, my Betty, with every fiber of my being, and will to the end of time. Please God, may it be soon that I can be with the only woman in all the world - - forever.

3/20/45 Tuesday noon in port

Forgive me if this letter is more than usually dopey, but a while ago I took a nasty knock on the head and it did me no good. I also overdid the writing the other day when I scribbled seven letters and mailed you a package. Really I don't feel like writing but this is my chance for the day since I'm on watch, so here goes.

The knock on the head came just after I had walked through the chow line and was going over to get a cup. Without warning, and for no apparent cause, the leg of one of the tables I told you are suspended against the ceiling, swung loose and struck me on the head. It staggered me for a moment, and I spilled half my tray, but recovered and went back for more food and then ate.

Result is that I have a big knob on my forehead, and a slight cut, plus a handsome headache. But I guess I'll survive - - no Purple Heart for sure.

There's little to tell you about today and I know of nothing coming up. I rolled out of my rack about 7:30, had one soggy slice of make-believe toast and a few sliced peaches for breakfast then went to quarters. After which we had our pictures taken, not individually but the whole division in two groups. I expect I'll get one print some day, and I'll send it to you. After that it was work until we had to quit, then lunch and my head-whacking and here I be on watch. Which, just now is a good place to be.

First of all it gave me this chance to write to you, and secondly because there's a great deal of work to be done that wouldn't make my headache any more pleasant. Time was when my conscience would have bothered me to loaf while some of my work is being done, but not any more.

And honestly I hope that attitude, or at least a part of it, stays with me after I leave the Navy. When I think of all the hours I worked, when my own full share was done, just because I wanted to help someone or felt I was needed, I could kick myself. For every one of those working hours was an hour I might well have had with you. And if I didn't know it before I know now that all I really want in this world is hours and days, months and years with you.

Gosh, Bettsy how I'd love to be with you this night. Maybe we could go for a ride and just enjoy the country together. Remember one night we rode, and you talked, and at the end I kissed you? That was the beginning of many, many wonderful nights for us, my darling. Nights I shall never forget, nor days either and I want only to go back to that life with you and our little ones at the earliest possible moment.

Those memories, my Betty, are the greatest treasure any man could hope to have, and I want only to go back and make them live again. It's mighty comforting, in these lonely days and much more lonely nights, to know that you, too, want and are waiting for the same thing.

Yes, my dearest, I am lonely, and will be always so long as I must remain away from you. But this won't last forever and some day I shall have you in my arms and shall try to begin telling you - - I love you.

3/25/45 Sunday (I think) evening (I think) - - at sea

Obviously I'm not at all sure what day or date it is - - life is like that again - - but having let you down yesterday my conscience just won't let me slip past again. There's no way I can gauge in advance how much or how little I shall be able to write now, but at least you can be sure I've not forgotten.

Quite the contrary, you've been in my thoughts and dreams even more than usual these past two days; I am so hungry for the sight and sound and touch of you, just to convince me that those years of ours were not a too-wonderful nightmare. (Now what in the hell made me write that?) Guess that I was thinking faster than these shaking fingers can follow, saying to myself the years were a dream and this is the nightmare. But anyway, you'll know what I'm thinking, that the essence of it all is and always will be - - I love you.

Of the two days there's little that can be said. Watch and eat and watch and sleep would just about cover it, with what spare time there has been for me devoted to the Dos Passos book of which I told you. It's good reading, a bit too much on the erotic side and vastly overdrawn. But the man is a beautiful word architect and I enjoy it much. Anyhow I've a good backlog of sleep, and hope I shan't mind too much having to stand the midnight to four tonight.

One little item: The toilet kit which I reported missing a couple of weeks ago turned up today, in a cranny where apparently I had placed it and then forgot. Was so delighted at the recovery of my favorite lotion that I promptly blew myself to a shave. And now I have two full kits - - against any similar future forgetfulness.

Mention of the lotion brings to mind two apparently dissimilar items I've been meaning to mention to you. Their similarity, and apparently my subconscious reason for thinking of them together lies in the men who practice them.

The lotion first: Increasing frequently of late I've been running across tremendous odors - - like the collected smells of all the (to recall an old phrase) Polish whorehouses in the world. And I've discovered that a surprising percentage of the men use lotion, hair oil, powder and, in at least a couple cases, perfume! The other day in the mess hall I couldn't eat because the boy across from me was so overpoweringly (and obnoxiously) "adorned." As a result I'm often loathe to use my old standby.

Second item is the "muscle men." It's my guess that upwards of 10 percent of the entire crew take regular exercises, straining at heavy dumbbells, bar bells, spring devices, etc. in pursuit of the body beautiful. Most of them work like dogs at it, too, stretching, straining, puffing until you wonder that they don't blow up and burst. Me, I've never been around much of that before, and it seems so silly; such a waste of energy. And their programs aim principally for huge biceps and shoulder muscles - - the kind that are most easily and most often displayed. They talk of "feeling wonderful" and "it's the best thing in the world for you. In passing: I've noted with amusement that when there's real physical work to be done, the "muscle men" usually are hard to find and not working.

Well, we were told today a little more about where we're going and why. Of course I can't tell you but I mention it here as a symptom of what I hope is a new policy of keeping the crew better informed. Anyhow I find it distinctly encouraging and hope it will continue and expand. Understand, too, that soon we'll be permitted to talk about the last operation, and when that day comes I shall be able to set you straight on quite a few things.

One more thing before daylight vanishes and I must quit: We're permitted to tell you now of our last operation; I haven't received a release yet, but have read it, and won't go into detail until I've had a better chance to study it; and of course I'll send my copy to you.

But for this letter, I can tell you I did have a date with your "hunch islands"; but <u>not</u> on the day you think I did. You see, my darling, the day I couldn't write we were torturing Tojo - - yep; we were on the Tokyo raid. I couldn't find time to write the first day, but did the second. <u>Then</u> we went to Iwo, which I'll always remember as one of ugliest, most God-forsaken pimples on the face of the earth. And after a stay there we went back to tease Tojo, found him hiding behind a snowstorm, and so went home.

There's a lot more I want to tell you, especially about Iwo, but that can wait. Meanwhile this much may salve your burning curiosity.

Would that be my good deed for this day? I hope so, for dusk is coming on me and I must say halt. But before I say that, perhaps you'd be willing to listen once again to our most oft-said phrase. I hunger for you, my Bettsy, and for all the lovely life we all of us knew together. I pray every day we may return to that life soon. 'Nite, my dearest one.

3/28/45 Thursday morning at sea

Time is mine for a little bit at least, and while all is tense it is hard for me to settle down to writing - - nonetheless I'll do what I can.

A long, pleasant night of sleep has done much to freshen me today. Nearly eight hours is the longest snooze in nearly a week, and lordy how I hated to roll out. Now Leroy and I are on watch, and if lucky we'll have the afternoon off and perhaps I'll be able to sneak another snooze. Well, I haven't yet gotten my copy of the last operation release for further study, but this should be almost as good a time as any to tell you what I can remember about it. Concerning the Tokyo raid, there really isn't much to be said. We weren't told officially where we were going, or when, until a day or so before the first strike. But curiously we weren't worried then. The carriers of a Fifth Fleet Task Force are very comfortable company indeed.

And the correspondents must have know what they were saying when they described the force as the mightiest striking force in naval history. Our press and radio reports told us - - and you - - of 1,000 and more planes over the islands, and the Nips had their hands more than full at home.

It was cold there, especially on the long night watches, and I'll never be able to give enough credit to the boys on the carriers who must have been freezing on the windswept flight decks as they loaded, fueled, armed and launched the planes. There never was a hitch in their smooth teamwork. The news told us that at times Tokyo was less than 100 miles - - 15 minutes by plane - - but all we saw was sea - - and our own lovely planes.

Coming back from that first raid we ran at night into a screen of enemy picket boats, the same ones which apparently had failed in their mission to warn of our approach. Fellows on watch that night told me later there was sporadic shooting as our force found them and sent them down. I wouldn't know; I slept like a babe all night.

Then it was Iwo, an ugly, desolate black island much smaller than I had imagined. All around it was an incredible concentration of the ships and boats and warships of invasion. When and how so many men could be at one time on that little island I never could imagine. But they were there, we could see endless streams shuttling onto the beach in the bobbing boats, and watch them slogging up the hill.

At one end of the island, Suribachi, the old volcano, stuck up like a wart on the level plain; at the other end a jumble of volcanic rock rose almost as high as the volcano, and it was there that we saw the only vegetation; gnarled, stubby trees and farther out the underbrush that seemed to thrust roots like claws digging into the island.

Destroyers were in close to the beach occasionally spurting orange flames as their guns fired at the cave-hidden enemy. Farther out the bigger ships were there, sometimes almost hidden behind the orange-brown smoke of their guns.

All the way to the horizon you could see transport cargo ships, alligator-jawed amphibian ships and boats and in and around and among all these, scuttling to the beaches and back were the smaller amphibs; the LCI's and LCVP's.

We lay out not too many thousands of yards off the island, and through field glasses I studied it pretty closely; the sunken ships on the beach, the wreckage of a dozen planes along the edge of the airfield; the gaunt steel skeleton of a gun emplacement on the skyline. I watched our shells smashing into the enemy positions, followed the tanks scuttling about hunting the enemy. Even without glasses we could see the spurts of red fire and black smoke where the flamethrowers were at work.

And at night the guns kept a continuous cover of star shells - - big ones that burned whitely - - hanging over the battle zones. They kept the place light as day, almost, yet we could see streams of tracer bullets spurting. Sometimes a bullet would lodge in a rock or something and glow weirdly for a moment. Others ricocheted off at angles like the ribs of a fan.

Always there were planes, our planes, overhead; spotting for the guns, circling, guarding us. But one morning the bombers came, to work on Suribachi. It was a sight I'll never forget. Clouds of planes buzzed like bees in formation overhead until they had picked their targets and time. The diving; roaring motors; guns spitting lead and a wavy trail of smoke; bomb bay doors opening and the bombs dropping out. As each plane leveled and pulled away two others seemed to take its place.

I could feel the concussions and watch the smoke rising, the rock crumpling to dust. When the raid had finished I could <u>see</u> the changes in the mountain. How anyone could possibly have lived through it, I can't conceive - - yet the Marines had a bitter fight before they reached the top. There were other raids, but none I saw approached that one in ferocity.

Those are some of the things I remember - - oh yes, one more. One day from my perch I watched through the glasses as the Marines assaulted a pillbox on the hill. From a trench I could see them aiming rifles, firing, then skulking from rock to rock inching upward as the clumsy looking little tanks crawled up to help. So far away, I could not hear the noise I knew was there. It was like watching a movie, a silent one, on a small round screen. I did not see the finish, but I know what it must have been.

As I said, those are some of the things I remember out of the kaleidoscope of my first invasion closeup. Perhaps others may come to me later, and some day I'll tell you the whole story. Probably you've guessed this has been hard to write - - it's now nearly six hours since I started and the afternoon is gone. Maybe there'll be a chance to write again this evening, if so I'll try.

But whether or not, my darling, you know I am thinking of you often, and remembering and wishing, wanting; loving you with all my heart until the day we can be together again.

3/29/45 Thursday evening - - at sea

Dearest Betty:
    I love you
    Tonie

3/30/45 Saturday evening at sea

You can see how far I got with that letter, and maybe this one will be no better so I'd better say now what's most important.

I do love you, my dearest, and always will. I'm lonely, too, for all of you; I want only to get back to being part of a family once more. That's the essence of it; there's lots more could be said on the subject but let it ride at that much for the minute while I try to find something that will make this less of an excuse for (and more like a real) letter.

Truthfully there isn't much I can say at the moment except that I'm quite tired, and most assuredly looking forward to a full night of real sleep, if we're lucky. I've spent so many hours wearing phones lately that my ears tingle every time I walk past a set - - and maybe they won't be so stick-outish when I come back.

To be perfectly frank, I've even lost track of the day and date, so badly that I can't quite bring myself to realize that yesterday was Good Friday and tomorrow will be Easter.

In the few minutes I lay awake in my bunk last night before dropping off to sleep I was remembering other Good Fridays, somehow recalling best those when I was a boy serving on the altar and making the long three-hour visit in church during the afternoon. And just now I recall where I was last year: arriving at Great Lakes and starting out on all this Navy business that has taken me so far from the ones I love and so changed all our lives. I'd rather forget that; just hope it will be over soon and we all can go to church together next Good Friday. Seems funny not to be able to go to Mass, but that's the way it is now.

Along the same line, I don't even remember when I last wrote to you; recall a quite long letter on Tokyo and Iwo, but I'm not sure whether it was Tuesday or Wednesday. As you can see I didn't get very far with my attempt on Thursday - - (to be strictly honest, all I did write then was the date; the rest I added this evening just to show you what I was thinking) - - and there was no chance whatsoever yesterday. Good Friday began at midnight Thursday when I went on watch and there wasn't a minute of writing time before I rolled into bed, dog-tired, at 8 p.m. And today began for me at 3:30 a.m.; up to now I haven't seen my bunk since then, and will be grateful to get into it so early as last night.

By the way, this letter will contain my copy of the Tokyo-Iwo release, which I obtained the other day. Hope I covered it all in the letter, for I don't think of anything else now and honestly don't feel like trying to remember. It all seems so far in the dim past.

Still no sight of mail, though we keep hoping day by day. A letter or so from you would do a lot toward making life more livable at the moment, and I know they're on the way. And there should be a pretty good batch for you with this one, which is some small consolation. (Oops, another interruption and I dropped my pen but it doesn't seem to be hurt.)

Guess now I'd better quit for tonight, my dearest, with the hope I'll be able to write again tomorrow. But whether I do or don't you'll know that always and forever I love you.

3/31/45 Sunday afternoon at sea

It's dammed near impossible for me to realize that this is Sunday, let alone Easter, but that's what the calendar says and who am I to dispute the late great Julian? Maybe I should argue instead with the guys who got us into this mess, but Adolph is a long way off and sinking fast, while Tojo and Hirohito yet remain a little too distant even for Frisco's big guns.

Anyway here I am just about as far away from you as I ever hope to get, on a sun-hazy afternoon; the sea flat, the wind pleasantly calm, and all about me hangs a queer quiet into which the rapid ticking of the director fits like an integral part. If I could just keep my eyes and ears closed for a little while it would be easy to believe the war is far away.

And I thought last Easter the strangest I ever spent! At least, then, I had some new clothes; rather ill-fitting blues, they were, but free and so I shouldn't kick. And there were some friends with me then, too; wish Jess were here now. My sartorial splendor, today, however, is confined solely to a much-needed bath, shave, and tooth brushing, which made me feel pretty good. Confess I needed all three, and a haircut, too, which I'm presently unable to get. However, I suspect this is the time for that special trim. Will advise you later on that.

As you have guessed already there's little to be said today. Got me my long sleep in good order last night and feel pretty pert right now though 5 a.m. to midnight is going to make this a long day. Might even treat myself to a nap when I finish this, which will be soon. I'm sitting now near my tub, with the phones on and a pair of binoculars slung around my neck.

Lordy, darling, how I wish and hope we'll not have to be apart any more Easters. Two is more than plenty, thank you, and it's no shame to confess I'm more than a mite homesick for all of you.

Chapter II
FRISCO AT WAR - PART FOUR
ROOSEVELT & HITLER DEATHS,
CATAPULT OPERATION, V-E DAY, FRISCO GETS A DOG
4/2/45 to 5/29/45

4/2/45 Tuesday morning (0100) at sea

Funny, when I tore this sheet from my tablet yesterday afternoon I knew I might not use it immediately - - but I didn't suspect I should be writing now.

This is my first watch below decks, and a queer one, for we know nothing about what's going on topside - - and have no responsibilities there. But the work isn't too hard, and there's light to write, so it won't be a total loss despite no opportunity for me to snooze.

Honestly, I'm physically unable at the moment to count up how little sleep I've had in the last week all I do know is that it hasn't been enough. Practically everyone sleeps as they can in the daytime, but somehow I never can get enough hours to make up for my night watches.

By the way, I haven't told you yet that the writing business which I mentioned previously has disappeared and I'm somewhat glad. It seems now we have a yeoman aboard, a former newsman I'm told, who will take over the press news.

To go back to the more routine things for a moment, yesterday was a long and busy one for me. Up at 3:30 to go on watch, spent the morning after breakfast cleaning and oiling our guns and getting my laundry folded and put away. Through the afternoon I was on watch, rubbernecking mostly, and got ready to write but gave it up. Snatched a half-hour nap before supper, then to my tub until 8, and finally to bed for 3 hours before I came on this watch. This morning I hope to spend sleeping, but don't dare even promise myself that.

Still no signs of mail, though rumors persist of its presence or imminent arrival. Truthfully I have become sort of inured to this blackout and don't mind it overly much except that I know it's much harder for you to get along without letters. At least I know where you are and approximately what you're doing - - which is more than you can say.

Chow has improved a bit as of late, and I've discovered a new method of filling the hole. When I've finished eating what I can, if I'm still hungry I go back to grab a slice or so of bread and usually can wrangle a hunk of butter to go with it. That helps surprisingly.

Did I ever tell you that sailors are the most amazing sleepers I've ever seen? Right now ten are awake; the eleventh has his shoulders on one deck chair (head dangling over the back), his hips on another deck chair (the two chairs are a foot apart) and his feet on a packing box another foot away and about a foot lower. He's been sleeping there for two hours, completely oblivious to the chatter, a constant stream of traffic and enough noise to frighten a civilian out of his wits!

Honestly I don't even remember what a bed with real sheets (let alone a certain bed with certain other very special accoutrements) feels like. Nor do I dare let myself think overly much about it, for obvious reasons. But when I do get back, you're as likely as not to find me sleeping on a stairway or some other dumb fool place, at least until I'm housebroken.

Wonder if you've gotten the package yet? I'll be interested in your reaction. Gee, it's warming to think about that - - and other things, anything connected with you and home.

Gradually I begin to hope that it may not be an eternity until we can begin making some of our dreams come true again, my darling. The news from Europe is wonderfully encouraging these days; the end there <u>must</u> be near, and anyone with half an eye can see the handwriting on the Pacific wall. But I can't help wish that the end were equally close here.

Wonder just what it will be like to go back to really living again, and how many difficulties and challenges we must encounter. As for you and I, I'm fairly sure they will be few and easy, but I'm not so sure about the kids and I, for I'll have to begin all over learning to know Buck and Chubbin and Fran. I've so many plans and dreams for them, for all of us together, that if only a very few of them can be made to come true we'll all soon be able to forget this long separation - - this hole in our lives

This interlude has taught me a lot, and shown me a lot I never would have known otherwise, but it couldn't possibly be important enough to compensate for having to be away from you. That, my darling, is because I love you.

4/9/45 Monday afternoon at sea

It occurs to me as I start this letter that I very possibly was entirely in error on both the day and the date of the note I scribbled so hurriedly last evening. However, the day and the date above are correct (I checked!) so while there may seem a gap it's not there.

Well, my long sleep last night materialized, glory be, and except for an unpleasant (?) very personal but brief interruption I snoozed away eight solid hours. That caught me up pretty well, but it begins to look as if I'll be back in the hole as quickly as I got out, for now it appears the only relief I'll have today during 20 hours of solid routine watches is about an hour and a half devoted to standing in line and bolting down my three meals.

I've spent the day thus far reading, when it might better have been devoted to writing. I've just now finished with a bad taste Will Irvin's "The Making of a Reporter" which I began yesterday, and the first few chapters of which I enjoyed so much. The last half degenerates into a very ordinary travelogue - - very dull to say the least.

To return to last night for a moment, I don't suppose you knew it but I was with you for a little while, in our own particular heaven, and it was very wonderful. Lord, my darling, I find it impossible to imagine how heavenly it will be to return to living our own lives. But since at this distance 'tis the nearest thing to heaven I can know I'm resigned to the aftermath. And I can never tell you what a source of comfort and courage it is to know that you are wanting and waiting too.

This morning during our brief respite for breakfast, I got out my pictures and gloated over them a bit, and do you know I've just now realized that the ones I enjoy most, with one exception, are those snaps I took before we left Philly. Trying to reason why, I've come to the conclusion that that they show our little ones as last I knew them, while the most recent pictures are of changelings; familiar, ours to be sure, but older and so obviously matured that I subconsciously wonder can I, do I really know them? It will be a thrill to hold them in my arms, to walk with them and talk with them and tuck them into bed at night and to try to make up all the hours we've lost together.

The exception is the smiling picture of you taken in front of the house, for it shows me you as I remember - - and you've never changed a whit from the wonderful one I found 15 years ago. By the way: remind me some time to tell you I love you.

I'm glad to hear you admit to curiosity about the package, for it's my favorite project at the moment. And I hope your curiosity will be further awakened when said package arrives. I'd love to watch your face when you open it - - or any time, preferably <u>now</u>, for that matter.

Which is a good place to stop It's coming along toward supper time and the wind and awkward writing position have about drained my patience. Besides I'm out of words except those that I always close with. And you know what they without me having to pen them.

4/10/45 Tuesday afternoon in port

I dood it! Here's how:

Even as I move in the dark of early morning, when usually my thoughts are blackest, I had no premonition of such a horrible deed. To be sure, I was grumpy and tired; yesterday was much, much too long and I had only four hours sleep. But to think - - I shudder.

Through the long rainy dawn watch I stood grouchily at my post, peering into the damp haze. My feet were wet; water dripped from my waterproof clothing: everyone was crabby, there was little talk. Some of the more hardy drowsed - - but I am not yet in that salt-crusted circle.

At last: Relief! Sloshing across the puddled deck I begin to feel a bit better. Soap, cold water, my toothbrush bolstered my morale. Hot cakes and canned grapefruit for breakfast helped too. As I got up to dispose of my tray and silverware, I began to feel almost human.

(Now all of these things have no direct bearing on the dastardly act I'm about to impart. I relate them here only to show that I began the day at least nominally pure in heart.)

Then came my downfall! As I turned from the table after stacking my tray, I saw a line, only a small line to be sure, but a line nonetheless. Now few sailors can resist a line. Be it a block long, with a hairpin salesman at the head, the average sailor will join it, shuffle slowly to the front, make his purchase (or do whatever those ahead of him in line have done) and then, wander away - - in search of another line.

As I say, this was a small line, little more than a beginning. Soon, I knew it would be longer and subconsciously sailors reserve a special spot in heaven for those of their ilk who are at or near the front of any line, can carry out their mission, while latecomers stare enviously, and perhaps may have an earlier chance at the next line. Past this line, this little line, this incipient one, I must go to reach my bunk. I started, but a force too strong for my weak will turned my sodden shoes from the chosen path. Before I realized it, I was IN that line!

For a long time it seemed - - we sat there or stood; talking perfunctorily or just staring. Beside me, a big, jolly North Carolinian, Doc Edwards, sat puzzling through the mysteries of the daily news sheet. When I think of Doc in after years, he will always be to me the white man best personifying Kipling's description of Fuzzy Wuzzy "at his 'ome in the Sudan."

"You're a poor benighted 'eathen

But a first-class fighting man"!

Absent-mindedly I counted the heads ahead of me; eight. Breakfast was over and the mess cooks come with brooms and mops to make all clean again. Charily we moved out of their way as they worked, watchful always lest someone preempt an earlier place in line. Oh, the LINE - - it had become much longer.

At long last a canvas-covered gate swung open. A white-garbed sailor, with a green eyeshade clamped around his stiff, sandy hair, beckoned to The First Man In Line. The First Man scuttled into the white-painted brightly lit room without even pausing to notice the envy of those behind him. Two others followed him. The rest of us shuffled ahead a step or two, settled down to wait again. Shortly, another gate swung open, and another white-coated sailor (this one had brick-red hair) beckoned. Only one man followed him. Four remained ahead of me. We shuffled up one more step.

A few minutes more and the first door opened and The First Man emerged smiling. We could see three white-coated men inside. Another man got up and took his place inside. Twice more this happened and only Doc stood between me and The Door. It might come any moment now! Again we waited; more patiently for the end was in sight. Out came a man from the second relay and Doc replaced him; another out and I was IN.

All this time I had been thrusting from my conscious thoughts the decision I knew I must make. Sure I will. Well, maybe not this time. Why not? When a better opportunity? Well perhaps we might wait- - Oh the hell with it. But I was In! Too late to turn back and the white-coated man was wrapping a sheet around me. My fingers must have been clenched as I whispered to him in a shaky voice. I could feel the others looking at me - - and I didn't dare return the stare.

A whirring, buzzing noise - - I thought of a rattlesnake. I could feel, sense rather, the white-coated man (this one was tall and dark, quite thin) moving deftly, silently behind me. I felt an odd tingle to my scalp. The buzzing continued, now louder, now softer. I could _feel_ it, as well as hear it. There was some perfunctory talk - - but not from me.

Now the white-coated man held carefully a gleaming, silvery instrument. He approached me from the side. No use trying to run, the sheet bound me firmly. But there was no pain, only a gentle, scraping rasp. Then the smell of something sweet, like flowers, and the shroud was lifted. I stepped down, mentally pulling my belt a couple of notches tighter.

As I slunk through the gate xxxxxxxxx [Censor at work again] there were less sneers and snickers than I anticipated. I ran the gauntlet of the still growing line. But I could feel a blush mounting on my naked knob! And I could hear the barber murmur "Next"!

All that was some hours ago and already I'm becoming accustomed to my nakedness. Matter of fact it feels rather comfortable

(Bet Lady Godiva was, too!) and within a day or so my friends will be past the jeering stage. Actually, there has been less than I anticipated, possibly because I had so little to lose. At any rate the deed is done, and in a good cause, too, for I feel quite sure that should I come home with anything remotely resembling a head of hair you will consider this war to be a little less than a total loss.

And I do hope you'll forgive the bit of fantasy. It's been a long time since I wrote anything just for the fun of putting words together that when the idea struck me I couldn't pass up the chance. Of course that, too, is a dividend for you, in words, for without it there would be precious little to write and it was fun, too.

Anyhow I'm relieved to find my knob not quite as horrible as I feared. Shorn of my once-luxuriant tresses, my head emerges as rather egg-shaped, a sloping (distinctly anthropoidal) forehead rising to a fairly distant point at the rear summit. There's an absence, though, of the bumps, knobs and scars that emerged on so many of the shaved heads. Wish I could get a picture to send you, but I'm afraid it's impossible. As for the future, I expect to have the dome re-shaven every week or so for awhile, then let nature take its course. After all, I had darn little to lose, and if the razor can bring out hairs on my chin, why not on my head?

So you see there is no length to which I will not go for you, even when we're so far apart. Does that not prove I love you?

4/12/45 Thursday morning

As might have been expected, the urge to write waned after my hair-destroying epic, so that I've missed one day, part of another, and Lord only knows how far I'll get on this. But at least I can start - - and tell you I do love you, with all my heart.

But the intervening hours have been busy ones, have given me a new version of my old life - - yesterday I helped edit and prepare the ship's press news. My own part was very small, but nonetheless it was fun.

What happened was this. A day or so ago another officer - - totally without newspaper experience but anxious to make improvements and willing or at least able to put some time and intelligent effort into it - - took charge. Somehow he had heard of my past work, and so I received an invitation to help.

I was delighted and more than glad to devote what time I can spare. So right after lunch yesterday I reported for duty, and we spent something like three hours editing the material and organizing it. The product was his, wholly. I made a few suggestions, mostly on points of basic newspaper policies and edited a piece or two of copy and when it was done I could feel a little of that old indefinable pride that used to come to me when I saw the papers streaming from the press; or picked up a paper and point to a story and say "I wrote that"!

I was to help again today but circumstances and that wench Morpheus (or should it be he?) intervened until now and it looks like I 'm out. Oh well, tomorrow's another day. This morning I was free, but after breakfast Sam and I had some work to do on the guns but when that was finished Mr. Konopka, the officer, wasn't quite ready to start. So I went back to my bunk, intending to just rest for a half hour - - well, you can guess the rest. Someone had to shake me else I should have slept through lunch and gone on watch hungry. Ever since I've been on duty, and by the time I finish tonight tomorrow's issue should be done.

I guess maybe I should report on my new hair-do, then on to some mail matters. Said hair-do is progressing nicely. I've the darlingest crop of blond fuzz (There even seems to be a <u>bit</u> where there was none before!) and am gradually progressing out of the razzing stage. So far I've managed a twice-daily brushing, which I hope will help. Time alone can tell.

I've had quite a haul of mail the last few days. I received four letters from you, one from Buck, three envelopes of clippings and a Time.

Turning to the older of your two letters, I regret to find I was writing dully in port. Wasn't 'specially conscious of it at the time, but thinking back I recall that I did sort of have the blues or at least wasn't very happy.

As for you doing a good job keeping your worries out of your letters, I'm inclined to think you have. Of course I <u>know</u> - - and have known since before this venture started last year - - that you worry about me. Conceited ass that I am, I'd be dammed upset if you didn't. But what I insisted that you escape was the fidgety, skinny, aging obsession of fear and incompetence that has gotten too many otherwise fine women down. I am satisfied that has not <u>and will not</u> happen to you. And I'm very glad and very proud of you. Remind me, some time, to tell you I love you, in addition to the aforementioned emotions. Thanks.

Turning to your more recent letter, which mentions receipt of Jess's, I honestly can not recall writing him a single thing I have not told you.

Your coat sounds interesting, and I feel quite sure I shall like it (assuming that you kept it). I'm so glad you bought it - - and amused that such a savings-conscious person as yourself neglected to mention the price. Scared I'd scold?

And Aha! The wench admits to curiosity about the package. Gosh, I'd like to watch her face as she opened it, and hear the exclamations - - x!x!xxx - - afterwards. Oh well, some day.

Look, toots, it's getting dark now and I gotta go. Give Bucky and Chubbin and Fran a special big kiss from their lonely Daddy, and maybe when I get back I'll <u>even</u> have <u>one</u> for <u>you</u>!

4/13/45 Friday morning at sea

And so a Missouri political appointment [Harry Truman], sponsored if not spawned by one of the foulest political machines in the modern era, became the executive head of the world's greatest nation at one of history's most critical moments!

The news has just come to me that The President [Roosevelt] is dead. And instinctively, as I always do in moments of emotional shock, I am turning to you and to words for some relief. This letter may never be mailed, but whether or not it is should help me untangle some of the confused thoughts flooding through my head. Then I'll see about sending it to you. Curiously, I have a hunch you, too, are writing similarly at this moment.

It is a hazy and pleasant morning. I am on watch and was sitting near my station devouring my new Time magazine when a blonde boy manning the phones near me remarked nonchalantly, as though to no one in particular: "You hear that? The president is dead; straight dope. Came from Radio II." For a second I failed to grasp what he had said, then I made him repeat it and dazedly turned back to my magazine. The printed words refused to make sense. I must have fallen for a moment into my old trick of staring absently at nothing.

Suddenly the dam broke, and a wave of depression swept over me. I felt I had to get up, get some air. Outside a couple of the men were talking (casually, it struck me) about the news. Someone asked me who would become president; I told them. "Who's Truman"? one of them asked, and I told them what little I could remember about the man at the moment.

Perhaps it was the dark mood into which I had fallen, but the most important thing about Harry Truman I could remember was that it was St. Louis' bribe-taking boss Tom Prendergast who put him on the federal bench, later sent him to the Senate where Truman fought to the last ditch to keep his patron out of jail.

Yes, the latter part of his Senate term he had been a good legislator, a staunch New Dealer, a thorough investigator. He talked soundly through the campaign and, I thought, made a smart move when after being investigated he announced he would stick to his job of being vice-president and not go stump-jumping for everything from health to Hottentots as did his predecessor. But

I could not forget Prendergast.

As you know, I am not now and never have been a whole-hearted New Dealer, although most of the time I was inclined to that side. I felt and feel I was right in voting for him in 1936 - - and against him in 1940. I am not so sure I was right last year when my vote was cast rather against entrenched Republican re-actionaries, for whom Dewey was the front, than for FDR. But since the death of Wendell Wilkie I have been more and more convinced that no man in our public life save Roosevelt was qualified and prepared to deal with Stalin and Churchill toward any real hope of attaining what we are fighting for - - an enduring peace.

Now he is gone. And in my darkened thoughts I am inclined to believe that the nation and the world could better have suffered the loss of every man and every ship in this operation than of that so-lively cripple in Washington.

The war will go on, its outcome a certainty, no matter what the enemies may do or how sadly we mismanage. The juggernaut of men and machines has attained such momentum it cannot be stopped short of its military goal. But the peace is a-building. The scaffolding yet is large enough for only three. And now, our architect-carpenter is not FDR of the sharp blueprint and deft touch but the political product of a Missouri mob.

It may be - - let us all hope and pray - - that Truman can and will carry on to the universally-desired end. But - - - - -

Firstly he lacks FDR's experience and unmatched prestige in world politics. It seems only remotely possible that he should have so complete a grasp of history, economics, and psychology on the world scale. And very obviously he does not have the personality that was so much an invaluable asset at the conference table.

Lack of that personality, with its unprecedented vote-getting power, may hurt as much at home. Harry Truman will not be able to align recalcitrant Senators and Congressmen with the thought that he will take the issue in dispute to the people. A substantial percentage of the Senate and a damm-near majority of the House who made it into office on FDR landslides and whose only hope of reelection was his backing of their candidacy, will owe no debt to his successor. Truman was not long ago a sitter on those same magic coattails.

He also inherits an extremely difficult to deal with heterogeneous cabinet and I wonder if he can make it work.

Out here life goes on without a perceptible change. A half hour after we on watch received the news by phone someone remembered to mention it to the rest of the crew via the public address system: A shrill peep from a boatswain's pipe; an every-day tone of voice: "Word has been received of President Roosevelt's death in Washington." Only that, nothing more. The ship sails slowly across the flat sea. Probably I am hypersensitive, but I know this is a moment in history

Beside me, Leroy sleeps not knowing, rather not caring. Back on the fantail the pinochle game goes on uninterrupted. It would be a good wager that aboard this ship at this moment more men are engaged in a vicarious discussion of sex than are considering what has just happened to us.

But much of the pressure inside me has flowed out through my pen. Thank you my darling, for being you whom I know will understand my deepest feelings.

4/15/45 Saturday afternoon

I seem to have really written myself out yesterday, so that I've no such urge as I've had but there's time to write and a conscience to pacify. When I say I wrote myself out I mean it literally, for my day's production must have been a good many thousand words. First of all there was that windy panegyric to you and then I went to work.

Then I expended the entire afternoon helping with the press

news, because we got out an extra edition with all the available details of the President's death. I wrote the story from several thousand words of copy received via radio. I'm hoping that the censors will clear to you a copy of what I wrote, not that it's anything exceptional or important, but it does seem a milestone of my journalistic career. Frankly, I never expected to write the obituary of the man elected to the presidency in 1944, much less write it where I am and under such circumstances. After that I turned to the regular news report and wrote (rewrote, rather) three or four other stories.

Anyhow, it was fun, albeit hard work; seemed like the good old days to have a typewriter clattering under my fingers and to be rushing toward deadline. And the work seemed to pull me out of the slough of despair into which the news had plunged me. Right now, my instinctive reaction is that his death was a horrible blow to all the world - - yet somehow I <u>hope</u> we'll muddle through to the end we all want.

As to the news today, Russia's declaration of war [a false report], I have only hearsay of the bare fact. And I feel quite sure it was distinctly a propaganda move designed to counter the worldwide psychological effect of FDR's death. I don't mean by the declaration itself, but the timing of it, coming just now. It's been obvious for some time that Russia would fight Japan, perhaps only giving us bases, and I believe the timing of the announcement was agreed to at Yalta, probably to come shortly after Germany's defeat.

But it seems to me only a morale move just now. Stalin most certainly does not intend to make Hitler's fatal mistake of fighting on two fronts, so until Germany collapses and probably for some time afterwards, the Russian declaration can mean next to nothing in a physical military sense.

On the other hand it extinguishes any flickering Japanese hope the Soviets would somehow be persuaded to remain aloof from the Pacific War. At the same time - - and this I think is much the most important just now - - it takes away from the heads of the Japanese state any lingering optimism they might have held that Russia could be, even in a nominal sense, their friend at the allied court in arranging a compromise peace.

In the midst of all the writing hullabaloo yesterday I collected a flock of mail. First the lovely valentines from Bucky and Sis, then a letter from each of my darlings, a flock of clippings and Mary Smith's Christmas letter to you! Need I say my head was in a total whirl? I recall at the moment two things.

Firstly your hat spree, which delighted me no end and I do hope you went ahead with the permanent and glove business. But I'm dubious about one thing: I can't see how, after all the buying; you had so much money left out of such a small start. Gosh I hope you spent enough to get a good coat, and didn't let your frugal instincts overcome you. And I'm glad you got the next money order, which I suspect you've already turned into bonds. If there's anything you or the kids need or want, though, I hope you'll get it instead.

Secondly, the kids' letters, which I thought much the best either of them has done. Thank you, Elizabeth darling, and I do hope you'll enjoy your "straw bonnet with cherries." Your writing is very good, getting better all the time, and I hope you'll send me lots of letters. And yours too, Bucky, I thought was the best you have done; neatly written, not a word misspelled and just full of news. Wish I could see you in your new long-pants suit and real man's hat.

To all of you, I'll write just as soon as I can, and I send you my love and prayers for the three grandest kids in the world. Thank you, darlings, and take good care of Mother for me until I can get back to care again of all of you.

Do I need - - should I say thanks to you too, my Bettsy? You know what a joy and comfort your letters always are, and some day soon I'll be able to tell you in person all about it.

4/22/45 Sunday morning

I'm at the typewriter again today trying to get a bit of writing done and you are the first order of business.

Two days ago for the second time within a week I've been shocked - - I mean that literally. But unlike the death of FDR which made me <u>think</u>, the death of Ernie Pyle [a famous War Correspondent] made me <u>feel</u>. Although I never had the good fortune to meet him or work with him, it was like losing a very close personal friend, almost one of the family. And to think he had to die on one of these little postage-stamp hells that we fight for out here - - like all the rest of them a place of no more importance than a pimple on the face of a pubescent school boy. Is there - - can there possibly be - - any justice in that?

I had just finished the press news when I happened to hear the radio broadcast he had been killed. It was too late then to put anything in that morning's issue so I wrote the story for the next day's issue. And so within the space of a few days, I have written the obituaries of two great Americans, both dear to the hearts of the people

More mail arrived; a half dozen letters from you, one from Buck and another from Jess. He and Vone at last are on their way. Where, they don't know, but it looks like an advanced island base and when Jess wrote (4/8), they were on the eve of their departure. He sounded happy.

Your letters bring several pieces of news - - and a worse piece that you don't specifically put in words. First there was news of Jay Hauger's death, and of course that was mighty unpleasant. At least it was good that Ray came through OK. Secondly, Mary's new love and her sudden determination to marry. Unfortunately, the letter in which you apparently told me what little you knew about the guy is hasn't arrived yet. The only thing I know is that his name is John. When I finish this I shall try to write to her.

But the implied bad news, <u>much</u> the worst, was the way <u>you</u> let bad news get <u>you</u> down. Damm and double damm, that is the sort of thing I've been bawling hell out of you about. You individually and all of you HAVE GOT TO KEEP YOUR CHINS UP. AND TO DO THAT YOU MUST BELIEVE - - - - I DO, and it is ever so much easier.

Don't try to hide things from me or sugar-coat them. It's important for me to know that you are doing that. Don't try and camouflage or conceal your real feelings. Pray and believe (and I suggest the church may be able to strengthen you in that belief if you so desire) that some of these days I will be coming back to you and the life and love we have known and will have again.

As to Mary, don't prejudge. When he comes to Somerset, Mother and Dad must have the courage to sit down and talk the whole thing over with both of them, frankly and honestly. I never have forgotten that talk I had with your Dad, and always have been proud that he told me (I can hear him say it yet as we sat there on the bench in the kitchen.) - - "x x don't wait too long." That seems centuries ago, yet looking back it seems to me that you and I can say we did the right thing; certainly we can say our marriage has been a success in every sense.

Turning back to me for a moment, I spent all but 20 minutes of the night in my tub. Yesterday morning I worked on the press news and right after lunch I rolled into my bunk where I stayed for four hours and when I crawled out I felt like the fag end of a week-long drunk. Last night it was watch until midnight, then five hours' sleep, and here I am writing when bed is beckoning. This afternoon I'm afraid I'll be back at newspapering again and tonight is the long midwatch but I guess I'll get by.

From my perspective, these letters provide my relief from battle nerves. After all, you and writing are my ordinary life and so enable me to escape this temporary one, even while I am telling you about it. Almost always feel choked up after a letter to you. It is very good to talk to you my darling, even at such long range. And it will be infinitely more wonderful when I can once again see and be with and hold tight all of you, forever and ever.

4/25/45 Thursday morning at sea
[This was probably Wednesday]

Had an odd experience just after I finished writing to you the other day. A boy from another division, whom I scarcely knew, came up and asked if I could talk to him for a little bit. Of course I assented, and sort of shyly he wanted to know if I could straighten him out a bit on religion.

He's of Spanish or Mexican descent, I judge of the type that takes Catholicism very seriously, and why he asked me to help I don't know except he felt he wanted to talk to someone older who also is a Catholic and I guess I'm both of those. Anyhow, it turned out that he was very much afraid he had committed a serious sin because he lately had doubts about the very existence of God.

I confess it pretty well stumped me because, I am no theologian. I did the best I could for him, told him what I could put into words of my own personal beliefs, then suggested that he talk with our chaplain. He seemed to be dubious about the advisability of a Catholic discussing such matters - - or any religious matters - - with a Protestant minister, but I assured him that the chaplain is here to serve all men of all faiths. Then I went up and spoke to Mr. McAllister, who said he would be glad to see the boy and help him in any way he could. I went back and sent Flores (that's his last name; I know only that much because everyone has his name stenciled on his shirt) up to the chaplain's room.

I didn't see him again that evening, but the next evening after supper he and two other boys were sitting on a top-tier bunk talking and called me to come up and sit with them. They were still talking religion. Flores said he had a good talk with the chaplain about the whole thing, although he's still not completely reassured.

Anyhow, it was a new experience for me, albeit I realize I'm in no way qualified to be even an unofficial father confessor.

Thinking it over, I've come to the conclusion that the boy's trouble is battle nerves. I feel he turned to his religion for support and courage, got to thinking and by some queer quirk his more obvious worries were transmuted into worries that he was losing his faith. Hope we can come across a priest reasonably soon and Flores can have a decent chance to talk it out with him.

All around us the water, wrinkled as a crone heaves gently, methodically up and down like the shallow-breathing chest of a sleeping person. Up ahead a battleship plods majestically, leaving a silvery streak of wake which we follow and sometimes cross. That ship is a huge impersonal mass of steel; looking at it I find it hard to realize that men are living and working there too. Further out a slim destroyer steps daintily, as impersonal as the battleship yet somehow it seems a more natural thing than the vast, unwieldy wagon. It seems so tiny, too, but they're deadly little rapiers, these "tin cans" of ours - - as the Japs know all too well.

Behind me now the boatswain's pipe shrills and the crane begins to growl, tugging a plane off the catapult to lower it into the hanger. Each toot or series of toots on the pipe is to the crane operator like a blueprint to a machinist. Whooo-EE-ee picks up; TWweet, tweet tweet - - hold it there; Tweet tweet-tweetle tee (trilled on a descending scale) let it down. A weird and wonderful invention that pipe, a relic of the old sailing days. With it not only does the boatswain direct the crane in any delicate operation; he calls us to meals (a different tune, or at least series of notes for each meal), orders the decks swept down, clothing removed from the drying lines, or a boat to get moving and a dozen and one other things from welcoming, or saying goodbye to a distinguished visitor aboard to calling our attention to verbal orders transmitted via the loudspeakers or supplementing the bugler's call to battle stations!

And did I ever tell you about the bugle? Let's see how many calls I can remember: Reveille ("of course, dammit; some day I'm going to murder the bugler"), attention, mail call, liberty call, pay call, general quarters and A-A defense to send us to battle stations, secure (stop doing what the bugle last ordered), swimming call, various calls for different motor boats (on some of these a set of extra notes on the end means "on the double" - - (do it damm quick), lights out and taps. Betcha that isn't half of 'em either!

I'm sorry I let you down on the writing front recently and am trying to make up for it today. Yesterday I slept through lunch and then worked on the press news. Last night, I got into a poker game and enjoyed myself for a long time too, until 2 a.m. It wasn't overly profitable, but I added $5 to our personal kitty so the evening wasn't a total loss. After the game broke up, I crawled into bed and slept like a babe until 7 this morning, when I ate and came on watch. Spent most of the time rereading your recent letter and then started this, broke off for chow and here I am again.

Wonder if <u>the</u> package has reached you yet, and if your curiosity has been aroused a little?

I gather from your letters that the present moments and hours and days slip past much more quickly for me than for you; yet the accumulation of time, the <u>distance</u> back to <u>our</u> life, probably is greater for you.

And, following very naturally, you ask in another letter if I think we "can all hope to be together in our own house a year from now." My answer to that is yes, I feel we <u>reasonably</u> are entitled to <u>hope</u> - - and I <u>believe</u> that I will be home for good in <u>1946</u>. This hopefulness is because the war has come a long way in the <u>past</u> year

The tide is moving **irresistably** with us, soon to be augmented by the vast weight of arms now crushing the last breath from Nazi Germany. And so while I am not ready to <u>believe</u> that I will be home to stay in 1946's April, <u>I say we can hope</u>! I can't wait to get back to you and ours Bettsy.

4/27/45 Friday evening

I'm typing this note down below and it's hot as hell despite the rather feeble efforts of a fan buzzing not far from my right ear.

There's little to report, except another long night of sleep, broken when I was called at midnight to go on watch, which resumed immediately thereafter until 4 a.m. when I was relieved, wandered below and promptly returned to slumberland at 8 a.m.

This afternoon we had our first lower-decks inspection in some weeks and there were no problems. While waiting for the inspection, I stumbled across another book and the 4-6 afternoon watch found me reading "Torpedo Junction" by Bob Casey of the Chi Daily News. This fascinating yarn is a story of his own experience in Pearl and with the fleet during the first two years of the war.

The sea has been unlike anything I've seen before, flatter than any mill pond you could imagine; without a wrinkle except the wake of our passing to mar the surface. No waves, only a steady heaving that seemed so permanent it reminded me of a Kansas wheat field on a still day. And the color! A deep, lively blue from which a silvery flying fish broke occasionally to go skimming along for many yards before falling - - PLOP - - back in leaving only a spreading ripple to prove you weren't mistaking what you saw. Altogether very lovely, I assure you, but not so lovely to look at as a certain girl I can think of - - without trying too hard.

I sat, that hour on watch this afternoon, looking at the lovely sea and thinking of the lovely girl and somehow I was very lonely, more acutely so than for a long time. It seems so horribly long since I saw all of you; more than a year now, except for that girl, and no prospect of when the lonely journey will end.

Lately I've been wondering what this vast sheaf of letters I've written will sound like to me when I come home to read them, and if in after years they will bring back something real to me or will sound like a very amateurish travelogue. There must be a helluva pile of these things now Bettsy; finding any difficulty with storage space? Too bad I can't save your letters.

Thank God the end of the war seems to be in sight. Moment by moment I expect the news from Europe that it is all over - - it is inconceivable that the Germans are continuing to fight. Out here in the Pacific we are so close to victory, but the end result is just as much inevitable, and the path plain before us. How can it not be plain to those we fight?

But just now the writing mood has fled me, and I think I'll call this a letter. 'Nite my dearest. It's dark, now, and I've the midwatch (12-4) tonight, so I think I'll be heading for my little bed. Wish instead I could be heading for another, ever-so-much-more-friendly one, but that isn't to be for at least a little while yet. But no matter the distance, I can always tell you goodnight, my darling.

4/29/45 Sunday night in port

Have you ever written a letter by moonlight? Neither have I - - until now - - so forgive me if this scribbling is even worst than usual. Anyhow, that should give you some idea of what kind of night this is. Seems such an occasion and such a setting ought to yield something special in the way of a letter, but I've no hopes for that and will be more than satisfied if I can discharge my daily duties even reasonably.

A number of events worth reporting on this very hot day, the first of which was Mass and communion for the first time in six weeks. I didn't serve; the priest brought his own yeoman. And all afternoon Svoboda and I worked up on the forecastle. Next I think was noon chow, which was turkey and all the trimmings - - our Easter dinner five weeks late because we were much too busy then. It was a grand meal, the best we've eaten in a long time.

But I had to go to work, hard work, afterward for Svoboda

and I worked for hours up on the forecastle cleaning the list of our guns in the broiling sun. I felt so tough when we finally finished that after my shower I just had to lie down - - so no work at all today on the press news.

Several mail calls today brought me a letter from you, one from Bucky, several papers from the Smiths and a couple envelopes of clippings plus the food package you mailed 2/17 which arrived in very good condition. I thank you my darling and shall save the chow against our next shortage or set of bad meals.

Your letter shocked me no end and I must confess that I failed to note the Allentown postmark until I started the text. The picture is not clear but I gather something happened and your dad became so ill you ought to go home. I'm glad you did go Bettsy and I pray that Dad is back on even keel.

And that seems to be the end of the "nightly" tome darling, sorry it's so short. My relief is here and it's nearly midnight, time for bed. 'Nite my dearest darling! Give our kids a special big kiss from their lonely Dad, and tell them I love them very much - - and you too, just in case you didn't know.

5/4/45 Friday evening in port

For 10 minutes I've been sitting here on the aft machine gun platform staring gloatingly at a piece of green paper which I fondly hope will surprise you a bit. But my gloating is not unmixed with guilt for I feel like a heel that I let you down so badly the last few days.

I have no excuse for we have done _less_ gun work than any previous stay in port. Yet still my days seem so very crowded. Part of that is of course due to the news press work, to which I have been devoting as much time as possible. But today I couldn't help for we had other work that kept us all afternoon.

I forgot to tell you that I wrote two other obituary stories recently. The first was Mussolini - - Il Duce. We didn't receive much in the way of background on him and I was surprised at how many facts I could dredge up from the dark recesses of my mind.

Then it was Adolph Hitler's death although I am skeptical of the facts of his demise. Suspect this whole Hitler business will wind up like the story of John Wilkes Booth - - there are some people who can <u>almost</u> prove the man who shot Lincoln is alive today; and others are willing to wager he was killed a couple of days later when a posse hunting the assassin burned down a barn in which he was (?) hiding. All sorts of fantastic answers are possible, even probable, and I doubt very much we'll ever <u>know</u> the <u>truth</u> - - about Booth or Hitler.

I do seem to be writing a lot of obits - - FDR, Ernie Pyle, Il Duce, Adolph's. It seems strange that individual deaths can mean as much, in so many ways, to a world which has for five years callously watched thousands of its best men dying violently daily.

Let's see, I dropped you with quite a jar the other evening, saying I might find a poker game for a change. Well, I did, and while it wasn't overly profitable it was enjoyable, and resulted in another last night which lasted longer, <u>was</u> profitable and also pleasant. The net result of the two is reflected in a money order a bit larger than I had anticipated. Its disposition I leave <u>solely</u> to <u>you</u>.

Today we worked all day so that there was no chance for me to help with the press news. And tomorrow we must work again, painting, but I hope to be through in time to lend a hand with the news. One of these days, right soon too, I'm going to be writing "It's all over in Europe." and I don't want to miss that.

A bit of news to report - - Ensign Moglever was transferred and we also lost Lt. Barrett, our junior division officer and a whale of a nice young chap who has been more than kind to me. He's young, about 24, was married last time in the States and his wife is expecting, which makes his reassignment just now a real break for he's hoping to be home for the big event.

These transfers, by the way, are routine things affecting the ship's personnel, both officers and enlisted men. Almost every time we come into port there are some, and while it never is any substantial fraction of the crew, nevertheless all the guys seem always to be hoping lightning will strike them next and they'll be sent elsewhere, preferably to the States, for a duration shore berth.

I think, my darling, that's about all the letter there is tonight. Had hoped for more and better but - - . 'Nite my dearest one. Tell my kiddies I love them and miss them much too much - - and just in case you hadn't heard it before remind me some time to tell you the same.

5/6/45 Sunday evening in port

What's more dreary than a rainy Sunday?

It seems <u>such</u> a long way back to my boyhood days when the thing I dreaded worst of all was a rainy Sunday, You've no idea how soakingly disagreeable is a load of drenched windblown Sunday papers. Carting them out the street, up the long hill, put every one in a <u>dry</u> - - try to find one!- - place where it won't blow away; fish in the pockets of your ought-to-be-wrung out clothes for change, stuff away the dollar bill that draws water like a blotter and sometimes it must have just floated out of your pocket.

The long jaunt to the outlying "mansions" - - there weren't near so many of them on Parson's Hill then as now - - with the wheelbarrow loaded with papers standing forlorn on a corner collecting more water; down the rocky, rough hill and up the street that's broad concrete now - - but wasn't then - - weaving from side to side to catch all the spread-apart houses. Mustn't forget Scott Brashear wants a Ledger and a Tele; and Ed Brill <u>must</u> have his press or raise H.

A long long wait at the deadbeat's house - - he hasn't paid for three weeks and that 30 cents is right <u>out</u> of <u>your</u> pocket - - until a blowzy woman from a Saturday night beering (Say that was some home brew!) sleazes to open the door a crack, clutch the paper and mutter something about pay-you-next-week before she disappears again. The closing door tells you another dime is gone to join the lost three!

The load is getting lighter, but not the rain, and you begin to wonder if you'll have enough for all of Jewtown. Must remember to save a Ledger for Curt Truxall, he's a TRUST; and a Ledger and a Tele for Metzgars, 'cause they always leave a quarter on the window ledge - - the extra nickel is YOURS, and it will help make up that one <u>you</u> had to trust; 40 cents, Damm! They'd better pay up next week or <u>No</u> papers!

Home stretch at last but still it pours. Put Harvey Stahl's paper well back on the porch, those people <u>never</u> get up on Sunday; another side trip up the hill. (Is Ed Darr still a TRUST or should I collect?) And remember to save the last two New York Times for Father Manning and Katherine Snyder. Either one might save you something some day; the Rev. John P. is in the soul business but at the moment Katherine is the more important for <u>she's</u> a <u>high school teacher</u>.

Done at last! Pick up the handles and trundle the wheelbarrow back through the alley. Dad grumping and fuming at the sock-soppy papers left over – "What the <u>Hell</u> did you do-miss half your route"? And the phone ringing and people moaning and "No Mrs. - - - - - - that boy's not back yet but he's down there somewhere and won't miss you" or "You say he left you a - - - - - - instead of a - - - - - - (Tone of extreme irritation) Well I've told him a dozen times you wanted yours changed and just as soon as he comes in we'll take care of it"!

Settle up, recite the list of TRUSTS and stack the dimes on the damp dollars but there never seems to be enough money. Dad figuring, counting, checking off the TRUSTS again, tapping the tiny shiny stacks of dimes with his pencil.

"How many did you trust today by yourself? Only one? Still

leaves you 30 cents (or 80 or something else) short. What <u>did</u> you do with that money"? (<u>very</u> exasperated). - - long pause. You stand and squirm and try to imagine; he just sits there in the big high-back chair at the funny old roll-top desk that always seems in complete confusion.

A customer comes in or a dozen of them if the Lutheran Church is just out and he gets up to drop the dimes into the dingling register. When it's all over he comes back, figures it all out again.

"Well, what do you expect me to do about it - -"?

And he leaves the question dangling there while you fidget then slowly, carefully he counts out the big round half dollars and the quarters and dimes and pennies - - you know he almost always takes all or most of the loss himself but he grumps so that even when you <u>know</u> he doesn't mean a damm word of it you worry.

There - - the pile is counted out and he hands it to you! Treasure - - and maybe a Sunday afternoon penny ante game at Jim Anspach's or Duckie's. - - (Ducky was in and done a long time ago and he always sold more papers and got done first and his money was right.) "I don't see why he can do it and you're always late and wrong"! - - in sort of injured tone - - (But you know he wouldn't trade sons for a couple of worlds. And it makes you feel pretty good).

Past the candy counter, snitch a piece real quick and "Dad can I have some to take home for the girls, too"? More grumping, then an absent-minded "Yes" as he counts the money into the drawer. Mustn't make a mistake, you almost <u>hear</u> him think - - but you know damm well the total on the register almost never agrees with the money when <u>he</u> goes to check up! So candy for the girls you get too, knowing that when Dad comes home he'll have two cigar boxes under his arm; one full of neat rolls of change, each wrapper carefully initialed CAW so the bank will know from whom it came, and the other chock full of green mint leaves and tootsie rolls and chocolate drops for after-the-Sunday-dinner.

Out again, and up, the wheelbarrow rumbles emptily toward home and the garage where it will gather dust until next Sunday. Still raining but you don't seem to mind so much now that you're rid of the soggy smelling papers. Home at last, now to read until dinner time. Funnies? No, I read them long ago on the route, in the rain. Where is that book? Mother bustling in the kitchen, the girls scooting around or thumping the piano: smell of roast beef and mashed potatoes all through the house; a chorus of "Mother – can – I – have – the – pan" as the dull clack of the spoon on aluminum tells you it's - - goodie, hope it's chocolate - - and why can't we have lemon pie once in a while - - cake and thick fudge icing. Curl up in the big leather chair to read and lick chocolate off sticky fingers and wait for Dad.

Really, my darling this letter ought to be addressed to Mother and Dad, because for once it is their letter and not yours. Ashamed of myself too, for not having done something like it more often for no one knows better than I the debt I and we owe them and never will be able to repay. And I know all too well I have neglected them shamefully, seeming to write all the letters to you and for you when they too have been in my thoughts and heart a very great deal. So I can only hope that this little memory out of a past that seems so very long ago will reassure them.

And I made my Mother's Day and Father's Day communion combined this morning.

This day hasn't been much to report, for as I feared last night the schedule didn't work out. Matter of fact the only thing I got done was this most important letter.

Woke about 8, went to breakfast and just wasn't feeling like working so - - we didn't. Loafed around until 10 o'clock when the Catholic party left on an LCI for Mass on another ship. It was past noon when we got back, and raining, so all I did was eat and roll into bed, where I stayed until 5. Up and ate (again!), fiddled around a bit and here I am still scribbling as the second movie starts.

Anyhow, my darlings I think this is all the letter that's in me tonight. For so many words I haven't said much, but the bulk and background of it all you should know now by heart. There's no need to repeat it again for you and all of you.

5/8/45 Tuesday afternoon in port

It's a dreary, rainy, day of a kind that seems to have become right frequent of late, and of course it's raising hob with our plans, which in turn have raised hob with my work.

We were scheduled again for a practice shoot - - which shot the day just as did the one yesterday. This was my first time with a new teammate however, and while the type of shooting we did wasn't sufficient enough on which to base a fair judgment and besides it was his first time on a director.

Still no letters written, and it begins to look like I'm destined to be a distinct failure in that line this time. And I want so much to write to the kids, to tell them how I love them and miss them. Please tell them their Daddy hasn't forgotten - - and never will - - and that I'll write just as soon as I get a chance. Seems such a shame to let them down, too, for the mail today brought me two more of the missing letters, one from you and one from Buck and Sis. Both were grand, too, and so very well done I can't believe they were written by the youngsters I left behind. Guess they just aren't little ones anymore. And Fran too, even though he can't write, must be growing far beyond my poor powers to imagine. Lord how I'd love to seem them all and hold them in my arms, just to be sure that they are real and they are ours. Will, too, one of these days.

Last evening I was on watch until nearly midnight when, I found a poker game with a seat for me. When the game broke up about 1:30 I was the big winner - - not in cash, for the others had borrowed from me, but come payday there will be another money order go into the mail for you.

It occurs to me to wonder, so <u>very</u> casually, how you all are reacting to V-E Day. Tomorrow, from the fragmentary radio reports I get, seems to be officially it, and introspectively I'm amazed that it means so little to me. Trying to figure out why, I get the self-impression that the whole thing is anti-climatic.

Then too there is the personal equation. Europe seems so very far away, and from the day I entered the Navy I knew <u>this</u> was to be my war and somehow have come to regard that other war as something distant, impersonal and not very important (to me). Logically, I know that latter part is silly. Men are and have been fighting and dying there longer, on a vastly more bloody scale, than this war out here has or will know

War, except for the part of it immediately around you, is something so very impersonal. And the little bit of it that is <u>yours</u> is, by contrast, all-important. Did a bomb or a shell hit that other ship? Too bad, you sort of say, and go on looking out for the <u>bastard</u> who's out to get <u>you or your ship.</u>

See those soldiers storming the hill? White puffs of smoke around them; long squirts of flame and oily smoke out in front of them, and from the distance hear faintly the currump and the softer rattle like a stick drawn across a distant picket fence. See the bombers circling high then slowly nose over, glide down and from their bellies four black eggs go hurtling earthward as the slow-looking plane levels, then climbs twisting, turning the hell away from there. Four brownish clouds of dust rise lazily - - and a hunk of the hill isn't there when the dust blows away.

It's fascinating to watch always. But you never, or very seldom, stop to think that the currump was a huge Jap mortar shell that may have hit a dozen men, or that some men (thank God not ours!) are dying horribly in that licking red tongue of black-shrouded fire spurting from the flame throwers, or crumpling before the lashing whip of bullets from the rattling machine gun. This hill, sure some Japs died when the bombs hit and the earth disintegrated; lovely, let's get on with the war.

But let one lone bomber turn toward your ship. You shake, all over; your guts churn round and round. This is it! All around you the guns roar but the only one you hear is your own, that overly faintly. The silvery tracers stretch out towards the plane; you see other tracers, but you watch yours, and twiddle the little dials to change the line. And suddenly, beautifully, the tracers are a white string spun from the gun to and into the plane. And you see the bright gold bursts like stars in a summer night! Bursts - - your bursts - - on that plane.

In he comes, into the storm of fire that you feel rising all around to a terrific crescendo. He turns a little, as though to retreat, then quietly seeming in perfect peace, rolls over on his back, starts down, down, down to the shiny blue waters. A wisp of smoke, light blue smoke, comes from the fuselage. And you note the ugly red ball of fire there, remembering suddenly there were others on the wing, you saw them as he rolled so gently. Down, down down, still the tracers streaking all around him and suddenly SPLASH! A little geyser erupts on the calm sea and when it disappears so has the plane. Gone! For good!! That bastard won't be back! Hurray! We got him!

You feel wonderful. The shake is gone; your guts unshaken as though by magic The roar that you almost failed to notice, gives place to quiet; the smoke of the guns is gone; slowly the black dots that were deadly ack-ack bursts a moment ago drift astern and dissipate in the bright sky. Now there was a fight, you think subconsciously. Yet the others on the hill must have been so much fiercer, more deadly - - and it wasn't over in a minute or two, may go on for hours and days. And yet - - well one was my war, the other ------------?

On the same scale that is the way that we of the Pacific regard that other war. Something fascinating, terrible - - and yet not our war, in the personal sense. Yes, we are glad, more than glad it's over. We want all of the European-based military to have a chance at home - - but will be more than glad to move over and give them place beside us just as soon as they can get here to help finish <u>our</u> war so we can <u>all</u> go home.

All of which, my dearest, may seem strange and a little silly to you, as it would to me before I came aboard Frisco. But that's the way I and most of my shipmates feel - - our war is out here. A weird world we live in! And a weird way to go about telling a gal you love her isn't it? As usual, I had no such thing in my mind when I started but the words just kept coming out and here I am winding up the longest letter in a long time.

'Nite darling one, sleep tight with your comfortable pillow, and soon I hope I shall be there to take my very rightful place for all the rest of our days and nights.

5/14/45 Monday afternoon

Dear Bucky:

Yes, I know it's been a long time since I sat down to write to you, but I hope you will understand that it was only because my time has been pretty full, not that I have forgotten you. Matter of fact the opposite is true for I think very often - - and wish - - for those happy days we had together and I hope soon we will be having again.

By the time this reaches you, I suppose school will be over and you starting on the long summer vacation that, as I remember, always seemed to disappear so quickly. There are lots of things you and I could be doing together with that vacation if the world were different. Seems to me you ought to be almost ready to learn to swim and dive - - and I'd love to be teaching you.

And I often wonder if there are still fish in some of those holes that were my favorites when I was a boy; we must investigate together some day, if not this summer perhaps next. Then there's the playground, where I suppose you will be playing ball 'most every day, and I hope you'll get a chance to see some real baseball at the high school. By the time we get back to Philadelphia I ought to be able to take you to see Joe DiMaggio as I promised so long ago. Joe, you know, is in the Army, although I'm not sure whether he's in Europe or somewhere in the Pacific. Anyhow there are ever so many things we can do together, and will have to hurry after I come back to make up for all the lost time.

Glad you enjoyed the few little shells I was able to send you though I know you would have had a lot more fun picking them up on the beach and swimming there. The big rolling waves won't let you swim very much but it's good sport just to jump into them and be tossed head over heels up on the beach. (Remember how you used to laugh and squeal when I bounced you or tossed you on the bed?)

Did I ever tell you how we send off and receive the airplanes we carry? I think not, and since that's what we were doing when I started this I thought I might try.

First of all the planes are kept on a catapult, which is in some ways like the turntable you have seen at railroad yards: a set of tracks, not very long, that can be turned to point in any direction. Of course the planes always go off to one side of the ship. These planes are old-fashioned biplanes (that means they have two wings) and on the bottom instead of wheels they have a float, that permits them to land or take off from water. A smaller float is attached near the end of each lower wing to prevent the plane being tipped over - - although a big wave or a clumsy landing sometimes does that anyway.

On the catapult the float fits into a sort of car that rides the tracks, slides along to the end with the plane and stops as the plane keeps on going. To get the plane flying, the catapult is pointed out over the side of the ship, the pilot gasses the motor until the propeller is going full speed, and then a shell, big as a cannon shell but without any bullet, is fired in a special chamber where the power of the explosion actually shoots the plane along there by running along the catapult, until, when the plane gets to the end, it is going fast enough and does keep on flying.

They also can be lifted off the catapult by the crane, set down on the water where they float like a boat, and take off from there just as a wheeled plane takes off from an airport, by running along on top of the water until they are moving fast enough to fly. But the catapult is easier and quicker.

When a plane is ready to return to the ship, the pilot flies back and circles around and around, just as the carrier pilots do, until he is ordered to land. If the ship is stopped he just lands on the water, taxis alongside and the crane picks up plane and pilot, lifts them right up on to the catapult. If the ship is moving - - and this is an operation that requires great skill and is thrilling to watch - - the pilot circles until the captain begins making a big turn with the ship. Big ships sort of skid in a turn, like an auto on a dirt road, and they leave a sort of flattened-out place on the water where for a moment there are no sharp breaking waves. The effect of the turn is to make a little landing place on the water.

Meanwhile a platform, called a sea sled, has been hung over the side of the ship and is being dragged along in the water. The sea sled, which trails a net of heavy rope, jumps and plunges from one wave to another in rough water and you wonder how the pilot will manage to hit it but he does, landing on the slick water, taxiing alongside, until the crane can pick up the plane and lift it onto the catapult again. The ship keeps right on, without stopping or slowing.

Well Sonny, guess that's enough sea story for this time. Tell Chubbin and Fran I haven't forgotten them either and will write just as soon as I can, maybe tomorrow. Be a good boy, Bucky, and don't go running around too much this summer. Always let Mother know where you want to go and she'll ok anything within reason.

And keep your letters coming, for they mean a great deal to me away out here where there are no kids and especially not the boys and girls I love more than any others in the world.

All my love, Your Dad

5/15/45 Tuesday morning

Dear Fran:

Your turn now, fellow, for even though you can't read as of yet you're entitled to a letter when I have written already to Bucky and Sis.

There's not much out here of interest for a boy your size. It's a dull, rainy morning, the kind of day that keeps you indoors when you would like so very much to be playing in the yard. That kind of day isn't very pleasant for me, either, for to write I must find some shelter and of course everyone else on watch has the same idea, with the result we are all crowded on one tiny little platform.

Anyhow it's hard for me to write under such circumstances which means the product will be (isn't it already) even more feeble than my usual letters - - which is feeble indeed. To tell the truth I would a whole lot sooner be with you than here, helping you grow up, and enjoying it more than I care to think about just now, but I guess it wasn't destined to be that way. Somehow you and I have missed out on a lot of the good things Bucky and Sis and I had together but I'll do my best to make them up to you when I come home.

Whoops, time out, here's a bit of a story: I've just had my first look at a Pacific Ocean fish! Seems one of the boys had hung a baited line over the fantail and when a couple others hauled in the line this fish was hooked. And they brought it up flopping on the deck. Not only was it flopping but it was grunting like a pig wallowing in the mud! I got down in time to get a look at it, but can't tell you what kind it was although someone suggested it was a dog fish. The thing was about two feet long, very fat, with a white belly and an olive drab back with brown spots a little smaller than a dime. Its mouth was round, with hard bony ridges instead of teeth, and it had the biggest brown eyes of any fish I've ever seen; eyes like a calf, I thought. I guessed its weight at 12 pounds.

Then they unhooked the fish after a few minutes, threw it back in the water where it floated belly up for a few minutes then slowly wiggling its fins it swam away and is by now, I guess, back at the bottom with the rest of the tribe, nursing a sore jaw and telling about the strange things on top of the water. A big boat floats and there are funny-looking things called people that have hands and feet instead of fins and walk upright in the air, when any fish knows the only sensible way to move is to swim under the water.

Guess that's your sea story for this time Sonny. Be a good boy for Mother and one of these days I'll come walking home to you and we can all begin living again.

Loads of love from Your Dad

(Personal You need not share this with the family!) 5/16/45

My own darling:

Since all three of your children have had a letter of their own methinks it time for you again, and besides I'm in the mood for a wee bit of talk with (or more literally to) that girl.

First off a bit of business you told me not to mention in the shared letters, and that is I heartily approve of the Allentown money and am only too glad you had it and used it as you did, and if you need or feel you want more, here it is and no strings attached - - which was exactly why I hurried the last money order to you. After all I owe them a debt no money could ever pay, for didn't they give me the most wonderful girl in the world?

To answer your question, it has now been a week or more since I touched the press news, and from the looks of things it will be some days longer before I get another chance for as we go to sea this time I have entirely too much work remaining undone - - through no fault of mine. Because of which I've missed the handling of V-E Day, a day incidentally which created hardly more than a ripple of comment on shipboard as I wrote the other day

As you may have suspected from some of my more recent letters, I'm suffering from what you once aptly called an acute case of internal combustion. The reason, of course, is obvious - - and so was the remedy when I awoke quite suddenly this morning. Oh well, such is life without a wife. But I have been dreaming - - and wishing - - very often of coming home to you, even for a little while, if not to resume the life we both love and want. Even one minute with you, my Bettsy, would be the grandest thing in the world if I could not have more.

Nine months since Chicago when last I held you in my arms, could feel you close to me and know that you heard even my whispers. Lord, dearest, it must have been ever so much longer than that, for in contrast our 10 years together seem to have been only a minute. And every second, every heartbeat I have been away from you I have missed you and wanted you more than anything in the world.

Yet somehow, it is good to feel, to <u>know</u>, that nothing nor any other person ever could fill the tiniest part of that void. I told you long ago I never could want or have another woman, and if nothing else this past year - - and whatever lies ahead - - will have proven that beyond any shadow of doubt. Yes, I feel sure that you <u>know</u> that too, but I repeat it here in the hope that the repetition may help you be just a little less lonely. I'm selfish enough, I confess, to be glad you are lonely and miss me, yet I should like to ease it just a little if I could. Is that strange?

By the way, I was dreaming this morning of that third honeymoon we've planned. Lord I wish we could be starting on it tomorrow and would be coming back to the only kind of life we both want, together. It's now nearly 15 years since that June afternoon I first saw you, and I promise you I'm as hungry now for the sight and sound and presence of you as I was that first morning after I fell in love.

Need I tell you I love you I love you, want you, need you, my Bettsy? I think not - - but I say it again so you may be very sure!

5/19/45 Saturday evening

For 20 minutes I've been sitting here trying write but my tub mates are in a talkative mood and so I haven't even been able to start until I just now very rudely told them to get the hell away so I could at least write a couple of lines.

I've about come to the conclusion all my recent letters must have been horribly dull - - just meaningless words, a dreary recital of days about which I can tell you only the very small things even if there were something else to write, which there isn't. Often of late I've regretted not having started and kept a diary for when this is all over I'm sure the days and events will have so merged in my memory as to be a confusing jumble - - and I know I should like to have an accurate record and know also too much now must now be left unsaid for these letters to be of much value. However, from here on in I'm resolved to write more interesting letters - - or else!

By some saving grace, here is today's "or else." Did I tell you we have a dog?

Yes, that's right, a dog; and not only a dog but the cutest little all-black pup you could ask to see. He's playful as pups always are and so small now I don't suppose he's destined to be very big. He has glossy black hair, and a dinky tail he carries jauntily curved over his back. All the crew is fond of him, and naturally he's much petted and pampered; fed from the galley, I expect, and of course he has the run of the ship. Strangely I've heard no one mention a name, if he has one, but my own suggestion is "Shanghai."

The story back of the dog is an amusing one. I don't know the dog's breed, suspect it's just ("dog"), but it's at least possible his ancestors came from Nippon, for he was acquired by a sailor on an atoll once Jap-occupied and now in our hands and so far as I know dogs are not native on Pacific atolls. Anyhow this sailor, a big, fat baby-faced youngster, was stationed on this atoll and somehow he got himself this dog. It (he, the dog) was the joy of his (the sailor's) life, the light of his love in this God-forsaken hole.

Came the day when a cruiser (ours) anchored in the harbor, and some time thereafter there went ashore a recreation party, bent (sic) on refreshionment (a sort of compound word of my own devising). And in this refreshionment party was a certain officer whom I shall call Nemo - - the Homeless One. And so it came about that Nemo (whether before or after the refreshionment I know not) espied the dog and the thought came to him that he would be the ideal mascot for the cruiser riding at anchor in the harbor. The owner of the dog was summoned and asked (?) would he care to give to the cruiser a mascot, this dog.

To the amazement of all present, the owner replied in the negative to Nemo. And on further inquiry declared and expounded at length on his love for and his attachment to, this dog. At the end, dramatically, he is said to have remarked "The dog is mine. He goes where I go. Life without him would be worthless" (or words to that effect)!

Even so was it done!

Now Frisco has a mascot. And Frisco also has a new crew member, a big, fat baby-faced youngster, who is now contrasting life on a coral atoll with life on a cruiser. So is the dog, who might be called "Shanghai"!

With which, my darling, I bid you goodnight.

5/20/45

5/21/45 Monday morning

The above is not for effect, for although I actually did write it 24 hours ago I have no excuse for not going on to fashion some kind of a letter except that I did not feel like writing, even to you, and so stopped right there. And the sheet is used because I've discovered I'm running short of paper so must husband my resources until I get a chance to purchase more.

Still no mail and though it seems interminably long a back-check shows that it's only two weeks since the last letter arrived. I unashamedly confess here and now I'm downright hungry for a letter from you in much the same way I'm hungry for the presence of you.

The intervening days since my last letter have been much the same as those before them and the others immediately ahead of me. Seems a fantastic way to fight a war, sleeping, eating, standing watch, and sleeping some more when I'm not plain loafing, but I've learned war is like that and so am resigned to it for so long as I must. Yet every second of it only whets a finer edge on my hunger - - yes it actually _is_ hunger - - for you and our family and the free life we all love and want.

This is another of those cool, misty days we've been having lately, and while the temperature is far more comfortable than the heat of the not-so-long-ago days, there's nevertheless something dispiriting about being surrounded by a wall of gray. We get a shower or two every day, but they're only a drizzle which do nothing to clear the atmosphere.

My sole work of the two days has been on the press news this afternoon, but that wasn't overly much. Not a conspicuous record is it? But something new has developed there, and it will probably result in my first interview with the executive officer.

It started last evening when Ensign Rowell who has replaced Ensign Konopka in charge of the press news, told me he had been advised that the executive officer has ordered that henceforth no stories concerning the Army's points-for-discharge system shall appear in the paper. Well of course that's an out-and-out abridgement of freedom of the press; in a small way one of the things we're out here fighting for, and because of my peculiar personal interest in that freedom, the thing made me hopping mad! Well this ensign is new on the ship, and while he said he felt as I did about the order, he also didn't quite know what he could do about it.

I feel I'm fully qualified to dispute the point, and I certainly am so minded. So I proposed to discuss the matter with the exec, if the order is not rescinded before I get to him through the devious channels of Navy protocol and procedure.

Actually such a situation could occur only once in a blue moon in the Navy - - I mean an enlisted man taking any issue with the second ranking officer on the ship. There is not only the wide and deep crevasse between the enlisted men - - the untouchables - - and the officer caste, but a further hurdle beyond that is the gap which separates the junior officers from the seniors and another smaller one setting aside the department heads. Strange that democracy should be so lacking in the Navy of the world's greatest democracy.

Now I don't mean that the officers, especially the junior officers up to and including some full lieutenants, aren't courteous and friendly and helpful when they get the chance. Nearly all of them are that and some much more while a few hold themselves snottily aloof. But they live in an entirely different world, with a different code of rules and conduct, and except in comparatively infrequent cases the meetings between enlisted men and officers are only those routine things necessary to the proper operation of the ship. Generations of Navy men, inheritors of the old British-Spanish-Dutch traditions of the ruling class, accelerated by the natural situation that only the wanderers, the wastrels and the uneducated are attracted to the life (or thrust into it) of a Navy enlisted man in peacetime, have built the caste system on a rock that no mere war can destroy.

I am not, I hope railing childishly at this situation; it is here and I must recognize it and know I can never change it. But my inbred Quixotic instincts make me feel good when I've a chance to break a lance against it.

What, Ho! Bring on the white charger! Tomorrow I ride! With love and kisses to the far-away fair lady. (Wish I had a pair of her pink you-know-whats for a battle flag.) I am

Your most obedient servant

C. Anthony Welsh, Jr.

S1/C

5/24/45 Thursday evening

I write tonight with a shattered lance; Quixote, having charged the windmill, nurses a numbed posterior while Sancho Panza pursues the white charger against the possibility his master may ride again. From which jumble of words you should deduce I have had my interview with the exec and it turned out as I had every reason to believe - - even while in my always overly-optimistic heart I hoped for something better.

He was courteous to receive me, and listened attentively to what I had to say. But he replied in effect that_this press is different; that even while we fight for a free press for the world (among other things), that we may not necessarily expect to read a free press. That in his judgment "The Navy is of necessity an autocratic institution." and repeated publication ("continual harping," he called it) of the discharges and prospects under the Army's point system would be detrimental to morale. "The press news already," he told me "has reported the existence of the system; we all know that a number of men are going to be released. Why then keep harping on it"?

And I suggested to him that this is only the first item of what would undoubtedly will be many more in the time between now, V-J Day and the time when all of us who so desire may go home. Hypothetically, a situation might arise that would find us in the Western Pacific or somewhere else far away with no prospects then of going home while other Navy men, and crewmen of other ships were being discharged. Would he then withhold that news? His reply was consistent. He absolutely would withhold it if morale was being adversely affected.

There the matter stands, for the interview was terminated abruptly when he was called away. As we were leaving he remarked that besides, nothing prevented the men from obtaining the same information, denied in the press news, from the radio, their hometown papers, and such magazines as Time. My parting remark was something about "Doesn't that make the censorship pretty futile"? Exit the exec smiling, his order intact and in force.

What have I accomplished? Nothing, I think, except that I faintly hope that he may in the future be chary of expanding the ban to include other subjects. Personally I probably have gotten myself on his list as a presumptuous nebbynose ("In the old Navy I'd have thrown the stupid ass in the brig for so much as thinking he had any right to question an order, let alone the audacity to approach me"!)

As to whether - - or what - - to attempt any further protest I am now in doubt. So much for that pro tempore. But you'll be hearing more from me on the subject, I suspect.

There's been quite a bit of incoming mail; seven from you and one each from Bucky and Sis Tuesday, two more from you and a note and two papers from the Smiths yesterday, one from your folks and two issues of Time today. When I tell you I'm all caught up on my reading - - that means a couple times through the letters - - including the magazines, you should have pretty clear picture of how my time has been spent.

Incidentally I acquired another John Dos Passos book yesterday but have barely started it. Golly that guy writes beautiful words, even when they're hard to follow, but his characters annoy me. Every one in a Dos Passos book is a libertine or worse - -and dammit little people just aren't like that! (This book is "Manhattan Transfer").

There are some things in your letters I want to note, but I believe I'll let them slide at least until tomorrow, for there isn't much longer to write (This letter is long enough now!) and my usual perch on the platform is, as usual, becoming a bit cramped.

Miss me a bit, my Bettsy? Yes I know you do, but it's always nice to hear it. And if it's any consolation I miss you, too: muchly, for always when I've a problem you're the best solution in the world. Anyhow, my darling, good night, sleep tight and remember our days together. Did I ever tell you I want you always?

5/29/45 Tuesday evening

A wee bit of slightly delayed mail today, letter from you and each of the kids. They had been slightly held up somewhere for I previously received later ones, but nonetheless I was a wee bit extra glad to get them for yours reported receipt of the money order and your weekend with friends.

Before getting into your letter, I want to enlighten you some more about a pet peeve of mine - - the muscle men aboard ship. Day by day I find more of them puffing, grunting and sweating over their wasteful labors. Right now there are two of them hard at it within three feet of me and I find it very annoying. Annoying also is the fact that down on the well deck are a half hundred or so cases of ammunition, waiting to be carried forward a hundred yards or so and then stowed in the magazines. Now there's real exercise, and useful too. But will these punks do that? Hell no, they'll grunt and groan over their silly dumbbells and bar weights - - and admire their manly? muscles. And when there's work to be done they go hide, almost without exception!

Now back to the important stuff. Gosh, if you get a surprise and a thrill out of that one [a money order in the package], the next one should really be a bang. Pleases me no end, too, 'cause I like to do such things to you. Wish I could do it every day, but obviously I can't and perhaps it's just as well for it probably soon would become boresome. However, I'm a mite surprised Mother didn't then and there earmark a part of it for that new set of Wearever pans <u>you're</u> going to buy her.

I'll be interested, of course, to know what you do with this one and the next, for if you don't need them the choice is entirely yours. However, it doesn't seem to me to be wise to convert them to cash; certainly not to keep the cash around the house. If you feel you've plenty of cash in the checking account, then war bonds or a savings account would be the logical choice.

As to your seam-bursting, I'm not sure whether the calendar ought to reassure me - - or start me really worrying. Whoops! Low punch but I couldn't resist it. Anyhow I can always <u>hope</u> some of the new avoirdupois is bulging out in the right places. After all these years, wouldn't it be nice to have me acquire some hair and you suddenly turn sweater girl? "Optimist" she snorts.

This has been a peaceful and quiet day, and a long one, too, for a change. But last night! Oyay! As I told you I had the midwatch, from midnight to 4:30 reveille, and it poured dogs, cats and kitten britches all the time. Result was no sleep and a very, very unpleasant time for all. But I crawled into bed for an hour before breakfast, then took a shower, ate and went right back to bed until noon.

That refreshed me considerably and so this afternoon I got most of the press news out myself and then just lazed around for a couple of hours. To top it all off, there were the letters and an edible supper so that if you hadn't guessed it before, you now know your husband is feeling right chipper at the moment.

The kids' letters too (you needn't tell them this) amused me as always. Chubbin is so simple and direct in everything she says and Bucky is so definite, so emphatic. I always enjoy them so much and often wish I could find the opportunity and the words to write them more often. Guess you can understand how very difficult it is to find something in this out-of-the-way place I can tell them about. Tried something a little different with Chubbin's last letter but I'm afraid didn't succeed too well.

By the way, did I tell you that Bucky's letter (from me) was rejected by the censor? I got it back in our first batch of incoming mail, fixed it at once and sent it through but instead of his being the first it will be the last received. Just thought I'd note that here in case you're curious about the patched up letter.

I seem, my darling, to have run on a bit longer than usual this evening; strange, for the bugle interrupted me and I'm finishing now in the sweltering, crowded mess hall. Almost always hot down here, although during that cold South China Sea trip it was necessary to heat the place a couple of days.

Need I tell you Bettsy I'm very lonely for you, wishing always that that I could be with you always - - or even for a minute if I could have no more? Please know this!

Chapter 12
FRISCO AT WAR - PART FIVE
OKINAWA BATTLE DESCRIPTION,
"LOPSIDED MOON" POEM COMPOSED
6/4/45 to 6/30/45

6/4/45 Monday evening

Fair warning now that this won't be much for I'm just not in the mood for writing. Which, plus weather handicaps, is why I haven't written earlier today, after passing you up yesterday.

How a character who used to love rain - - probably I would even now if That Girl were with me - - I certainly have acquired a bellyful. I really intended to write this morning on watch but squatted on my usual platform perch I found the wind too stiff to handle paper. Then finally it poured - - I mean POURED - - and for the last hour I just sat hunched up trying to keep dry. Honest, it rained so hard that it flattened the waves around us! And the little whitecaps that had been crowding the surface before finally quit because they discovered whenever they poked their heads up a million raindrops pounced at once, driving them back into the sea.

Most of the intervening hours since last I wrote have been spent in reading all of Thomas Wolfe's "Look Homeward Angel." And by damm I'm through with fiction for a while - - except maybe westerns. They're always sane and dependable. Perhaps it's my imagination, or unfortunate selection, but it does seem to me that every recent book I've gotten my hands on has been written by a lunatic about madmen. And the hell of it is that every one of them is built of beautiful words but every one of them is crazy, in thought and deed.

Well, yesterday we had church services of a fashion, rosary and a couple of hymns but I want so much to get to Mass. And the tragedy of it was that not far away was Father Holland, you'll recall the priest for whom I served at Great Lakes and who came aboard to say Mass while we were docked at San Pedro. I had seen his ship a week ago, and saw it again yesterday afternoon.

Still playing along with the press news, but I seem to have least partially lost interest. Scuttlebutt says this evening the exec has been promoted from commander to captain, which could mean a shift from here. Maybe then - - but wait and see.

Haven't yet gotten around to my second head shave (for which dutiful reminder I thank you) but firmly expect to do so tomorrow morning. And I begin to be a wee bit - - a WEE bit-optimistic.

Incidentally, you wondered some time ago if you would have, in the ship, a rival for my affection (?). Just in case I neglected to reply at the time I hasten to say now the answer is "NO," very definitely .While I feel I'm mighty fortunate to be on her, especially in this latter phase of the war, I've no great love for this "pig iron S.O.B." as she often is called by some of the more disgruntled members of the crew. But on the other hand, since I know the ship, and some of the men, I confess to a great interest in her story and very probably shall endeavor to collect every-thing I can that has been written about her when I come home.

A dribble of mail today, including (loud cheers) my first copy of Life. Your letter was 5/24, telling of your housecleaning spree, the carnival and some mail - - quite a day. Please tell Dad I fully sympathize with him in the midst of all that house cleaning for I'm fully aware what terrors (and tearers) you and Mother are when you get started.

And <u>what</u> a spendthrift you have become. A whole dollar and 70 cents literally thrown away at the carnival! Have you, woman, no idea of the blood, toil and tears required to earn that that money? Please see that it does <u>not</u> happen again. (Aside to Bucky: Your mother is a natural-born tightwad. Son, wait til I come home and the next time we find a carnival we'll have a real blowout. I enjoy 'em too. Bet she wouldn't even let you go see the hootchy-kootchy. Maybe you should have asked Grandpa to take you; he <u>never</u> misses one of those.)

As for the few pennies I sent you, you already have my approval of the last previous disposition and unless you need something or can find something better I suppose there'll be a repeat performance. It's fun to dream of spending them <u>with you</u>.

There, guess that does it, my darling. And if I do say this is a poor excuse for a letter, but at least it's a letter. Anyhow, as usual talking with you has made me feel <u>much</u> better and as always I thank you for being you. Goodnight, my dearest.

6-5-45 Tuesday afternoon

<u>Ode to a Vanished Glory</u>
Here sits the sailor, all shaven and shorn
(Poor sailor; his noggin looks so cold, so forlorn)
 He's sacrificed hair (?) on the altar of hope
To please the fair lady - -My god Whatta dope!
"But it wasn't my Idea"! she snorts, in defense.
(Nonetheless you know, Madam, you've caused this expense.)
So keep right on hoping, and I will hope, too,
That some day there'll be HAIR where it once lushly grew!

Now you should be convinced I love you. Not only have I gone and "dood it" again but have actually grown lyrical (?) over it. Imagine sonnets to a lady at <u>my</u> age, and him married 10 years.

He <u>must</u> be daft.

The "dooding" was not without incident. I had been in the chair a couple of minutes this afternoon and half the job was done when the bugle blew, and of course the barber and the barberee had to run - - what a sight I was! But after a little I was able to go back down again, to have the other half removed, and I am once again "Egghead" "Skinhead" and all the other nicknames I acquired last time.

It's been another gloomy day of intermittent rain; for a while a heavy swell was running and causing quite a roll, but now the sea is flat and the gray mist clouds of rain closing in. Phooey, for I'll be on lookout in a little bit, not free to seek shelter. My watch last night was an easy one for after standing my lookout stretch I curled up on the lockers and went to sleep, awaking some time after midnight to stagger below blessedly to bed. Slept soundly until 7 then got up to eat.

Went shopping afterwards for some new stationary and then for a change Sam and I did a bit of work. That took most of the morning and I was able to get my shower before going to lunch and starting my watch. No press news work today because of said watch.

In between I've found time to read through - - and I <u>do</u> mean read - - my new Life, and was delighted to find it the issue (4/2) carrying the story of Ernie Pyle and how he grew. Read everything in it, then passed it along to be circulated.

Damm, here comes the rain, soaking everything exposed, but it's later than I thought and I guess I'll not have a lookout this afternoon. Don't know whether to be mad or glad, for while it means I'll stay dry now, it also means a lookout from midnight to 1 tonight (when I'd <u>much</u> rather sleep and may get wet anyway). One of these dammed-if-you-do-dammed-if-you-don't propositions, I guess.

Sense the punk letter Bettsy, but I guess that a bit of poetry (?) drained the well for I seem to have run out of words. Anyhow

I love you with all my heart, and am only waiting for the moment I can tell you about it in person.

6/8/45 Friday evening

There is something about this lovely day that takes me back a whole year, to last summer and Lake Michigan. Maybe it's the haze-blue sky that's comfortably filled with fleecy-white clouds over sparkling blue water that's tossing enough to set free the whitecaps in occasional showers of spume. Or it may be the bright sunshine glinting from the waves, doing its valiant best to drive the chill out of the fresh-blowing breeze. Or it might be just plain nostalgia - - or all of these things combined.

Right now I have reposing in my hip pocket a copy of Time, and in the other pocket my half-read volume of Mr. Allen's "Bedford Village" - - which, by the way, is a delightful story and has caused me to neglect completely my newly acquired Dickens. "Bedford Village" is not only a grand relief from my recent dosages of would-be aphrodisiac fiction but it's a swell yarn in its own right. And as the Scotsman says, 'tis a tale of mine own couture and knowing every foot of the road makes it that much more fascinating. I heartily recommend it for all of you.

This has been another sunnily lazy day, and I've done next to nothing to justify my existence. On watch all the morning, I helped get out the press news this afternoon, showered and shaved then read my Time until supper. As I started this I was munching on a sandwich of good old rat-trap cheese that would have been truly tasty if accompanied by a cold glass of milk or a ditto bottle of beer. Or - - much, much nicer - - a warm smile from That Girl

The mail today also brought me a note from you. Your sandwich in the Monday night letter literally set me slathering, and it was a dirty trick. Damm it's been nearly 8 months since I tasted tomato, or lettuce, or whole wheat bread or fresh milk! When I get back to civilization the first time I run into a restaurant I'm going to order a cup of coffee, a glass of milk and a whiskey-and-soda and drink them in that order; bing, bing, bing. Then I'll see what's to eat.

In thinking of our future the thought came to mind the fact we'll be facing the old house-hunting problem one of these distant days and I'm sure you'll be interested in the enclosed clipping which is straight dope from a recent Navy publication. And I tell you here and now I expect to take advantage of it before I have paid one more year's rent.

As I see it, the bottom is going to fall out of the over-inflated real estate market right shortly, and we ought to be able to get the kind of a house where we want it for a decent price. Under that circumstance, and the absence of a down-payment requirement of a couple thousand bucks, we'd be foolish to go on paying rent, can instead pay rent to ourselves to pay off the mortgages. And wouldn't it be nice to own <u>our own</u> home, the kind of a home we want with a yard for the kids and one of those shiny tricked-up kitchens with all the gadgets? Plus all the new furniture I told you about a while back? Well, a guy can dream, can't he?

Once again I look forward to your reply with more than a modicum of interest.

And one more time, my dearest, I bid you good night. Don't think I'll tell you tonight that I love you. Planning a post-war house ought to be de facto evidence of that so I'll not bother. Besides, you know it anyway.

This letter was found in Chuck's safe deposit box after his death. Unfortunately a water mark rendered the end of the letter unreadable.

Somerset, Pa June 10, 1945
Charles Dear,

Daddy and I have talked and thought of you all day and this

seems the only way we can how to tell you how happy we are to have you for our very own boy. We were bursting with joy and happiness on that first June 10 – and today it is an even deeper love and pride we have in you. We both feel that year by year you have come closer to our hearts and it's wonderful to feel that never once in our lives have you brought us anything but joy. It's a poor way to say it, sonny dear, but I know you understand. And looking at these sons of yours we are forever finding reminders of your childhood – expressions, remarks and actions. We are so glad to have this part of you with us while you must be so far away. And Betty and Elizabeth – Elizabeth is just a duplication of Mary – while Betty is just the dearest girl any son ever brought home to his parents. I'm sure Betty has told you of the fun we get out of living and working together and we understand when her very lonesome moods come over – and stand by as well as we can – She and Daddy are wonderful friends – and keep up a continual joshing and ragging of each other that would only be possible between true friends. We live a happy life here – all centered around one aim and prayer to have you back soon again with us.

Just now Betty and I are puzzled – Daddy laughs at us and says we might as well look for a needle in a hay stack as try to locate you in the Pacific. We watch all communiqués, New York Times, etc., and can't decide if you are with the big task force back at Okinawa or just patrolling. Feel you are not at Borneo – as only light units are announced as there (though the Japs say otherwise). Also we read one brief article that said all main Jap airfields had been moved to northern Japan to be out of reach of the B-29 range and we wondered if the fleet would dare go that far up enemy waters with the carriers. So you see how we spend our evenings in arm-chair strategy.

Dick Irwin was in the store the other day to see Daddy. He has been on a destroyer – named it but Daddy did not recall the name but sounded like the one Navy announced this week as lost – the Luce – If he comes in again we will get his number to send you – Also McNamara (the cemetery salesman) was in today. He is in the SeaBees – and apparently is in a crack outfit – Says they have expert men in every field that you can imagine. – Has had quite a tour of duty in the Pacific. His big worry today is how to get his car to New York. Stored here it has 1942 plates on it and state policemen and the ration board can give him no help. However S.P. told him people have been know to take a chance and get away with it.

6/12/45 Tuesday morning

Just in case you didn't already know it, let it be said here and now your husband is a lazy lout. There wasn't any good reason for not writing yesterday; I just didn't, and here I've been sitting for hours doing nothing until a half hour ago the whiplash of conscience drove me to pick up pen - - and it took another 30 minutes to achieve a start as feeble as this!

It is for a lovely change, a sunnily hot day and I'm enjoying it minus my shirt in hopes of picking up a few vitamins (besides it's comfortable!). As you can guess from the morning heading, I'm on watch, and just plain loafing. Anyhow, I had the longest, most pleasant unbroken sleep in a month last night, which may be what makes me dopey (I mean more so than usually!).

Perhaps a little story will help get me started, and this amusing incident is fresh. A youngster named Brinton, one of the real boys of the crew, came up here to write a little while ago, copiously armed with stationery, pen, and of all things, a pocket dictionary.

He's only a little bit of a fellow, baby-faced, downy-cheeked, doesn't look a day over 16. He might be 18, for he's been on board here a year or more, but if he is, his looks and squeaky voice belie it. Anyhow he sat down and was writing assiduously. (It's easy to imagine the product, a boy's boyish letter to his Mom.) I was reading but happened to glance up a couple of times, noticed him leafing diligently through the dictionary, a puzzled frown on his face.

Finally he gave up, turned to one of the other guys here and asked how a word was spelled. Eventually, when the other guy started getting a "z" where no "z" should go, I butted in with the correct spelling. He listened, asked me to repeat, leafed through the dictionary, then asked for another repeat and looked again. At length he snorted "Well it ain't in the dictionary." then asked me to spell it again, slowly, letter-by-letter as he wrote it. Then he went on with his letter. (That's amusing enough I think. But the payoff was the word. I have no familiarity with the things, except once, long ago, a special fur-lined model, but I had no difficulty spelling BRASSIERE!)

- - Footnote: Later he asked me how to spell the plural of BODY! <u>Must</u> be <u>some</u> letter!!!!

With which bit of humor I shall hie me off to chow in a much better frame of mind. More letter later.

After chow it was mail call, a bath and a sweaty snooze, so it's now 5 p.m. Anyhow, the mail was grand, even though it didn't include a letter from you. The reason? - - one from Joe Brennan reporting on his leave in Somerset and his more-than-welcome words of you and the kids did me more good than anything a doctor (or psychiatrist) could have prescribed. I'll send it along in a day or so, when I've devoured it sufficiently and replied.

Missing out on my letter yesterday most certainly didn't deprive you of much, for there just wasn't a dern thing worth saying. I tried all morning, without a whit of success to sleep, then had to spend the afternoon on watch. Later I got into a quarter limit poker game - - and lost my shirt! ($7.60 to be exact) and that made me mad as _ _ _ _ cause there wasn't a poker player in the bunch! So the rest of the evening I just sat around reading and in due time went to bed.

Probably it will surprise you to hear it, but I'm sick and tired of going to <u>that</u> bed, perhaps especially because I always seem to start remembering and dreaming which only makes the darn thing so much the less pleasant. But then I suppose the same thing happens to you, and perhaps more often for there are around you so many more things to give nostalgia a nudge.

Incidentally, I am reminded now that for a long time I've meant to thank you for an expression that cropped up in one of your letters. It was something to the effect that some experience wasn't "fun any more because my partner isn't here." You know, that was awfully nice, to think of you thinking of me as - - not your husband, or the man who pays (?) the bills, or the father of your children, or even your lover - - but as your partner. For partnership, and especially partnership in and for life, means so vastly more - - you could have said nothing nicer. Think this will be an acceptable letter, Bettsy? Neither do I but there isn't much daylight left so I'd best be saying goodnight once more. It will be lovely to be able to tell you that again - - in person with you close enough to hear me if I whisper.

6/16/45 Saturday evening

I am guessing, as I start this, that it will be little more than a note for I've been reading so much of "Nicholas Nickleby" today that I've neglected my shower. And sadly, also needing a shave, I must get there while daylight lasts. Anyhow there's little to be said, for it has been a long, but by and large, routine day.

One thing, however, is new: we are at long last permitted to tell you we were in on the invasion of Okinawa. It's official now and I'm enclosing the handout which is only a little less informative than usual. Of course that leaves me with a writing job to do tomorrow and I'm hoping I can wangle a typewriter for it because I'd like to tell Harley and Mary, too, as much as I can about what it's been like. Seems a long way back to April but I guess I can remember enough to make a coherent story.

One other thing of interest, I've a new boss on the press

news, a Lt. Coral whom I hadn't met until this afternoon. The Ensign has been shifted to a new assignment, which seems usually to be the case as soon as someone gains enough experience to handle the thing. The new man (as was his predecessor), is a former school teacher. However, the pressure of the job has eased immeasurably with the end in Europe so it's much easier to catch on. Although my own interest is flagging, I'll give him as much help as possible.

Well, I guess summer really is here, for this is the third consecutive day of boiling sun, and as happened once before during a hot spell past my lips have chapped and cracked most uncomfortably. Reminds me oddly enough of Kipling's poem from "Child's Garden of Verse":

In winter I get up at night
And dress by yellow candle light;
In summer quite the other way
I have to go to bed by day.

There's something of the same anomaly in chapped lips, usually due to cold, being caused by heat.

And that my darling, seems about the letter for today. Such a letter, too, for a guy who passed up his gal yesterday (just sort of felt I ought to address it to Mother and Dad on that date) but honest I'll try and do better tomorrow.

6/17/45 Sunday afternoon

Another lovely hot day finds me on watch, my tummy pleasantly full and my pen loaded with a fresh supply of ink so this should be at least a long letter and I hope will compensate for the sleazy job I've been doing lately. Managed that shave and shower after last evening's note then went back up topside, made my daily blue book entry and then just loafed around until time to go on watch.

It was a lovely moonlit evening and so I sat awake through the first two or three hours, just looking, talking a little and thinking, wishing a lot. Need I tell why, or about whom, I was thinking? I rather imagine not, but for your guidance my thoughts were many thousands of miles from here. Strangely, I wasn't melancholy; it was more than pleasant, this time, to be remembering and imagining. Anyhow, it was a lovely evening, one I'm sure you would have enjoyed. Eventually I drank a cup of coffee and, being relieved from watch wandered below and to bed. Next thing I knew it was broad daylight, most everyone else up and stirring.

Breakfast this morning was beans, oatmeal, a piece of cake and an apple. I ate the latter two. While we're on the food subject, may I report that I am at last learning to drink - - with no great relish, yet - - the stuff called "mud." Not mess hall mud for that's more vile than any bootleg whiskey I ever bought - - which is some kind of vile. But the mud the crew is eternally brewing in the pots which are part and parcel of every watch station is, I find, palatable when diluted about 1 to 2 with water. But I yearn for a cup <u>of coffee with real cream</u>!

Started to read this morning, finding "Nicholas Nickleby" pretty fair going, but was suborned into a penny ante game and wasted the last three hours of the morning. Net loss: my time and $1.10. Actually I should have been writing for last night I promised myself this would be the day of the Okinawa story, and this is the best available time and place to start.

Probably because it was my first full picture of invasion, Okinawa was fascinating to me. Of course it was a fearsome sort of fascination; something like a bird must feel under the eyes of a snake, but that part slides into the background with time and the other picture stays sharp and clear.

Always before we had operated with the carriers and the big, sleek new battleships and the curious cruisers that were only dreams on paper when the Japs struck Pearl Harbor. This time we joined the pre-war fleet, much of it that the same Japs thought they had smashed forever at Pearl Harbor. Remember the long-ago movies of the fleet in battle line, the stately, tubby battleships plodding through the waves, spray splashing from their bows? That was the picture I looked at day by day as we advanced on the enemy.

It was a clear bright Palm Sunday when we came out of the dawn mists to find Kerama Retto weaving sharp-pointed green hills out of the blue water. It was a lovely place to look at, real land, when you haven't seen anything but yellow-palm-thatched coral and black volcanic ash for half a year. Those hills rise sharp from the sea, fringed by only a thin strip of sandy beach. Trees, there were, and, perched on almost every hillside, stairways of terraced fields built by the people to husband their land and keep from sliding down into the sea. In the little flat places at the foot of a notch between hills we could see tiny houses grouped in tiny towns. Some of the houses had tile roofs brick-red in color. From a distance they looked neat, clean and orderly - - and very deserted.

On one beach a long Japanese-type rowboat lay brown against the white sand, its blunt bow and stern tip tilted like a double-barreled snub nose. I did not then, nor afterward, see any people there. Roads zig-zag up and down the hills, seeming to lead from nowhere to nothing. High up on one cliff a bare spot was scraped across the hillside, showing plainly the round black mouths of two caves. We wondered if the Japs hid in there, waiting.

Between and among these island hills glinted blue water sparkling in the sun. Later we were to find that water sheltered a busy anchorage from which we drew as we needed the sinews of war - - fuel, food, firepower. And it came to acquire the sobriquets of "Suicide Gulch" and "Death Valley."

That Palm Sunday we steamed slowly past, firing a few shells, starting a few fires that ran snakily up the hills through dried grass. That evening we steamed away. Next morning we came back before the sun to find all the ships of invasion had materialized during the night; the big transports and cargo ships, the lumbering LST's, and all the mosquito swarm of the amphibs suddenly there. It seemed like magic. Some rocked lazily at anchor, some steamed slowly, and the little boats darted like water bugs on a quiet pond. We shot some more; we could see the troop-laden assault boats going in and the amphibian tanks clumsily splashing shoreward.

And right there we got our first breath of the Kamikaze - - Japan's "divine tempest" suicide fliers. A plane strange to us darted from a cloud a half mile away flying fast, a few hundred feet above the water. I watched as it sped, on a level course, toward a destroyer. And the guns raged, spat out orange fire and orange smoke and ugly black clouds that came into being all around the plane. Suddenly he tilted, dove down toward the sturdy little ship lying still in the water. Down, down the plane dove and to me looking on, it seemed that all that side of the ship was a blazing inferno as every gun on her bellowed and flamed. But on and on the plane came, now trailing a wisp of grey smoke.

As just as suddenly as it started it was all over. The plane, never seeming to vary one iota from its deadly dive, slid over the top of the destroyer (by inches it seemed to me) struck the water and disappeared in a white geyser. I'll never forget the feeling of admiration that surged up in me as I watched that little ship fight and win. Some of her guns were still firing a second or more after the plane passed over. Then clumsily she turned and steamed away, went on about her business in a simple "matter-of-fact" way. I have seen many such attacks since then, but I'll always remember that one.

It was the next day or perhaps the day after that, that we got our first look at Okinawa. From Kerama, the big island [Okinawa] is only a blue haze on the horizon, but we came up close for a good look at the nearest thing to civilization in a long time. As the handout says, our station was Naha and the airdrome, and we got a good look at the shelled out city that not long ago was as big and populous as Johnstown. There were some big buildings there, 3 and 4 stories high, and we could see that one looked like a church - - or the remains of one. The dock section looked as though it once had been very like a similar area of Philadelphia, and there were suburban sections stretching out into the valleys with some big, wealthy-looking homes among them.

The island itself was fresh and green; a run of sandy beach giving way to gentle hills rising slowly toward the middle of the island where the higher ridges lay. It was interlaced with roads that looked surprisingly smooth and wide wandering among the fields and over the hills. And everywhere you looked - - if you looked closely - - were little hamlets of a half dozen houses clustered together; in valleys, along the roads, in a copse of trees. In those days we saw no people; later there were a few but we were never certain whether they were civilians or Jap troops. Several times we saw horses, shaggy, diminutive things they seemed through field glasses, standing in the fields. Once I saw one all alone, forlorn on a tidal flat.

All that week we bombarded, patrolling slowly up and down our section by day, fighting off air attacks morning, noon and night. Bombarding soon becomes a boresome task. You stand long watches; get little sleep; the roar of the big guns rings in your ears day and night and often, when you must stand too close, the concussion of the guns is like a physical blow. Sometimes it felt as though I were being sharply slapped on the throat. Where the shells land you see only grey-brown blobs of smoke and shattered earth. Curiously, the snapping crackle of the five-inch guns I found more annoying than the deeper rumble of the eights. Sometimes from a distance we felt the jarring thud of the 12-14 and 16-18 inch battleship guns. But there are, sometimes, amusing little incidents.

One was the day we bombarded the lighthouse. Now the lighthouse stood on a promontory of rock at the entrance to Naha Bay. The rock, on the three sides we could see, rose 75 feet or so from the water on two sides and the land on two sides. It was level on top, and there was built the round lighthouse, some 60 feet high, and a pleasant-looking house which I guessed was the residence of the light keeper. Both were solid-looking buildings of tile or large size mosaic brick, topped by the neat brown tile roofs that mark the better buildings of Okinawa.

Obviously, the place was an excellent observatory, from which Jap binoculars could chart our moves, and eventually it might be an easily-defended fort. So we were told by phone that would be our target, and the eight-inch guns went to work. The first salvo was over; we could see the brown dust and rocks fly. The second was a little short, and a corner of the rock crumpled into the sea. The third was to the right, and a corner of the house caved in.

Fourth salvo - - all this in five minutes - - was "on target." A great cloud of smoke and dust sprang up and when the wind lifted it away, as a stage curtain goes up, the lighthouse had vanished completely! We went on to other targets. There were a couple of huge radio towers between the lighthouse and Naha airdrome. One was toppled by a ship one day, and the same night the other disappeared. On the airdrome were the gaunt steel skeletons of two hangars, either never finished or else burned out which we left alone. We left alone, too, some cleverly contrived dummy planes the Japs had left on the airstrip to cause us to waste ammunition. But we blew the hell out of some underground hangars and neatly demolished a couple of real planes the Japs thought they had hidden safely.

All that week we bombarded and Easter Sunday brought a big-scale duplication of Kerama. Saturday night we steamed away from a deserted island. Sunday morning before dawn hundreds of ships were there. Then began the real bombardment, and for an hour or more shells of all sizes rained on the beach and the adjoining hills. Slowly and deliberately, while we shelled, the little landing craft circled, loaded, circled again and then in lines moved toward the beach. With them went the rocket ships and, as the guns on the warships stopped, they laid an even more all-encompassing rain of death and destruction on the area. It's awesome to watch flight after flight of rockets spring up from the little ships, spurting fire for a moment, then gone again.

The sound came out to us - - whoosh, whoosh, whoosh - - then a solid roaring as they struck and exploded. A great cloud of dust covered everything. The troops went ashore. That first day, the fate of Okinawa, the course and ultimate outcome of the battles, was sealed and delivered to us. The soldiers and marines swarmed out onto the beach, raced almost unopposed up the hill and by nightfall held Youtan and Kadema airstrips. This you have read, I know, but I was there and I tell you it was true and vastly important.

Through that week the carriers and planes of Task Force 58 stood between us and Japan, covered us with an aerial umbrella that, while it didn't keep out all the rain of planes, enabled most of the Kamikaze to attain their divine objective of death for the emperor with comparatively little trouble. And as we held and developed and began to use Youtan and Kadema the pressure gradually eased.

Not that it was easy or pleasant. I have no records but it's my recollection that we were under air attack for 18 or 20 consecutive days and nights. The bugle seemed to be blowing almost hourly, and we griped, lost sleep - - and the Japs lost planes and pilots.

When the attack started we were in Kerama, taking on ammunition, and as one of the guys laughed later, "We used up more in shooting our way out than we loaded while we were there"! That was the day "Suicide Gulch" started. For a long time after that we kept on bombarding, moving with the troops toward Naha, watching through field glasses a little of the fighting - - tanks, men and guns streaming along the Okinawa roads; watching the houses burn as the troops routed the Japs. Now it was day and night shelling, and if possible we lost more sleep.

Star shells, some silvery and some golden - - ours and the Japs - - lighted the nights. Yellow and ruby red arches across the night sky were the tracers of the big shells. (Ernie Pyle wrote of "red hot shells, visible 10 miles at night" but he really was seeing the same tracers.) Ernie wrote, too of our nightmare AA (antiaircraft) barrage, that I saw and never will forget.

Hagushia anchorage was jammed with ships, hidden under a dense cloud of artificial smoke, when the three planes came in quite high. Searchlights, long fingers of white poking up into the black night found them, held them, lost them, found them again as the battle went on for more than an hour. Each time a shaft of light caught and held a silvery dot of plane, all the other lights would swing to it until the plane became a fly caught in a basket web lacing the entire sky; spread at the bottom, all converging to that one pinpoint, diffusing above each on its course to infinity. And each time the lights caught and held the guns below would open up, spouting red and gold tracers in a rainbow curve that, too, seemed to hold the plane at its apex. Eventually the planes were shot down or went away.

And before I forget it two other things: first the fliers, who as always kept watch over us day and night did a marvelous job! And they were attacking, too, bombing, strafing and rocketing day in and day out. Sometimes at night, too, we could see tracers spurting jumptisiously from the air toward the ground and knew our planes were working.

It was at Okinawa that I saw for the first time one of our planes shot down by the enemy. Four fighters were attacking a gun placement, four went in, and only three came out. It seemed to all of us that we had lost a friend, that pilot whom we never saw. But the all-time high for me in air attacks, for sheer ferocity and destructiveness, remains the raid on Suribachi at Iwo.

The other thing I wanted to note was the work of the little boats, the pickets of the vast screen that warned us of the approaching enemy - - and very often themselves kept the same enemy from approaching closer. Theirs was long, lonely and hard duty, and we of the big ships know it and are grateful to them, proud of them too.

When we left Okinawa the troops had moved down to, and all but stalled at, the Slivui line. Behind them were green fields and hills, little wooded patches and towns. Ahead of them the constant rain of shells ripped away the green of tree and bush and grass, leaving the ugly yellow dirt and rock where the Japs holed up and died. But Okinawa, especially, as I saw it first, remains the first real earth, the nearest thing to civilization I have seen in a long time.

There Bettsy is the story I've been wanting to put down for a long time. Undoubtedly there are parts I've omitted, and all of it you have read in the papers but perhaps my eyes will bring it into sharper focus for you. I hope so, for when I get home I'll have no time, for a long time, to be spinning you sea stories. You see, I'll be too busy telling you I love you.

6/19/45 Tuesday evening

A new project (perhaps it's not exactly new, just blossomed) has brightened an otherwise dull day for me, so let's talk about that first. It stems from the Okinawa letter that I wrote you day before yesterday, which you should have by the time you get this one.

I typed the sensible parts of your letter and sent it to Harley and Mary. I had the good sense to make two carbons, and last evening while some of us were sitting around in the mess hall doing nothing in particular I gave it to Sam and Will to read. They liked it, and still without any special idea I gave the copy to a couple of other guys to read and it circulated throughout the ship.

Now quite a few guys asked for a copy for themselves, some going so far as to offer to buy it. The idea took shape that I might put all my operations letters, the one about the typhoon, my haircut story and the yarn about the night in the mess hall and put them together into book form. You previously suggested we do something with the letters when I come home. Otherwise there's next to nothing to report of the day. I've had only a brief nap since 4 a.m., spent the morning reading and loafing, the afternoon on the press news and reading and here I am on watch after supper. It's been a murky sort of a day, but pleasantly warm and not too boresome. Chow at noon was the most tasty pork chops I've had in many a moon, and that helps. I shall not however, comment on either breakfast or supper.

My reading was first the completion, and partial re-reading of "East by Southwest." Secondly I reread, and revered your four letters of yesterday, about which more later, and thirdly I pitched in on "Nicholas" for a bit.

Now to your letters, and right away I want to thank you for the <u>full</u> name of my new brother-in-law. So it's Mrs. Mary Lyons, is it? I like it. Now please get me the address.

Glad to hear that Bucky and Chubbin were so very good for Mary's wedding procession and I was very sorry to have missed out on the biology (genetics, more properly) lesson with Bucky, for that was one I'd hoped to share with you. But your account tells me indirectly that you got past that first big hurdle beautifully and I'm very proud of you.

Thank you, my Bettsy, for the back pat on my "freedom of press" row and of course, you know by now I've adopted the answer you suggested. As to the importance of the story, it wasn't at all but it was the principle of the thing that I don't believe he or anyone else has the <u>right</u> to ban any piece of legitimate news for <u>any</u> reason

The point on the insurance policies, Bettsy, is that if we accumulate the dividends they will be paid up <u>years sooner</u>, instead of making just one premium a year easier. So I suggest see Wib soonest, and try to have them fixed that way - - unless he advises not to do it for some reason that doesn't occur to me now. We can depend on his advice.

Gosh I'm worried about this shoe business for the kids. It's not right that Buck shouldn't be allowed to go to the playground because of it and I hope you'll have gone to Johnstown to remedy it before this. And for the Lord's sake get 'em <u>at least two</u> pairs of sneakers <u>each</u> when you do.

Would it make you feel badly if, before saying good night, I should remind you of that promise you made about something we didn't do in Chicago. and wished in a later letter that we had? This is as good a place as any to end this my Bettsy and (as usual) tell you goodnight and tell you (as always) I love you.

6/21/45 Thursday evening at sea

Loafed last night, just plain, simple, downright loafed for there was no other excuse for not writing. Instead I've been reading through, and I mean thoroughly through - - four issues of Life that I accumulated at recent mail calls. Of special interest was the pictorial story of FDR's death and Truman's accession and another issue with an editorial pointing with pride to the Navy and naming four outstanding ships, among them "the bloody San Francisco"! Incidentally, did I ever mention to you that we are, with the carrier Enterprise, the only two major ships of the fleet now afloat holding the Presidential Unit Citation?

I procured and read today, "Carrier War" - - and I'm sorry to say I can't agree with all the whoop-hurrah reviews. A good book, but I think it <u>not</u> so good as Bob Casey's "Torpedo Junction" nor in fact any better than the semi-official somewhat dry "Battle Report."

It may be that I've been reading too many war reports of late so that they have somewhat lost their savor, or that having seen Task Force 58 in action too little of it was new. And when you've <u>seen</u> a sky filled with blossoms of ack-ack fire, and the horizon lit by the orange flame of burning planes, words and pictures of other similar scenes lose their punch. No photo can convey the deafening roar of the guns that caused these bursts, nor the strange strained stillness that follows when the attack is interrupted or ended.

Tomorrow I think I shall have my head clipped for the third time, and then I expect to embark on the great experiment - - will hair, or anything worthy of the name, grow on those vast vacant spaces? I don't know; honestly I don't think so; but I shall continue to try.

Haven't thought or done any more about the writing project I mentioned the other day, but I guess there's plenty of time. Incidentally the copy put in circulation has disappeared - - as I suspected it would. And I'm not sure whether I'm mad because something of mine was taken or flattered because something by me was of sufficient interest to swipe!

Wherein it's worthy of note that sailors (I take this ship to be typical.) are, as a whole, more congenitally larcenous than any other group I can think of. Anything - - a hat, a towel, a bar of soap, a magazine - - left in the open only for a moment probably will not be there when you return to look.

We bring food aboard - - and half the crew swarms around to loot; oranges by the dozens; canned meat in 6 pound tins; gallon cans of peaches and pears; even a 100 pound sack of sugar to be used for coffee all disappear. Oranges, lacking cold storage, dry, and usually are thrown away. Guys go back to the mess line to swipe a half dozen slices of bread, put them in their lockers, and wind up throwing them away half the time. A can of stolen meat is opened for sandwiches with stolen bread in a late-night snack; the bread runs out, half the meat is thrown away. Ditto the canned fruit and the sugar.

Then on a long cruise the chow runs low; try to tell the men that had they not stolen so much to be wasted there would be enough for all, and they laugh; "Bull; I'll swipe twice as much next time to make sure I have enough"! To me it's very disgusting - - but it seems to be the way of sailors, and there's no use in my squawking.

Gosh, almost forgot, Fran's birthday is due Wednesday and I feel like a heel that he won't at least have a letter from me. I hate that I've fallen down on such an important occasion, especially because it's the little fellow I hardly know. Damm it to hell, I've missed two out of his three birthdays and don't want to miss any more. Please tell him his Dad is mighty sorry and will write him real soon.

Again the daylight is thinning, my Bettsy, almost time to say goodnight once again and go below to bed for we have the mid-watch tonight. Truthfully the loneliness and homesickness that plagued me so a few weeks ago have waned but still I think of you, long for you, every hour of every day. And so I will continue to do, as long as we are apart.

6/28/45 Thursday evening at sea

Another day brings me, miraculously, another letter from you after seven on Wednesday along with two from the kids and one from Don Reed, who's still in the Philippines. Also arriving was the June 18 Time which I finished already.

I did work awhile this morning, but not too strenuously because of the heat and expect to go to bed as soon as I finish this for the 12-4 watch is not an overly pleasant prospect tonight. The combination of work and watches has kept me away from the press news lately.

My days have been moderately active lately despite the heat and my nights interesting, for we've been playing a bit of cards and the diversion is pleasant. Our Beer Can #4 for our honeymoon has benefited from this nocturnal activity. The fact that it cuts into my sleep hasn't hurt either, until today. Last night we played until after 1, and since I had to go on watch at 3:30, I came up to the boat deck instead of my bunk - - sat around drinking coffee and talking until 2 when I spread a blanket on the deck and went to sleep until 6.

Damm it the words come ever more slowly than usual tonight. At the moment the only thing I can think of about which I might write come under the head of bitching and it's such a perfectly lovely evening I'm trying mighty hard to avoid that. Let's take a look at what's left of your letters after last night's abrupt ending.

Oh yes, Reed's letter and yours re the $15 check reminds me I've still heard nothing from Wunder. And so I guess I'll have to admit that our paths crossed only briefly and regret it for I liked him a lot. Anyhow I'm glad the money matter is off your mind.

Golly, girl that sure was some day you had a few weeks ago, what with the laundry, a doctor's appointment and company all bunched together. And I, having somewhat of a memory, know just exactly how you were feeling as events progressed. 'Twas at times like that in the past that I betook myself to the nearest bar, or meekly curled up in some quiet corner hoping the storm would pass me by.

Suspect Pat [Jean's dog] must have been hiding in the house all the time you were looking for him, but that's a sinking sensation and I'm glad it came out OK, like Bucky, he was in the attic "just looking."

By the by, have you checked on my golf clubs as you said you would? If they're rusting, as I fear, I wonder if Jean could take them out to the country club some day (Sunday would do) and ask Joe to buff them and see if he has anything in the way of preservative grease. I'd sooner keep them shiny by swinging but it looks like I'll play even less golf this year than the 36-hole low I dropped to in 1944.

One of your letters starts out by telling me you are feeling "very virtuous" and the little green-eyed man who walks around behind me slyly whispers "What's so unusual in that as to be worth reporting"? Which causes me to wonder, for the girl I married always was very virtuous (sometimes too much dammed so).

Frankly, Bucky and Sis' reaction to my "Ode to a Vanished

Glory" startled me no little. I wrote it with the thought it might give you all a laugh, but now since these very competent judges point it out I begin to believe I may have something of the eternal muse in me. ("He means bemused," she snickers.) Anyhow, if I can persuade the muse to move me I shall try to initiate a few stanzas for them.

There, think that's at least enough words for a respectable letter, even when they don't say anything. And having put them down for my beloved I confess to feeling considerably better.

It is, as I said, a lovely evening; the sun is gone now and soft, cool breeze replaces the burning heat. As I look back our wake stretches like a broad, bubbling road across the flat water to the sky that's almost a spectrum: baby blue at the water level, almost green beyond the horizon a bank of white clouds, and higher up a faint mauve fading to the gray of evening, overhead. The sea is so big, and so very empty as is my bed.

Goodnight, my own Betty. I want only you!

6-30-45

Writing this is going to be, for a time at least, very difficult. There's a blazing sun setting almost in my face and the reflection from the water, like a river of molten steel, multiplies the heat and the glare so that it's most uncomfortable. And will be until either we change course or the sun sets. I came up here to the platform after a good supper, all fresh and clean and ready to write. But now my clothes are soggy with sweat and I'm not sure but that the perspiration has drained away the will to write. However, we shall see.

The enclosure with this letter may come as a bit of a surprise to you, as I know it was to me for it's my first real effort of the kind. Probably you will have difficulty with it, but as the creator I know what it's meant to say and so can read into it a certain rhythm that the casual reader may not perceive. As I say, it is the first, but it may not be the last for truthfully I enjoyed doing it. And, I guess if the truth is told Bucky and Sis are co-responsible for the product because as I told you the other night I was amused by their reaction to "Ode to a Vanished Glory" and half-needed to really try my hand more poetry - - some time.

Some time arrived last night, between midnight and 1 a.m. for I had the first lookout of our watch. It was a peculiarly lovely night, brilliant, softly cool, more stars overhead than ever I have seen before. And the moon <u>was</u> odd, past the full stage yet not sharply lined, a sort of lumpy light hanging in the sky. And so, for lack of anything better to do I began fitting words together until at the end of my watch I had three stanzas. So I ran below for paper to jot them down and this afternoon ground out (with a great difficulty) the last. To be strictly honest, I'm a bit proud of the product, even while I know it isn't poetry and won't stand the test of proper scantion. But perhaps there may be others, better ones, I hope, and at least I think you will enjoy this one - - if so it will have been a complete success.

Well another day another dollar. Slept like a babe all last night (except for my watch) curled up atop an ammunition locker, the same one on which I'm sitting now and where I very probably shall spend this night. The darn thing is, I just measured it, less than five feet long and just 16 inches wide - - so you can tell approximately how much space I shall take up at night when I come home. Anyhow it's much too dammed hot and stuffy to be sleeping below. I'll go there if it rains, for the first drops never fail to wake me but otherwise the hard steel will make me a comfortable couch.

Inspection today, the first for me in a long, long time, and we were warned to expect more in the future, so it seems we're going back to the peacetime Navy - - and I want <u>no part</u> of that. However today's was in dungarees, working uniform, they're called, which was a break, but I expect to be hauling out a set of whites - - which I haven't donned in nearly 8 months. Suppose they're "yellow" by now.

Afterwards we worked, Sam and Chuck and I, hard and dirty all through the morning. But we took the afternoon off and I spent part of it doing a bit of shopping but was disappointed to find the one thing I wanted most, envelopes, not available. The remainder of my purchases, soap, cigs, a couple shirts, shoestrings, etc., trimmed my available capital to $12 - - the beer can profited nearly $1 - - but a couple of the boys owe me $5 each and tomorrow or next day should be pay day.

Then after stowing my stuff in the overcrowded locker, finished my "pome" and just sat around the rest of the afternoon gabbing and drinking mud. When I finish this - - soon, for the sun is setting and I'm now much more comfortable - - I'll have a little more of the same and then "crap out" - - which is Navy slang for going to sleep, anywhere, any time.

And there my dearest you have my daily report, such as it is. I could add a whole lot of words about how lonely I am for all of you, and what dreams I dream for That Day, but being a lazy person I'll just let you figure out "My Dream."

THE LOPSIDED MOON

The Lopsided Moon and I are friends
Keeping watch together in the star-filled night.
I share all my dreams with the Lopsided Moon,
And somehow the sharing helps make them more bright.
There's a pathway of silver across the sea
That leads from the Lopsided Moon to me;
And the brightest of dreams is that when this job's thru
I'll be sailing that pathway straight home to you.
Of when I shall sail, and what I shall find,
The Lopsided Moon helps bring to my mind
A myriad of pictures; of scenes old and new
And around them and through them moves each one of you.

Yes, The Lopsided Moon is a comforting friend,
Sharing my dreams, shining on Journey's End.
And when I come home (may That Day be soon!),
May it be by the light of the Lopsided Moon.

C.A.W. - - At Sea, June 1945

Chapter 13
FRISCO AT WAR - PART SIX
MASS MEDICINE THE NAVY WAY,
A VISIT TO A WAR-TORN ISLAND
7/4/45 to 7/29/45

7/4/45 Wednesday morning at sea

The old song used to say "Every day will be so sunny, Honey, with you" but I guess that applies only in God's country and not in the western Pacific. Very obviously I am not with you (loud and long laments) yet equally obviously every day of recent date is so sunny that it's becoming boresome - - and it's <u>hot </u>too.

Another blazing hot day, but I think I've managed to escape any more sun-burn damage while acquiring a bit more tan. All three of us worked all morning, and loafed all afternoon. The ship was again on "holiday routine" - - which is the Navy's way of saying loafing is permitted except for those routine watches and duties essential to the operation of the ship.

Slept atop my favorite locker again last night, and plan to return tonight and every night so long as the weather stays fair. Strangely enough I find it more difficult up here to get awake in the morning, although I sleep none too soundly. By the time I had washed and cleaned up this morning I had missed breakfast, but it was a small loss and more than made up at noon by a turkey dinner. I hit the jackpot; a large helping of white meat went very well with the gravy and stuffing, cranberries, olives and ice cream. Then I finished a book of Damon Runyan short stories, read a bit of Beard's "Basic History"'and got me a shower before starting on the Okinawa Invasion letter to the Smith's.

Wonder what you and the kids are doing today? Used to be that Independence Day was a big holiday, but personally it's sort of lost its appeal since fireworks were banned. Maybe I wouldn't even enjoy them now. But when I was Buck's age it was a big time and so much fun.

Now for some finances. Yesterday was payday, and my fund on the books is another $7 greater to the comfortable sum of $162. However the strain of nursing Beer Can # 4 finally was too much for me and since the ship is putting on an Independence Day bond drive I persuaded myself to peek. Courtesy of said Beer Can you will be getting an envelope from Washington to add to the others of our collection. Besides, opening the can was the patriotic thing to do; for once again the ship is short of silver and appealing for all hands to turn in their hoards. Felt quite virtuous depositing my jingling pocketful with the cashier, too.

Dammit darling, I wish I could be with you, even for just a little while. Even to pick up a telephone and talk for a bit, as we used to do, would help although I'd probably be tongue-tied too. But it's been so long now I guess I can get along for however much more time is to be taken away from us.

It's toughest of all to think of how I'm missing seeing our kids grow up, for all I'll ever know is how they were when I went away, and how they are when I come back; never how the transition came about.

But there, if I go on you'll be thinking me extraordinarily blue and homesick when that isn't the case at all. I'm just blurting out whatever comes into my head, and the only thing wrong with me is that I'm so far away from you and ours. With that I'll close Bettsy.

7/8/45 Sunday evening in port

I would have you know, young lady, that you are responsible for my having been up and around since 5 a.m. today - - and if that doesn't prove I love you damm if I know how to do it (at this long range).

You see I <u>really</u> was tired last night, and a half hour after finishing writing that poor excuse for a letter I was curled up here on the locker and knew nothing more until I awoke with the gray of dawn tingeing the sky. Not feeling like more sleep just then I wandered below for a drink and to check on the time when, as I entered the compartment, what do I see but a heap of letters - - 6 from you, one each from Buck, Peg and Joe, plus a new Time. So quite naturally I hunted a bright spot, read a couple of the letters and then came back up for the air is so much better here and by then it was light enough to go on reading.

Which I did until reveille at 7, then for a while I just lay here dreaming until time for breakfast. After that Svoboda and I worked a little (very) and then loafed and stood my watch. This was the <u>third</u> official "holiday routine" day within 8, an unprecedented event.

Anyhow, and especially because of your letters it's been a swell day. Gray and rainy all the time, but minus the oppressive heat and for that I'm thankful.

There was one other big event, too, Mass and communion although I was only able to sneak down for a few minutes since it came while I was on watch and couldn't find a full-time replacement. Seventh Sunday after Pentecost, and the last time I heard Mass was the Fourth Sunday of Lent. An awfully long gap but I guess it can't be helped. And the priest said he would come back again tomorrow or Tuesday which suits me swell.

I'm pleased to report that my personal work is in good order since I've folded and stowed away all my laundry since supper. But one of these days I must go into the laundry business on a big scale, for my blues and all but one suit of my whites have been crammed into my locker without so much as an airing for 8 months now. Hate like the deuce to start on the job, which I've been postponing for a long time.

Also tomorrow should be my liberty day, and if all goes well I'll be setting foot on real, dirty dirt for the first time in a long time. More about that tomorrow evening I hope.

Now to the letters. Peg's contained a set of new pictures that were most welcome, albeit a bit fuzzy. Since she says they were taken by you, it's high time for a scolding for film is scarce. Didn't I ever tell you the camera must be <u>still</u> to take a clear shot? Anyhow there was one really good picture of the kids and another of Buck and Sis in their Easter outfits. Lord, I can't get over how they've grown and changed!

Darn your story of the lemon pie. Fairly made my mouth water, I can tell you and by golly you'd better have at least 6 of them when I come in the door for I sure will be desiring some eventually and you'll <u>not</u> be having time for baking . . . . pies. But I can't imagine you, of all people, being frightened by a thunderstorm. Wish I could have been there to protect and console you.

You mention Democrats and I should specify here that I haven't had any later than March and now believe It's been stopped - - which is OK. They are so old when they do arrive and they're piled up so that it's difficult to read them. I still think, and I say I can prove, the paper's gone downhill since Jess left.

See Henry Baker Reilley is still writing editorials as political news - - which I find amusing and painful. Now if <u>I</u> were running the American _____

So, you cruel wench, not even from you can I find any sympathy in my direst need (not for sympathy, but at this distance it would help). But you'll be sorry. I'm going to save some of these letters and when next I get that not-tonight-dear-I'm-too-tired business I shall resurrect them and read them to you as a sort of gentle reminder.

Would that be a good note on which to stop? I rather think so, for there's a hidden, yet perfectly obvious meaning that will save me the trouble of repeating those three little words so oft written. 'Nite my darling.

7/9/45 Monday evening in port

Not much daylight left, so I'll jump first into an item of business then go on to report my day which has been almost entirely on the beach.

The business comes up in one of your delayed letters which I received a while ago in which you report receipt of a check for $72.21 as the 1944 income tax refund. My recollection is that the tax paid during my brief tenure as a civilian last year was $85 plus and according to my reckoning all of that should have been refunded. Seems to me there's enough dollars difference to warrant a checkup, and so I suggest you look up the duplicate copy I sent you

Lots more to be gone into on your letters but guess I'll be letting it slide until tomorrow so I can get on with the story of today. Which started out as an early eye-opener, for I was awake about 6 but just sat around until after 7 when I went down to breakfast. Then Dooley and I, who were going on the beach, decided to get a bit of work done first and we slaved up quite a sweat before the liberty party LCI arrived about 10.

That part of the outing, and much of the rest of it, was just like Ulithi. After what seems a nonsensically long delay it's finally decided everyone is aboard and the LCI shoves off, stumpily through the busy harbor until within 100 yards or so of the recreation area. Then it dumps anchor and stops, only this time there was no wait before the LCM (another smaller amphibs boat) came alongside. And we all piled in it and rode that last 100 yards to the dock. There we piled out.

The recreation area seems to be a low-lush-spit at the foot

of the hills, all grown up with coconut palms and green jungle vegetation. A stagnant little tidal creek cuts through it, of which more later. And on the way in we passed the oddest rocks, rising 50 feet or more, sheer from the water and literally covered with trees or shrubs. I can't imagine how the green stuff hangs on to the rock, let alone finds anything to nourish it.

On the whole this place is much like Ulithi's recreation island (Did I ever tell you its name, Mog Mog?) only it seems larger and better developed. From the pier we walked through the grove, past several concrete basketball and handball courts to the beer area where the officers in charge of our party brought the beer and distributed it. Refrigeration units installed on the island keep the stuff good and cold.

Each of us got one sandwich and two cans of beer, which may be why I found the liberty dull for two cans just isn't enough to really cool you and there didn't seem to be any to be bought that we could find. Not even at $1 a can. So we drank it quickly, and while drinking watched a half dozen native youngsters paddling a double-outrigger canoe in the creek I mentioned and diving for coins the boys throw to them.

The little beggars might have been almost any age from 3 to 10, but 5 or 6 would be my guess and they swam like fish; laughing and chattering all the time and I didn't once see them fail to come up with any silver coin thrown to them. "Hey Joe, Throw" they kept calling, and every time a glinting coin flipped through the air and splashed in the water they turned up their brown bottoms and went swimming down after it. Sometimes I know they must have caught the coins in the water, only a couple of feet deep; others they dug out of the black rock bottom. But they come up grinning, coin pinched between thumb and forefinger, calling "Hey Joe, Throw"! It was about as good as a circus.

Then I wandered down to the beach past the baseball fields to the bazaar. We're technically forbidden any intercourse (about which many of the boys are vocally grieved) with the natives, and are not permitted to go outside the barbed-wire surrounded compound. But the native merchants are not to be denied.

They have set up little shops against their side of the barbed wire, built crude counters and covered the whole thing with thatched palm. There they sit, all the family from grandma to the youngest babe crawling in the muck, all day long. There's a long row of these "stores," mostly side-by-side and in the intervals others less enterprising or energetic simply peddle their wares through the fence. And the universal cry is "One dollah; one dollah, Joe." All sailors are Joe here. Nope I don't know why.

Their merchandise is mostly shells, sold separately or strung into necklaces, etc. The handiwork is extremely crude, but the shells alone are pretty and there are many kinds and colors; small medium and large. Also they sell grass skirts, gaily colored and very, very sketchy; little hempen sandals that are truly pretty handcraft; odd-shaped hats woven from some flat palm frond; crude little wooden slippers and clumsy, wicked-looking souvenir bolo knives, too dangerous for toys, too small to be useful.

Of course I walked all along the line looking, and eventually with the few dollars I had bought a couple little things which I'll pack up and send to you some day. There was much haggling, some loud, some funny, some profane, but in the vast majority of the cases it seemed to me the diminutive natives won hands down. It was "One dollah-two dollah-three dollah, Joe" or no sale. And all they wanted was Uncle Sam greenbacks, silver did not interest them - - I tried.

Oh yes, one of the most prominently-displayed items in trade was Jap invasion money; some pesos, some guilders. Little urchins waved whole fistfulls of it squeaking "One dollah, Joe. You buy Joe - - one dollah." And I wondered if they hadn't collected this money from the Japs just as they are now raking in our greenbacks

The natives are all tiny people, much smaller than I had imagined, brown of skin, quite regular features and many of them really pleasant-looking. They seemed to understand only a smattering of English, but their quick brown eyes missed only a smattering of tricks. All of them wore what appeared to be factory-made clothes, the women in ill-fitting, colorless dresses that stressed black and white. Nearly all were barefoot. Many of the men wore khaki that might once have been some army's issue.

They were not only selling, they were buying and bargaining, too. An orange - - we had some with our lunch - - was as good as a dollar; a cake of soap worth 2 or 3: and they were hungry for twine which they use for necklaces. I saw one ball sold for $15 cash and was told another went for $25. And jewelry! Some of the men and women (who I am very sure couldn't tell time) sported wristwatches. Others had rings and bracelets and necklaces. One girl wanted to know if I'd dicker for my dog-tag chain. I told her no, I needed it.

Some of the more uncouth stood around trying to figure out how to go about making a pass at the girls, and I heard a few crude remarks but these dignified quiet little people seemed to have that situation well in hand. Some of the girls conceivably might have been attractive but I did not see anywhere any attempt to capitalize on this, even as a means of attracting customers to the shops. Mom, Pop and the kids were there in most of them, and they were no less annoyed than the couple of shops where mother and daughters, or a couple of sisters, presided at the counter without male aid.

It took me an hour or more to see all this, but there was little variety in the merchandise and when the cramped sales lane began filling up I moved out, back to the recreation area and just sat around for about two hours until it was time to board our LCM and reverse the travel route back to the ship.

Gambling here is officially barred and I still think its unfortunate, but guess it can't be helped. Not that I wanted to gamble, for even with the desire I would have had no capital, but there's so damm little to do on such a place, and rules or no rules these boys with money will gamble somehow, sometime. I did see one crap game, of a surreptitious sort, but it wasn't exciting,

All in all it was a poor liberty, and having seen the natives, the only new thing once, I've no great desire to go back. Incidentally the first civilians I've seen or talked to in 8 months didn't mean as much to me as I expected, although I did a kick out of the kids. For kids are kids, any color time or place and what pappy won't enjoy others when he can't see his own?

But my own is really what I want and need, and I suspect if the truth were told I'll not really enjoy anything until I'm close enough to tell you - - - - - - - - - - - - - .

Yep, here I go again and I guess this has run its course long enough at least to drag me down into the sweltering mess hall, and so I guess it's goodnight once again Bettsy. One more day gone from the total lost to us. How many more will we lose? Only the Good Lord knows and he also knows I love you.

7/11/45 Wednesday evening in port

More mail today and if it keeps on piling up I shall never be able to answer it - - but I love it. I speak specifically of your two mis-numbered letters, about which I had been wondering. Anyhow I am now all caught up to July 2 and so the deluge should slow to the daily trickle.

Damm I just (too late) remembered I wanted to listen to the radio this evening. Some of the guys caught the tail end of a broadcast (Jap, I assume) at noon which claimed the U.S.S. San Francisco was sunk, and I wanted to learn more about it, if possible. I assure you it's a very strange feeling to be at the bottom of the ocean, especially when you haven't had so much as a salt water swim or shower in weeks. Guess this about the 'steenth time the Shamboes have "sunk" Frisco, and if they don't cut it out they're going to wake up some morning to find they have lost the war to a Navy that sailed exclusively on the bottom of the ocean.

Seriously though, I'm afraid the report may have reached you and caused some undue worry and so I wish here and now to put it in the same class with the report of his death which Mark Twain told a reporter was "grossly exaggerated."

Well it's been another gray, rainy (and pleasantly) day but in between showers we did manage to get a bit of work done. Now the guns, magazines and lockers are all shipshape but we still have a mess of rust and paint to chip, and then the painting. Oh well, guess it will get done some day.

Went to the movie again last night after mailing your letters. Sat through the very dullest movie I've seen in years (some kind of alleged farce-mystery that was neither funny nor mysterious) simply because I hated to go to bed in the bake-oven compartment. When it was over I did try to find a place topside but the rain soon settled that and I had to go down. It was a punk night and I had a helluva time getting awake to go on watch at 3:30. I've slept about one hour since then.

Below now, just in time to hear (radio) some squitch squalling a tune (?) about "Saturday night is the loveliest night of the week." A lousy tune, but somehow that one phrase out of it makes sense to me - - and I'm afraid you'd agree.

Speaking of radio, I suppose you know that Armed Forces Radio Service, through stations on a number of islands, brings us newscasts relayed via short wave from the States and of course most of the top-drawer network shows, minus commercials.

Your letter today contained the family snapshots on Mary's wedding day, and to put it mildly I was delighted. First of all was a new set of you and the kids and while I could have asked a little kinder treatment for some of the others, the shots of Buck and Chubbin were delightful. Then there was my first look at my new brother-in-law, sizable guy, ain't he? I know now what Buck meant when he spoke of them as our two great "lovers." Can't speak for John but Mary is as radiant as any sunrise I ever saw.

Then too there were the two Dick's both looking grand

although my kid cousin apparently didn't shoot up so far as I thought. And finally, Dad, sticking his bald knob - - boy I <u>can't</u> be that bald - - and puckish grin in back. And he's plump as a tub of butter, too. Must be too much brew; I recommend temperance, if not total prohibition. Anyhow, Pappy, you look <u>swell</u> and it makes me feel good all over.

P.S. to Mom - - Honest all the camera ever wants to do is tell me the truth about you. Why don't you loosen up and let it - - or must I always be snapping you with your slip showing (or I might have caught you coming out of church the other day) so you'll forget to pose? 'Sall right Honey, guess you and I just aren't photogenic like your husband and your grandchildren.

As for you, wench, despite all your boasts of weight-gaining you look skinny to me so keep on with the milk, etc. (no cracks about crackers, pls; causes nostalgia, heartburn and "I funks") and if necessary I'll go for a new wardrobe, or at least a dress or two. Orders, Madame!

Well I used to begin and end the day with orders for you (yeah, I know they weren't always obeyed, especially those at the end) and guess I might as well start getting back in the habit. Besides it is (always) too damm hot down here so goodnite my Bettsy.

7/15/45 Sunday morning at sea

Dear Buck:

How are you doing? Since you always start your letters that way I guess I can too!

To start off, I'm inclined to scold you a bit, for your recent letters haven't been nearly so neat or well-written as they were for a while, but on second thought perhaps I'd better not scold, for at least you have been writing, which is more than I can say for it's been just about two months and I know that's much too long.

But as I have explained before, we don't have a whole lot of opportunities to write and every day when I write to your mother

I'm thinking of all of you, too, so you really get more letters than the occasional few I write to you.

This is a sunny, hot morning, and down on the fantail (that's what we call the deck at the stern of the ship) quite a few men are loafing and taking sunbaths. Me, I can't do that just now for my nose is still peeling and pretty sore. One of the gun crews is at work, too, chipping off the old paint before putting on new, and it seems sort of funny to see the four barrels of the gun pointing up at the sky.

Four barrels may sound like a funny sort of a gun, but what it is, really, is four separate cannon on a single mount, so that all are aimed at the same target all the time. And we can fire any one of the guns alone, or fire them all together. Makes quite a racket, I can tell you, when they're all shooting.

My friend Chuck Svoboda is on watch on another gun, and he's wearing the phones because he happens to be lookout just now. You see each gun has a set of phones, over which the officers give us orders of what to do and when to shoot. The phones are something like those a telephone operator uses; two earpieces that clamp over your head, a mouthpiece that sort of sits on your chest and is held by a strap around your neck. And they have a long wire, or lead, (Betts. Pronounced leed) so you can walk around while wearing them or using them.

Time out for a bit, Sonny, must go to lunch.----------------
Lunch was fried chicken (not nearly so good as it sounds; I think they use sparrows) and now I'm back on topside loafing after standing a very brief watch. However the situation has changed quite a bit and now we're in port with small boats buzzing all around. Pretty soon the mailman will be shoving off in one of them and I hope he'll bring me back a letter from you.

Which brings me back to where I started. It's swell the way you've been sticking to your writing, Son, for it means a whole lot to me to have those letters coming in so regularly; it's real proof you haven't forgotten. But I like to see each one done better than the one before, and that wasn't so the last time, looked like you were in an awful hurry to get it done. I know you can and will do better.

One more thing: Mother told me you asked why the other guys get mad when you strike out playing baseball. Don't you worry about that, just step in there and take your cut, and run them all out, as hard as you can, even when it looks like you're a sure out. And everybody strikes out some times, even Joe DiMaggio - - so don't you get mad when your side needs a run and some one else strikes out. Make up your mind you'll get that run next time.

Lots of love, Your Dad

P.S. How's the Latin coming along? Will you be ready to serve Mass soon?

7/15/45 Sunday morning at sea

Dearest Fran:

Well big fellow, I seem to have missed out on another of your birthday parties and since two out of three is entirely too many I'm sort of counting on not missing any more. Anyhow I know you had a good time and it sounded to me as though you collected quite a flock of presents.

Too bad you can't be going to vacation school with Buck and Sis, but you will be next year and anyhow it gives you more time to spend with your mother, which I envy you a great deal. Hope that when I come home you won't mind too much if I take up some of her time. After all, I saw her first.

Hear you got a big kick out of going into the newspaper office and watching the machines at work. That's fun isn't it? I remember that when I was a little boy I used to do the same thing, and perhaps that's what got me started toward the newspaper business. When we get back to Philadelphia I'll make it a point to show you through my office and I'll bet there are enough clicking teletypes to keep you interested for a while. Buck and Sis used to enjoy them, when you were too small to go.

Do you have lots of fun with Pat? I'll bet you do, romping and playing in the big yard there, and I'll bet you can't ride your bike fast enough to keep in front of him. There used to be a grape arbor in the middle of the lawn where the long flower bed is now and I played tag around it with Mickey, who was only a very little dog but lots of fun.

And I wonder if they are still using the wading pool at the playground. Mother hasn't mentioned it in any of her letters but it seems to me that you ought to try it. Buck and Sis both are too big now for that.

Do you know Sonny that it's very hard for me to write to you; steaming along these strange waters where there's nothing but clouds, ocean and some distant mountains to see. I find it difficult to think of anything that will interest you. But some of these days we'll be together again and walking and talking and it'll be lots easier, and much more fun, to get acquainted. But at least I can tell you that I do love you very much, and miss you much too much. We'll have lots of fun when we can be together.

Always, Your Dad

7/15/45 Sunday evening in port

Through dint of much (?) energy applied to the pen I now hold in hand, said pen then being in contact at various times with one of several sheets of paper, my conscience is much clearer this evening and I begin to hope in the not-too-far distant future my correspondence debts will be paid. I made a good start for at long last I've written to those three sprouts of ours.

And before I go any further with this I apologize for the nasty, bitchy letter that I wrote this morning. I could withdraw it now but I think I'll let it go anyway just to show you what a distinctly dismal person you are (or were once, remember?) married to. But honest, honey, I promise that after I come back all will be sweetness and light. These past 15 months have shown me how wonderful you and home are; I doubt that I'll even growl very much when you burn the pans!

It's a gray, sultry still evening after a brief but very hard shower that broke just before supper. I had finished (for the time) writing and sat here for a long time watching it roll down from the steep hills. Gradually it started across the bay like an almost solid wall of water and when it struck the ship I couldn't see 100 feet. But it soon passed on and now only vagrant white clouds cling to the hills, hiding the peaks and roofing the valleys.

It's now about 6 o'clock, and that gives me plenty of time to finish this before dark. Then a shower and perhaps, if we have a second show as usual I'll see the movie. For tonight it's Irene Dunn and Charles Boyer in "Together Again."

There's really good news this evening, for the water rationing which plagued us has been called off. Guess they've been over-hauling some of the machines which turn salt water into fresh. Because for the past few days we've been able to get fresh water for bathing during only 3 specified one-hour periods daily. Which makes for a mad scramble, with everyone trying to get in at the same time, and besides it isn't always convenient to take a shower when the water is on.

Last evening, for instance, I had worked quite late and then galloped up to get clean. You can imagine my reaction when, just after I'd gotten all of me nicely lathered and had just stepped under the shower to rinse off, the water was turned off, and there I was all sudsy. Of course I was able to go to another shower room, two decks lower, and rinse myself with the salt water but that improved my disposition only slightly.

Tomorrow we must get down to the grind of chipping and brushing and painting. Damm but I hate that kind of work (It's both hard and dirty and as you know I'm allergic to that stuff.) but it must be done so here we go - - I'm ready!

I'm not making a definite report as yet but I'm beginning to lose what little hope I had that my "grand hair experiment" might work. It's been nearly two months now since my second scalping and I'm sorry to say that my forehead remains all too high and my crown sports only a practically invisible coat of fuzz. Nevertheless I shall make one more effort; next time we go to sea I'll acquire another scalping and then will see what happens.

There, I guess that cleans up the amount of my moment so I'll drag out your saved up letters so hang on for a ride on the merry-go-round.

Much surprised at your easy acquiescence to my home-buying plan. It really is a plan, and I'm quite serious about it. However we'll have to wait a wee bit I guess, to find out where, at least. Meanwhile assume you're saving appropriate ads and ideas re plans, equipment, etc.

Thought you'd enjoy my "wee bit green" reaction, so I couldn't hold it out on you. Myself, I'm not a bit ashamed of it, for you're no more a one-man-woman than I am a one-woman-man. Love me?

And so you ain't sorry for my aggravated internal combustion. Well all I can say Toots is that you're asking for it and ------- ------ (that's one sheet I'm <u>saving</u>!) and so long as you're gloating, I may as well remark that it's with me again, and I'm not sure whether I'm mad or glad. Very disconcerting

I'm shocked no end by your reckless extravagance of late and especially by that crack about spending our whole bank account. Along that same line, tomorrow should be payday and I expect to draw $50 and just stow it away somewhere as an emergency reserve. I also expect to collect $55 that's owed me, which will be my working capital but I don't intend to be caught again without ready money.

You and Mother both know, from long experience what I think about locked doors, and I should have laughed myself silly to see you running to check on a "kidnapping." Don't suppose it will do any good renew the protest at this late date but just suppose I should come home inexplicably late at night and find all the doors locked. Then I either would have to go to a hotel or get everyone up (probably by blasting off the front porch). Now I ask you, wouldn't it be much easier for all concerned if the door were left unlocked and I could just walk in and go to bed, then let you find me in the morning? Think of all the trouble and fuss that would be saved.

With which pleasant suggestion I think I shall say goodnight once again. Dusk is coming on and I need that shower so I'll be hoping to continue with more words tomorrow. Until then dearest when I'll be telling you once more that I love you.

7/20/45 Friday evening in port

Here I are again on the same old perch but I warn you here and now I must stop when darkness comes for we're on watch and I can't go below until we're relieved, which will be after the first movie. Furthermore, I'm a bit late starting for since chow I've been busy giving the good old "Navy polish" to my best shoes in preparation for the inspection tomorrow and that takes some little time. Anyhow I guess I'm ready for the dammed inspection, although our paint-work is in horrible shape. Otherwise the guns are good, the magazines excellent, and my personal gear as neat as any.

Last night after writing, I dropped in, entirely by accident, on one of the little parties that occasionally develop on shipboard, and even had a sip or two of an alky cocktail (?) that didn't taste half bad. Then I ankled off to the movie (can't remember the name, if indeed, I ever knew it) and then to bed about midnight.

Up at 7 this morning, worked from quarters until noon and for two hours more this afternoon, since when I've just been sitting around gassing. By the way, the pants I had been wearing, one of the two pairs issued when I came in 16 months ago, finally wore through at the knee and so I ripped the legs off, shed my shoes and sox and shirt and wandered around in the rain very comfortably indeed. Rather wish we wore shorts as the British sailors do, but it's not de rigueur in this Navy.

Speaking of showers reminds me to report this has been the warmest and most pleasant day since we pulled in here. And we even had a few glimpses of sunshine, and the showers were scattered and warm, not at all hard to take! I finally got to confession today, for the first time since <u>March</u>, but no Mass. The priest came aboard from another ship just to hear us, for it's been a long time.

Well, quite a few of the boys were AWOL this morning when a surprise general muster was ordered at quarters, among them Sam and Will. Seems they've been more than anxious to taste the forbidden delights of the island, even if it isn't very civilized, and so hopped a ride on a beach-bound boat.

They returned this afternoon, muddy, bedraggled and broke, having spent $150, all that 3 of them had, in slightly more than 24 hours. Curiously enough the two culprits are avoiding me, probably because they know I'll bawl the hell out of them if I get a chance. But from some of the others I've heard pretty wild tales and I don't doubt they're true (mostly). Among them: a lady companion for the night is readily available at the equivalent of about $30 - - or $5 an hour; liquors and food very expensive but obtainable; ask me some time about one boy who proudly displayed abrasions on his knees!

Not for me. Don't know whether it's because I'm old-fashioned or just plain old. But it would have been a fair guess you have something to do with it. Worst of all, I'm afraid it may go extra hard with Sam this time, who has been in scrapes before and has been for some time past in the bad books of one of the minor powers - - that be, our chief gunners mate. I'm hoping it won't be too bad, but am keeping my fingers crossed.

Not much light left, now Bettsy, for the movie already has started. But gee I wish you could sit beside me and enjoy this evening. The water is flat calm, undisturbed by the breeze that cools us, but furrowed by the white washes of small craft scurrying between the ships and the beach. Over on the island the lights have come on and the gray-hanging clouds that hide the tops of the hills around us seem to be preparing to creep down the valleys. And the lights are on, some of them, on the ships, too, with the crews clustered wherever the movie screen is perched. It could be a completely lovely place and time, with you. That my darling, would be true anywhere anytime! I pray every day that "anywhere anytime" will come soon.

7/26/45 Thursday evening in port

I'm feeling quite a bit better this evening, thank you, although not yet up to par. But I'll hope to be there, or thereabouts, tomorrow for it's back to work again with all four guns to be cleaned and our painting still undone. As for the lack of a letter yesterday, there's three reasons - - my sinus problem, watch all morning, and then I got into a poker game after lunch, going to bed when it broke up at 9 p.m. And I might as well report that it was an unfortunate game, too. Guess I might have known my luck couldn't last. Anyhow, I now am, for the first time insolvent. I still have the $50 I drew last payday for an emergency fund, and I'll not use that. But meanwhile I am without operating capital, and I owe $2 more than the other guys owe me. Phooey! And that ends poker until payday.

To fill in the gap since my Saturday letter, I did go to the movie that night. Sunday morning I got off watch long enough to go to Mass and communion, and in the afternoon I went to the liberty island. (I can prove I'm not well; we were issued three cans of beer; and I gave one of mine away! Didn't taste good, even though it was Duquesne.) Came back on the ship for supper, and then bed.

The ship's plan of the day this morning called for the names of all personnel with newspaper, advertising, publicity, etc. experience. The request was repeated at quarters and my name was submitted. We'll see what happens.

It's been a very sunny, very hot day, more so than any in quite some time, and my poor proboscis, what with the sun and the sniffles, is unpleasantly tender. Unfortunately, I'm still not in a writing mood and I've decided to postpone my tale of liberty until I've had another opportunity to examine the place, which may be tomorrow. Anyhow I'm not going to miss any more chances to go ashore, and perhaps after I go again I can spin you a fairly interesting yarn, for I enjoyed the place.

We're all hoping there will be some mail for us here this evening, but I for one am not optimistic even though I've had only one letter from you dated later than July 2. But there will be a batch catching up one of these days. Lordy I'm dirty this evening. Haven't done much today, either, for I lay around on watch all morning and spent most of the afternoon in my tub for another practice shoot, after which we greased and stored some ammunition. Oh well, when I finish this I'll have me a shave and a shower that should remedy the dirt.

Have I ever told you about mass medicine, or the Navy way? I assure you it's quite different from anything I've seen in civilian life. It seems there are quite a few of us so annoyed by head colds at the moment, and so we line up in the morning for sick call at 8 o'clock. The Pharmacist Mates ask each guy in line what he thinks is wrong with him and those reporting colds are set aside in a separate line, 14 to a relay. Each one gets a thermometer to suck, and after a suitable interval one of the PhM's goes down the line picking off each thermometer. If any man shows sufficient fever he's clapped pronto into bed.

The rest of us, still standing in line, are each handed a small (whiskey) glass containing a couple drops of clear, oily, lemon-flavored liquid - - which we toss down. Then a PhM, with a sprayer containing white liquid, moves down the line spraying each man's nostrils. He's followed by another PhM, with a sprayer containing brown liquid, who sprays each throat and adjures each man to swallow it. Then the first PhM comes back with a big bottle from which he shakes 6 pills per man with instructions - - 4 now, 2 before lunch. And we all walk out to give place to the next relay, 14 men treated in little more than the time it would take for two. Oh yes, the bottle from which the pills are shaken is labeled A.C.P. - - which scuttlebutt says means "All Common Purposes" or "All Common People."

The nose spray was a bit rough on me this morning, for I got a full charge of the stuff right on my tender sinus and for a minute or two I thought the top of my head had come off. But it didn't. (Doggone it I must be coming a hypochondriac. There I go complaining again and that will never do.)So here I stop, my Bettsy, and I begin to believe that maybe tomorrow I'll be able to write a decent letter. At least I'll try. 'Nite dear and I look forward to sweet dreams of you and ours.

7/28/45 Saturday morning in port

Funny how the best laid plans go astray, for here's a whole, broiling day gone and not a line written up to now. And to complicate my problem, I'm even further behind for two more letters from you arrived today, bringing me up to July 18. Not bad, eh?

But I just did not feel like writing this morning. Instead I decided to see if the sun could boil away the remnants of my cold and so spent the morning loafing and reading, clad only in a pair of shorts. Sweated copiously, of course, and tonight said cold is barely a memory. This afternoon, instead of working, I swapped with another guy and made my second trip to the recreation island. Went with Svoboda and we had a swell time roaming all over the place.

It's only a pinpoint of an island at the mouth of the bay but back in the days before the Japs came it must have been a lovely place. Down along the beach there are patches of creeping bent grass, the remnants of what once must have been a lovely lawn. And nearby are the shells of three or four buildings; generous concrete porches, stately white arches and pillars. Oddly the bare concrete foundations mark the sites of other buildings, completely destroyed.

We rode from the ship on an LCM, docked beside and clambered over the waterlogged, rusting hulk of what once was a sturdy little inner-island steamer. Ashore we received our four cans of beer each and Chuck and I each drank three before starting on our travels. By that time the gang had split up, some to play softball, others seeking a secluded spot for crapshooting, still others like ourselves to wander. Aside from the small area adjacent to the dock, the island is quite hilly, overgrown with brush and pitted and pocked by war's passing, twice.

The first time was a helluva fight, from all the evidence I've seen of whole areas where trees were blasted 6 or 8 feet above the ground as by a giant, pulverizing swath. The stumps still stand, more than three years later with graying frazzled tops poking through the dank undergrowth newly sprung up. And the defenders were not fighting empty-handed, for when the end came they spiked the big guns, blasted the huge concrete emplacements and wrecked their underground communications systems so they would be of no use to the Japs.

Back against the hills are two or three huge, two-story concrete buildings that I guess once were barracks for the garrison. Only shells now, the bare walls have been adorned (?) by scrawled signatures of countless wandering sailors, and by some unknown artist with a penchant for charcoal drawings of Amazonian, very voluptuous and reasonably nude wenches.

The walls of these buildings, once smooth and shining, are pocked everywhere by small arms fire and shrapnel. In places you can see where a machine gun sprayed stretches yards long, the round-sprawled bullet craters evenly spaced in an almost straight line. Sprawled, too, are what's left of the concrete gun emplacements. On the floor of one I found what appeared to be a mortar hit, a shallow pit from which radiated concussion lines much like the radii of some circular chart.

And the hills and valleys are pocked, too, huge craters from which must have been aerial bombs: others, marked by a long furrow leading to the crater, from heavy artillery, perhaps naval guns. And other, smaller ones, like round red sores in the green grass, from lighter artillery and mortars. Often it's difficult to tell whether these are from the old war, when we were yielding as slowly as we could, or this new war when we came back much more rapidly. Not many months have passed but the jungle grows fast hiding its sores.

Clambering over the hills, I waded (literally) through waist-high grass and at times, through brush as thick as I ever encountered, even though I was following trails fairly well tramped out by others as curious as I. And at times, in little ravines, in open fields, at vantage points on the edge of the hill I came across little holes, slots really, in the ground that I knew were man-dug forts for both offense and protection - - foxholes.

And when I had climbed enough, and seen all I thought interesting, I drifted down to the beach and there picked my way among the rocks, and the washed up flotsam and jetsam, back to the starting point, ready to come back to the ship. In all I don't suppose I walked 3 miles, but it was much the longest foot journey in many a moon and I enjoyed it. Incidentally, I picked up a few more shells and some pieces of shrapnel I think will interest Bucky.

At the end we encountered the first real on-shore accident I've found in the Navy. Waiting for the boat, a man off another ship fell from the seawall, somehow, to the hard sand beach 6 or 8 feet below and when I saw him being carried up to the pier I knew at once he had a compound leg fracture. We found a stretcher and brought him out to Frisco and I suppose by now he's sleeping after the setting operation. Who he was I haven't any idea, but he gets my vote for a man with guts for despite one of the worst fractures I've ever seen he never once whimpered.

There now, I've told you the story that was on my mind last week. Now tomorrow (this said with my fingers crossed after my failure to make good today) maybe I can get on with answering the mail. Almost dark now and I must run, Bettsy, for I sadly need that shower tonight. But as always, I must say goodnight my darling and perhaps, just for a change it might be well to add I love you.

7/29/45 Sunday afternoon at sea

I've plenty of time, and the will, to write today but right now I am dubious as to just how much I'll get done, for I've an ache in my right knee that makes me uncomfortable any way I sit. However it may be I'll become sufficiently engrossed in putting words together to enable me to forget the knee - - I hope.

No movie for me last night, to speak of, for after finishing your letter I stood around gabbing until there barely was time for my shave and shower before the first show ended. I did see a little bit of the second, a comedy made up of old footage (circa 1920) of Mack Sennett and Keystone Kops stuff that I enjoyed. But "Belle of the Yukon" was to my mind the poorest, least interesting big time movie I've ever smelled. I got up and left in disgust after 5 minutes of it.

Finally went to bed some time after midnight, and slept right well. This morning we worked for a half hour or so, since when I've been just plain loafing. By the way, we had fried chicken for dinner, a fairly ordinary Sunday meal, but this one was different. My piece of chicken not only was edible - - but actually delicious.

Remember a long time ago I wrote about the mess hall, and mentioned a boy named Valentine Pena. He's our new (?) hand, a queer little youngster who's been on the ship for something over three years. We call him "VP" (his initials) or "Cisco" (for what reason I really wouldn't know). He's a happy, slightly irresponsible youngster who, like so many others has matured out here, makes you think at times he's a little boy, and at others that he's a little old man. I enjoy him lots, and we get along fine.

Just before we left the States he was one of several guys who went AWOL and nearly missed the ship. As a result he was court martialled and his heart nearly broke when his GM2/C rate was taken away and he went back to seaman. He was so proud of it, and thinks now he ought to get it back, but I doubt that he ever will unless he gets some powerful help from above.

"Cisco", like most of the boys of Mexican or Spanish descent, speaks with a decided accent, and after he came back aboard he told a story on himself that was uproariously funny. (Better explain here that Cisco speaks of all girls as "squaws" and he dearly loves every one of them.)

Anyhow it seems the S.P.'s had picked him up after a night, or several, of uproarious partying and had handcuffed him prior to returning him to the ship. Pretty disheveled and bedrazzled, he must have been quite a sight standing in the bus station. Somehow the S.P. wandered away. And a pretty "squaw" who I guess felt compassionate at seeing the little guy so messed up and manacled (or maybe just curious), walked up and asked him what he had done. Cisco, not one to disappoint a lady, replied with emphasis: "I keel a guy and boy you should have seen that squaw take a hike." Cisco laughs. As I said, I do enjoy him.

Gosh this is a lovely day, blazing hot sun, brightly blue sea and the green wake stretching behind us. Overhead a few white clouds hang lazily. You'd be in seventh heaven with all this heat and sunshine. Wish I could pack you a few bushels and bring them home to you.

Before starting into your letters again, one of the most recent ones contains your plea for help on a Christmas package and I guess I can't deny you that. But honest it's hard to tell you what I want, for there is so little I can use, need or keep. Best of all I want another <u>good</u> picture of all of you. And I could use a cheap pocket knife, a Boy Scout knife (complete with bottle opener!) would do very nicely. Beyond that there's nothing I can think of but food, in which line a fruit cake, if you can find one in a sealed tin box, would be swell. Otherwise <u>small</u> packages of cheese, tongue, shrimp - - things of that sort. You know what I like.

There is one other item, but I'll be needing a new diary before Christmas. I've been right faithful with this one and at the same rate it should last until November. Don't know where you got this one but it suits me well and if you can get a duplicate I'd like it

6/25 – Gosh I'm glad your pappy really got enough energy to write - - or maybe that proves he isn't well? Anyhow you tell him Bob and I are counting on that trout fishing and deer hunting - - and he'd better have a frig full of cold ones when we arrive.

Assume you'll keep me informed on Dick. I know the young punk won't write but if and when he gets out here (God forbid) I'll sure try to see him if our paths cross. Yep, I'll probably crave milk just as he did, or perhaps worse for Air Force men in Britain must have been able to get a little and I haven't tasted the real stuff in 9 months.

6/26 – Thanks much for getting Fran's birthday present when I couldn't. Makes a guy feel sort of ancient to think of the baby as 3 already - - and imagine Bucky in fourth grade!

7/1 – Hope you've made that Johnstown trip long before you get this; if not please go as soon as possible. Don't want any barking dogs needing care when I come home. Nor shall I grieve <u>too</u> much if you do buy a couple of dresses. Just make sure they fit your fanny. Nothing is too good for my sweetheart!

7/2 – Hah! See you too disapproved of "Belle of the Yukon." Having no memory for movies, nor names or actors, I'd forgotten your gripe.

Sorry Toots, but I'll have to stop here for the sun is getting at me and it's unbearable. May write more tonight.

7/29/45 Sunday evening in port

Here I are again, same old perch, mountains all around and the cool of a lovely evening shoving aside the memory of a broiling day. Out on the boat deck half dollars clink merrily as the boys indulge in their latest pastime, pitching at a crack (for nickels).

Down on the well deck the crowd is rallying for the first movie, and I see the same thing going on aboard other ships around us. The dark green jungle stands silent at the water's edge. Small boats scurry bouncily across the rippled harbor. A fading sun sheds golden light on the mountaintops. Signal lights white and red and green blink mysterious messages.

Not having anything to do with the messages, I've no idea what they say. Sometimes I amuse myself by concocting imaginary ones like:

From: Commanding Officer, U.S.S. Whoozis

To: Commanding Officer, U.S.S. Whatzit

Appreciate advice soonest if any Scotch aboard; I'll bring ice cubes and White Rock."

Maybe that isn't the way it goes, but it's hard for me to imagine how it does work because there are so many types of blinks.

Anyhow it's extremely difficult, at times like this, to realize this is war, a deadly serious business that has dragged me away from all I love for more than a year now, and will keep me away God only knows how much longer. But there's no denying this seeming make-believe war is vastly more bearable than the real thing when you're haunted day and night by the bugle and the bong-bong-bong of the general alarm. It is a summons that takes away even the will to ignore; the most profound sleeper is awake at the first bong, and on his way at the second. I'll never forget the first time I heard it, when I had no advance warning even of what it meant or what I should do. I was new out here then — a long time ago.

We were tied up beside another ship, when something, somehow, set off the ship's alarm. And instantly we were all galvanized into action. I was far forward on the forecastle when it happened, and I remember feeling I <u>must</u> <u>do</u> something. Then I saw other men running on both ships - - and next I remember I was pantingly putting on the phones at my battle station. (Which was, I learned, the right place to be, even for a false alarm.)

Now dusk is on us - - it comes quickly here - - and the sun has slid down behind the mountains leaving only a streamer-like orange-painted cloud to mark its passageway. Out to sea a lonely patrol boat prowls the horizon beneath a bank of purple clouds. Inland a white cloud has obscured the pointed peak of one mountain, seems poised to creep down its side for an evening prowl in the valley. Ashore the yellow lights blink on like an amber necklace dropped 'round in the bay.

The bugler's call seems, literally, to say musically "Let's Start the Movies"! In a minute attention will be called on the well deck as the big shots arrive for their reserved seats. Then the projector flicks on, and the movie starts amid howls, whistles and applause. (Not many of us care what the movie is. Of course an effort is made to get the best available but most of the men, and officers too, do religiously sit through anything on the theory it's better than the real life we've been seeing and living for so long.)

Well my darling, you can plainly see I'm not now, nor have I been, in a mood to go back to your letters. Instead I've chosen this as the best substitute for putting my arms around you and settling down in real peace. If I could only do that I think I should have some words for your ear; (the words) possibly would (probably will) be a bit monotonous and repetitious. But when that time comes I hope you'll forgive those infractions because I'll keep saying them over and over! I hope you never get tired of hearing me say them.

Chapter 14
FRISCO AT WAR, PART SEVEN
VISITS TO MANILA, THE ATOM BOMB,
THE WAR IS OVER, DEVASTATING NEWS
8/2/45 to 8/26/45

8/2/45 Thursday morning at sea

Two days in a row now I let you down, out of sheer laziness, but I've finally browbeaten myself into picking up the pen and while this probably will be only a note I think I can promise to do better tonight.

For all the interval there seems surprisingly little to say. The sea, being a bit rougher than other cruises in the recent past, has evoked the old reaction - - sleepiness. Not that I've done any more snoozing than usual, but what I get just doesn't seem to be enough.

About the most interesting thing, I suspect, that I can report is our whereabouts through May and June and as you already guessed it was Okinawa. So we were there for the start and the finish and I guess saw just about as much of it as any ship in the fleet. The handout this time is unusually well done, and I'll enclose it with this. Later I hope to expand on it a bit.

Of the days since I wrote, there doesn't seem much to be

said. Day before yesterday I did take my bothersome knee to sick bay, and the doctor, without x-raying, said it probably was the same old trouble - - a piece of loose cartilage from a long-ago football game. He gave me an elastic bandage and orders to exercise the knee, besides being careful with it. Today the thing feels a good bit better, though not yet comfortable. Also we've gotten a bit of work done, but the practice shooting we've been having (We're having more of it right now but at the moment I've nothing to do.) leaves us with all the guns to clean again. But given two or three decent days we should get the situation in really good shape.

Found time to read a book – "Piloting Comes Natural" by Frederick Way, Jr., not much of a story in itself but of interest to me because it concerns steamboating (recent) on the Ohio River out of Pittsburgh and boats and places at least vaguely familiar to me. Think Dad would enjoy it. Haven't yet tried "Brave Men" but will one of these days, although I need to do a bit of studying - - just in case.

Further I must report that luck finally seems to have definitely turned against me in cards. Yesterday was payday and I drew $30 "liberty money" but last night a game got going and in about two hours I succeeded in losing $35. That makes three deficits in a row, which hasn't happened to me before, and not only leaves me without operating capital but has my "emergency" fund reduced to $38.

Oh well, I still have $103 on the books and since I will not go below that, nor can I (will I) touch what I have already sent home to you, we're bound to show a substantial profit. By the way, have you received that extra envelope from Washington of which I told you last month?

Time runs out rapidly, Bettsy, and so I'd best tack on an au revoir here and get ready to dream of you.

8/3/45 Friday evening in port

Don't know exactly what's come over me lately, but here's another day and evening I've been slacking; not a line written and the first movie already under way. Another large haul of mail arrived last night, too, which makes me an even bigger heel for failing to take pen in hand. Five letters from you, one each from Buck, Sis and Rusty and a paper from the Smiths.

Mother dear, many thanks for my new medal. I found it last night in the first letter I opened, and first thing this morning attached it to the chain where it will stay. I'll hope to return it to you soon, in person.

Another very good movie last night "Thrill of a Romance," and Lauritz Melchior was absolutely wonderful. He's grand and so human I almost believe he can bring opera down to the level where I can understand and enjoy it

The letters arrived between movies, and I read the latest before going to bed at midnight to sleep again on a most delectable pillow. And again this morning I was reading happily in the early hours I used to see only on the other end of the day.

Could have gone ashore [the city of Manila] this morning with the first liberty group but for some reason decided against it, possibly because I didn't know Walts was going and couldn't see anyone on the list for company. So I turned this one down and now it develops I'll be going Sunday - - and perhaps to Mass ashore for the first time in many, many months.

As a result, Sam, Chuck and I worked hard all morning to get the four guns all cleaned up and now we have only the painting to do and all will be lovely. Expect to pitch into that tomorrow when Chuck will be ashore.

This afternoon I managed a haircut (trim) and a bath and shave, spent an hour or so sunning myself and then, with the rest of the stay-aboards, watching the liberty party return. Lord what a rowdy bunch - - I'm almost afraid to go. Fights, drunks, rip-roaring hell raising, Whoo!! But they seem to have had a swell time, the nearest thing to real liberty in so very long.

Sidelight: Frequently in the past we've been warned of the very high percentage of social diseases in the area. The warning was repeated at quarters this morning before the men left - - and each man, before he went down the gangplank was handed the common preventatives, with adjurations to go to a prophylaxis station.

Be that as it may, this remains by long odds and even from this distance, the most interesting place I've seen in all my travels. You've no idea how strange it seems after so long to see 5 or 6 stories of buildings – real buildings! - - shining yellow squares of light in the night and to watch the crawling white lights that you know are auto traffic on real streets.

And here too is the utter devastation that in all my war I have not seen at close hand. Even from this distance it is apparent, the jumbled rusting masts and superstructures of sunken ships; black blotches on tall white buildings that mark the path of fire; the gaunt steel skeleton of what must have been not long ago a huge and beautiful church, towering above it the familiar cross.

Yet in the midst of all this I took time out a bit ago to watch the most colorful sunset I ever have seen. It had been a gray, dull evening until suddenly the sun lighted the whole western sky into a sheet of orange flame. Beneath the sky of fire a bank of blued steel clouds hid the horizon all but obscuring the dim outlines of the purple mountains rimming the bay. And in the distance the lights blinked on in the tall white buildings behind the forest of ships. Did I say it was lovely?

And so having, after a fashion, brought you up to this moment I'm going to call it quits for tonight. Lately your letters have been chiding me about writing so briefly but I hope this, and future ones will appease you a bit.

Nite, my darling. And do forgive me if sometimes I can manage only notes. My will, and ability to write may waver at times, but my love for you grows with every hour I must be away. And, in case you didn't know, that's some hours by now, how many we don't know.

8/6/45 Monday morning at sea

No letter last night, which is not surprising in view of the fact that yesterday was my nearest thing to a real liberty in nine months. But my alibi is not quite the common one, for I didn't so much as have one drink!

But walk! Hellzfire we walked and walked and walked some more until at the end my recently-bothersome knee was so painful I could neither walk nor stand nor lie down with any degree of comfort. I did try to write, actually brought out my gear after supper, but gave it up as a bad job and went to bed at 8. Today it's much better, thank you, and so I'll try to make it up to you with two letters - - if I can find more envelopes for this is the last.

First of all I think you'll be interested to hear that I did make the picture grade; though disappointingly I must confess. Anyhow, I have these prints and a negative which I'll try to get in the mail in the next day or so, and you can judge for yourself. Also I picked up a couple of small souvenirs, and must remember to look for packaging materials.

As for the liberty itself, it was grand; as I predicted in another letter much the most fascinating place I've seen. The incredible debris, the swarming streets, glimpses of the old, normal life; the sights, the sounds, the smells. Yes, I was as fascinated as you would have expected me to be.

We left the ship, wearing whites, about 9 a.m., a whole bunch of us jammed into an LCM that ploughed through the greasy harbor water, past rusting hulks of half a dozen ships, and up the river to the liberty landing in the heart of the city.

As we got off the boat I happened to drift in with Swafford, the little GM1/c I told you of long ago, whom I never have either known or wished to know well. But a moment's conversation disclosed that neither of us were looking for female companionship - - called locally "pom-pom" or "babo" - - or very thirsty and so we stuck together all through the day. And I think we wound up better friends than either of us had previously though we ever would be.

First we wandered a bit through the business district, gaping at the burned, blasted buildings, the constant jostling traffic and hordes of people. Then I wanted to see Russ Brines in the AP office and located an Army telephone only to discover he was away. But Dan Schedlen, the chief of bureau, was there and invited us up to his office - - which was only a block away.

Surprise No. 1 of the day was to find an elevator - - a real elevator, actually working! - - waiting to take us up to the fourth floor office. The building of course was much less damaged than most of the others around it, but at that there was nothing left on the ground except the walls and pillars supporting the upper floors. At the office I met Schedlen, Spencer Davis and a native who comprised the staff at the moment. Most of the morning work seemed to have been cleared up and we stood around a while talking shop

Afterward Swafford and I continued our tour. Every bridge across the river had been dynamited by the Japs, and repaired by our engineers who threw Bailey bridges across the missing spans. Traffic roars across them now in an unending stream; trucks, jeeps, cars, ambulances and horse carts bumper to bumper. We crossed one on the pedestrian lane, a narrow boardwalk just wide enough for two streams of motley humanity flowing in opposite directions, into the older part of the city.

Here the Jap Royal Marines made their death stand, and if the newer part had seemed wrecked this was a shambles. There are no words of mine to tell you how huge buildings were blasted in crumpled piles of stone and concrete and twisted steel. Huge holes bored through two-foot walls showed where artillery shells went in; and the outward bulging walls testified to the force of the explosions within.

We found wicked-looking barbed wire entanglements; a few rusted Jap cannons and some exploded but not quite disintegrated shells that might have been ours or theirs. A couple of bullet-ridden orange streetcars lay on their sides in a clump of weeds; at some places the rails remained in the center of the broad four-lane streets; at others they were twisted ribbons of rust thrown into the rubble of a building. In some places areas blocks square had been leveled to the base, black earth and there were pitched the tents of Army units and, nearby, civilian refugee camps.

Around and through these camps, in the streets, everywhere we went were hoards of brown youngsters, playing jabbering, squalling, scampering, flashing friendly smiles, begging cigarettes and gum, hawking fistfuls of Japanese money and big round copper coins. As I've tried to tell you I got a tremendous kick out of them, especially one friendly little fellow who took my hand and walked a block or so, jabbering away.

It must have been nearly noon when we got back across the river, and by then I was hungry. But the first restaurant that looked decent from the outside wasn't inside so we settled for a cup of coffee and went on our travels.

Everywhere in the business district little shops, selling handmade curios, some junk jewelry and the omnipresent Jap money, have been thrown up in the burned out street floors of the buildings, in the vacant spaces where buildings used to be, along the sidewalks. There were little brown men, haggard old crones in tattered dresses, kids everywhere smiling in a friendly mystified way as though wondering what manner of people are these soldiers and sailors crowding our streets.

Bars are everywhere, selling mainly local whiskey (?) and in a few places genuine stateside stuff; from second-floor drink-and-dance honkytonks comes the tinny rattle of a piano, the soughing of a saxophone, the blare of a trumpet. Through the windows you can see white-garbed sailors dancing with the brown-skinned girls. Mostly they (the girls) are a fairly good looking lot, dressed after our own style; smiling, bright-eyed little wenches not at all hard to look at.

The bars, are, by the way, almost as cheap as any available entertainment by Stateside standards. A drink of local whiskey is 50 cents and up, stateside when you find it, $3; the drinks are very small. I bought some food; coffee 20 cents; cucumber salad, consisting of 8 slices of cucumber and two leaves of lettuce, 75 cents; an egg sandwich, $1.25; slice of papaya 50 cents; 2 slices (very tiny) of bread, 50 cents. By contrast, a woman costs from $3 up.

But the whole trouble, it seems to me is inflation. I didn't feel they were trying to gyp us at all, but scrambling to exist. And the inflation started when the Japs were on the way out, they dumped reams of paper money, tiny cheap-printed cheap paper stuff whereas when they first came, intending to stay, they produced currency that at least was solid-looking. When we recaptured the banks, I was told, we found them jammed to the gills with this worthless paper; you can buy a whole bundle, worth hundreds of dollars at face value, for 50 cents. And of course the black market flourishes; you can sell and buy cigarettes, soap, watches, anything of that sort, for prices as fantastic as you're charged for local goods. Anyhow, the effect of the whole place is like walking through some fantastic tatterdemalion version of an Arabian Nights bazaar - - and I loved it.

We went on with our walk, as I said, through this jumbled humanity and battered masonry, past curio shops, food shops where they sold queer little pastries and had greasy-looking meats on display; past a movie theater where the waiting lines stretched 3 blocks in each direction and on to the part of the old residential area where the war passed by without scorching.

There were fewer service people here off the beaten path; little shops, more dirty houses jammed together along the narrow streets and the numerous alleys; a slimy stagnant creek crossed by rickety arched wooden bridges, and little pony carts everywhere, drawn by the smallest horses I've ever seen but hauling 3 to 6 passengers besides the driver. And kids, kids and more kids!

We found one fantastic house, hidden from the street, reachable only by stepping from stone to stone through a slime-filled 4-foot alley. The place was of gaudy red, orange and yellow tile, had a Shinto shrine and a formal Japanese garden in the rear where stone bullfrogs sat on the edge of a pool. And atop the whole thing was a cross, put there I guess at the insistence of the priest! The five-foot cement wall around the place was studded with what looked like jade - - and proved on closer investigation to be shards of green glass. A sign proclaimed no admittance to anyone except persons concerned with the owner-occupant's real estate business and others "by special appointment only." Further, the sign said, the place was closed Sundays and Catholic holidays!

By this time we were both tired and my knee quite painful so we headed back towards the liberty landing and en route met a couple of (sober) Frisco guys on shore patrol duty who remarked there was a nice bar nearby. At this point I was ready for a drink and we agreed to try it. But when we started up the stairs we were called back and told admission would be $1 - - so we said to hell with it and that was as close as we came to a drink. I guess it was a drink-and-dance joint and all we wanted was the drink.

Eventually we did get back to our first stomping ground. And there we found a really nice looking restaurant that was reasonably clean inside (It even had tablecloths!). There I ate my meal. Swafford said he wasn't hungry but I suspect he didn't trust the food. Neither did I, so I picked very carefully but it must have been all right. Papaya, by the way, is a sort of melon, of no especially pungent taste; it looks like a long cantaloupe and the meat is about the same color and consistency.

Then we shopped a bit, collected my pictures which had been

taken in the morning and by then it was after 4, with the liberty expiring at 5. Lordy there were a mess of drunks there, staggering, lying on the ground, shouting and fighting. Sam, Will and couple more came up to me, all boiled. Will bled from top to toe from a gash on his head where he'd been clouted by a billy-club by an SP. Sam, until then, was in good physical shape. But they left me after a bit, went to another bar, got into another fight and when they came aboard on a later boat Sam had to go to sick bay to have two stitches in his lip where someone had hit him. They're wild, riotous boys, but nevertheless I like them and we get along swell, even when they're drunk.

As we waited for the boat the rain began and my clothes, which had remained fairly clean until then, soon were a mud-spattered mess. Eventually I got back to the ship OK, grabbed a bit of supper and then tried to sleep after failing to write. Took a while, but eventually I dozed off and my knee is much better today.

Now there my dearest, is an account of my first liberty and also my first letter of the day. I'll surely be able to write at least a little this evening so I will not say goodbye or good night.

8/6/45 Monday evening in port

The rain has stopped but in the mountains all around us little white clouds nestle softly against the green and there's a mistiness in the air that hints of more rain tonight. I hope not for we have the 12 to 4 watch and rain is never pleasant. Anyhow it's peaceful and quiet here, which I'm enjoying.

A few more odds and ends on my liberty.

I spoke of inflation in my earlier letter; despite which I couldn't understand how come I'd spent $16. Well all prices and sales are in pesos, and the money interchanges freely with ours at one peso = 50 cents. Shortly after we got ashore, and while I was looking for the AP office, I dropped into an Army financial section to make inquiry and bum a phone. While there I had a $10 bill changed into pesos and last night when I was trying to account for my money I suddenly realized I had gotten only 10 pesos for $10. Perhaps he was intentionally gypping me, but it's my guess that the sergeant was mystified by a $5 surplus when he checked out at the end of the day.

Lots of little stands along the streets sell fruit, but none looked very clean and I didn't buy. There were bananas (smaller than the kind we're used to at home); pineapples, also small; papaya (pronounced pa-pie-ya), something that looked like a small avocado, and another that looked like an oversize lime. With my papaya I was served a tiny green fruit that the waiter called a lemon. It was no bigger than a marble, green like a lime, and tasted rather like a flat orange. I tried in two restaurants for fresh sliced pineapple, but no luck. Some of the guys bought pineapples and the bite I had was quite good.

The little pony carts so common in the residence areas also are seen near the liberty landing although they must keep off the main traffic arteries. Most of their business there is steering sailors and soldiers to the various houses. Several of the drink-and-dance joints operate small trucks as free taxis from the landing. Usually they're baited with a tasty-looking damsel or two.

The officers, I assume, are taken to another area for liberty, for in all my travels I saw very few, only one from the ship and he was on Shore Patrol. He came along while Swafford and I were admiring some gorgeous little birds in a shop, warned us "You can't take them aboard ship, you know," and moseyed along. Swafford was incensed, claiming the guy just wanted to flout his authority. I guessed he was trying to do us a favor, assuming rather naturally that we'd been drinking, might buy and then have to throw them away. (Birds and most animals are prohibited as a health menace, psittacosis and such things.) The birds were lovely; wings covering a spot of pure white, and stubby pyramid-shaped beaks of coral pink.

We found one especially gorgeous shop (I mean the contents, for the shop itself is only a slightly-larger-than-usual cubicle in another blasted building). In one case were carved ivory bracelets, amply large to slip over your hand, with a chain of quarter-inch high elephants, marching trunk to tail around it, 150 pesos; gorgeous hand-embroidered silk mandarin robes from China, red and deep green, 250 pesos; four magnificently-carved teakwood chests, fitted with brass, each 600 pesos; and a pair of Chinese gods (Evil and Good, identical until you looked closely at the facial expressions) also carved from teak, not yet fully cleaned of the dust from wherever they were hidden from the Japs. I didn't even ask that price.

Everywhere the people were courteous, friendly, trying to understand and to meet our requests. In one very nice little tailor shop I stopped to chat quite a while with the neatly-dressed, apparently well-educated proprietor. Among other things he warned me to be aware of pickpockets. And the kids, as I said, were a real treat to me even when they were almost annoying with their cigarette-begging and pleas to buy something, anything.

On the other hand I was at times disgusted with the boorish behavior of some of my compatriots (not from our ship). I can forgive a guy for getting quietly, even fighting drunk, but I've small patience for those who drink until they pass out and then must lie in any filth in which they happen to fall. And even less for those who become tipsy and begin trying to lay hands on any girl they see, or cursing or browbeating decent natives whom they, the besotted idiots, feel are their inferiors. And worst of all, the guy who staggers up to a ten-year old boy offering cigarettes "if your sister got pompom." I damm near got into a fight over that.

I'd heard quite a few stories of small boys, pimping for their sisters, but in all my travel I only once heard a youngster calling to a serviceman "Hey, Joe! You want pompom"? However in this case I believe the kid thought only he was playing some kind of a game. I'm convinced the stories were largely fictitious.

Anyhow, it was a swell outing, one I'll remember for a long time and one part of the cruise I'll really enjoy telling you about.

Aside from these letters I haven't done a thing all day for it's been raining steadily until just a little bit ago. Perhaps tomorrow we'll get back to work for we've still quite a bit of painting ahead of us. At any rate I hope to have gotten out of the letter-writing doghouse with you with this outpouring.

My knee, by the way, feels much better tonight thank goodness. It really was giving me fits last night but I've kept the bandage on today, as I should have yesterday, and the improvement is pleasing.

With which bit of hypochondria I'll be signing off again, dearest. Wish to gosh I could be sure how much longer I must continue saying good night at this unpleasantly long range but since I can't we'll have to settle for hope.

But regardless of how long it's been, Betts, or how much longer it must last, I couldn't be loving you a whit more had I been in your arms every minute of the time (which I wish I had been). So give Bucky and Chubbin and Fran an extra big kiss from their long-absent Dad, and tell them I'm only waiting for the day when we all can be together again.

8/7/45 Tuesday evening in port

I don't think this will be much of a letter for I'm hot and tired tonight and besides I've got a good excuse. It's been a sunny, hot day and we finally got over the hump on our work with the last chipping and scraping job. Hooray, now we've only some paint to slap on and from there it's a shoo-in.

And all the day I worked in the sun without a shirt; you should see me. Remember how brown my arms used to get back when I was playing golf almost every day? Well the whole upper half of me is now four shades darker than that, the swellest coat of tan I've collected in all my life. Hope I can preserve it until I get home.

By the way, Madame, how's for a financial accounting? Don't recall having had one in some time and in case you didn't know it, I am a mite interested in that horde of ours. (Nope, I am not going to put the bite on you for a loan.) At the moment I'm not too healthy what with $4 in my locker, $18 owed to me and $108 on the books but what I have will be ample. Need to do a bit of spending though, as soon as I can get around to the canteen; stamps and stationery (I had to bum this envelope from Walts.) are the major items.

If this "atomic bomb" announced today fulfils the long-ago prediction of scientists as to what would happen if we ever learned to control atomic energy it may be the final straw on the camel's back, and perhaps would explain why the high command has apparently decided to give the airmen a chance to finish it off the cheap (relatively) way.

Movie-time Bettsy and I think I'll go for the show sounds funny tonight and I can use some of that. And as I said I've a good excuse this time for not writing because from your letters today it's apparent you're not reading what I do put down. Hope by now you're blushing with shame at such a lousy guess - - but if you aren't better go back and read again.

Despite which I love you with all my heart and maybe - - just maybe - - will be back to scribble more but forgive me if I'm unable.

8/8/45 Wednesday evening in port

I cut you off very abruptly last night for a third-rate movie "Up in Mabel's Room" but I guess I just wasn't in the mood to write for I couldn't get back to it. Nor am I very much in the mood tonight, for without being able to ascribe a reason to myself I'm sort of jittery. Perhaps I'll talk it out this way, in which event you may wind up with a helluva bunch of words.

Probably the cause of my jitters is that all day we've been talking about this atomic bomb and listening to breathless radiocasts of what it did to Hiroshima and what it likely will do to the rest of Japan. Of course it seems obvious that if all we've been told is true the <u>thing</u> must bring Japan to its knees (or obliterate her entirely) in a very few months, if not weeks or days.

And of course that end result, the end of the war and a definite prospect of coming back to life and love to stay, is pleasant to contemplate. But I'm scared: as one communication said, "mankind has found the way to destroy itself" and even if it does win this war the atomic bomb means that if war erupts again no person nor any place can be even relatively safe. That may mean you or I or our children or our children's children - - but in any event it would nullify completely the ideal that brought me out here.

It's been another broiling day, thus enabling me to acquire even more suntan for I had two hours this morning and a similar stretch this afternoon sitting on the boat deck wearing only shorts. Honestly, I've become quite vain about my brown and it will be an awful disappointment to me if I can't maintain it until I can exhibit it to my favorite audience.

Aside from that we got a bit more work done towards our painting cleanup and Sam and Chuck got a bawling-out from the boatswain when I was absent on watch. Seems we painted <u>more</u> than the bosun had authorized - - he only wanted a patch-up-the-most-rust job - - and just the day before the gunnery officer had been wondering rather pointedly why the painting wasn't done and when we'd get it done! That, my dearest, is the Navy way!

The day brought a bit more mail, one letter and some clippings from you and two copies of Life. While I'm on the subject, I recall that a couple of times recently you made rather caustic remarks about me writing too briefly - - yet I notice some other people's letters chop off pretty short too. And I'll wager I've written <u>more words</u> over this absence than you although I must confess you've written more letters.

Your letter today was written the day of Churchill's election defeat, and since you profess eagerness to know my reaction it occurs to me that I haven't put it down on paper for you; if in truth, I've had a conscious appraisal of it.

His defeat was a much less serious thing in my mind than the death of FDR. Churchill, after all, was more the front, the symbol, for Britain's war effort while FDR was not only that but the actual directing head. And, again looking back, I think Churchill knew what was going to happen; that would account for many things, especially why Atlee actually had a seat at the Potsdam table rather than just being a ringside spectator. Churchill isn't done; the British (witness Lloyd George) don't cast a defeated politician into the exterior darkness as we do. And it may well be that Atlee-Truman-Stalin will be more effectively functioning than the original Big Three.

The big difference will not show in the remainder of the war, nor so very much in the peace, I think, as in the postwar world. The Labor Party in Britain is another name for Socialists - - Socialism of the Karl Marx-Engels school - - and in another country that same set of principles gave birth to the Communist Party. The Labor Party in Britain won the election on a program of socialization of industry, greater benefits for all the people, an almost complete Marxian plan, excepting only communal ownership and use of land.

What's going to happen, in the post-war world, when American private industry must compete in the market places against such a fully-developed program in Russia, a nascent one in Britain and possibly similar programs in other European countries? The leftists rising to power there now have a clear track from England and a push from Russia. Can we hold our own lives with our familiar methods? Or what changes may be forced in business, government, industry, finance? These are the questions raised by

British ballots, and I think we can well leave them unanswered until we wind up the business at hand.

Which will be enough pontificating for one evening. But anyhow, I've gotten some words on paper and, in case you're curious, perked myself up no little but must stop now. Nite my darling.

8/10/45 Friday evening in port

Guess I'm just plain lazy for, as has become the usual of late, I don't feel like writing this evening. However recent letters that started out with some such kind of admission have wound up as unusually long products and perhaps it will recur tonight

Real achievement of the day, as far as I personally was concerned was completion of our painting and if you don't think that's a big job all my recent moans have been wasted. There still remains, and I guess there always will, considerable work to be done but from here on it's going to be easier and we'll be coasting. Nor are we sorry. This daytime heat is pretty rough, especially in the afternoon when a tool left exposed to the sun soon becomes too hot to handle. So we'll do what needs to be done in the mornings, and let it go at that.

The news today - - Russia's attack and another atomic bombing - - seems in the wake of the past few days to be quite a letdown although actually it's far from that. Of course what we're all waiting for is to hear from Tokyo and it's too soon for that; even in such a predicament, if she does decide to give up, she certainly will observe the diplomatic amenities. First move, I think, will be a request for an armistice to discuss (?) terms although an armistice might be difficult to obtain on all the myriad fighting fronts out here.

And Lordy if it doesn't come, should the Japs elect to fight on to the utter finish as did Germany, there's going to be a mess of howling-mad disappointed Americans out this way. As the Pennsylvania Dutch say: "This it will make"! Anyhow, we're all waiting - - I've had that feeling of marking time for something big to happen - - and hoping the end has come. Just in case it does work out, the next question will be how soon and with the hope of gaining some minor fame as a prophet I think I can tell you that for me the prospects are it will be reasonably soon. Just what that word "soon" may ultimately mean I am not sure. But I think it a sound guess I'll be in the first 25 % discharged.

There are a lot of reasons for that, and a lot of guesswork in the reasoning. But after it's over I don't think we'll be stuck out here too long or patrolling or something similar. And once we get back to the States it would be reasonable that I never should have to come out again. That latter statement hinges on my interpretation of what the Navy point system is going to be; I feel fairly sure it will duplicate the Army plan.

But I have enough time in service and overseas service too, to meet ordinary requirements. I think the credit will be the same as the Army plan. Also our three kids will give me a maximum score in another section which will match the Army plan. On the other hand I don't believe the Navy will rate battle participation stars as heavily as the Army; comparatively the sailor earns more of them with vastly less danger than the soldier. I should guess my minimum of three (Luzon, Iwo, Okinawa; there might be others) will be worth 3 to 9 points. Which won't discount my family credit, in comparison to the single guy who's been out here a long time. (I'd guess that <u>more than half </u>of this crew is entitled to wear 10 or more battle stars; and a helluva lot of them 15 and up! Doubt very much that any one man in the entire infantry has so many.)

And the Navy may introduce a new factor onto the table - - age - - because young single men are vastly better suited for this life, especially in the (slight break; I'll tell you later) peacetime Navy. Perhaps one might be a point or two for each year over 25 - - and if something like that turns up I'll be even further ahead. At any rate I seem able to ascribe some reason for my optimism, eh?

The break of which I spoke: we're having one of those Navy

"happy hours" down on the well deck, a sort of home-talent revue. And never did I see a guy have so much bad luck in one song. The singer was one Pat Patterson, who, the program says used to sing with Jan Garber. He was in the midst of "I'm in the mood for Love" when the bong bong bong of the general alarm broke in, and the PA blared news of a fire in one of the crew's sleeping compartments. Out of the jam-packed well deck sprinted those concerned with the fire while the rest of the mob sat tight – until needed.

When the fire was pronounced over in a few minutes Patterson came back and resumed his song. Halfway through the first verse the bugle called everyone to attention for colors! He decided very wisely, when that was over, not to again attempt to claim "He's in the mood for love." But he did get off another song or two.

Bettsy here it's getting dark again and since I have the evening watch there'll be no chance to go somewhere else to continue. So once again, from far away, I bid you good night and wonder, my darling how soon we will all be together.

8/11/45 Saturday morning in port

Where to begin this, as much as the usual what-to-say is troubling me right now. For life goes on just as it has for the past weeks even as we wait for the official word it's all over.

In my heart I feel that it is; I cannot see that the Japanese offer represents an abridgement of unconditional surrender; further it is in line with our propaganda policy since Pearl Harbor. No nasty words about Hirohito, we'll need him to make the survivors lay down their arms when they are beaten. My very definite expectation is that acceptance will be announced by the Big Four sometime between 9 p.m. tonight and 9 a.m. tomorrow. That would be 10 a.m. to 10 p.m. Saturday August 11 in Washington, 5 a.m. to 5 p.m. in Moscow.

But what if it is not accepted? Still I believe the war is over, for with rejection would come a counter-proposal and probably a 24-hour ultimatum. And should the Japs reject that the unescapable bludgeons are ready to hammer them into line within hours or days. So I hope and believe I have fired my last shot at the enemy in this war. There is more to be said, but I think I shall let that wait until it is final; official; beyond the shadow of a doubt.

How did the news come, and how did we react? Rather strangely, I believe you'll think. Last night after finishing your letters, I lay down on a cot near the gun and dozed off, I guess. Somewhere along the way, a single shout, a whoop that broke through the noise of the movie below, woke me. (I learned afterward that I had slept more than an hour.) Foggily, instinctively I sensed that something had happened, the boy wearing the phones told me the news had just been relayed to him of a <u>reported</u> Jap surrender offer. I guess by then most of the crew knew of it, but there was no celebrating, visual or audible. Somehow we've been fooled too often by false rumors to put much faith in any.

Nobody on the boat deck seemed to have any more explicit information, but I recalled that our Marine Officer, Captain McInteer, was standing the officer-of-the-deck watch on the well deck and I went down to ask him. He repeated what I had been told; adding the information that it was an unsupported network report and then remarked what must have been almost the unanimous opinion of the crew. "It's wonderful news if it's true. But I'm taking it with a grain of salt, waiting until morning, until we can get some corroboration."

We talked a bit more, of related things, and later I wandered below to check the mess hall where a dozen oddly-silent boys listened about the radio speaker. We listened in silence as an announcer in far off San Francisco retold the story and added the news of lack of confirmation from the White House and London. Another announcer addressing the armed services, warned against premature celebration stressing "This is an enemy report."

I went back up, told Captain McInteer what I had heard (in case he had not had the opportunity to listen) then tried to interest myself in the movie, a poignant little thing called "The Clock." But the rush of other ideas blurred the dialogue; other pictures in my mind's eye obscured the screen. Need I be specific about those pictures? I think not.

When the show ended I went below and to find another knot of silent, curious, hopeful boys clustered about the speaker waiting for the midnight broadcast. We sat and talked for 15 minutes. When the announcer had nothing new I went to bed and, after a while, to sleep.

For the first time in many days reveille woke me up this morning at 6. I shaved in darkness, dressed, went topside to wait for the 7 o'clock news. When it came the surrender offer was official - - and we jumped from the "is it true" frying pan into the "will it be accepted" fire. We've been broiling all day, waiting for Friday night to end back where you are.

Up to now there's been no semblance of celebration here; I doubt that there will be much even when it is officially over. We man the guns, stand our watches; life goes on as before. That's not quite true of all the ships. One nearby turned out its band last night and we could hear the whooping on it and others. Two boys aboard another ship at the time said the movie there was stopped suddenly and over the PA system some optimist apologized for interrupting but added he thought they'd be interested to hear "You'll all be civilians soon. The war is over." But there has been no such outburst here as the radio says took place at Okinawa, or Guam, Manila or Pearl Harbor.

And there, my Bettsy, you have what I know and think to now. There's so much more to be said about what I feel, but somehow this blank white paper doesn't seem the place to say it.

Some day though, (God willing, soon) with my arms around you I shall try to say it, to tell you of this love of mine that has made those long months a lonely desert in my life for nothing can bloom without you. I look to see bountiful blooms soon!

8/14/45 Tuesday evening in port

Shamelessly I passed you by last night, without so much as a line, and it would be easy to take the same out tonight in this completely confusing situation. But the small voice inside won't let me, and perhaps it's just as well for perhaps talking to you will clear the fog a bit. You see the trouble is that I keep insisting, to others and to myself that I am certain this is all over. It must be so; it is so - - and yet I cannot shake that final glimmer of doubt until the end is confirmed officially.

And the news is so vague, so confusing, while we are flooded by the greatest deluge of scuttlebutt that has ever been poured into my always receptive ears. Honestly, the whole situation is like a passage from Alice in Wonderland - - it would be hilarious, if only it wasn't so all-important and so dammed personal.

Yet even while I gripe to myself I know it must be vastly worse for you, for of course you cannot know at <u>this</u> moment when it could be so very consoling, that I am safe and sound and well, in a backwater of war that must be as certainly as any place out here a safe haven from any random lashing of Japanese militarism in its death throes. I don't deny for a second that I'm more than glad to be here; I only wish every other sailor and soldier could be equally safe.

The war is won. The grimmest of all tragedies are the inevitable deaths and injuries that must come before all the formalities can be completed and hostilities ceased. Until now we have had to consider casualties as the inescapable toll that must be paid, each contributing in its small way to victory. Of such it might be said "x x that these honored dead shall not have died in vain." Now there is not even that consolation; the victory is won; further bloodshed can add nothing to it.

And so you see once again our Frisco is lucky. Now we need

only one more real break and my cup will be full. Could be; we're all waiting for the cheering (remember I told you of it once before?) to start and hoping - - - - - A lovely, indeed a beautiful thought.

Be that as it may I propose now to settle down to the facts of life, and correspondence. No longer have I any alibi for not writing for what was an envelope shortage is no longer the case as I managed to get to the store today and purchase 4 boxes (96 envelopes) of stationery. Now I simply <u>must</u> take pen in hand.

Among my other purchases at the store was a bottle of hair oil - - yes, you read alright, hair oil! - - and I now am embarked on The Great Experiment, testing whether that dome, or any dome so conceited and so denuded, can be revived. For obvious reasons I've had to by-pass the third scalping, in lieu of which I shall get a close cut, then have at 'em! As a matter of record, tonight is the first time I've made any attempt, with brush or comb, to achieve an orderly arrangement in many months. Surprisingly, it worked - - a little.

Otherwise there is not much to report for my two days. Quite frankly, I've been lazy, and enjoyed it. There's still some work to be done but now the meaning, the significance, of the guns is gone and I'm not much interested. On the other hand, my stage is now set for my self-made writing assignment of interviewing the ship's officers and writing stories about them for the press news and I expect to see the exec, and possibly the captain, tomorrow. That I'm looking forward to.

Yesterday was my liberty day, and a pleasant one it was. First of all I got four deliciously cold cans of Duquesne, which I drank with great relish. Then I guided Sam and Will on an exploratory trip to some of the old gun emplacements and finally we wound up swimming. When we had our swim, I saw a couple of other guys from the ship kicking a football around and went to join them for a bit. Nothing odd in that except - - I was naked as a newborn babe at the time. Eventually we got back to the ship. I loafed around for a while, went to the second movie and then to bed.

This morning I fiddled around a bit getting my interview matter organized, really thought I might see the exec today but wasted too much time, and spent the afternoon on watch. Meanwhile I've had ample reading, for the mail yesterday and today brought me a new Time and four copies of Life, all of which I've consumed.

And so have gone my days, Bettsy, waiting for the end and then the big news. I know this must be a trying time for you, too, my darling but I promise I'll do my best to make it up to you on that now-measurable distant day when I come home.

Have I even remembered to tell you I love you, and with all my heart? If not, remind me on That Day and I shall try.

8/15/45 Wednesday morning in port

Salt water sloshed over the well deck, sprinkling the little knot of men clustered about the radio speaker. Seamen scrubbed away; around the starboard gangplank the routine morning business of the ship went on as usual. A line of men leaning on the boat deck rail smoked, talked, plodded through the morning ship's press news. Nothing new there. Nobody seemed much interested - - in anything. The 7 o'clock newscast had said pretty plainly no announcement was likely for several hours. And everybody had been waiting so long, so very long that all the tang was gone from expectancy.

Besides, it was too big, too all important to be understood or even believed, this thing we have been waiting for. I know it seemed so to me; how much more so it would have for those others around me who saw and felt the deadly thud of torpedoes and bombs at Pearl Harbor; who lived through the hellish fire and shattering destruction of that night at Guadalcanal.

Static crackled through the broadcast, making the speaker in far-away San Francisco often unintelligible. It had rained, hard, all night and lightning played in the mountains like an amateur electrician testing the lights on a great stage. Rain was still falling, quietly, warmly, but no one minds that, out here.

Suddenly a scrawny little fellow dashed, whooping excitedly, from the radio, heading for the compartment where his friends were loafing. The other listeners clustered closer to the speaker. There was something electric in the air.

Then someone below shouted up to us "The war is over"! - - and we stood in stunned silence.

It was too big, too good, incredible this thing we had been waiting for, now that it was here, it was real, it was true.

I wanted to hear it for myself; got into the radar room just in time to hear the announcer: "I repeat: President Truman has just announced Japanese acceptance of the surrender terms"!

There wasn't even a ghost of a celebration under way as I walked out on deck. Nor did I celebrate; leaning on the rail, looking out across the flat gray water to the green hills I said a prayer.

A few of the irresponsibles began talking about firing the guns. The word came down from control: No shooting. I guess quite a few of us were remembering what happened at Okinawa a week or two ago.

We talked a little. Mostly about home, laughed, talked a little more. From the beach red and green and gold flares were soaring. A merchant ship spouted a plume of white steam; distantly we could hear the throaty roar of the whistle. Someone on another ship set off a smoke generator. Other ships followed suit and soon the river harbor was shrouded in gray.

Two bumbling old seaplanes that had just taken off buzzed methodically on their mission. The ever-routine bugle called us to morning quarters - - where, after the usual 10-minute wait, we were apprised that the ship is reviving the "lucky bag" for cloth-ing and equipment left astray; and that the radio isn't "official," we must wait for the formal orders!

Back to the boat deck we trooped, chattering a bit excitedly for the news seemed to be sinking in. A flutter of color hung from the foremast: the flag hoist spelled out: Victory – cease all present operations! (At least that's the way we read it.)

And soon the ship was at work, painting. Scaffolds hanging everywhere, the air filled with the soft, wet slap of brushes. We talked of home and how soon. Pay call was sounded, and I noticed that few men drew more than a couple dollars (guess my 15 would be about average). Funny, money begins to mean something now, with home and freedom in sight.

The morning passed swiftly - - I never saw the crew work more eagerly. At this rate the ship will be painted in two days! Oh yes, the captain summoned all the bad boys a few minutes ago; the fellows who stayed too long on the beach went over illegally or committed other infractions, and wiped all the slates clean as his V-J Day present

Down below the radio blares jazz at the moment. All morning it has been going full blast but since the big moment we listen only a little.

And that, my darlings, is about all there is to tell about V-J Day here, or at least about what it looked like. Perhaps I can tell you how it felt, but I'm not up to writing it.

There is one thing, though, something that has been stowed away in a conveniently forgotten recess of each of our minds since that October day we sailed from San Pedro. Each one of us can, and doubtless has in one way or another, said to himself: "Well it's over and by God I made it. I know now that some day I'll be going home, not in pieces, not in a box. I'm going home"!

Pretty crude and brutal, that, but now that the danger is over it's vastly easier to bring it out into the honest open. Yes, I know, I always have insisted to myself, as well as you, that I was sure I'd come back. And I was sure in a way, insofar as it was within my control and power. But hiding behind that the subconscious was the inescapable possibility that something - - - - - - -

I suspect you've been over the same trail pretty often yourself, and I know, too, that you'll not rest entirely easy until you have the evidence (my arms) around you. But I tell you the evidence will be forthcoming and and before too unbearably long; not right away, mind you, nor this month, nor the next, but reasonably soon.

And oh, my darlings, how wonderful that will be!

It can't be true that I've been away from you only 16 months; right now it seems that I've spent all of my adult life out here; dreaming about you, waiting, wondering. Wondering often if all those lovely years of ours were real or just a figment of my imagination. Wondering too, if they were true, and can we ever recapture them.

But now I know, and I shall wait as patiently as possible until we do begin to live again, hopefully very soon.

8/16/45 Wednesday evening in port

I don't need to go into any details on what happened today, nor my reaction, for I'm sure you must have sunk, too, at this alleged Navy point system in regard to being discharged. It has been, of course, almost our sole topic of discussion. And among the dozens of opinions I've heard, including those of the handful who passed the test, I have not found one man who thinks the system is fair.

No credit is being allowed for sea duty, hazardous duty and/or combat action - - a gross injustice. Of particular concern to me is the lack of dependency credit -- no allowance for children. Even the kids aboard feel strongly that a man with children should have preference in discharge over one who has, for instance, a working wife who will be able to support herself. Further the "system" is mathematically unsound, in that it attempts to build with too few bricks - - in future months as the critical score is lowered to permit more discharges there will come a time when more men than are planned to be discharged are grouped at a single point level. And in order to avoid releasing too many men the whole group will be held up.

In short the whole thing strikes me, and many others, as a Typical Navy Fuss-Up. Nor do I think it will be changed unless extreme pressure is brought to bear on the home front.

Whew! How's that for a gripe, a doozy of a bitch? Feel mildly improved, too, at having got it off my chest.

Actually the thing possibly does not mean that I, personally, must stay in service much longer than I anticipated. The whole matter of getting out is still dependent on so many things and I haven't yet lost my confidence that when I get back to the States it won't be much longer.

Which reminds me of the day's one concrete accomplishment. I did have my talk with the exec, and he gave me a clear track for my plan to write stories about the ship's officers for the press news. Tomorrow afternoon I go to visit him again and possibly the captain. The others will follow in a few days if I make the grade. Hope to have the first story, possibly two of them, ready for Sunday after next and, if all works out according to plan, there will be three others on each of the two succeeding Sundays. Of course that's a batch of work but I think I'll enjoy the writing, and I know I'll get a kick out of talking to these guys.

Also this afternoon I went to the recreation island again with Svoboda, swapping my chance to go tomorrow. Didn't do much; 3 cans of beer, then gabbing for a while and a bit of a swim. Nothing exceptional, but not a bad way to pass the afternoon.

Otherwise I've done nothing all day, which is just about what I expected - - except planning for the future. I'm lazy and admit it - - So what?

Incidentally, we have had nothing on this ship even remotely resembling an end-of-the-war celebration, strange as that may sound. Last night for a while the harbor put on a moderate display of fireworks - - colored signal flares and rockets, and some illumination rockets that arched high into the sky and then burst leaving brilliant gold flares that hung for minutes. Frisco's contribution was a half dozen red and green signal flares, swiped from our life rafts by a couple of demonstrative youngsters. They went off with a pop, arched 20 or 30 yards then dropped into water with another pop. That was all.

Perhaps there was too much similarity between the colored lights and the colored tracers we had been seeing for too long. But nonetheless the biggest and only real important fact is the end is here, and return home has come within the realm of measurable time. We are all celebrating, down in our hearts, even while we gripe as usual, particularly about the stupidity of the points system.

I've wasted more than enough of life by being away from you. Every minute more is painful. I love you, want you always! I want to come home, now!

8/18/45 Saturday evening in port

Another do-nothing day leaves me, again, with little or nothing to write but I hope I can do better than last night.

Lordy, this weather would be right up your alley, broiling hot all day long under the blazing sun, yet always (or almost always) a bit of breeze going and shady spots are comfortable. And at dusk the temperature drops with the sun so that it's always pleasant sleeping topside; sometimes in the cool evening hours a blanket is comfortable.

All of which leads me to the fact that I spent the whole afternoon sunning myself, dozing and just sitting around in my shorts. By the way, since I've learned how coolly comfortable they (shorts) are, I've added several pairs to my post-war wardrobe plans. Of course during that time I got nothing done except to gossip a bit, chewing over the seeming-endless flood of scuttlebutt that flows in one ear and out the other for all sensible people. However I did mange to get my nose and forehead cooked to a crisp again, so once more they're coated with zinc oxide ointment - - making me look like some circus clown who neglected to wipe away his makeup.

This morning we stood captain's inspection again, and I guess we'll be doing it about every Saturday. To be perfectly frank about it, I think it's a good idea, it helps force some of these dopes (there are only a few) to clean themselves up once in a while and the only unpleasant feature is standing around waiting for the thing to start.

The remainder of the morning was devoted largely to filling out two questionnaires, one on our point system status, the other on our service records as applied to award of operations ribbons and combat stars.

My own list of the latter is impressive enough to make the casual observer believe I've really done something: Presidential Unit Citation (without star), American Area ribbon, and Asiatic Pacific ribbon with 3 stars now authorized (Leyte, Luzon and Iwo Jima operations; Okinawa will be the fourth), and the Philippine Liberation ribbon with one star.

The point questionnaire was based on this original Navy announcement and of course my total still comes to 34.5. Whether or not there has been or will be changes I don't know; most of our scuttlebutt concerns that and all kinds of weird stories are afloat.

While I'm recovered somewhat from my original shock and anger at the plan (?), I continue to insist, in chorus with everyone out here that it is not fair. However a checkup I made today shows I'm not too-far wrong in my original estimate that I would be in the upper fourth of the list to be discharged.

Meanwhile my personal attention is turning more towards completion of the war. The radio evinces less concern at Japan's delay in signing than a lot of us feel. If her radio is correct, that members of the royal family are being sent to the many fronts to order the men to lay down their arms it would appear that Hirohito is doing everything within his power to get it over, apparently in hopes of retaining a greater share of his own powers.

In that light, his apparent reluctance at sending surrender delegates, and McArthur's rather casual acceptance of the delay, seem more than a little strange. My guess is that there's internal dissension in Japan that perhaps might blossom into an Army coup d'e-tat in an attempt to force him out and continue the war. And we must not, will not, relax our vigilance one iota until the occupation of Japan and complete disarmament of her forces are effected.

It seems to me that here is a situation unique in all military annals: a nation so completely defeated as to volunteer unconditional surrender - - before the conquering powers have even come in contact with her major land forces. That was true at the end of the Russo-Japanese War, except that Japan did not claim (nor would Russia have conceded) the right to occupy the loser's homeland.

But even so I cannot keep my thoughts from turning more toward home. That is where I want, with all my heart, to be, and where I hope I and all the rest can be soon. How soon? I don't know; I wish I did. But I do know I will be there some day in the not too distant future.

8/20/45 Monday morning in port

Dear Buck:

Lots of letters from you since last I had a chance to write, and I thank you very much for they're swell, every one of them. But much as I enjoy letters from you I'm hoping you'll not have to write many more. It will be lots nicer when we can be swimming and talking and playing together, won't it?

Perhaps you're wondering why, now that the war is over, I can't be coming home right away. Well Son, the surrender means only the end of the fighting and before I come home there are a great many things that must be done to make certain there can be no second Pearl Harbor. Japan must be occupied, her armies disbanded, their guns and planes and ships taken away and her factories controlled so they never can make any more. All that takes time, but I hope it won't be too many more months. And I'll be coming back to you just as soon as I can.

Have you served a Sunday Mass yet? I'm very glad and proud you have learned to be an altar boy and you must never forget that it is a very great honor and privilege. Wouldn't it be nice if, some day, we could serve together? Perhaps we'll ask Father Gartland; guess you know that I, too, have been serving although it isn't always possible to get to Mass, even on Sundays.

I was sorry to hear about the time you were playing with matches in the garage. That was bad, Buck, and you're much too big for little-boy stunts like that. It's very dangerous, for you and everyone, and I'm sure you'll not do it again.

Yes, I've been swimming a bit, and I even have been doing a little bit of diving for there's a fairly good board on the dock at our recreation island. But it will be lots more fun to swim with you and I'm counting on doing a good deal of it next summer.

Your badminton games sound like fun, like something I want to try, too. Don't believe I've ever played that but I used to play a lot of tennis and they're a little bit alike. Bet an ice cream cone I can beat you.

And as I said before, I hope that will be soon. Me, I'm tired of writing letters. So long for now; be a good boy, take care of yourself and the rest of the family until I can get back to my job. Much Love From Your Dad

8/20/45 Monday evening in port

A rainy day; no place to go, to sit, to read or write; in short not a dammed thing to blunt the edge of boredom has just raised very h---- with my always good intentions.

All the morning on watch, without another thing to do, I managed only three scrawny scraggly little notes to the kids that I am very sure don't say a darn thing. At the last minute I dropped a couple of hunks of Jap currency in each envelope as sort of a conscience-saving offering; hope they'll help.

Mail today brought me your letters to me right up to the edge of victory day, and rereading them I sense that you, too, must have had some prescience the end was near, yet didn't dare let yourself say it. Anyhow I was glad to see the absence of any unusual anxiety, which I had feared. Sometimes I think you're pretty wonderful, sometimes.

There has been, however, one redeeming feature of the day, my talk with the exec, which I enjoyed muchly. There were a lot of things I wanted to about the piece but overlooked them in the rush, but by and large I think I got most of what I need and already have written a draft. Not finished yet, but I hope to do that tomorrow.

I knew he was quite young for a commander, and especially so for one who is executive officer, second in command, of a big warship; but I didn't expect him to be only 29. Physically he's a solid six-footer, about 195 I should judge, brown hair cropped short with a hint of grey creeping in. His face is a strong one, aquiline nose, a slightly jutting jaw, only a few lines. He speaks clearly, crisply, makes decisions without delay and (it strikes me) is thoroughly willing to abide by them. Fond of sports, he was quite a basketball and baseball player at Annapolis, looks like he could still be a hefty opponent at either. Smokes many cigarettes, with an air of enjoying them; my guess is he'd be a pleasant companion for a bit of drinking.

Regular Navy, but not a whit obnoxious about it; thoroughly understands that the vast majority of the men are only anxious now to get home. Yet he feels the future importance of the Navy as a keeper of the peace; feels a lot of the men would be doing themselves a service to stay in, even while recognizing that improvements - - retirement, pay, etc. - - are necessary to attract a sufficiently high caliber of men.

If all the senior officers were as human as he, the Navy in war or peace would be much more habitable. Less of his gold braid has been wasted stiffening his neck than is true of some several ensigns I've seen. Perhaps that largely reflects his former assignments; two years in submarines, three in destroyers, in addition to two years on a more-formal cruiser before coming here. He's seen a lot of the War - - Pearl Harbor, the Solomons and his ship was rammed and all but sunk the night before the Attu invasion. Back home (near New York) are a wife and a five-year-old son. No, this was a strictly business talk; we didn't get around to details about kids.

When we were through he thought the captain, too, might be available. I've been looking forward to that, too, of course. Anyhow the exec came back in a few minutes with an odd sort of smile on his face, took an outline of questions I'd drawn up said the skipper will fill it in, then send for me to complete it when he was ready. The smile, I judged, was occasioned by the skipper's reaction, which must have been a bit on the irritated side. The exec said the skipper "didn't want a lot of blah," apparently under the impression that I'd probably want to make a great hero, or something, of him.

Anyhow it's as pleasant a pastime as I can think of to slur over the inevitable wait until I can come home. The news today, however, does seem a great deal better and at last it begins to seem that the war is ended. Now to get the surrender signed, the occupation completed and I'll really start counting days.

Right now I'm going to count off a night. No letter for Mom and Dad, either, durn it, but maybe tomorrow. 'Nite Bettsy.

8/22/45 Wednesday evening in port

As if another day of rain-forced inactivity were not enough

to depress even my spirits, I've just watched my friend Sam get himself into another mess - - but <u>good</u> - - and right now I'm really lowdown. Damm that boy. Sometimes I don't believe he has <u>any</u> brains.

But before I forget it, my best reason for writing tonight is to apologize to Chubbin for chiding her yesterday because, apparently, she missed out on a letter for me. I felt like a heel when the letter arrived today, in a separate envelope with a couple of clippings. And a very swell letter it was, my Blondie, just chock full of news ("MOTHER BURNED AN OTTER PAN"). And darling I will be coming home to you at the very first minute. It will be very wonderful to hold you in my arms again.

To get back to Sam, I don't know just yet what it's all about but he was on the beach today and along with quite a few others, came back roaring drunk, on black market beer or bootleg island whiskey, I assume. He seemed happy and having a good time when I saw him in the chow line. When I left the mess hall after eating, a couple of other drunks were having a bit of a mouth battle but I kept on going for I didn't give a hoot what happened to either one. Five minutes later I came back to find a table and some benches upset, Sam and one of the first belligerents thrashing about on the floor with four MAA's prying them apart. Eventually it took three of them to hold Sam; the other guy didn't seem at all anxious.

Aside from booze I haven't any idea what started the row or what it's all about. But I'm afraid Sam really is in trouble this time. And I'm really fond of the boy. He's got a lot of good in him - - and this is a helluva time to get messed up. I'll go into it tomorrow, but can't see any way I can help except maybe to try to prevent it from happening again. And speaking of Sam reminds me I've neglected to report on two more of my friends.

Walts is no longer a mess cook - - he finally made gun striking and friend Will is one of only five reserves in our whole division with enough points (49) to go home. At 22 he's had more than

4 years service! For two days now he's been going around like someone in a dream, and writing endless letters to his wife. He deserves it!

The mail today also brought a copy of Time which gave me a pleasant afternoon of reading.

One other thing I accomplished today: I finished and turned in the story on the exec (no reaction yet, nor word when I'll see the skipper).

Not much of a record for a whole day is it? But dammit there's nothing you can or want to do in a rain like this. But rain or no rain the open-air movie goes on - - but not for me. Already the mob is gathering, huddled under rain clothes and waterproof covers. Doesn't make sense to me.

One of the clippings Chubbin sent hit home with me. It concluded with the statement "I'll yield to no man, or woman either, on my desire to get back to living"!

Guess that's a good place to end this tome for that thought has been the beginning and the ending of everything for me for a long time. That, my darling, is because I can't wait to be with you – forever!

8/24/45 Friday evening in port

Don't see how I can write much this evening, (when have I said that before?) for there isn't a damm thing to say except I'm still sitting around on my big fat grass waiting - - and don't even know what I'm waiting for. Meanwhile I've been dodging showers. For a change there have been occasional dry moments today, and a couple of times the sun actually appeared, but the only thing on which we can depend is that it will rain again, very soon. Such a place!

However I did write one more letter today to Reed, finally answering his last letter. I got a big laugh from it, as I'm sure you will too, and am enclosing it. He's a swell guy and I know you'll like him when we get together some post-return day.

Aside from that, the only progress I can report for the day is that I got my first story back from the exec, approved with only some minor changes in phrasing. It came second-hand so I've heard nothing further on who's next, or when. And I don't see that I can do anything else other than sit tight.

Golly but it did rain last night; so hard that it drove me below to sleep for the first time in weeks. I had brought my bedding up to the locker about 8:30 and had just laid down, planning to miss the movie because it was drizzling, when a whistling squall blew up from another direction.

Now the platform is dry in ordinary winds, being sheltered beneath another overhanging platform and by the bulkhead when we're moving or headed into the wind as is almost always the case when at anchor. But this squall came from the side and for some reason the ship was slow swinging into it so that for 15 minutes the rain just sheeted in. I managed to keep my bedding fairly dry by retreating into the most sheltered corner but even so my clothes were soaked and when the rain let up a bit I, very disgusted, carried the stuff back down and went to sleep. However I did very well, thank you, woke at 6 a.m. reveille and have been loafing around ever since. I'm told it rained even harder about 2 a.m.

However, I'll try it here again tonight - - with my fingers crossed.

And there, Bettsy, is the nearest thing to a letter I have in me tonight. I hope to improve tomorrow but it's dern difficult when you're doing <u>nothing</u> ----- but sitting and waiting.

Nite, darling, and don't let this miserable scrivel mislead you. It won't be long now!

This was enclosed in the August 24, 1945 letter.

Philippines June 6, 1945.
Dear Chuck:

Excuse me please for not writing but I have tried several times to write a long interesting letter and once I succeeded but the censor thought it was too interesting and gave it back to me. Our skipper is the censor and he Don't have to look very far for the guy who wrote the letter. Your letter must have been pretty interesting too before the man blacked out your beautiful description of the Frisco. Right now I don't know enough about anything to get my tail in the door if I shot the works so here goes.

Life On the PT 282 is somewhat like being in a cage with a dozen Jack (Randazzo) Vagkicas, two Spearings and a smattering of Stoner's, Mahelich went home THANK GOD, he had been out a little too long anyhow and that may have had something to do with his outlook on life. The food on a small boat is everything we heard it was, only more so. We eat out of cans when we are not getting base chow and base chow is something like our service school chow without the frills. When we have the opportunity we make a bumming trip around to any big ships that are within the cruising radius of our limited fuel capacity and right now we are in the money, for two days we were one of the only two PT's in the harbor and bumming was good. We got cheese, bacon, ham apples and the tail end of a beef, our reefer holds almost as much as a small ditty bag, so now all we have to do is eat like hell before it all spoils, we also got some pork loins and some of that rare old fashioned stuff called butter and that is something.

I think that we have been pretty close to each other at times but have no way of being sure, we were at Tacoban and Mindoro in Feb and went from Mindoro to Palwan on Mar 1st, the Palwan invasion was a sort of a wet fizz but very very safe and that is the way I like my invasions, we had the pleasure of visiting the Culion Leper Colony about a month before it was liberated, we were the first white folks to visit the place since the Japs took over and we got quite a welcome, the non leper citizens had a party for us and most of the crew had quite a time but you know what a cautious soul I am and there were a lot of critters running around who were definitely not non lepers and after one look at a few of them I went back to the boat like a scalded dawg.

If I try to stretch this one out and make it interesting like the other unmailed editions it will probably meet the same fate so I think I will knock it off, in the meantime I will look real hard for Svoboda's nose hanging over a rail and sniff for Walts pipe, I have seen several craniums with the same sheen as yours so I guess I will have to depend on the other guys for identification.

As Ever

Don [Reed]

8/26/45 Sunday evening

Almost I passed you up this evening, but just didn't feel right about it so here goes while the time lasts - - there isn't much of the latter for when I failed to write earlier in the day, I neglected to take into account that I had the evening watch.

Oh, yes, I suppose I will for some time to come. The Navy, having been caught napping once, does not intend that it shall happen again. And I guess there will be the usual at sea watches so long as I remain in the service. Frankly I don't mind; we all can afford to lose a little sleep, and an occasional watch helps in keeping track of the time if nothing else.

For a change, a minor miracle in fact, we've had no rain for 24 hours now, and I've been sunning myself all day.

Mass this morning, for the biggest congregation I've seen at sea, many men coming aboard from other nearby ships. There were 130 communicants - - and one queer moment.

Don't think I've mentioned it before, but we've acquired a couple of monkeys as pets since coming into this area, one of them only a tiny thing. And just before Mass this morning, while Father O'Mara was making some announcements, this tiny one came ambling into the hanger and proceeded to hide under our improvised altar. I coaxed him out and carried him away. After Mass I remarked to the padre that it probably had been the first time a monkey had attempted to attend his services - - but the padre hadn't noticed the byplay!

Anyhow I loafed the rest of the morning, did a bit of the laundry and sat in on the match with boxers from another ship. There were some pretty fair scraps and our ship won 5 matches with the other a draw.

And there you have my day. Not much, is it - - nor can this letter be for I sneaked out to the movie and now, nearly midnight, I'm scribbling beneath a dim light in an upper passageway. Show tonight was "Eadie Was a Lady"; not a bad class B musical if you get a kick out of burlesque - - and I do. There were a couple of scenes right out of old burlesque routine - - and I wondered whatever happened to that strip dancer I met in Philly a couple of years ago. Remember?

But now, darlings I must get off to bed. Sorry to have slighted you so but at least there's this little something to prove (?) Guess what it is.

Chuck's father passed away very unexpectedly on August 25 but he was not yet aware of it. He was informed about the death on the afternoon of August 27.

Chapter 15
THE LONG SAD ROAD HOME
8/30/45 to 9/15/45

8/30/45 Thursday evening at sea

It's going to be very difficult for me, at least at first, to resume writing again but I know I must, for you, and so I'll do my best. Forgive me if it isn't much or doesn't make sense.

The intervening three days have dulled a little the initial shock and have enabled me to catch hold of myself after dangling at the loose end of a rope in a bottomless hole. And I'm ready to go on, to do whatever must be done.

Dad would have wanted it that way; for all of us.

I'm not going to report on those missing days; a little of it, so much as I could write, is in my diary and some day you'll read it there. But most of it is locked up inside me and I am sure neither my pen nor tongue can open it.

But I think you will want to know how the sad news came to me: I had spent almost all of Monday afternoon with the captain; I had gone there to get the biographical data of which I spoke, and we had drifted mostly into football, talking for hours of people we knew and games we had seen. He's a swell guy, the skipper, and I haven't so enjoyed a bull session in a long time.

When I came out, his orderly said the chaplain wanted to see me, and all unsuspecting I went down to his cabin. He offered me a seat, and then told me as easily yet quickly as possible. I say I was unsuspecting when I went there: yet I knew what was coming before the words were out - - the one thing I have dreaded since I left you 16 months ago.

That was about 4 p.m. August 27, our time. I read the two messages twice, there, but even yet do not specifically know what they say. I recall noticing that they were dated Philadelphia, August 26, and said this "evening". And I guessed that he had died Sunday evening - - which would be Monday morning our time, and 8-12 hours before I knew it.

Of course the most important thing now is to get home, and as I said in Mother's letter this morning only a formality of approval, and the much more pressing problems of transport remain to be solved. How soon I cannot even guess; it may be only days until I start; more likely it will be weeks, possibly even months. Nor can I say how speedy it will be if and when I leave this ship.

But I will be home, before the year ends, I am confident. And my job, whatever it was, is done out here while I know you need me. I want to help. And don't worry about me needing money. I have upwards of $125, which should be more than ample.

That, I think, fills some of the holes I left in Mother's letter - - I would sooner have gone through Okinawa and the typhoon together than write that, and finally did it only at the last minute before our mail was taken off the ship to a destroyer for transfer to regular postal facilities.

One more item before I say goodnight. Censorship was lifted today to permit our telling where we have been recently. As you guessed, it was the Philippines. First in Leyte Gulf, near the town of Tacoban, and the native trinket stands were on Samoa, where our recreation (?) isle was. Later we steamed from there through Sunigao Strait to Subic Bay on the southwestern coast of Luzon - - the mountains I spoke of that looked like home were part of

Bataan Peninsula. Our liberty area there was tiny Grande Island, in the very south of the bay.

Later we went to Manila, as you should already have guessed. Going in and coming out of Manila Bay we got a close-up look at Corregidor, and of course Bataan was by then familiar. And we went back to Subic Bay, where, but for the ill fortune of a few hours delay, I might now be started home. But - - - - - - - -

So much for this first letter I'm sorry to have missed you these days when you needed all the possible help, but the letters could not have reached you before the one I wrote this morning to Mother, and would only have been so many meaningless words. Goodnight now, my darlings: keep well and be strong until I can come to you. And until then I send all my love

Charles

Chuck always ended his letters with "Tonie" or "Your Tonie". Sometimes in jest he used "CAW" or "C. Anthony Welsh." This was the only occasion in the 400 plus that used the formal "Charles" in a serious vein.

9/1/45 Saturday evening at sea

Yesterday I told myself I was through writing, for a while at least, and so there was no letter last night. But today I'm not so sure, hence this letter, and perhaps, others to follow it. But they will not be daily, nor even regular, but I'll try to keep them frequent enough to keep you from worrying.

You see I have been granted an emergency leave. The exec has been most kind - - so has everyone - - and not only cleared the details as rapidly as possible but has promised to start me on my way "at the first opportunity." When that will be neither I nor he can say because of the uncertainties of the situation; it may be only a matter of days, even tomorrow, or it could be weeks. But I'm sure he'll do his utmost.

There is of course the possibility I may be home before this letter arrives for I intend to press my hardest for air transportation. If I am to be of any real aid to Mother it is of course imperative that I get there at the earliest moment possible. And surface transportation would surely require weeks and might even stretch out into months. But I can't know if I will succeed until I arrive at some air base and make the try; and if I do not reach home before or within a few days of this letter it's a sure guess I've failed and must travel some slower way. So please, don't go worrying; not now.

However you will stop writing as soon as you get this, for it's very doubtful that any more mail can catch up with me, even that which is on the way. And I can get along without mail for that stretch.

My orders will be for a 30-day emergency leave, dated from my arrival in the U.S., at the end of which I am to report to the Naval District, Philadelphia, for reassignment. And so it would seem certain I'm ending my cruise on Frisco, possibly even my sea duty if all goes well. Further I shall have solid grounds (I think) on which to base a request for an immediate discharge, especially in view of the fact that it would be only a comparatively few months until my normal release via the point system. We will go into that more fully when I do get home and see how you are and what has developed.

It's pretty awful to be away out here, at a time like this, with no way of knowing - - - - - -

But then I suspect I am worrying you, too, even now that the war is over. Wish there were some way of telling you that I am all right, and will be. I've gotten pretty well over that awful shock, although I must confess I'm restless and quite moody. All the thrill, all the fun is gone from the idea of going home to you, but that can't be helped, I guess.

There, you see Bettsy I still can't write sensibly. I'm ashamed of myself, but will get over it in time.

Anyhow, there's little more to be said. These past two days at sea have been idle ones. Stand watches and just sit around while the ship rocks slowly across the water. How can anyone write sensibly about that - - especially when you're waiting? And trying to think.

So goodnight once more, my darlings, and now I can say I will be seeing you soon. I wish it was under happier circumstances.

9/8/45 Saturday evening in the Yellow Sea off Korea

Aboard U.S.S. Chiwawa

So nearly as I can tell from my diary it is just a week since I wrote you, which is a long time for me and must seem doubly so for you. And while I still hope and pray I can beat the letter home I'm writing it just in case my try should fizzle.

In which event I think you'll be glad to know I am on my way to you, traveling just as fast as The Good Lord (and the not-so-good Navy) will let me. If I knew, I now could and would tell you when I'll be there, but I don't know now, and may not be able to even guess after I get a yes or no on air transport.

This much may be recorded: (censorship now being ended). My cruise on Frisco is over, ended last Monday [September 3] and since then I've been a passenger on the U.S.S. *Chiwawa* (AO68) a tanker - - cruising aimlessly up and down a patch of the Yellow Sea between China and Korea.

Our task force - - Maybe I'd better start at the beginning. You know I was just leaving Subic Bay in the Philippines when the radiogram reached me. Then 'Frisco, with her three sister ships, New Orleans, Tuscaloosa and Minneapolis and some destroyers, went to Okinawa for a rendezvous with the battle cruisers Alaska and Guam to become Task Force 71 (the cruisers Intrepid, Antietam and Cabot are included, but they stay 50 or so miles further out to sea) and go into the Yellow Sea, the first U.S. surface ships there since the start of the war.

We went up the China coast, past Shanghai, and steamed into the harbor at Tsingtao looking for a couple truant Jap destroyers.

They weren't there and we steamed right out again. V-J Day found us in sight of Korea, listening to the radio broadcast; we were 1,000 miles <u>west</u> of Tokyo!

Monday the task force fuelled and I said goodbye to my friends, was hoisted up in a breeches buoy and pulled on a rope across 60 feet of water. Simple as that. The tanker then planned to unload her fuel and leave for Okinawa, the first stage of my journey home. But my luck was still bad for our orders were changed and the ship dawdled around for four days, fueled Frisco and the others again on Thursday, and the carriers Friday.

But today, at long last, we dumped the remainder of the load onto another tanker and now are heading for Okinawa at a sluggish 10 knots per hour. Don't know yet whether we'll get there Monday or Tuesday ------------- But what a relief it is to be on the way!

Once there I shall try, <u>hard</u>, for air travel priority, and if I should get it the probable route will be Okinawa to Guam, to Eniwetok, Johnston, Pearl Harbor and either Frisco or Los Angeles. If I fail, I'll try to get to Guam, where perhaps Si Uhl can help me get in priority or at least I have a chance to get on a warship that would be homebound faster than a tanker or (God forbid) a cargo ship.

When I reach the States I'll phone. Meanwhile I'll write enough at least to keep you a little informed, if there's need for writing. For my usual journal, you'll see it all in my diary which I'm keeping as faithfully as possible. Funny how the urge to write (letters) has evaporated after so long. All I can think of is I must get home, fast, and so I hope there'll be no need for letters.

Too bad, too, for here I am at the time I wished for so often, <u>all</u> censorship removed, and legally I can write all I know. Which, however, isn't much. The task force is in this area to support occupation landings in North China, and Southern Korea. At first the landings were scheduled for September 1, then advanced to September 7, and I believe finally were made today. However we weren't in that close, in fact haven't seen land for some days. But it's not far away, witness the bugs, mosquitoes and flies in the air, and dainty brown-gray Chinese sparrows that light on the ship to rest, then fly away again.

Truly the war seems to be over. Last night, for the first time in all my experience at sea, the four tankers of our group and their escorting destroyers were lighted at sea - - a much lovelier sight, to one who spent so many nights in darkness, than you would think. And tonight the crew is seeing a <u>movie</u> on the open cargo deck!

Nevertheless reminders are constantly with us. Daily, almost hourly, we sight, shoot at and explode some of the millions of mines the B-29's sowed in here to disrupt Jap shipping. They go off with a helluva bang, and I shudder to think of what that would do to a ship that stumbled into it - - which I'm afraid is likely to happen to some ship some day before all the mines are destroyed or sink of their own accord. However by tomorrow we should be out of the mine belt, heading into the peculiar yellow-green water from which the sea gets its name. Really the color change is astoundingly definite, not just some mariner's fairy tale as I had half expected.

And there you have the trivia of me at the moment. But what of you ------------? Yes, I know you can't answer but my heart is listening, my brain trying to think. And I'm hoping and praying to see the answer for myself very soon.

This letter was found in Chuck's safe deposit box after he passed away. Assumedly it was not mailed and was given to him by his Mother when he returned home from the Navy.

Somerset Pa.
Sept 9 – 1945

Charles Darling – Unbelievably soon, your letter came today. Betty and I, and the other children, have grieved so for you and how the news would come to you. We have prayed that Betty's daily letters would reach you first after we knew that the Red Cross – working frantically could not reach you, first in time to get you home while Daddy was still with us – and then to go with us on our last ride with our darling. And Sonny I must tell you the feeling in my heart on that day. The happy day when I walked smiling to the altar with Daddy and all the times we had gone so happily to church together – I walked as close to him as I could on that last trip to the altar and I didn't cry. – I didn't even need the support of Dick's (Sr.) arm – who walked with me because you could not be there. My darling he always was and always will follow me all the days of my life. And you say those were the words you would have liked to say to him – Don't worry Charles dear – Daddy knew your deep love for him as you knew his for you and all the children – his family was his whole love – and no matter what the need or call he stood back of us all – and, God willing, I will carry on as he would want me to do – And I'll tell you here your Betty brought great joy to his life this last year and a half. There was a deep bond between them, their great love for you, and he loved her as truly as any child of his own. I think the feeling that you and daddy sensed when you said good-by, must have been that it was good by and God bless you. To Betty and me, it was the fear we were saying good-by to you. Betty's letters must have reached you by this time – telling you how short it was and how everything possible was done. On Sunday morning the 19th he felt sick as he opened the store – called home – and at 6:30 A.M. I had him home in the car and in bed – In ten minutes Dr. Barchfield was here – thought it would be a light attack – back at noon – at seven Dr. Shaffer back in town was here – and still seemed to think it would come out all right. But Monday – Tuesday – brought no improvement. Wednesday Dr. Houpt – came in on the case, consulted with the heart specialist and the newest heart drugs were used – oxygen – special nurses on every minute – and Friday afternoon the end came – with us all praying and without any struggle. Daddy was anointed on Wednesday and answered the prayers with us – just before the oxygen mask was put on. As you did and just as Daddy had trained me to do, Daddy had everything prepared. All deeds, policies, insurance and everything were in proper order in the bank vault. For the past couple of years I had power of attorney and signed all business checks. Now the business goes on as the Chas. Welsh News Agency – with my name underneath. There will be no change – and positively no sale. The house is clear but I will have to pay inheritance taxes on it, the car, the business and the bank account. Allowed to choose my own appraisers, I chose Mr. Neilan and Mr. Doherty. For work I have a big boy, Francis Casey to open the store – start the boys – and check on all the bundles – come in at four and get the evening boys out. Two other high school boys – one responsible for all day stuffing – and one in charge of Sunday stuffing – under Francis – and a capable flock of carriers.

Marguerite [Carey] collects – and I go to the store from 10 A.M. until 4 – take care of all book work and contacts with field men. And Charles – it is a blessing that I can carry on – for I don't know how I could stand it to stay home and look at the empty chair and rooms.

And when you get home we can tell you many little things we are still unable to write. And I thank God for guarding you and we all pray for you every day – your safety and the day when you will be back again. Your little children are looking forward to "when my daddy comes home".

Good night dear and God bless you forever
Mother

The Last Letter

Sept. 14, 1945 Friday evening

Area Barracks, Hawaii

Another letter, and from the looks of things at the moment I'll have to write more - - not many, I hope.

However the dateline should tell you most of what you want to know; that I'm a good many thousands of miles closer to you; temporarily stalled but nonetheless on my way. How soon? I can't know, but I do hope I can be on the mainland within a week to 10 days from this date; and perhaps by the time you get this I will have already talked to you by phone. I'm considering phoning from here Monday, for excepting the radiograms I've had no word from you in a month, and of course am not expecting any now.

I still find it difficult to write, although I have managed to keep up my diary in lieu of letters. But I'll do what I can to keep you informed while I must stay here, and hope it won't be too much longer.

To tell you, how I got here, the tanker anchored in Buckever Bay, Okinawa, the morning of September 11. I and the others went ashore in a motor launch, and at 5 o'clock that evening I climbed into an Air Transport Command (Army) plane at Kadema Airfield and we took off for Guam. There was nothing to the ride; the huge four-engine C54 stripped to the barest essentials was just like riding a very barn-like bus over the Turnpike. We arrived at Apra, on Guam, about 1 a.m. then were transferred to NATS (Naval Air Transport Service) at Agana.

Got a few hours sleep, talked to Si Uhl by phone, and at noon next day climbed into another C54. This one was a NATS plane and a very deluxe transport with real seats, meals aloft - - all the comforts of the plushest Pullman! First stop Eniwetok, then Kwajalein, then the long flight to Johnston (all are islands of course). And at Johnston the plane was laid up; seems a gas tank was leaking although we passengers knew nothing about it.

So I went to bed again, after a heavenly shower and a swell meal, only to be routed out at 2 a.m. – there was space on another NATS plane, this one like the first and at 3 we were off, landing at

John Rodgers Field, Honolulu about 8 a.m. [September 13, 1945]

(Curiosity: Quite a few thousand miles of salt water separate Guam and Johnston, yet we landed at Johnston <u>before</u> we left Guam!! By virtue of crossing the dateline and so regaining the day I lost last November.)

And at Honolulu the air transport ended, abruptly, unpleasantly, and very unexpectedly. I had feared bottlenecks at Guam and Kwajalein - - they were there but Si helped me at Guam and I was lucky at Kwajalein - - had anticipated trouble there.

But our requests for air priority here were, almost literally, laughed at. We got the story that the returning POW's are taking all of the planes. And we were hustled into a bus, sent here to the receiving barracks and told we likely will get surface transportation to the States.

When? The Good Lord only knows, if anyone does. There are thousands of men, maybe tens of thousands, in barracks, awaiting transportation. Quite a few of them are also on emergency leave, some have been here ten days or more, they say. The rest are about equally divided, I think between men awaiting transport home for discharge and others in transit for duty in the States, on ships now there, etc.; some have been here ten weeks or more I'm told.

I can learn nothing of what's in store for me, nor do I see any possibility of help. No one gets to see the chaplain - - he almost certainly could not help, and he is effectively hidden behind a guard of yeomen outside his office. I may be entitled to liberty Monday, and <u>if</u> I am and <u>if</u> I go I'll see if the Red Cross in Honolulu can do anything - - but I doubt it.

My only chance here was Tubby Braucher and this morning I went out of bounds to hike five miles to his office. And my original guess that there was nothing to be done was right. Nevertheless, it was good to see him and we had a nice talk in the few minutes I could stay and still avoid detection. He did have news that several CVE's (small carriers) fitted as emergency transports will be leaving in the next few days. There's a chance (and I fervently hope) I can be put on one of these. But I don't know -------------------. They would make Frisco in 3 or 4 days; a regular transport would take a week or more, a freighter twice as long.

Meanwhile I lie around in a jam-packed barracks. I've nothing to do, so far, although sooner or later there will be some kind of work; it's cool and fairly clean and the chow is fairly good. But it's a hellish life when I want so very much to get back to you.

As I said, I may call from Honolulu. If not Monday perhaps the next liberty, if I'm still stuck. Otherwise I'll phone from wherever I hit on the west coast (Frisco most likely; San Diego or Bremerton are possible). And I guess that's all I can say right now. Yes I know it isn't much, but the diary will fill in the holes.

And, as I said I can't write when all I can think of is you, and how you are and how you're faring. Yes, I know it's tough for you, or tougher, than for me, but hold the fort and I'll be with you at the first minute possible.

All my love to you and ours,

Your Tonie

P.S. If you're still map conscious, you'll find Aica, a town on the northwest edge of Pearl Harbor. The barracks is near the town, and I am presently in 406.

- 30 -

This is the final letter. In journalism parlance, -30- signifies the end of an article or story. However, this is not the end of Dad's "Long Sad Road Home" saga but unfortunately, there was a huge void.

As stated in the Prologue, the decision was made to read and transcribe the letters in chronological order. This seemed to make sense at the time and made it very interesting for the transcriber and for Dad. As the letters were completed (over a four-year period) they were shared and discussed with him. We never jumped ahead, following the chronology religiously. Regrettably time ran out and Dad passed away without an opportunity to discuss how and when he arrived home from Pearl Harbor. How sad! How foolish!

My sister, brother and I had no personal recollection of the final steps of his journey. All we knew or cared about at the time was that our Dad was coming home – to stay! We vividly remember him stepping out of a bus in front of the house in Somerset.

Following his death in 2008, a search of his safe deposit box yielded another "Treasure," an envelope which shed some more light on the final stage of his journey. Dad had written the following on the envelope "This twenty dollar bill was won in a crap game aboard the USS *Baltimore* en route from Pearl Harbor to the states."

The USS *Baltimore*, thankfully, was a cruiser of the same class as the *San Francisco* and not a tanker or a freighter. The stateside trip from Pearl Harbor would only take 4 or 5 days. We assumed he landed in San Francisco and found his way home from there, probably via an airplane and then the above-mentioned bus ride.

A piece of correspondence found in his personal effects following his death provided additional insight into his "Long Sad Road Home." Dad wrote that his ship's end of the war assignment was to proceed to Inchon, Korea. On the evening before the ship was to sail from Subic Bay, Dad received the message about his father's death. The Frisco's skipper, Captain John E. Welchel, immediately approved an emergency leave request but it couldn't clear the Command Task Force before the dawn departure from Subic Bay. With Dad still aboard, the ship proceeded to the Yellow Sea just off the coast of Korea where he boarded a tanker, the USS *Chiwawa*, for the first step of his journey. From there it was Okinawa, Guam, Eniwetok, Kwajalein, Johnston and Honolulu and then San Francisco. The correspondence made no mention of how he got from there to Somerset.

In February, 2010, all of the pieces of the puzzle came together when Joan and I opened an old briefcase of Dad's that my sister had brought to our house in Virginia. In it was the diary, referred to in his letters, that he started on May 30, 1945. His entries filled in the blanks about his final journey from Pearl Harbor to Somerset.

The diary indicated that when Dad arrived at Pearl Harbor on September 14, 1945, it was jammed with men from all services waiting for transportation back to the states, and air transport was impossible. However, he was fortunate to board the *Baltimore* on September 16, 1945, and the ship docked in San Francisco five days later. He went ashore and called home immediately.

Dad had to undergo some processing before his final departure and in the usual Navy fashion there were delays and long waits. While there, he saw his old friend Duckie Neilan and his wife Lib and another Somerset acquaintance, Red Sabin. After two days in San Francisco Dad boarded a train for Chicago which followed the same route as the trip from Great Lakes to Shoemaker a year earlier. From Chicago he took another train to Johnstown and then a bus to Somerset and home, arriving October 1, 1945. His odyssey was over!

Epilogue

As indicated in his diary, Dad arrived in Somerset on October 1, 1945. The reunion was joyous, although tinged with sadness because of the death of his father. According to his sister Margaret, Mom and Dad did take a one-week honeymoon journey to parts unknown.

In November Dad made a trip to Philadelphia where he was officially discharged from the Navy. He remained in Somerset through the end of the year, enabling the family to celebrate Christmas together. However, work and the Associated Press beckoned and he returned to Philadelphia in mid-January, 1946. Correspondence and childhood memories indicated that our family relocated to Prospect Park, a Philadelphia suburb, after the school year in Somerset ended.

In September, 1955, the Associated Press transferred Dad to Pittsburgh, and the family was on the move again. Four years later it was on the road once more – this time to Louisville. The family was much smaller this time because my sister and I were in college and Fran was the only child to accompany Mom and Dad to Kentucky.

The Associated Press reassigned him for the final time in April, 1961, to the New York City office. No children were involved in the move since Fran was now in college. Mom and Dad settled in Metuchen, New Jersey, a location selected because of its proximity to the city and the fact that my sister, now called Betty, lived there with her family. In 1965, his mother finally sold the newspaper business in Somerset and joined them in Metuchen. She passed away in 1973.

While in New Jersey, Dad was very active in his church, Saint Francis, the seat of the Diocese of Metuchen. He played golf regularly, was a frequent blood donor and was involved with the Associated Press Credit Union and its Veteran Employee organization. Dad and Mom were very supportive of my sister's family and he was a surrogate father to her four children after the death of her husband Jack. He finally retired in 1978, albeit reluctantly and not by choice.

Dad continued to keep busy in retirement with the church, golf, the AP Credit Union and grandchildren. He was also involved with the Veterans of Foreign Wars and participated in numerous USS *San Francisco* reunions held throughout the country. He drove cancer patients to and from treatment and served a stint as a United States Census worker. Dad and Mom also travelled frequently, visiting Fran and his wife Maria in Florida and my wife Joan and me in Virginia and later in Florida.

Mom passed away on Christmas Day, 1994, leaving a huge void in his life. The support that he received from my sister and her family helped him deal with his loss. However, he didn't slow down at all, continuing with the above-mentioned activities including travel, golf and attending ship reunions.

In 2003, he moved into Clara Barton, a retirement community not far from his home and very close to my sister's residence. In 2006, he relocated to a Veterans' facility in nearby Menlo Park, New Jersey. Dad was somewhat frail but kept moving, enjoying his grandchildren and great-grandchildren and dining out. One of his grandsons periodically took him to church, a source of great comfort. Although wheelchair bound, he attended a number of USS *San Francisco* reunions accompanied by his daughter Betty. He also maintained an affiliation with the VFW Post 9626 in Edison, New Jersey and served as Grand Marshal for the community's annual Memorial Day parade just a month before his death on June 23, 2008. He was buried back home in Somerset with Mom and his parents.

He lived a long and remarkable life and was the patriarch of a large and loving family. It is only fitting that his legacy lives on via the publication of his "War Letters" and their inclusion with his other papers in the Associated Press Corporate Archives in New York City.

Taken at my sister's home in Metuchen, NJ
on the occasion of Dad's 92nd birthday.

THE USS *SAN FRANCISCO*

Since many of Dad's letters detailed life aboard ship, it is pertinent that some information be provided about this proud vessel. The *Frisco* was one of the most storied Navy warships in World War II, participating in many historic battles and earning seventeen Battle Stars and two Presidential Citations. However, its roots go well back beyond the 1940's.

The first *San Francisco* was a steel-hulled cruiser whose keel was laid in August, 1888, at the Union Iron Works Shipyard in San Francisco, California, and was launched in October, 1889. She was active in the Spanish-American War and during World War I spent considerable time laying mines in the North Sea. After the war, the ship prowled the waters of the Atlantic and the Carribean before being decommissioned in December, 1921. Her name was changed to *Yosemite* before being sold for scrap in April, 1939, nearly fifty years after the original launching.

The second *San Francisco* (CA 38) was born prior to the demise of number one. A construction contract was signed in October, 1930, and the keel laid a year later at the Navy's Mare Island Shipyard near Vallejo, California. She was launched in March, 1933, and commissioned in February, 1934. Her home port was Pearl Harbor on the island of Oahu. The "new" *San Francisco* was the first of seven New Orleans class cruisers to be launched during this time frame. She initially participated in numerous peace-time maneuvers and training exercises on both coasts, the Caribbean, and the Pacific.

After war broke out in Europe in September, 1939, the *San Francisco* put to sea as a member of the newly-formed Neutrality Patrol, delivering provisions to patrol squadrons stationed in San Juan, Puerto Rico. She continued to provide support in the Caribbean area before returning to Hawaiian waters and participating in fleet maneuvers in March, 1940. Two months later, she entered Puget Sound Navy Yard in Bremerton, Washington, for overhaul and weapons upgrade. Upon completion she sailed back to Pearl Harbor for tactical exercises in the Pacific.

The ship was moored in the Pearl Harbor Navy Yard for another overhaul when the Japanese attacked on December 7, 1941. Fortunately, she was not damaged and moved out to join Task Force 14 to relieve Wake Island which was under Japanese attack. She was en route when Wake fell to the Japanese and the Task Force diverted to Midway Island before returning to Pearl Harbor.

In early 1942, she was engaged in the Samoan Islands and New Guinea. In April of that year, she sailed back to Mare Island for further refitting with more sophisticated weaponry. She provided escort service for small-troop landings and joined the expeditionary force for the initial landings in the Solomon Islands. The *San Francisco* was an active participant in the second Guadalcanal landing (Second Savo) and also provided cover for additional landings. In November, 1942, the ship engaged enemy air and surface units in the "Battle of Guadacanal" (Third Savo) and sustained severe damage from an aircraft crashing on the aft conning tower. Reports indicated that she received 45 enemy hits and suffered over 200 casualties, including 24 fatalities. She sailed back to Mare Island for extensive repairs and a major overhaul.

In March, 1943, the *San Francisco's* assignment involved the repatriation of the Aleutian Islands. After the recapture of Attu and Kiska Islands, she returned to Pearl Harbor and spent the rest of the year in action in the area around the Gilbert and Marshall Islands. This activity continued into 1944, coupled with additional sorties on Truk and Palau in the Carolines, New Guinea, Saipan and Guam. In October, 1944, major overhauls and repairs were required and the *San Francisco* went back to Mare Island. It was here that Dad began his journey with the ship.

When the overhaul was completed, the *San Francisco* was off to San Diego, California for refresher training and then proceeded to Pearl Harbor before being anchored at Ulithi in the Caroline Islands. She took part in strikes against the Japanese on Luzon in the Philippines and withstood the effects of a massive typhoon, losing two crewmen in the process.

In January, 1945, she joined operations in the Philippines, Formosa and Indochina including a high-speed sweep in the South China Sea. This was followed by participation with the carrier task force in a raid on the Japanese mainland, striking air-fields in the Tokyo area and Honshu. The cruiser then took part in the pre-invasion bombardment force at Iwo Jima followed by another carrier strike on Honshu. She was part of the Task Force 54 invasion of Okinawa and returned there after a brief respite, shelling positions on the island. She was anchored at Leyte when Japan surrendered on August 11, 1945. Her post-war assignment was in the Yellow Sea patrolling the coasts of China and Korea. It was here that Dad's tour on the ship ended following his father's death on September 25, 1945.

The *San Francisco* made port at Jinsen Bay, Korea shortly after the Japanese forces in Korea formally surrendered. She continued to patrol the Yellow Sea and later anchored at Tsingtao, China. In November, 1945, the *San Francisco* departed China for Pearl Harbor and then it was homeward bound for San Francisco and a final overhaul stop at Mare Island. January, 1946, found her en route to the Philadelphia Navy Yard via the Panama Canal. She was placed in inactive reserve there and was decommissioned on February 10, 1947. This fine lady's life ended in September, 1959, when she was sold and subsequently scrapped. However, this proud ship will be forever remembered at the Land's End

Memorial at Point Lobos, California, just south of the Golden Gate Bridge. The ship's bell and navigating bridge windscreen constitute the centerpiece and plaques memorialize the officers and enlisted men who gave their lives at Guadalcanal.

Long live the USS *San Francisco* – and she does in the form of a Los Angeles class nuclear attack submarine which was launched on October 27, 1979, and is still in service today.

CPSIA information can be obtained at www.ICGtesting.com
Printed in the USA
266356BV00001B/4/P